CONTENTS

DEDICATION

*This book is dedicated to the greatest Cub of them all, **Ernie Banks**, whose passing on January 23, 2015 deeply saddened baseball fans everywhere. Rest in peace, "Mr. Cub."*

ACKNOWLEDGMENTS

I would like to express my gratitude to the grandchildren of Leslie Jones, who, through the Trustees of the Boston Public Library, Print Department, supplied many of the photos included in this book.

I also wish to thank Troy R. Kinunen of MEARS Online Auctions. com, Kate of RMYauctions.com, Pristineauction.com, Mainlineautographs.com, Ben Grey, ChrisB Photography, and Ben Fenske, each of whom generously contributed to the photographic content of this work

INTRODUCTION

The Cubs' Legacy

Originally founded by Chicago businessman William Hulbert in 1870 to provide a professional challenge to Cincinnati's Red Stockings, the team that eventually came to be known as the Chicago Cubs served as one of the founding members of baseball's first professional league, the National Association, when that entity formed one year later. Initially dubbed the "White Stockings," the team from the Windy City remained in the National Association until 1876, when Hulbert spearheaded the formation of the National Base Ball League. Playing their home games at Street Grounds on Chicago's south side, the White Stockings emerged as one of the infant league's most formidable clubs after signing former National Association stars Albert Spalding and Adrian "Cap" Anson. With Spalding posting 47 victories and Anson batting .356 and driving in 59 runs over the course of the 66-game schedule, the White Stockings captured the first-ever NL pennant in 1876. However, after Spalding retired following the conclusion of the campaign to tend to his burgeoning sporting goods business, the team entered into a brief period of mediocrity, before reestablishing itself as a National League powerhouse by winning three straight pennants, from 1880 to 1882.

Although Hulbert passed away during Chicago's successful pennant run, the White Stockings continued to flourish under the leadership of player-manager Anson for another decade, during which time Spalding assumed ownership of the ball club. Christening newly-constructed West Side Park with back-to-back league championships in 1885 and 1886, the White Stockings remained perennial pennant contenders throughout the 1880s, with first baseman Anson, catcher/outfielder Mike "King" Kelly, and pitcher John Clarkson (53 wins in 1885) serving as the anchors of the team.

Anson, who went on to become the first player in major league history to accumulate 3,000 hits, established himself as one of the nineteenth century's greatest stars, compiling a lifetime batting average of .331, while amassing 1,879 RBIs, 1,719 runs scored, 3,011 hits, 528 doubles, and 124 triples. Unfortunately, Anson, whose forceful personality and greatness as a player enabled him to wield an extraordinary amount of influence in baseball circles, failed to demonstrate as a person the same wonderful qualities he displayed on the playing field. Stubborn, recalcitrant, and narrow-minded, Anson provided much of the impetus for baseball remaining segregated for another sixty years with his adamant refusal in the mid-1880s to compete against black players.

Nevertheless, with Anson serving as the dominant figure in Chicago for more than two decades, the White Stockings gradually became known as "Anson's Colts," or the "Chicago Colts." That moniker remained affixed to the team until a 59-73, ninth-place finish in 1897 cost Anson his job, prompting the local newspapers to begin referring to the ball club as the "Orphans."

Chicago, which began playing its home games in newly-constructed West Side Park II in 1893, remained out of contention until 1903—one year after James Hart purchased the club from Albert Spalding and turned over the managerial reins to former Boston Beaneaters skipper Frank Selee. Although Selee remained at the helm for less than three full seasons, being forced into retirement after contracting tuberculosis, he laid the groundwork for the franchise's next period of excellence, assembling the legendary double play combination of shortstop Joe Tinker, second baseman Johnny Evers, and first baseman Frank Chance, while also acquiring star pitchers Mordecai "Three Finger" Brown and Ed Reulbach. With Chance taking over as manager midway through the 1905 campaign, Chicago ended up capturing four of the next six National League pennants—a period during which the team permanently adopted the nickname "Cubs." Although the Cubs ended up losing to the crosstown rival Chicago White Sox in the 1906 World Series, they posted a phenomenal record of 116-38 during the regular season that gave them the best single-season winning percentage (.763) of baseball's "modern era." Following their disappointing loss to the White Sox in the 1906 fall classic, the Cubs captured the next two National League pennants as well, after which they twice defeated the Detroit Tigers in five games in the World Series. Despite winning 104 games in 1909, the Cubs failed to earn their fourth consecutive league championship, placing second in the senior circuit to a powerful Pittsburgh Pirates team. However, they captured their fourth pennant in five seasons the following year by once again posting 104 victories, before falling to Connie Mack's Philadelphia Athletics in five games in the World Series.

Although the Cubs failed to return to the fall classic in any of the next three seasons, they remained a consistent contender, finishing second once and third twice, as ownership of the team passed from Charles Murphy to Charles Taft. However, they regressed somewhat following the departure of Frank Chance, posting just two winning records over the course of the next five seasons, while going through five managerial changes. The Cubs finally returned to prominence in 1918, two years after they moved from West Side Grounds into the newer Weeghman Park when an investment group headed by advertising executive Albert Lasker and Charles Weeghman, the proprietor of a popular chain of lunch counters who previously owned the Chicago Whales of the short-lived Federal League, purchased them from Taft. Led by star pitcher Hippo Vaughn, the Cubs captured the 1918 NL pennant, before suffering a six-game defeat at the hands of the Boston Red Sox in the World Series.

Another period of mediocrity followed, with the Cubs not finishing in the first division in five of the next eight years as their managerial carousel continued. However, things finally began to turn around after William Wrigley, who changed the name of Weeghman Park to Wrigley Field after he assumed sole ownership of the team in 1921, hired Joe McCarthy to manage his ball club prior to the start of the 1926 campaign. Within three years, McCarthy had the Cubs back in the World Series, with Rogers Hornsby leading the way by capturing 1929 NL MVP honors. Unfortunately, the Cubs suffered their third consecutive defeat in Series play, losing to the Philadelphia Athletics in five games. But they remained strong contenders under McCarthy the following year, finishing a close second in the NL race, just two games behind the pennant-winning Cardinals, with their hard-hitting outfield of Riggs Stephenson, Hack Wilson, and Kiki Cuyler providing much of the offensive firepower. In fact, Wilson put together arguably the most prolific offensive season in franchise history, hitting 56 home runs, batting .356, and driving in a major-league record 191 runs for the runner-up Cubs.

Oddly enough, the 1929 campaign began an interesting period in Cubs history during which they won the National League pennant every third year, finishing first in the senior circuit in 1929, 1932, 1935, and 1938, despite undergoing numerous managerial changes. Piloted at different times by Joe McCarthy and player-managers Rogers Hornsby, Charlie Grimm, and Gabby Hartnett, the Cubs nevertheless remained an elite team, placing in the league's top three each year from 1929 to 1938, and winning at least 90 games five times, en route to earning four more World Series appearances. However, each season ended on a sour note, with the Cubs losing the aforementioned 1929 fall classic to the Athletics, before dropping the 1935 Series to Detroit in six games and being swept by the Yankees in both 1932 and 1938. Standout performers for the team during this period included second baseman Billy Herman, third baseman Stan Hack, catcher Gabby Hartnett, and pitchers Lon Warneke, Guy Bush, Charlie Root, and Bill Lee.

With Chicago's front office being headed by Phil Wrigley following the death of his father in 1932 and the subsequent passing of general manager Bill Veeck Sr. one year later, the Cubs slipped into their next period of mediocrity, finishing well out of contention six straight times between 1939 and 1944. However, the absence of many of the game's best players due to the nation's involvement in World War II enabled the Cubs to experience one brief moment of glory in 1945. Led by NL MVP Phil Caveretta, who topped the senior circuit with a .355 batting average, the Cubs captured their sixteenth pennant, before falling to the Detroit Tigers in seven games in the World Series.

It was during that 1945 fall classic that the infamous "Curse of the Billy Goat" came into being. With the Cubs ahead in the Series 2-games-to-1, Wrigley Field served as the backdrop for Game Four. Leading to a bizarre series of events, one of the fans in attendance, Billy Sianis, purchased two box-seat tickets—one for himself and the other for his goat. As odd as that in itself may seem, things didn't really get interesting until Mr. Sianis began parading his pet through the stands during the early stages of the contest. Following numerous complaints about the unpleasant odor of the animal, Phil Wrigley demanded that the goat leave the ballpark. Angry over being forced to leave the stadium, Mr. Sianis uttered the following words on his way out, "The Cubs, they ain't gonna win no more." The Cubs subsequently lost Game Four, and then the Series as well, before beginning the darkest period in franchise history the following year.

After being one of the National League's most successful franchises for much of the first half of the twentieth century, the Cubs began in 1946 a twenty-one-year run during which they posted a losing record 18 times, finishing out of the second division just once. Losing at least 90 games in

11 of those seasons, the Cubs suffered defeat 103 times on two separate occasions, placing last in the senior circuit a total of five times. Nevertheless, in spite of their consistently poor performance, Cubs teams during this period featured several outstanding players, including pitcher Ferguson Jenkins and sluggers Hank Sauer, Ron Santo, Billy Williams, and Ernie Banks, who captured league MVP honors twice.

Led by Banks, Santo, Williams, and Jenkins, the Cubs experienced a brief resurgence under manager Leo Durocher, finishing with a winning record six straight times between 1967 and 1972, while placing second in the newly-formed National League East on three separate occasions. However, following the departures of those star players and the firing of Durocher, the Cubs once again drifted into mediocrity, acquiring the nickname "Loveable Losers" by failing to post a winning record for 11 straight seasons, even though their roster featured standout players such as Bill Madlock, Bill Buckner, and Bruce Sutter at different times.

Following the passing of Phil Wrigley in 1977, his son, William Wrigley III, assumed control of the team, continuing to run the organization until 1981, when the Wrigley family ended its sixty-five-year association with the Cubs by selling them to the Tribune Company. After getting off to a slow start under their new owners, the Cubs rose to the top of the NL East standings under manager Jim Frey in 1984, advancing to the postseason for the first time in thirty-nine years by compiling a record of 96-65 during the regular season. Yet, even though they featured the league's Most Valuable Player in Ryne Sandberg and the circuit's Cy Young Award winner in Rick Sutcliffe, the Cubs failed to make it past San Diego in the NLCS, losing to the Padres in five games, after earlier holding a 2-0 series lead against their Western Division counterparts.

After subsequently posting a losing record in each of the next four seasons, the Cubs returned to the playoffs under manager Don Zimmer in 1989, only to lose to the San Francisco Giants in five games in the NLCS. More uninspired play followed, with the Cubs finishing above the .500-mark in just two of the next eight seasons, during which time they transitioned to the NL Central Division in the league's new three-division setup. However, led by NL MVP Sammy Sosa, who began an extraordinary five-year run by hitting 66 homers, driving in 158 runs, and scoring 134 times, the Cubs made the playoffs as a wild card in 1998 by defeating the Giants in a one-game playoff. They ended up exiting the postseason tournament quickly once again, though, suffering a three-game sweep at the hands of Atlanta in the opening round.

In spite of Sosa's prodigious slugging, the Cubs posted just one winning record over the course of the next four seasons, before capturing their first NL Central title under new manager Dusty Baker in 2003. They even managed to advance beyond the first round of the playoffs, recording the franchise's first postseason series win in ninety-five years by defeating the Braves in five games in the NLDS. But then, in an all-too familiar scenario, the Cubs suffered a devastating defeat at the hands of the wild-card Florida Marlins in the NLCS, losing in seven games after earlier holding a 3-1 series lead. Making the loss particularly hard to swallow was a play that took place during the latter stages of Game Six. Apparently on the verge of clinching the National League pennant, the Cubs entered the top of the eighth inning in front by a score of 3-0, with arguably their best pitcher, twenty-two-year-old right-hander Mark Prior, on the mound. Everything soon fell apart, though, after Florida second baseman Luis Castillo hit a foul ball down the left field line that Cubs left fielder Moises Alou appeared to have an excellent chance of catching. However, just as Alou reached into the stands to snare Castillo's drive, a Cubs fan by the name of Steve Bartman attempted to catch the ball, deflecting it away from Alou. Having failed to record the inning's second out, Prior subsequently walked Castillo, after which shortstop Alex Gonzalez committed a costly error that eventually led to the Marlins scoring eight times and evening the series at three games apiece. The Cubs lost Game Seven as well, preventing them from making their first World Series appearance in fifty-eight years.

With that ignominious defeat weighing heavily on them, the Cubs failed to make it back to the playoffs until 2007, when they captured the first of their back-to-back NL Central titles under manager Lou Piniella. However, they suffered a three-game sweep at the hands of the Arizona Diamondbacks in the opening round of the postseason tournament, before experiencing a similar fate against the Dodgers the following year.

Meanwhile, after real-estate mogul Sam Zell acquired the financially troubled Tribune Company in December 2007, he set about finding a suitable buyer for the Cubs. The Ricketts family eventually proved to be the perfect fit, purchasing a majority interest in the ball club in 2009, bringing to an end the Tribune Company's twenty-eight-year ownership of the team.

The Cubs initially experienced very little success following the change in ownership, posting a losing record five straight times between 2010 and 2014, as on-field leadership of the team passed from Piniella to Mike Quade, to Dale Sveum, and finally to Rick Renteria. However, things began to look up shortly after Tom Ricketts fired general manager Jim Hendry and signed Theo Epstein away from the Boston Red Sox. After being named club President, Epstein replaced Hendry as GM with Jed Hoyer and hired Sveum to be his new manager. Although the hiring of Sveum proved to be a mistake, Epstein later hit pay dirt when he lured Joe Maddon away from the Tampa Bay Rays following the conclusion of the 2014 campaign. In his first year as Cubs manager, Maddon led a young Chicago team to a record of 97-65 that earned them the right to face the Pittsburgh Pirates in a one-game playoff to determine the league's wild-card entry into the playoffs. After defeating the Pirates by a score of 4-0, the Cubs needed only four games to dispose of the St. Louis Cardinals in the NLDS. However, they subsequently lost to New York in the NLCS, being swept by the Mets in four straight games.

Brimming with confidence following their strong showing the previous year, the Cubs entered the 2016 campaign as odds-on favorites to capture the National League pennant. Living up to their advanced billing, they ended up posting a regular-season record of 103-58 that represented the best mark in either league. The Cubs then advanced to the World Series for the first time in seventy-one years by defeating the Giants in four games in the NLDS, before winning a hard-fought six-game NLCS with the Dodgers. They subsequently punctuated their magical season by mounting a memorable comeback against the Cleveland Indians in the fall classic that saw them overcome a three-to-one game deficit to claim their first world championship in 108 years.

Having exorcised the demons of the past by winning the World Series in 2016, the Cubs seem poised to establish themselves as perennial contenders for the NL flag. Featuring a young nucleus of players that includes sluggers Kris Bryant and Anthony Rizzo, budding stars Kyle Schwarber, Javier Baez, and Addison Russell, and standout pitchers Jon Lester, Jake Arrieta, and Kyle Hendricks, the Cubs appear to have a bright future ahead of them. Their next World Series appearance will be their 12th, with their 17 National League pennants tying them with the Braves for the fourth most in the history of the senior circuit (the Giants have won 23, the Dodgers 22, and the Cardinals 19).

Although the Cubs have proven to be one of the National League's more enigmatic teams through the years, they have featured many exceptional players, several of whom have attained notable individual honors while performing in the Windy City. The franchise boasts 11 MVP winners and five Cy Young Award winners. The Cubs have also featured 22 home run champions and 13 batting champions. And, despite spending much of their time pitching in windy Wrigley Field, Cub hurlers have led the National League in ERA 13 times and strikeouts 16 times. Meanwhile, 40 members of the Baseball Hall of Fame spent at least one full season playing for the Cubs, 22 of whom had several of their finest seasons as a member of the team.

FACTORS USED TO DETERMINE RANKINGS

It should come as no surprise that selecting the 50 greatest players ever to perform for a team with the rich history of the Cubs presented a difficult and daunting task. Even after I narrowed the field down to a mere fifty men, I found myself faced with the challenge of ranking the elite players that remained. Certainly, the names of Ernie Banks, Ryne Sandberg, Ron Santo, Billy Williams, and Ferguson Jenkins would appear at, or near, the top of virtually everyone's list, although the order might vary somewhat from one person to the next. Several other outstanding performers have gained general recognition through the years as being among the greatest players ever to wear a Cubs uniform. Gabby Hartnett, Andre Dawson, and Mark Grace head the list of other Cubs icons. But, how does one differentiate between the all-around excellence of Ryne Sandberg and the extraordinary hitting ability of Ernie Banks, or the pitching greatness of Ferguson Jenkins and the outstanding offensive skills displayed by Billy Williams? After initially deciding who to include on my list, I then needed to determine what criteria to use when formulating my final rankings.

The first thing I decided to examine was the level of dominance a player attained during his time in Chicago. How often did he lead the National League in some major offensive or pitching statistical category? How did he fare in the annual MVP and/or Cy Young voting? How many times did he make the All-Star Team?

I also needed to weigh the level of statistical compilation a player achieved while wearing a Cubs uniform. Where does a batter rank in team annals in the major offensive categories? How high on the all-time list of Cub hurlers does a pitcher rank in wins, ERA, complete games, innings pitched, shutouts, and saves? Of course, I also needed to consider the era in which the player performed when evaluating his overall numbers. For example, modern-day starting pitchers such as Carlos Zambrano and Jake Arrieta are not likely to throw nearly as many complete games or shutouts as either Mordecai Brown or Ferguson Jenkins, who anchored the Cubs' starting rotation during the first decade of the twentieth century and the 1960s, respectively. Meanwhile, Hack Wilson had a distinct advantage over Andre Dawson in that he competed during an era far more conducive to posting huge offensive numbers. And Deadball Era stars such as Frank Schulte and Heinie Zimmerman were not likely to hit nearly as many home runs as the players who performed for the team after the Major Leagues began using a livelier ball.

Other important factors I needed to consider were the overall contributions a player made to the success of the team, the degree to which he improved the fortunes of the ball club during his time in Chicago, and the manner in which he impacted the team, both on and off the field. While the number of postseason appearances the Cubs made during a particular player's years with the ball club certainly entered into the equation, I chose not to deny a top performer his rightful place on the list if his years in Chicago happened to coincide with a lack of overall success by the team. As a result, the names of players such as Hank Sauer and Glenn Beckert will appear in these rankings.

There are three other things I wish to mention. Firstly, I only considered a player's performance while playing for the Cubs when formulating my rankings. That being the case, the names of magnificent pitchers such as Grover Cleveland Alexander and Greg Maddux, both of whom had most of their finest seasons while playing for other teams, may appear lower on this list than one might expect. In addition, since several of the rules that governed nineteenth century baseball (including permitting batters to dictate the location of pitches until 1887, situating the pitcher's mound only fifty feet from home plate until 1893, and crediting a stolen base to a runner any time he advanced from first to third base on a hit) differed dramatically from those to which we have become accustomed, I elected to include only those players who competed after 1900, which is generally considered to be the beginning of baseball's "modern era." Doing so eliminated from consideration nineteenth century standouts such as John Clarkson, Clark Griffith, Mike "King" Kelly, and Cap Anson—perhaps the era's greatest player. And, lastly, there is the case of Sammy Sosa, who, based purely on statistics, deserves to be included among the top two or three players on this list. However, there is little doubt that Sosa accumulated his exceptional numbers through the use of performance-enhancing drugs, greatly diminishing, at least in this writer's opinion, his offensive achievements. That being said, I felt compelled to drop Sosa several notches in my rankings, although I found it impossible to exclude him completely.

Having established the guidelines to be used throughout this book, we are ready to take a look at the 50 greatest players in Cubs history, starting with number one and working our way down to number fifty.

1

ERNIE BANKS

In spite of the superb hitting of Billy Williams, the brilliant pitching of Mordecai Brown, and the all-around excellence of Ryne Sandberg, the decision made here to exclude nineteenth century star Cap Anson from these rankings made Ernie Banks the only possible choice for the number one spot on this list. Spending his entire nineteen-year career in Chicago, Banks earned the nickname *Mr. Cub* with his exceptional on-field performance, sunny disposition, and perpetual love of the game of baseball. The most popular player ever to don a Cubs uniform, Banks appeared in more games (2,528), accumulated more plate appearances (10,394), and compiled more official at-bats (9,421) than any other player in franchise history. Banks also holds franchise records for most extra-base hits (1,009) and total bases (4,706), while ranking behind only Sammy Sosa in home runs (512), and Cap Anson in hits (2,583) and RBIs (1,636). Banks excelled his entire time in Chicago despite playing for teams that rarely contended for the National League pennant, ending his career with more games played than any other player in baseball history not to make a postseason appearance. Yet, even though he played for mostly mediocre teams, Banks won two NL MVP Awards, earned 11 All-Star selections, four *Sporting News* All-Star nominations, and hit more home runs than any other player in the game from 1955 to 1960. Through it all, Banks remained one of the sport's great ambassadors, expressing his love for the national pastime with his famous catch-phrase, "It's a great day for a ball game; let's play two!"

Born in Dallas, Texas on January 31, 1931, Ernest Banks displayed little interest in the sport that eventually became his passion as a child, finally developing a love of the game of baseball during his teenage years. An outstanding all-around athlete, Banks lettered in football, basketball, and track while attending local Booker T. Washington High School. However, since his school did not have a baseball team, Banks honed his skills on the diamond playing shortstop for the semi-pro Amarillo Colts.

Discovered by Negro League legend Cool Papa Bell while at Amarillo, Banks signed with the Kansas City Monarchs shortly after he graduated from high school, remaining in Kansas City for one year, before being drafted into the United States Army. Banks then spent the next two years in the military, spending much of that time serving as a flag bearer in the Forty-Fifth Anti-Aircraft Artillery Battalion at Fort Bliss, where he played with the Harlem Globetrotters on a part-time basis. Following his discharge in 1953, Banks rejoined the Monarchs, for whom he compiled a batting average of .347, before being sold to the Cubs during the latter stages of the campaign. Reflecting back on his time in Kansas City years later, Banks said, "Playing for the Kansas City Monarchs was like my school, my learning, my world. It was my whole life."

Immediately added to the Cubs' roster upon his acquisition from Kansas City, Banks became the first player of African American descent to play for the team when he made his Major League debut on September 17, 1953. Starting 10 games at shortstop during the season's final two weeks, Banks batted .314, knocked in six runs, and hit the first two home runs of his storied career. After assuming the starting shortstop duties the following year, Banks appeared in every game for the Cubs for the first of six times in his first seven seasons. Although he performed somewhat erratically in the field, committing a total of 34 errors, Banks had a solid rookie season, concluding the campaign with 19 home runs, 79 RBIs, and a .275 batting average. Banks subsequently emerged as one of the league's most formidable batsmen in 1955, when he began an exceptional six-year run during which he clearly established himself as the best shortstop in the game. Here are the numbers he posted over the course of those six seasons:

1955: 44 HR, 117 RBIs, 98 Runs Scored, .295 AVG, .345 OBP, .596 SLG, .941 OPS

1956: 28 HR, 85 RBIs, 82 Runs Scored, .297 AVG, .358 OBP, .530 SLG, .887 OPS

1957: 43 HR, 102 RBIs, 113 Runs Scored, .285 AVG, .360 OBP, .579 SLG, .939 OPS

1958: **47** HR, **129** RBIs, 119 Runs Scored, .313 AVG, .366 OBP, **.614** SLG, .980 OPS

1959: 45 HR, **143** RBIs, 97 Runs Scored, .304 AVG, .374 OBP, .596 SLG, .970 OPS

1960: **41** HR, 117 RBIs, 94 Runs Scored, .271 AVG, .350 OBP, .554 SLG, .904 OPS

*Please note that any numbers printed in bold throughout this book signify that he player led the National League in that particular statistical category that year.

Banks' 248 home runs and 693 RBIs during that six-year stretch led all of Major League Baseball, earning him six consecutive All-Star selections, four *Sporting News* All-Star nominations, five top-10 finishes in the NL MVP voting, and MVP honors in both 1958 and 1959, even though the Cubs finished well out of contention both years. Banks placed in the league's top five in home runs and RBIs in five of the six seasons, topping the senior circuit in each category twice. He also finished second in the league in runs scored twice and slugging percentage once, ranked first in total bases once, and led the league in games played in five of those six seasons, failing to do so only in 1956, when a fractured hand brought his streak of 424 consecutive games played to an end. Furthermore, Banks hit five grand slam home runs in 1955, setting in the process a single-season record that stood for over thirty years.

In addition to compiling huge offensive numbers, Banks worked diligently on improving his defense, gradually turning himself into one of the top defensive shortstops in the game. In fact, he led all players at his position in fielding percentage three times during the period, committing only 12 errors in the field over the course of his MVP campaign of 1959. Banks earned Gold Glove honors the following year, when he led all NL shortstops in assists, putouts, double plays, and fielding percentage.

In spite of the prolific numbers Banks posted on offense, he did not present a particularly imposing figure at the plate. Standing 6'1" tall and weighing barely 190 pounds, Banks lacked the physical attributes of a prototypical home run hitter. However, he had powerful thighs and tremendously quick and strong wrists that enabled him to wait longer than most batters before starting his swing, with an opposing player once noting that he often "hits the ball right out of the catcher's mitt."

Bill Furlong further elaborated on the primary source of Banks' hitting prowess in *Baseball Stars of 1959*, writing, "His wrists are the secret of Banks' success. Instead of taking the big Ruthian type swing of the lively ball era, he swings his bat as if it were a buggy whip, striking at the ball with the reflexive swiftness of a serpent's tongue."

Meanwhile, Banks chose to maintain a positive outlook in spite of the lack of success the Cubs experienced during his peak seasons in Chicago, with famed sportswriter Arthur Daly noting, "He rejoices merely in living, and baseball is a marvelous extra that makes his existence so much more pleasurable." In discussing his ability to retain his inner peace and zest for life while playing for a non-contending team, Banks stated, "You must try to generate happiness within yourself. If you aren't happy in one place, chances are you won't be happy anyplace."

Hampered by a knee injury he originally sustained while serving in the military, Banks saw his streak of 717 consecutive games played come to an end in 1961, when, appearing in 138 games, he hit just 29 homers, knocked in only 80 runs, scored just 75 times, and batted .278. His range at shortstop reduced considerably by his ailing knee, Banks also saw significant action at other positions over the course of the campaign, starting 23 games in left field, before moving to first base during the season's final weeks. Instructed on the finer points of fielding the position by Cubs' coach Charlie Grimm during the subsequent offseason, Banks became the team's full-time first baseman in 1962. Adapting well to his change in positions, Banks ended up leading all NL first sackers in putouts, assists, and double plays, while also experiencing a resurgence on offense, earning his eighth straight All-Star selection by hitting 37 homers, driving in 104 runs, scoring 87 times, and batting .269.

After contracting the mumps during the early stages of the 1963 campaign, Banks ended up suffering through a dismal season in which he hit just 18 homers, knocked in only 64 runs, and batted just .227. However, he rebounded somewhat in each of the next two seasons, totaling 51 home runs and 201 RBIs from 1964 to 1965, while leading all NL first basemen in putouts both years. Although Banks never again reached elite status during his time in Chicago, he remained a productive player for another four years, topping 20 homers three more times, surpassing 100 RBIs once more, and earning his final two All-Star nominations. Voted the "Greatest Cub Ever" in a 1969 *Chicago Sun-Times* fan poll, Banks found himself reduced to part-time duties by 1970, spending his last two seasons with the Cubs serving as a back-up first baseman and occasional pinch-hitter. He announced his retirement following the conclusion of the 1971 campaign, ending his career with 512 home runs, 1,636 RBIs, 1,305 runs scored, 2,583 hits, a .274 batting average, a .330 on-base percentage, and a .500 slugging percentage.

After retiring as an active player, Banks spent three years working in the Cubs' front office and serving the team as an on-field coach, before finally leaving the game he loved so much. The members of the Baseball Writers Association of America elected him to the Hall of Fame shortly thereafter, voting him into Cooperstown in 1977, the first time his name appeared on the ballot.

Although Banks remained away from baseball in an official capacity for most of the next four decades, he continued to serve the national pastime well, often expressing to others the joy he felt in being fortunate enough to spend much of his life playing the game. Summarizing the attitude Banks took with him to the field each day, actor and lifelong Cubs fan Joe Mantegna wrote, "He never complained about his team's bad luck or bad talent, never stopped playing the game with joy, never stopped giving his all, never lost his proud demeanor, and never acted like anything but a winner. He was a symbol of the Cub fan's undiminishing resilience. If he could be happy to come to the park each afternoon, then so could we."

Unfortunately, Banks developed dementia in his later years, dying of a heart attack at a Chicago hospital on January 23, 2015, just eight days before his eighty-fourth birthday. Following his passing, Cubs Chairman Tom Ricketts released the following statement:

> *"Words cannot express how important Ernie Banks will always be to the Chicago Cubs, the city of Chicago, and Major League Baseball. He was one of the greatest players of all time. He was a pioneer in the Major Leagues. And, more importantly, he was the warmest and most sincere person I've ever known. Approachable, ever optimistic, and kind hearted, Ernie Banks is and always will be Mr. Cub. My family and I grieve the loss of such a great and good-hearted man, but we look forward to celebrating Ernie's life in the days ahead."*

Career Numbers:

512 HR; 1,636 RBIs; 1,305 Runs Scored; 2,583 Hits; 407 Doubles; 90 Triples; 50 Stolen Bases; .274 AVG; .330 OBP; .500 SLG; .830 OPS

Career Highlights:

Best Season: Banks had his two finest seasons in 1958 and 1959, earning league MVP honors both years. In addition to leading the NL with a career-high 143 RBIs in the second of those campaigns, Banks amassed 351 total bases, which represented the third-highest total in the senior circuit, and finished second in the league with 45 home runs and a .596 slugging percentage. However, while Banks knocked in 14 fewer runs the previous season, concluding the 1958 campaign with a league-leading 129 RBIs, he established career-best marks in homers (47), runs scored (119), hits (193), triples (11), total bases (379), batting average (.313), slugging percentage (.614), and OPS (.980), finishing either first or second in the league in seven different offensive categories. It's a close call, but Banks proved to be a bit more dominant in 1958, making that the best season of his career.

Memorable Moments/Greatest Performances: Banks had the only 5-for-5 day of his career on September 29, 1957, when he doubled three times and singled twice during an 8-3 victory over the St. Louis Cardinals.

Just one day after going 4-for-4, with a homer, 3 RBIs, and 3 runs scored during a 12-4 win over Philadelphia, Banks continued his hot hitting against the Phillies on June 4, 1958, sparking an 11-5 Cubs victory by collecting 3 hits, a pair of homers, 4 RBIs, and 4 runs scored

Banks helped pace the Cubs to a 13-8 win over the Cardinals on May 1, 1963 by driving in a career-high 7 runs with 2 homers and a single.

During an 8-2 win over the Houston Astros on June 11, 1966, Banks accomplished the rare feat of recording 3 triples in one game. He finished the contest 3-for-5, with 3 RBIs and 1 run scored.

Banks led the Cubs to an 8-4 victory over Philadelphia on July 17, 1968 by going 3-for-5, with a pair of homers and 6 RBIs.

Banks tied his career-high mark in RBIs on May 13, 1969, leading the Cubs to a 19-0 rout of the expansion San Diego Padres by knocking in 7 runs with a single and a pair of 3-run homers.

Banks hit 3 home runs in one game on four separate occasions, accomplishing the feat for the first time on August 4, 1955, when the last of his 3 round-trippers—a 2-run blast in the bottom of the eighth inning—proved to be the decisive blow of an 11-10 victory over the Pittsburgh Pirates. He finished the day 4-for-5, with 7 RBIs and 4 runs scored. Banks again reached the seats three times against Pittsburgh on September 14, 1957, hitting 3 solo homers and scoring 4 runs during a 7-3 win over the Pirates. Although the Cubs ended up losing their May 29, 1962 match-up with the Milwaukee Braves by a score of 11-9, Banks had another huge day at the plate, collecting 4 hits, 3 homers, and 4 RBIs during the defeat. Banks' last such performance ended in futility as well, with the Dodgers defeating the Cubs by a score of 11-8 on June 9, 1963, in spite of his 3 homers and 4 RBIs.

Banks experienced one final moment of glory on May 12, 1970, when he stroked his 500th home run over the left field wall at Wrigley against Atlanta right-hander Pat Jarvis during a 4-3, 11-inning win over the Braves. Banks' solo blast in the bottom of the second inning made him just the ninth player at the time to reach the 500 home run plateau.

Notable Achievements:

- Hit more than 30 home runs seven times, topping 40 homers on five occasions.
- Knocked in more than 100 runs eight times, topping 120 RBIs twice.
- Scored more than 100 runs twice.
- Batted over .300 twice.
- Finished in double digits in triples once (11 in 1958).
- Surpassed 30 doubles twice.
- Posted slugging percentage in excess of .500 eight times, topping the .600-mark once (.614 in 1958).
- Led NL in: home runs twice, RBIs twice, total bases once, slugging percentage once, and games played six times.
- Finished second in NL in: home runs twice, runs scored twice, triples once, total bases once, slugging percentage once, and OPS once.
- Led NL shortstops in: assists twice, putouts once, double plays once, and fielding percentage three times.
- Led NL first basemen in: putouts five times, assists three times, double plays once, and fielding percentage once.
- Holds Cubs career records for most: extra-base hits (1,009), total bases (4,706), sacrifice flies (96), games played (2,528), plate appearances (10,394), and at-bats (9,421).

- Ranks among Cubs career leaders in: home runs (second), RBIs (second), runs scored (fifth), hits (second), doubles (third), triples (seventh), bases on balls (eighth), and slugging percentage (eighth).
- Hit three home runs in one game four times (August 4, 1955 vs. Pittsburgh; Sept. 14, 1957 vs. Pittsburgh; May 29, 1962 vs. Milwaukee; and June 9, 1963 vs. Los Angeles).
- 1960 Gold Glove winner.
- 1967 Lou Gehrig Memorial Award winner.
- Two-time NL MVP (1958 & 1959).
- Finished in top five of NL MVP voting two other times.
- Two-time *Sporting News* NL Player of the Year (1958 & 1959)
- Four-time *Sporting News* All-Star selection (1955, 1958, 1959 & 1960).
- Eleven-time NL All-Star (1955, 1956, 1957, 1958, 1959, 1960, 1961, 1962, 1965, 1967 & 1969).
- Member of Major League Baseball All-Century Team.
- Number 38 on *The Sporting News'* 1999 list of Baseball's 100 Greatest Players.
- Elected to Baseball Hall of Fame by members of BBWAA in 1977.

2

RYNE SANDBERG

The premier second baseman of his era, Ryne Sandberg exhibited a rare combination of power, speed, and exceptional defense over the course of his career that made him one of the finest all-around players ever to man the position. One of only three players in baseball history to have both a 40-homer and a 50-steal season during their careers, Sandberg is also one of just three second basemen to hit as many as 40 home runs in a season, becoming in 1990 the first second sacker to lead his league in that particular category since Rogers Hornsby topped the senior circuit with 39 round-trippers in 1925. In all, Sandberg surpassed 25 home runs six times and 30 stolen bases five times during his career, en route to amassing 282 homers and 344 steals as a member of the Cubs, with both figures placing him among the franchise's all-time leaders. An exceptional defender as well, Sandberg won a total of nine Gold Gloves, more than any other second baseman in MLB history, with the exception of Roberto Alomar (10). Along the way, "Ryno," as his teammates and Cubs fans affectionately called him, went four full seasons without committing a single throwing error, leading all players at his position in assists seven times, fielding percentage four times, and double plays turned once.

Born in Spokane, Washington on September 18, 1959, Ryne Dee Sandberg seemed destined for a career in baseball from the moment his parents decided to name him after New York Yankees relief pitcher Ryne Duren while watching a game on television earlier that summer. A three-sport star at Spokane's North Central High School, Sandberg received numerous offers to attend college on a football scholarship after being named the starting quarterback on *Parade* magazine's All-American Team upon graduation. Sandberg, though, chose to pursue a career in baseball instead,

Courtesy of MEARS Online Auctions

Ryne Sandberg established himself as one of
the greatest all-around second basemen in baseball history
during his time in Chicago

explaining his decision years later by saying, "I knew it would be a lot easier on my body than football."

After being selected by the Phillies in the twentieth round of the 1978 amateur draft, Sandberg spent the next three years working his way up the ladder in Philadelphia's farm system, primarily as a shortstop, before making his Major League debut with the club on September 2, 1981. Serving the Phillies mostly as a late-inning defensive replacement during the season's final month, Sandberg collected one hit in just six plate appearances.

With most Philadelphia scouts viewing Sandberg as nothing more than a utility infielder, the Phillies completed a trade with the Cubs during the subsequent offseason that sent Sandberg and veteran shortstop Larry Bowa to Chicago for shortstop Ivan De Jesus. Although the Cubs initially envisioned Sandberg as a center-fielder, they chose to play him mostly at third base during his first year in Chicago. Acquitting himself well at the hot corner, Sandberg committed only 12 errors in 156 games, while also doing a solid job on offense, earning a sixth place finish in the NL Rookie of the Year voting by hitting 7 homers, driving in 54 runs, batting .271, stealing 32 bases, and ranking among the league leaders with 103 runs scored.

The acquisition of veteran third baseman Ron Cey prior to the start of the ensuing campaign prompted the Cubs to shift Sandberg to second base—a position he manned for the remainder of his career. Adapting well to his new position, Sandberg ended up earning the first of his record nine consecutive Gold Gloves by leading all NL second sackers in assists (572), double plays (126), and fielding percentage (.986). Meanwhile, he again posted solid numbers on offense, finishing the year with 94 runs scored, 37 stolen bases, and a .261 batting average.

Sandberg subsequently emerged as a full-fledged star in 1984, leading the Cubs to the NL East title by hitting 19 homers, knocking in 84 runs, batting .314, collecting 200 hits, stealing 32 bases, and topping the senior circuit with 19 triples and 114 runs scored. He also once again led all NL second basemen in assists and fielding percentage, committing only 6 errors in the field all season long, including going 61 consecutive games at one point without making a defensive miscue. Sandberg's brilliant all-around performance earned him the first of his 10 straight All-Star selections, the first of his six *Sporting News* All-Star nominations, NL MVP honors, and the admiration of Cubs manager Jim Frey, who commented,

"He has the most consistent approach to the game I've ever seen. He's similar to (Al) Kaline. You could watch Kaline play for five years and look back and say 'I've never seen him mess up a play or make a mistake.' I know we use the word consistent a lot, but in Sandberg's case it applies."

Sandberg followed up his MVP campaign with another outstanding year in 1985, placing in the league's top 10 in eight different offensive categories, including home runs (26), runs scored (113), hits (186), stolen bases (54), and batting average (.305). Although Sandberg proved to be somewhat less productive at the plate in each of the next three seasons, he remained the senior circuit's top second sacker, averaging 16 homers, 68 RBIs, 75 runs scored, and 27 stolen bases from 1986 to 1988, while compiling batting averages of .284, .294, and .264. Sandberg also led all players at his position in assists in two of those seasons and finished first in the NL with a fielding percentage of .994 in 1986, committing just 5 errors in the field all season.

Sandberg reached the 30-homer plateau for the first time in 1989, when he earned a fourth place finish in the NL MVP voting and his fourth Silver Slugger by hitting 30 homers, driving in 76 runs, batting .290, and leading the league with 104 runs scored. He topped that performance the following year, though, earning another fourth place finish in the MVP balloting by leading the league with 40 homers, 116 runs scored, and 344 total bases, while also ranking among the leaders with 100 RBIs, 188 hits, a .306 batting average, a .559 slugging percentage, and a .913 OPS. Sandberg's 40 home runs made him just the third second baseman in MLB history to reach the seats that many times in one season, with only Rogers Hornsby (1922) and Davey Johnson (1973) previously accomplishing the feat. He also established a then MLB record by stringing together 123 consecutive errorless games at second.

Sandberg put up big numbers in each of the next two seasons as well, concluding the 1991 campaign with 26 home runs, 100 RBIs, 104 runs scored, and a .291 batting average, before hitting 26 homers, driving in 87 runs, scoring 100 times, and batting .304 the following year. He also led all NL second sackers in assists both years and posted a league-leading .995 fielding percentage in 1991, committing just 4 errors in the field over the course of the season.

Sandberg's stellar all-around play continued to earn him the respect and admiration of his coaches and teammates, with former Cubs manager

Don Zimmer stating on one occasion, "He made so few errors that when he made one you thought the world was coming to an end. Then he hits 30 or 40 homers and scores 100 runs. I saw them all...I saw the best second basemen who ever played, and in my opinion Ryne Sandberg is the best second baseman who ever played baseball."

Greg Maddux, who spent six seasons benefiting from Sandberg's tremendous defensive work at second, suggested, "Having Ryne Sandberg play second base behind you was like having a security blanket. You name it and he could do it—offensively, defensively, on the bases. In his prime, he was probably the best all-around baseball player I've ever seen."

Andre Dawson, who competed against Sandberg as a member of the Montreal Expos before joining him on the Cubs in 1987, admired his former teammate for more than just his playing ability, commenting, "As an opposing player, you marveled at what the guy could do because he could beat you in so many ways. Then, when you played with him, he's the type of individual who, every time you heard people talk about him, they wanted their kid to grow up like Ryne Sandberg. He was special. Everyone knew that."

Former Cubs GM Dallas Green also held Sandberg in extremely high regard, saying, "It's not often guys like Ryno come along. He was one of the cleanest-cut professionals I've ever known and one of the great leaders I've seen. Ryno provided leadership without ever having to say a word."

Limited by injuries to just 117 games in 1993, Sandberg finished the year with only 9 homers, 45 RBIs, and 67 runs scored, although he still managed to hit .309 and earn his 10th straight All-Star selection. However, after starting off the 1994 campaign poorly, suffering through a 1-for-28 slump at one point and hitting only .238 by mid-June, Sandberg chose to announce his retirement at only thirty-four years of age on June 13, telling the assembled media, "I am certainly not the type of person who can ask the Cubs organization and the Chicago Cubs fans to pay my salary when I am not happy with my mental approach and my performance." Sandberg later revealed in his book, *Second To Home*, "The reason I retired is simple: I lost the desire that got me ready to play on an everyday basis for so many years. Without it, I didn't think I could perform at the same level I had in the past, and I didn't want to play at a level less than what was expected of me by my teammates, coaches, ownership, and most of all, myself."

Sandberg ended up sitting out the remainder of the 1994 season, and all of 1995 as well, before his love of the game drew him back to the playing field. Returning to the Cubs in 1996, Sandberg hit 25 homers, knocked in 92 runs, and scored 85 others, although he also batted just .244 and struck out a career-high 116 times. But, while Sandberg failed to display the same consistency at the plate he demonstrated throughout most of his career, he remained an exceptional fielder, committing only 6 errors in 1,234 innings. Sandberg spent one more year with the Cubs, hitting 12 homers, driving in 64 runs, scoring 54 times, and batting .264 in 1997, before retiring for good at season's end. In addition to hitting 282 home runs and stealing 344 bases over the course of his career, he knocked in 1,061 runs, scored 1,318 times, accumulated 2,386 hits, and compiled a lifetime batting average of .285.

After initially keeping a low profile in retirement, Sandberg later took on various jobs that again placed him before the general public, including a brief stint as a radio analyst on ESPN. Sandberg eventually returned to the ball field as a manager in the Cubs minor league farm system, before accepting the position of manager of the Philadelphia Phillies on September 22, 2013. He remained in that post until June 26, 2015, when he handed in his resignation.

Elected to the Baseball Hall of Fame in 2005, Sandberg delivered a rousing speech at the induction ceremonies in which he expressed his love and respect for the game, the manner in which he feels it should be played, and the disdain he feels towards the showmanship that has become such an integral part of the national pastime in recent years. Speaking of his election to the Hall, Sandberg stated, "If this validates anything, it's that learning how to bunt and hit-and-run and turning two is more important than knowing where to find the little red light at the dugout camera."

Sandberg added, "I was taught you never, ever disrespect your opponent or your teammates or your organization or your manager, and never, ever your uniform."

Displaying the team concept he retained inside him throughout his career, Sandberg suggested, "Hit a home run—put your head down, drop the bat, run around the bases, because the name on the front is more—a lot more important than the name on the back."

Sandberg's playing ability and tremendous character prompted former teammate Lee Smith to proclaim, "Ryne Sandberg is probably the best thing that ever happened to the Chicago Cubs. On the field, he was almost perfect. Off the field, he was perfect."

Career Numbers:

282 HR; 1,061 RBIs; 1,318 Runs Scored; 2,386 Hits; 403 Doubles; 76 Triples; 344 Stolen Bases; .285 AVG; .344 OBP; .452 SLG PCT; .795 OPS

Career Highlights:

Best Season: It would be difficult to disagree with anyone who wished to present the notion that Sandberg had the finest all-around season of his career in 1984. En route to earning NL MVP honors, Sandberg hit 19 homers, drove in 84 runs, stole 32 bases, topped the senior circuit with 114 runs scored and 19 triples, placed second in the league with 200 hits and 331 total bases, and also ranked among the leaders with 36 doubles, a .314 batting average, a .520 slugging percentage, and an OPS of .887. Furthermore, Sandberg led all NL second basemen with 550 assists and a .993 fielding percentage. Nevertheless, the feeling here is that Sandberg proved to be slightly more dominant in 1990, when, in addition to leading the league with 40 home runs, 116 runs scored, and 344 total bases, he finished second in slugging percentage (.559), third in hits (188), fourth in OPS (.913), sixth in RBIs (100), and 10th in batting average (.306), establishing in the process career-high marks in six different offensive categories.

Memorable Moments/Greatest Performances: Although the Cubs lost their April 23, 1982 matchup with the Pittsburgh Pirates by a score of 12-10, Sandberg had his breakout game as a member of the team, going 3-for-4, with a pair of homers, 3 RBIs, and 4 runs scored.

Sandberg once again performed valiantly in defeat against San Diego in the 1984 NLCS, concluding the five-game series with a .368 batting average and a .455 on-base percentage.

Sandberg proved to be the difference in a 7-3 victory over the Padres on July 9, 1985, scoring 3 times and knocking in 4 runs with a single and a pair of homers.

Sandberg had a huge game against Atlanta on August 21, 1985, leading the Cubs to a 9-5 win over the Braves by going 4-for-5, with 2 home runs and 6 RBIs.

Sandberg paced the Cubs to an 11-6 victory over Houston on May 27, 1990 by going 4-for-5, with a pair of homers and 4 RBIs.

Sandberg came up big in the clutch for the Cubs during a 6-5, 13-inning win over Pittsburgh on July 1, 1991. After bringing the Cubs to within 1 run of the Pirates with a 2-run homer in the bottom of the eighth inning, Sandberg drove in the game's winning run with an RBI single in the bottom of the 13th. He finished the day with 4 hits and 3 RBIs.

Sandberg proved to be a one-man wrecking crew later that month, leading the Cubs to a 7-5 victory over Atlanta on July 27, 1991 by knocking in 5 runs with a pair of homers.

Sandberg still had some big games left in him after he returned to the Cubs following a 1 ½ year hiatus, with one of those coming on August 9, 1996, when he helped lead them to an 11-9 win over the Montreal Expos by driving in 5 runs with a grand slam homer and a solo blast.

Still, there is little doubt that Sandberg experienced his finest moment more than a decade earlier, on June 23, 1984, when, during the latter stages of an 11-inning, 12-11 victory over the Cardinals in a nationally televised game at Wrigley Field, he delivered a pair of memorable game-tying home runs off St. Louis relief ace Bruce Sutter. After tying the score at 9-9 with a solo blast off Sutter in the bottom of the ninth inning, Sandberg again homered off the future Hall of Fame pitcher in the ensuing frame, this time with two men out, one man on base, and the Cubs trailing by a score of 11-9. Sandberg finished the day 5-for-6, with a career-high 7 RBIs. Following the contest, which came to be known as "The Sandberg Game," Cardinals manager Whitey Herzog proclaimed, "One day, I thought he [Sandberg] was one of the best players in the NL The next day, I think he's one of the best players I've ever seen."

Notable Achievements:

- Batted over .300 five times.
- Hit more than 20 home runs six times, topping 30 homers twice and 40 homers once (40 in 1990).
- Knocked in 100 runs twice.
- Scored more than 100 runs seven times.
- Topped 200 hits once (200 in 1984).
- Finished in double digits in triples once (19 in 1984).

- Surpassed 30 doubles six times.
- Stole more than 30 bases five times, topping 50 steals once (54 in 1985).
- Posted slugging percentage in excess of .500 four times.
- Led NL in: home runs once, triples once, runs scored three times, and total bases once.
- Finished second in NL in: hits once, slugging percentage once, and total bases twice.
- Led NL second basemen in: assists seven times, double plays once, and fielding percentage four times.
- Ranks among Cubs career leaders in: home runs (fifth), RBIs (seventh), runs scored (third), hits (fourth), doubles (fourth), extra-base hits (fourth), total bases (fifth), stolen bases (fourth), bases on balls (ninth), games played (fourth), plate appearances (fourth), and at-bats (fourth).
- Two-time NL Player of the Month.
- 1984 *Sporting News* Major League Player of the Year.
- 1984 NL MVP.
- Finished fourth in NL MVP voting twice (1989 & 1990).
- Nine-time Gold Glove winner.
- Seven-time Silver Slugger winner.
- Six-time *Sporting News* All-Star selection (1984, 1988, 1989, 1990, 1991 & 1992).
- Ten-time NL All-Star (1984, 1985, 1986, 1987, 1988, 1989, 1990, 1991, 1992 & 1993).
- Elected to Baseball Hall of Fame by members of BBWAA in 2005.

3

MORDECAI BROWN

Spending his entire career pitching in the shadow of the great Christy Mathewson prevented Mordecai "Three-Finger" Brown from garnering the type of accolades he otherwise would have received. Nevertheless, the right-handed curveball artist rivaled Mathewson as the National League's premier hurler for much of the first decade of the twentieth century, establishing himself in the process as one of the Dead Ball Era's greatest pitchers. The ace of Chicago's pitching staff for most of his nine seasons in the Windy City, Brown performed particularly well for the Cubs from 1906 to 1910, a period during which he helped lead them to four pennants and two world championships by compiling an overall record of 127-44 and posting an ERA well below 2.00 each year. Over the course of those five seasons, Brown led all NL hurlers in wins, ERA, and innings pitched once each, complete games and shutouts twice each, and WHIP on three separate occasions. In all, Brown won in excess of 20 games six times, topping the 25-win mark on four separate occasions. He also compiled an ERA under 2.00 six times, establishing along the way a twentieth century record for the lowest single-season ERA of any pitcher with at least 200 innings pitched (1.04 in 1906). The Cubs' career record-holder for most shutouts (48), Brown also ranks among the franchise's all-time leaders in several other pitching categories, including wins (second), ERA (second), WHIP (second), and winning percentage (sixth). He also continues to rank among MLB's all-time leaders in ERA and WHIP. Brown accomplished all he did even though he spent his entire career pitching with a badly mangled right hand he injured during a childhood accident.

Born in the farming community of Nyesville, Indiana on October 19, 1876, Mordecai Peter Centennial Brown owed his unusually long name to his year of birth, which marked the first American Centennial. Brown's life changed forever at the age of seven, when he caught the index finger on his right hand in his uncle's corn shredder, forcing him to have it amputated above the knuckle. Just a few weeks later, Brown reinjured the same hand when he stumbled while chasing a rabbit, breaking the two middle fingers and damaging the pinky finger as well. Although the broken fingers healed badly and the pinky finger remained paralyzed, Brown eventually turned his handicap into an advantage, learning that the unusual manner with which he gripped a baseball forced it to move in an extremely unconventional manner.

Brown first learned to pitch by aiming rocks at knotholes on the barn wall and other wooden surfaces on his parents' farm. He later decided to pursue a career in baseball while working in the coal mines of western Indiana as a teenager—a period of his life that also earned him the nickname "Miner." After getting his start in semi-pro ball as a third baseman with various local mining teams, Brown transitioned to the mound in 1898 with the encouragement of a co-worker, who helped him learn how to grip and throw a baseball with his injured hand. Using his tremendous determination to overcome the initial pain he felt whenever he handled the ball, Brown eventually came to realize that his unorthodox grip gave his pitches a natural downward movement, which Fred Massey, his great-nephew, later described: "It didn't only curve—it curved and dropped at the same time. It made it extremely hard to hit, and, if you did hit it, you hit it into the ground because you couldn't get under it." In addition to his extraordinary curveball/sinker, Brown developed an extremely effective fastball and changeup.

Having perfected his pitching repertoire, Brown began his minor league career in Terre Haute of the Three-I League in 1901. After dominating minor league hitters for two years, Brown joined the St. Louis Cardinals in 1903, at the somewhat advanced age of twenty-six. Appearing in a total of 26 games for the last-place Cardinals, Brown performed relatively well as a rookie, compiling a 2.60 ERA and tossing 19 complete games, even though he finished the season just 9-13. Dealt to the Cubs during the subsequent offseason, Brown arrived in Chicago with little fanfare, with few people expecting the twenty-seven-year-old right-hander to amount to much.

However, with the help of his devastating curveball, Brown soon emerged as one of the National League's finest pitchers. After compiling a record of 15-10, throwing 21 complete games, and finishing among the

Courtesy of the Bain Collection at the Library of Congress

Mordecai Brown proved to be one of the
Dead Ball Era's greatest pitchers

league leaders with an ERA of 1.86 and a WHIP of 0.965 in his first year with the Cubs, Brown won 18 games, completed 24 of his starts, tossed 249 innings, and once again placed near the top of the league rankings in ERA (2.17) and WHIP (1.056) in 1905. Brown then began an extraordinarily successful five-year run during which he annually ranked among the NL leaders in most statistical categories for pitchers. Here are the numbers he compiled over the course of those five seasons:

> 1906: 26-6, **1.04** ERA, 144 Strikeouts, **0.934** WHIP, **9** Shutouts, 27 CG, 277.1 IP
>
> 1907: 20-6, 1.39 ERA, 107 Strikeouts, **0.944** WHIP, 6 Shutouts, 20 CG, 233.0 IP
>
> 1908: 29-9, 1.47 ERA, 123 Strikeouts, 0.842 WHIP, 9 Shutouts, 27 CG, 312.1 IP
>
> 1909: **27**-9, 1.31 ERA, 172 Strikeouts, 0.873 WHIP, 8 Shutouts, **32** CG, **342.2** IP
>
> 1910: 25-14, 1.86 ERA, 143 Strikeouts, **1.084** WHIP, 6 Shutouts, **27** CG, 295.1 IP

In addition to leading all NL hurlers with 27 wins in 1909, Brown finished second in the league in victories three other times during the period. He also finished either first or second in WHIP all five seasons, placed in the top three in ERA each year, and topped the circuit in saves three times. The Cubs captured the National League pennant in four of those five campaigns, failing to do so only in 1909, when they finished second to the Pittsburgh Pirates despite winning 104 games during the regular season. After suffering a stunning defeat at the hands of the Chicago White Sox in the 1906 World Series, the Cubs won each of the next two fall classics, emerging victorious over the Detroit Tigers both times, with Brown leading the way by posting a perfect 3-0 record, while holding the Tigers to 13 hits and no earned runs, in 20 total innings of work. Brown's brilliant pitching so impressed Ty Cobb that the Detroit great later proclaimed, "'Miner' Brown is one of the greatest pitchers in the history of baseball, and a remarkable fielder at all times."

Meanwhile, in discussing the effectiveness of Brown's best pitch following the conclusion of his playing career, Cobb commented, "It was a great ball, that downward curve of his. I can't talk about all of baseball, but I can say this: It was the most deceiving, the most devastating pitch I ever faced."

Legendary New York Giants manager John McGraw also held Brown in extremely high esteem, regarding the Chicago right-hander and his own Christy Mathewson as the two best pitchers in the National League. Mathewson, himself, expressed his admiration for his rival when he stated, "Brown is my idea of the almost perfect pitcher...It will usually be found at the end of a season that he has taken part in more key games than any other pitcher in baseball."

Over the course of their careers, Mathewson and Brown faced each other a total of 25 times in head-to-head competition, with Mathewson holding a slim 13-11 edge, including one no-decision. Most of those contests turned out to be classic pitching duels, with both men stifling the offenses of their opponents. Chicago player-manager Frank Chance felt extremely confident any time Brown took the mound, even against the New York Giants great, stating on one occasion, "Let's get one run ahead with Brown in the box, and we are sure to win."

Orval Overall, another member of Chicago's starting rotation, marveled at the determination and poise Brown consistently displayed on the mound, saying, "Brown, to my way of thinking, is the most courageous pitcher in the history of baseball....Cool as a deep-sea fish and brave as a lion, nothing fazes him."

Although the Cubs failed to win their fifth league championship in six years in 1911, Brown had another outstanding season, concluding the campaign with a record of 21-11, a 2.80 ERA, 21 complete games, 270 innings pitched, and a league-leading 13 saves. However, his period of dominance ended the following year when he found himself limited to just 15 appearances by a sore arm. Released by the Cubs at season's end, Brown joined Louisville of the American Association, who subsequently traded the thirty-six-year-old hurler to the Cincinnati Reds. After posting a record of 11-12 for Cincinnati in 1913 Brown jumped to the St. Louis Terriers of the rival Federal League. He spent the next two years in that short-lived circuit, compiling an overall record of 31-19, while splitting his time between St. Louis, Brooklyn, and Chicago. Reacquired by the Cubs prior to the start of the 1916 campaign, Brown ended up spending his final big league season pitching for the team with whom he experienced his greatest success. He retired at season's end with a career record of 239-130 and an ERA of 2.06, which places him third all-time among pitchers with at least 1,500 innings pitched, behind only Ed Walsh and Addie Joss.

Following his retirement from the majors, Brown returned to his home in Terre Haute, where he continued to pitch in the minor leagues and in exhibition games for more than a decade. He also coached and managed in the minors until 1920, when he opened a filling station in Terre Haute that served as a town gathering place and an unofficial museum for the next twenty-five years. Plagued by diabetes in his later years, Brown lived until February 14, 1948, when he passed away after suffering a stroke at seventy-one years of age. The Baseball Hall of Fame opened its doors to him the following year, with the members of the Old Timers Committee electing him posthumously.

Although the childhood injuries Brown suffered likely would have discouraged most people from pursuing a career in any professional sport, the Hall of Fame pitcher possessed the will and determination to make his handicap work for him in a positive way. Looking back at his career years later, Brown recalled, "That old paw served me pretty well in its time. It gave me a firmer grip on the ball, so I could spin it over the hump. It gave me a greater dip." Yet, Brown added, "I always felt if I had had a normal hand, I would have been a greater pitcher."

Cub Numbers:

Record: 188-86; .686 Win Pct.; 1.80 ERA; 206 CG; 48 Shutouts; 39 Saves; 2,329 IP; 1,043 Strikeouts; 0.998 WHIP

Career Numbers:

Record: 239-130; .648 Win Pct.; 2.06 ERA; 271 CG; 55 Shutouts; 49 Saves; 3,172⅓ IP; 1,375 Strikeouts; 1.066 WHIP

Cub Career Highlights:

Best Season: A strong case could certainly be made that Brown had his greatest season in 1908, when he posted career-best marks in wins (29), WHIP (0.842), and shutouts (9). However, he failed to lead the league in any statistical category. On the other hand, Brown finished first in the senior circuit with a 0.934 WHIP, 9 shutouts, and a 1.04 ERA in 1906, establishing in the process a twentieth century record for the lowest single-season ERA compiled by a starting pitcher. Nevertheless, the feeling is that Brown had his most dominant season for the Cubs in 1909, when, in addition to leading the league with 27 victories and a career-high 32 complete games and 342 2/3 innings pitched, he finished fourth in the circuit with a career-best 172 strikeouts and placed second in ERA (1.31), WHIP (0.873), and shutouts (8).

Memorable Moments/Greatest Performances: Ironically, Brown turned in one of his finest efforts in a losing cause, coming out second best to Christy Mathewson in one of the greatest pitching duels ever. With the two hurlers matched up against one another in a June 13, 1905 contest between the Cubs and Giants, only one batter on either team reached base safely via a hit all day. However, while Brown surrendered just one safety to the Giants, Mathewson no-hit the Cubs, earning a 1-0 victory over his Chicago counterpart in the process

Although the Cubs ended up losing the 1906 World Series to the White Sox in six games, with Brown taking the loss in the Series finale, the ace of the Cubs' pitching staff performed brilliantly in Game Four. After losing a hard-luck 2-1 decision in the Series opener, Brown, working on just two days of rest, evened the fall classic at two games apiece by tossing a two-hit shutout, in defeating the Sox by a score of 1-0

Brown proved to be practically unhittable in both the 1907 and 1908 World Series. Facing Detroit both times, Brown clinched the world championship for the Cubs in the first of those campaigns by defeating the Tigers, 2-0, allowing 7 hits and recording 4 strikeouts in the process. Even more impressive the following year, Brown won the Series opener in relief, before tossing a 4-hit shutout in Game Four. He finished the Series 2-0, with an ERA of 0.00, having allowed the Tigers just 6 hits and no earned runs, in 11 total innings of work.

Nevertheless, Brown considered his October 8, 1908 performance against the Giants at New York's Polo Grounds to be the finest effort of his career, telling John P. Carmichael in *My Greatest Day in Baseball*, "I was about as good that day as I ever was in my life." With the Cubs and Giants meeting in a one-game playoff to determine the National League champion, Chicago manager Frank Chance chose not to start Brown since the ace of his team's pitching staff had either started or relieved in 11 of the Cubs' last 14 games. However, with Christy Mathewson on the mound for the Giants and Cubs starter Jack Pfeister struggling during the early stages of the contest, Chance decided to call on Brown before things got out of hand. Out-pitching Mathewson the rest of the way, Brown silenced New York's bats, giving the Cubs a 4-2 victory that put them in the World Series for the third straight year.

Notable Achievements:

- Won at least 20 games six straight times, topping 25 victories on four occasions.
- Posted winning percentage in excess of .700 four times, topping the .800-mark once.
- Compiled ERA below 2.00 six times, posting mark under 1.50 on four occasions.
- Posted WHIP under 1.000 five times.
- Threw more than 300 innings twice, tossing more than 250 innings three other times.
- Surpassed 20 complete games eight times, topping the 30 mark once (32 in 1909).
- Threw 9 shutouts twice.
- Finished in double digits in saves once (13 in 1911).
- Led NL pitchers in: wins once, ERA once, WHIP three times, complete games twice, innings pitched once, shutouts twice, saves four times, and putouts once.
- Holds Cubs single-season records for lowest ERA (1.04 in 1906) and lowest WHIP (0.842 in 1908).
- Holds Cubs career record for most shutouts (48).
- Ranks among Cubs career leaders in: wins (second), ERA (second), WHIP (second), winning percentage (sixth), innings pitched (fifth), and complete games (fourth).
- Ranks among MLB career leaders in ERA (sixth) and WHIP (10).
- Holds twentieth century MLB record for lowest single-season ERA (1.04 in 1906).
- Four-time NL champion (1906, 1907, 1908 & 1910).
- Two-time world champion (1907 & 1908).
- Elected to Baseball Hall of Fame by members of Old Timers Committee in 1949.

4

BILLY WILLIAMS

Blessed with a near picture-perfect swing, Billy Williams spent 14 full seasons in Chicago, during which time he established himself as arguably the best pure hitter in Cubs history. Ranking among the franchise's all-time leaders in virtually every offensive category, "Sweet Swingin' Billy," as he came to be known, displayed remarkable consistency in his years with the Cubs, never batting any lower than .276 as a full-time player and topping the .300-mark on five separate occasions. The 1972 NL batting champion, Williams also hit at least 20 homers and knocked in at least 84 runs thirteen straight times, surpassing 30 homers on five occasions, reaching the 40-homer plateau once, and driving in more than 100 runs three times. Over the course of those thirteen seasons, Williams averaged 28 home runs and 98 RBIs, while posting a composite batting average of .298. Extremely durable as well, Williams missed a total of only five games between 1962 and 1970, at one point setting a new National League record (since broken) by appearing in 1,117 consecutive games. The left-handed hitting outfielder's consistently excellent play earned him six NL All-Star selections, four *Sporting News* All-Star nominations, one *Sporting News* Player of the Year Award, two runner-up finishes in the league MVP voting, and eventual induction into the Baseball Hall of Fame.

Born in Whistler, Alabama on June 15, 1938, Billy Leo Williams attended local Whistler High School, where he played basketball, ran track, and served as a 155-pound defensive end on the gridiron, earning in the process a football scholarship to Grambling College. Nevertheless, baseball remained Williams' first love, prompting him to play semi-pro ball as a teenager with a Negro League farm team called the Mobile Black Bears, since Whistler High did not have a baseball team of its own.

Discovered by the legendary Buck O'Neil while playing at Mobile, Williams signed with the Cubs as an amateur free agent in 1956, after which he spent the next four years advancing through the Chicago farm system. Although Williams performed well at each minor league stop, he became extremely discouraged shortly after he earned a promotion to the Class AA San Antonio Missions in 1959 due to the racial prejudice he subsequently encountered. Williams, who later recalled in his autobiography that he had never previously experienced overt racial discrimination, became so disenchanted at one point that he left the team and returned home. However, O'Neil eventually persuaded him to return to San Antonio, and, by season's end, Williams had advanced to Triple A Fort Worth and even appeared in 18 games with the Cubs.

Williams subsequently spent most of the 1960 campaign at Triple A Houston, where he hit 26 home runs and batted .323, making such a strong impression on batting instructor Rogers Hornsby in the process that the legendary Hall of Famer exhorted the Cubs to promote him to the Major Leagues, telling team management, "I suggest you get this kid Williams to Chicago as rapidly as possible because there isn't anybody on the Cubs right now who can swing a bat as well as he does. It's silly to keep him in the minors any longer." Promoted to the Cubs during the latter stages of the campaign, Williams started 12 games in left field, batting .277, hitting 2 homers, and driving in 7 runs, in 47 official at-bats.

After claiming the Cubs' starting left-field job early the following year, the twenty-two-year-old Williams went on to earn NL Rookie of the Year honors by hitting 25 homers, knocking in 86 runs, scoring 75 times, and batting .278. He improved upon those numbers in 1962, finishing the year with 22 home runs, 91 RBIs, 94 runs scored, and a .298 batting average, en route to earning his first All-Star selection. Williams followed that up with another strong performance in 1963, concluding the campaign with 25 home runs, 95 RBIs, 87 runs scored, a .286 batting average, and 36 doubles, which placed him third in the league rankings.

Although Williams established himself as one of the senior circuit's foremost hitters by the end of his third season, he failed to distinguish himself in the field. Possessing only marginal defensive skills when he first arrived in the big leagues, Williams led all NL outfielders with 11 errors as a rookie. In fact, he went on to commit at least 10 miscues in five of his first nine seasons with the Cubs. Williams also lacked outstanding instincts in the outfield. However, through hard work and dedication, he

Courtesy of MEARS Online Auctions

A model of consistency during his time in Chicago, Billy Williams averaged 28 home runs and 98 RBIs from 1961 to 1973

eventually turned himself into a slightly above average outfielder, leading all NL left-fielders in putouts three times, assists four times, doubles plays four times, and fielding percentage on three separate occasions. Furthermore, even though left field remained Williams' primary position throughout his career, he had a strong enough throwing arm to spend a significant amount of time in right field as well.

Williams had a big year in 1964, earning his second All-Star nomination and first *Sporting News* All-star selection by driving in 98 runs, scoring 100 times, batting .312, placing second in the league with 33 home runs, and finishing third in the circuit with 201 hits and 39 doubles. He followed that up with another exceptional performance in 1965, once again earning NL All-Star honors by ranking among the league leaders with 34 home runs, 108 RBIs, 115 runs scored, 203 hits, 39 doubles, 356 total bases, a .315 batting average, a .377 on-base percentage, and a .552 slugging percentage.

Williams continued his outstanding play over the course of the next four seasons, averaging 27 home runs, 92 RBIs, and 97 runs scored from 1966 to 1969, while posting a composite batting average of .284 and continuing his lengthy string of consecutive games played. Yet, in spite of the extraordinary consistency Williams displayed year after year, he remained largely overlooked and underappreciated by the masses because of his understated manner, quiet demeanor, and uncharismatic personality. Still, his teammates and opponents fully appreciated his playing ability and knew how much he meant to the Cubs. Veteran pitcher Bob Locker commented, "It's kind of funny. Here's a guy who does it the way it's supposed to be done, day-in-and-day-out, according to the book. And people don't notice him because he's not flashy—only good. It makes you wonder."

Longtime teammate Don Kessinger stated, "Billy Williams is the best hitter, day-in-and-day-out, that I have ever seen. He's unbelievable. He didn't hit for just one or two days, or one or two weeks. He hit all the time."

"Billy Williams," said Cubs manager Leo Durocher, "never gets excited. Never gets mad. Never throws a bat. You write his name down, in the same spot every day, and you forget it. He will play left, he will bat third. Billy Williams is a machine."

Pittsburgh Pirates slugger Willie Stargell, who once called Williams' smooth, compact swing "poetry in motion," expressed his admiration for his fellow left-fielder during the latter stages of his career by proclaiming,

"Billy is the best left-handed hitter I ever saw. But, for all you hear about him, you'd think he was playing in the dark. Can he hit the ball hard? I remember one time I was playing first base and he stung one through my legs before I could even move my glove. Bam. It was gone. I always keep my eyes open when Billy is batting. He could hurt you, know what I mean?"

Pittsburgh second baseman Dave Cash added, "When I got to the Pirates, I found out there were guys who weren't half as good as I had heard they were. But when I saw Billy Williams I said, 'This man is a ballplayer, and nobody writes about him.'"

In addressing the lack of notoriety he received throughout most of his career, Williams wrote in his autobiography, "People say I'm not an exciting player. I go out there and catch the ball and hit the ball and play the game like it should be played."

An extremely cerebral hitter, Williams approached each at-bat with a specific plan, carefully studying the tendencies of the opposing pitcher from the dugout and on-deck circle. He also became an expert at recognizing pitches on the way to the plate, revealing, "The way the ball spins—fastball. The arch of the ball—curveball. When I get into the box, the only thing I look at is the hand and the ball. I try to pick up the ball as close to the hand as possible. If I'm lucky, halfway to the plate I should know what the pitch is going to be, by the spin, by the arch." Williams' exceptional pitch-recognition, compact swing, and quick wrists enabled him to establish himself as one of the league's premier power hitters even though he stood 6'1" tall and weighed only about 180 pounds.

After laboring in near-obscurity for almost a decade, Williams gained general recognition as arguably the National League's finest all-around hitter in 1970 by hitting 42 homers, driving in 129 runs, batting .322, and topping the senior circuit with 137 runs scored, 205 hits, and 373 total bases. Williams' extraordinary performance earned him his third *Sporting News* All-Star selection and a runner-up finish to Johnny Bench in the NL MVP balloting. After a solid 1971 campaign in which he hit 28 homers, knocked in 93 runs, and batted .301, Williams had another monster year in 1972, earning *Sporting News* Major League Player of the Year honors and another second-place finish to Bench in the MVP voting by placing among the league leaders with 37 home runs, 122 RBIs, 95 runs scored, 191 hits, 34 doubles, and a .398 on-base percentage, while topping the circuit with

348 total bases, a .333 batting average, a .606 slugging percentage, and an OPS of 1.005.

While Williams' brilliant play gained him widespread acclaim for the first time in his career, the professional manner with which he conducted himself continued to earn him the admiration of his peers, with long-time opponent Joe Torre noting, "He leads his club with his bat and, just the way he plays, I think he knows if he blows his stack, he might affect a lot of the young kids, and Billy feels that kind of responsibility to his teammates, and it carries over."

Meanwhile, Chicago sports columnist Bill Gleason wrote, "The leader of the Cubs is, of all people, the quiet man of the clubhouse, Billy Williams. Billy Williams, who seldom speaks in a voice that can be heard beyond his own cubicle, who wouldn't say 'Rah! Rah!' if Phil Wrigley promised him a $10,000 bonus for each 'Rah!' is the man to whom the Cubs look for leadership...He combines the dignity of Ernie Banks, the determination of Ron Santo, and the competitive fires of Randy Hundley, and he plays every day, every night."

Williams spent two more seasons in Chicago, hitting 20 homers, driving in 86 runs, scoring 72 times, and batting .288 in 1973, before seeing his numbers slip to 16 home runs, 68 RBIs, and a .280 batting average after he assumed a somewhat diminished role the following year. With Williams turning thirty-six during the 1974 season, the Cubs elected to trade him to Oakland for young second baseman Manny Trillo and relief pitchers Darold Knowles and Bob Locker following the conclusion of the campaign. Williams left Chicago with career totals of 392 home runs, 1,353 RBIs, 1,306 run scored, and 2,510 hits—all of which continue to place him among the franchise's all-time leaders. He also compiled a .296 batting average, a .364 on-base percentage, and a .503 slugging percentage while playing for the Cubs.

Williams ended up spending two years in Oakland, serving the Athletics almost exclusively as a designated hitter during that time. After helping the A's capture their fifth straight AL West title by hitting 23 homers and driving in 81 runs in 1975, Williams hit just 11 homers, knocked in only 41 runs, and batted just .211 the following year, prompting Oakland to release him at season's end. Williams subsequently announced his retirement, after which he spent one year away from the game, before accepting a position as a minor league instructor for the Cubs. Promoted to Chicago's major league coaching staff in 1980, Williams remained in the Cubs organization for another 15 years, before spending his final four seasons in uniform serving on the coaching staffs of the Oakland A's and Cleveland Indians. Williams later returned to Chicago, where he continues to serve the Cubs as a senior advisor. He also has been a member of the Hall of Fame Veterans Committee since 2011, contributing significantly to the 2012 induction to Cooperstown of longtime friend and teammate Ron Santo. Honored in 2010 by the Cubs, who unveiled a statue of him outside Wrigley Field, Williams is appropriately depicted as a man finishing a perfect swing.

Cub Numbers:

392 HR; 1,353 RBIs; 1,306 Runs Scored; 2,510 Hits; 402 Doubles; 87 Triples; 86 Stolen Bases; .296 AVG; .364 OBP; .503 SLG; .867 OPS

Career Numbers:

426 HR; 1,475 RBIs; 1,410 Runs Scored; 2,711 Hits; 434 Doubles; 88 Triples; 90 Stolen Bases; .290 AVG; .361 OBP; .492 SLG; .853 OPS

Cub Career Highlights:

Best Season: Although Williams performed extremely well throughout the 1960s, he had his two most dominant seasons in 1970 and 1972, earning a runner-up finish in the NL MVP voting both years. The initial inclination would be to identify the 1972 campaign as Williams' greatest season since he earned *Sporting News* Major League Player of the Year honors by finishing third in the National League with 37 home runs and 191 hits, placing second with 122 RBIs and a .398 on-base percentage, and topping the circuit with 348 total bases, a .333 batting average, a .606 slugging percentage, and a 1.005 OPS, establishing career-high marks in each of the last three categories in the process. However, Williams actually posted slightly better overall numbers in 1970, when, in addition to finishing second in the league with career-best marks in home runs (42) and RBIs (129), he ranked fourth in batting average (.322) and led all NL players with 137 runs scored, 205 hits, and 373 total bases, reaching career-high marks in each of the last three categories as well. It's an extremely close call, but we'll go with 1970 as Williams' finest season.

Memorable Moments/Greatest Performances: Williams helped lead the Cubs to a 9-5 win over the Philadelphia Phillies on June 17, 1964 by driving in 5 runs with a triple and 2 homers.

Williams had a huge day at the plate on July 17, 1966, hitting for the cycle, knocking in 2 runs, and scoring 4 times during a 7-2 victory over the St. Louis Cardinals.

Williams helped pace the Cubs to a 13-5 win over the Braves on August 21, 1968 by driving in a career-high 7 runs with a homer, double, and single.

Just two days after collecting 4 hits, a pair of homers, a double, and 4 RBIs during a 10-3 win over the Phillies, Williams turned in an epic performance against the Mets, leading the Cubs to a lopsided 8-1 victory over the New Yorkers on September 10, 1968 by hitting 3 homers and knocking in 6 runs. After reaching the seats twice against New York starter Dick Selma, Williams delivered his final blow of the contest against rookie hurler Nolan Ryan.

Williams helped lead the Cubs to a 9-5 victory over the Giants on May 19, 1971 by driving in 6 runs with a triple and a pair of homers.

Williams turned in an exceptional performance against Houston on July 11, 1972, going 8-for-8 during a doubleheader split with the Astros. After collecting 3 hits, 3 RBIs, and a homer in the 6-5 Game One loss, Williams led the Cubs to a 9-5 win in the nightcap by hitting safely in all 5 of his trips to the plate, homering again and scoring 3 runs. In addition to going a perfect 8-for-8, Williams finished the day with 2 homers, a double, 4 RBIs, and 4 runs scored.

Williams again feasted off Houston pitching 10 days later, going 4-for-6, with a homer, double, and 6 RBIs, during an 11-3 win over the Astros on July 21, 1972.

Williams had a huge game against San Francisco on August 26, 1972, leading the Cubs to a 10-9 victory over the Giants in 10 innings by going 5-for-6, with a homer, 4 RBIs, and 2 runs scored.

Williams hit a number of memorable home runs during his time in Chicago, with one of those coming on August 11, 1968, when his 2-out, 3-run inside-the-park homer in the top of the 15th inning gave the Cubs an 8-5 win over the Cincinnati Reds. Williams again came up big in the clutch on May 12, 1970, when his leadoff homer in the bottom of the ninth inning off future Hall of Fame reliever Hoyt Wilhelm knotted the score with the Braves at 3-3. The Cubs went on to win the game by a score of 4-3 two innings later on a walk-off RBI single by Ron Santo. Williams provided further heroics on April 6, 1971, when he gave the Cubs a 2-1 victory over St. Louis on opening day by homering off Cardinals great Bob Gibson in the bottom of the 10th inning.

Notable Achievements:

- Hit more than 20 home runs thirteen straight times, topping 30 homers five times and 40 homers once (42 in 1970).
- Knocked in more than 100 runs three times, topping 120 RBIs twice.
- Scored more than 100 runs five times, topping 130 runs scored once (137 in 1970).
- Batted over .300 five times, topping the .320-mark twice.
- Surpassed 200 hits three times.
- Finished in double digits in triples twice.
- Surpassed 30 doubles seven times.
- Posted slugging percentage in excess of .500 six times, topping the .600-mark once (.606 in 1972).
- Compiled OPS in excess of 1.000 once (1.005 in 1972).
- Led NL in: batting average once, runs scored once, hits once, extra-base hits three times, total bases three times, slugging percentage once, OPS once, games played five times, and plate appearances once.
- Finished second in NL in: home runs twice, RBIs three times, doubles once, triples once, total bases once, and on-base percentage once.
- Led NL left-fielders in: putouts three times, assists four times, double plays four times, and fielding percentage three times.
- Holds Cubs single-season record for most games played (164 in 1965).
- Ranks among Cubs career leaders in: home runs (third), RBIs (fourth), runs scored (fourth), hits (third), extra-base hits (second), doubles (fifth), triples (eighth), total bases (second), bases on balls

(fifth), slugging percentage (seventh), OPS (ninth), games played (third), plate appearances (third), and at-bats (third).

- Hit three home runs in one game vs. New York Mets on September 10, 1968.
- Hit for the cycle vs. St. Louis Cardinals on July 17, 1966.
- Two-time NL Player of the Month.
- 1961 NL Rookie of the Year.
- 1972 *Sporting News* Major League Player of the Year.
- 1972 *Sporting News* NL Player of the Year.
- Finished second in NL MVP voting twice (1970 & 1972).
- Four-time *Sporting News* All-Star selection (1964, 1968, 1970 & 1972).
- Six-time NL All-Star (1962, 1964, 1965, 1968, 1972 & 1973).
- Elected to Baseball Hall of Fame by members of BBWAA in 1987.

5

RON SANTO

The National League's premier third baseman for much of the 1960s, Ron Santo hit more home runs (253) and knocked in more runs (937) during the decade than any other player who manned the position. A nine-time NL All-Star and five-time *Sporting News* All-Star selection, Santo topped 30 homers, knocked in more than 100 runs, and batted over .300 four times each, en route to earning four top-10 finishes in the league MVP voting. An exceptional fielder as well, Santo won five Gold Gloves over the course of his career, leading all NL third sackers in putouts and assists seven times each, double plays six times, and fielding percentage once. The longtime captain of the Cubs accomplished all he did despite playing his entire career with diabetes—a condition that later cost him both his legs and, eventually, his life.

Born in Seattle, Washington on February 25, 1940, Ronald Edward Santo grew up near old Sicks Stadium in Seattle, where he received his introduction to professional baseball by assuming numerous odd jobs for the Seattle Rainiers—then the top farm team for the Cincinnati Reds–working as an usher, in the press box, and in the clubhouse, Santo recalled years later, "I shined Vada Pinson's shoes and then, three years later, I am playing against him." A three-sport star at Seattle's Franklin High School, Santo excelled at football, basketball, and baseball, starring on the diamond as both a catcher and a third baseman.

After signing with the Cubs as an amateur free agent in 1959, Santo began his minor league career as a catcher, before eventually moving to third base. Working extensively with manager Grady Hatton on improving his throwing technique while at Double A San Antonio, Santo later credited Hatton with preparing him to play the hot corner at the major league level, stating, "He [Hatton] helped me tremendously at third, especially in correcting my throwing. I had been taking my time, daring the runner to beat my throw. It was strictly high-school stuff. Grady taught me to come up throwing and get rid of the ball immediately."

Promoted to the big leagues after less than two full seasons in the minors, Santo arrived in Chicago just four months after celebrating his twentieth birthday, hitting 9 homers, driving in 44 runs, and batting .251 in 95 games with the Cubs, after making his major league debut on June 26, 1960. Appearing in every game for the first of three straight times the following year, Santo emerged as one of the senior circuit's top third basemen, hitting 23 homers, knocking in 83 runs, scoring 84 times, batting .284, and setting a Cubs record by starting a league-leading 41 double plays at the hot corner. Displaying the same aggressive approach to hitting he carried with him throughout his career, Santo drew praise from Cincinnati Reds second baseman Johnny Temple, who commented, "If there is such a thing as a take-charge hitter, it has got to be Santo. When he steps to the plate, the kid literally defies the pitcher to throw the ball because he isn't bashful when it comes to swinging the bat."

Although Santo subsequently experienced difficulties at the plate in his second full season, batting just .227 and scoring only 44 runs despite hitting 17 homers and driving in 83 runs, he began a string of seven straight seasons in which he led all National League third basemen in assists, establishing in the process a new Cubs record for third sackers by throwing out 332 runners. Meanwhile, Santo's 161 putouts at third placed him first among players at his position for the first of six straight times.

Bouncing back in a big way on offense in 1963, Santo earned an eighth place finish in the NL MVP voting and the first of four consecutive All-Star nominations by hitting 25 homers, driving in 99 runs, scoring 79 times, amassing a career-high 187 hits, and batting .297. He followed that up with an even stronger performance in 1964, earning another eighth place finish in the MVP balloting by hitting 30 homers, scoring 94 runs, batting .313, finishing second in the league with 114 RBIs, a .564 slugging percentage, and a .962 OPS, and topping the circuit with 13 triples, 86 bases on balls, and a .398 on-base percentage. Santo also earned Gold Glove honors for the first of five straight times by leading all NL third basemen in putouts, assists, and double plays. Santo, who possessed a powerful throwing arm and exceptional range and quickness in the field, received rave reviews for his defensive work, with Cardinals manager Johnny

Courtesy of MEARS Online Auctions

Ron Santo hit more home runs and knocked in more runs
than any other third baseman during the 1960s

Keane commenting, "He always was a good hitter, but his arm seems to be stronger and more accurate than ever."

With Cardinals third baseman Ken Boyer on the downside of his career, Santo clearly established himself as the National League's best player at the position in 1965, a season in which he batted .285, scored 88 runs, and finished among the league leaders with 33 home runs, 101 RBIs, 88 walks, a .378 on-base percentage, and a .510 slugging percentage. After Leo Durocher replaced Lou Klein as Cubs manager prior to the start of the ensuing campaign, "Leo the Lip" took to his new third baseman immediately, proclaiming, "When it comes to all-around work, nobody is close to him. Ron is the best in the league, both offensively and defensively. He's one of the most aggressive players in the league—a born leader."

Santo had another big year in 1966, hitting 30 homers, driving in 94 runs, scoring 93 times, batting .312, leading the league with 95 walks and a .412 on-base percentage, and establishing a new NL record for third basemen by collecting 391 assists. Although Santo's string of four consecutive All-Star nominations ended the following year, he had one of his finest all-around seasons, earning a fourth place finish in the NL MVP balloting by batting .300, knocking in 98 runs, finishing third in the league with 31 homers and 107 runs scored, topping the circuit with 96 bases on balls, and breaking his own record by accumulating 393 assists.

Although Brooks Robinson gained general recognition as the finest defensive third baseman in the game during the 1960s, there were those who considered Santo to be his equal. Cubs left-fielder Billy Williams, who spent more than a decade playing behind Santo in the field, discussed his former teammate's defensive skills:

> *"Was Brooks Robinson a better fielder than Ron Santo? I played left field behind Santo in Chicago all those years and I'm telling you that sucker was quick. I saw him make plays that nobody else could have made. He was out there every day, hurt or not, he had marvelous instincts, and he could hit."*

Despite batting just .246 in 1968, Santo had another productive year, earning his fifth All-Star selection by hitting 26 homers, driving in 98 runs, and leading the league in walks for the third straight time. He followed that up with a sensational 1969 campaign in which he earned a fifth place finish in the NL MVP voting by batting .289, scoring 97 runs, placing second in the league with 123 RBIs, and also ranking among the league leaders with 29 homers, 96 walks, and a .384 on-base percentage.

It was during the 1969 season that Santo became known for performing a ritual at the end of every Cubs home victory. After spontaneously running down the third base line, leaping in the air three times, and clicking his heels on each jump following a particularly satisfying win at Wrigley Field on June 22, Santo made this routine part of his regular post-game regimen at the behest of manager Leo Durocher, who felt it helped motivate the team. However, he discontinued the practice shortly after the Cubs began their infamous September swoon, following claims made by Cubs fans and the local media that it symbolized the overconfidence that many felt led to the team's downfall during the season's final month.

Santo had another extremely productive year in 1970, hitting 26 homers, driving in 114 runs, and batting .267, before his offensive numbers began to fall off somewhat the following season. Yet, even though he totaled only 58 home runs over the course of the next three seasons and never again came close to knocking in 100 runs, Santo earned three more All-Star selections and one more *Sporting News* All-Star nomination. The 1973 campaign proved to be Santo's last year with the Cubs, who elected to trade him to the crosstown rival Chicago White Sox for four players on December 11, 1973. Santo ended up spending just one year with the White Sox, serving them as a part-time player, before announcing his retirement at season's end. He finished his career with 342 home runs, 1,331 RBIs, 1,138 runs scored, 2,254 hits, a .277 batting average, a .362 on-base percentage, and a .464 slugging percentage. At the time of his retirement, Santo trailed only Eddie Mathews among major league third basemen in career homers and slugging percentage. Meanwhile, his 6,777 total chances, 4,532 assists, and 389 double plays at third base remained National League records until Mike Schmidt eventually surpassed all three marks.

One of the most durable players in the game, Santo missed only 23 of a possible 1,595 starts from 1961 to 1970, taking the field almost every day despite being diagnosed with diabetes at the age of eighteen. Given a life expectancy of twenty-five years at the time, Santo begged those familiar with his situation not to reveal his condition to others, fearing that his illness might force him into retirement. Since the methods of regulating diabetes during the 1960s and 1970s were not as advanced as they are today, Santo gauged his blood sugar levels based on his moods. On those days he believed his blood sugar to be low, he typically snacked on candy bars in the clubhouse. Santo later said, "I was always careful not to give myself a shot of insulin in the locker room in front of anybody. I always did it in private." He also revealed that the disease drove him on the field, saying, "It was one reason I played so hard. I kept thinking my career could end any day. I never really wanted out of the lineup. The diabetes thing was hanging over my head."

Former Cubs teammate Randy Hundley said none of Santo's teammates realized he had diabetes until one night in St. Louis, when he made a bad throw to first base and went down on one knee in pain. They later learned he had the disease for six years. Hundley said, "We kidded him about it quite a bit, made his life miserable at times."

Santo revealed his struggle with diabetes to the general public for the first time during "Ron Santo Day," held at Wrigley Field on August 28, 1971. The disease later necessitated the amputation of both legs below the knee: the right in 2001, and the left in 2002.

Following his retirement, Santo joined the Cubs' broadcast booth in 1990, working as the color commentator for WGN radio. He subsequently developed a reputation for his unabashed broadcast enthusiasm, which often caused him to emit groans and cheers over the airwaves. As excitable as Santo became when a member of the home team made a great play, he proved to be just as vocal in expressing his displeasure over Cubs' miscues. Santo continued to entertain fans with his emotional style of broadcasting until 2010, when he died of complications from bladder cancer at the age of 70, on December 3, 2010. Upon learning of his broadcast partner's passing, Pat Hughes said, "He absolutely loved the Cubs. The Cubs have lost their biggest fan."

Hughes noted that, with all the medical problems Santo had "he never complained. He wanted to have fun. He wanted to talk baseball....He considered going to games therapeutic. He enjoyed himself in the booth right to the end."

Meanwhile, Cubs Chairman Tom Ricketts released a statement saying, "My siblings and I first knew Ron Santo as fans, listening to him in the broadcast booth. We knew him for his passion, his loyalty, his great personal courage and his tremendous sense of humor. It was our great honor to get to know him personally in our first year as owners....Ronnie will forever be the heart and soul of Cubs fans."

First eligible for election to the Hall of Fame in 1980, Santo spent the next thirty years being bypassed for induction into Cooperstown, first by the members of the BBWAA, and, later, by the members of the Veterans Committee. Yet, through it all, Santo maintained a positive outlook, telling a cheering Wrigley Field crowd on the day the Cubs retired his number 10, "This is my Hall of Fame!" Meanwhile, former Cubs second baseman Ryne Sandberg announced during his 2005 Hall of Fame acceptance speech, "...for what it's worth, Ron Santo just gained one more vote from the Veterans Committee." The members of the Golden Era Committee inducted Santo into Cooperstown posthumously seven years later.

Cub Numbers:

337 HR; 1,290 RBIs; 1,109 Runs Scored; 2,171 Hits; 353 Doubles; 66 Triples; 35 Stolen Bases; .279 AVG; .366 OBP; .472 SLG; .838 OPS

Career Numbers:

342 HR; 1,331 RBIs; 1,138 Runs Scored; 2,254 Hits; 365 Doubles; 67 Triples; 35 Stolen Bases; .277 AVG; .362 OBP; .464 SLG; .826 OPS

Cub Career Highlights:

Best Season: Santo had several outstanding years for the Cubs, any of which would make a good choice here. Yet, even though he posted comparable offensive numbers in 1966, 1967 and 1969, the feeling here is that Santo had his finest all-around season in 1964. Although somewhat overshadowed by fellow third baseman Ken Boyer, who captured NL MVP honors, Santo finished in the league's top five in seven different offensive categories, placing fourth in total bases (334) and second in RBIs (114), slugging percentage (.564), and OPS (.962), while topping the circuit in on-base percentage (.398), triples (13), and walks (86). Santo also ranked in the league's top 10 in home runs (30), batting average (.313), hits (185), and doubles (33), while leading all players at his position in putouts, assists, and double plays.

Memorable Moments/Greatest Performances: Santo fashioned one of the longest hitting streaks in franchise history in 1966, hitting safely in 28 consecutive games from May 31 to July 4, a period during which he went 39-for-101 (.386), with 7 homers, 20 RBIs, and 23 runs scored.

Although the Cubs ended up losing to the Dodgers by a score of 4-3 in 13 innings on August 18, 1960, Santo had his breakout game for the Cubs, going 3-for-4, with a pair of homers, including a solo shot in the bottom of the ninth that sent the contest into extra innings.

Santo helped lead the Cubs to a 16-5 mauling of the Cincinnati Reds on June 28, 1961 by homering twice, collecting 4 hits, driving in 7 runs, and scoring 4 others.

Santo led the Cubs to a 10-2 rout of the Milwaukee Braves on August 29, 1965 by going 4-for-4, with a pair of homers, 4 RBIs, and 4 runs scored.

Santo defeated Philadelphia almost single-handedly on September 21, 1965, driving in 6 runs with a single and a pair of homers during a 7-5 win over the Phillies. Santo delivered the game's decisive blow in the bottom of the eighth inning, when he hit a 2-run homer off future Cubs teammate Ferguson Jenkins.

Santo hit game-winning walk-off homers against Atlanta on consecutive days in May of 1966, giving the Cubs an 8-5 victory over the Braves on the twenty-eighth of the month by taking Ted Abernathy deep with two men out and two men on in the bottom of the 12th inning, before delivering the decisive blow of a 3-2, 10-inning win against Billy O'Dell the very next day.

Santo had the most productive day of his career on July 6, 1970, when he hit 3 homers and knocked in 10 runs during a doubleheader sweep of the Montreal Expos, Particularly effective in Game Two, Santo led the Cubs to a lopsided 14-2 victory over the Expos by hitting a pair of homers and driving in 8 runs.

Notable Achievements:

- Hit more than 20 home runs eleven times, topping 30 homers on four occasions.
- Knocked in more than 100 runs four times, topping 120 RBIs once (123 in 1969).
- Scored more than 100 runs once (107 in 1967).
- Batted over .300 four times.
- Finished in double digits in triples once (13 in 1964).
- Surpassed 30 doubles four times.
- Compiled on-base percentage in excess of .400 once (.412 in 1966).
- Posted slugging percentage in excess of .500 four times.

- Led NL in: triples once, walks four times, on-base percentage twice, sacrifice flies three times, and games played twice.
- Finished second in NL in: RBIs three times, walks once, slugging percentage once, and OPS once.
- Led NL third basemen in: putouts seven times, assists seven times, double plays six times, and fielding percentage once.
- Holds Cubs single-season record for most games played (164 in 1965).
- Ranks among Cubs career leaders in: home runs (fourth), RBIs (fifth), runs scored (eighth), hits (seventh), extra-base hits (fifth), doubles (ninth), total bases (sixth), bases on balls (second), sacrifice flies (second), games played (fifth), plate appearances (fifth), and at-bats (fifth).
- Ranks sixth all-time among MLB third basemen in assists (4,581).
- Three-time NL Player of the Month.
- 1973 Lou Gehrig Memorial Award winner.
- Five-time Gold Glove winner (1964, 1965, 1966, 1967 & 1968).
- Finished in top 10 of NL MVP voting four times, placing in top five of balloting twice.
- Five-time *Sporting News* All-Star selection (1966, 1967, 1968, 1969 & 1972).
- Nine-time NL All-Star (1963, 1964, 1965, 1966, 1968, 1969, 1971, 1972 & 1973).
- Elected to Baseball Hall of Fame by members of Golden Era Committee in 2012.

6

FERGUSON JENKINS

The last pitcher to win at least 20 games in six consecutive seasons, Ferguson Jenkins accomplished the feat while serving as the ace of Chicago's pitching staff from 1967 to 1972, a period during which he established himself as one of the top hurlers in all of baseball. Spending eight of his 19 big league seasons in the Windy City, Jenkins posted a total of 167 victories for the Cubs, while also setting franchise records for most strikeouts (2,038) and most starts (347). A true workhorse, Jenkins threw at least 20 complete games six times and tossed more than 270 innings in seven of his eight seasons with the Cubs. Meanwhile, Jenkins' outstanding stuff and exceptional control enabled him to lead all NL hurlers in strikeout-to-walk ratio three times, with the hard-throwing right-hander compiling a ratio of better than 4-to-1 on three separate occasions. Jenkins' superb pitching during his time in Chicago earned him three All-Star selections, three *Sporting News* All-Star nominations, four top-three finishes in the NL Cy Young voting, and Cy Young honors in 1971, when he became the first Cubs hurler to capture the award.

Born in Chatham, Ontario, Canada on December 13, 1943, Ferguson Arthur Jenkins attended Chatham Vocational High School, where he lettered in ice hockey, track and field, and basketball. Taking up baseball as a teenager, the tall and slender Jenkins spent his earliest days on the diamond playing first base, before gradually transitioning to the mound. Encouraged to develop his pitching skills by Philadelphia Phillies scout Gene Dziadura, who discovered him at the age of fifteen, Jenkins worked with Dziadura all through high school, before signing with the Phillies as an amateur free agent shortly after he graduated in 1962.

Jenkins spent the next three-and-a-half years advancing through the Philadelphia farm system, spending time at Miami, Chattanooga, Buffalo,

Courtesy of MEARS Online Auctions

Ferguson Jenkins won at least 20 games six straight times for the Cubs from 1967 to 1972

and Little Rock, before finally being summoned to the big leagues by the Phillies during the latter stages of the 1965 campaign. Making seven relief appearances over the season's final three weeks, the twenty-one-year-old Jenkins won two of his three decisions and compiled an ERA of 2.19 in just over 12 total innings of work. After earning a spot on Philadelphia's pitching staff the following spring, Jenkins found himself headed to Chicago when the Phillies included him in a five-player trade they completed with the Cubs on April 21, 1966 that sent Jenkins and outfielders Adolfo Phillips and John Herrnstein to the Windy City, in exchange for pitchers Bob Buhl and Larry Jackson.

Jenkins spent most of his first season in Chicago working out of the Cubs' bullpen, concluding the 1966 campaign with a record of 6-8, an ERA of 3.31, and 148 strikeouts in 182 innings of work. However, after being inserted into the starting rotation during the season's final month, Jenkins remained a full-time starter the rest of his career. Establishing himself as the ace of Chicago's pitching staff the following year, Jenkins earned his first All-Star selection and a runner-up finish in the NL Cy Young voting by going 20-13 with a 2.80 ERA, placing second in the league with 236 strikeouts, finishing third with 289⅓ innings pitched, and topping the circuit with 20 complete games. He followed that up with an equally impressive performance in 1968, finishing the year with a record of 20-15, a 2.63 ERA, and 20 complete games, while placing second in the league with 260 strikeouts and 308 innings pitched.

Although the Cubs faltered down the stretch in 1969, winning just 8 of their final 26 games, with the overworked Jenkins going just 2-4 in his last six decisions, the 6'5", 210-pound right-hander posted outstanding overall numbers nonetheless. In addition to going 21-15 with a 3.21 ERA, Jenkins led all NL hurlers with 273 strikeouts and ranked among the league leaders with 23 complete games, 311⅓ innings pitched, and 7 shutouts. Jenkins had another big year in 1970, earning a third-place finish in the NL Cy Young voting by compiling an ERA of 3.39, placing near the top of the league rankings in wins (22), strikeouts (274), and innings pitched (313), and leading the league with 24 complete games, a WHIP of 1.038, and an excellent strikeout-to-walk ratio of 4.567.

Jenkins' exceptional control, which enabled him to lead the league in fewest walks allowed per nine innings pitched on two separate occasions, made him a pleasure to play behind, with longtime teammate Billy Williams stating, "Jenks made it easy for us outfielders. When he pitched,

I could move to get a jump on the ball. When [catcher Randy] Hundley gave him a target inside, I could move to anticipate the hitter, since I knew Fergie was always on target."

Chris Cannizzaro, who spent one season in Chicago serving as the Cubs' primary catcher, also praised Jenkins, commenting, "He is just a super pitcher. It's a treat just to play with a guy like that. He has great stuff and great control. But, best of all, he's a competitor. He pitches from behind as well as anybody I've ever seen. He never gives up."

Feeling that the ability to consistently throw strikes represented one of the keys to being a successful pitcher, Jenkins later explained, "I tell youngsters to make the batter do half the work. Throw strikes. If the batter takes them, he'll strike out. If you don't throw strikes and give up a walk, you get angry with yourself, your catcher is disappointed, your manager is mad, and the pitching coach is unhappy. In today's baseball, the guys by far don't throw enough strikes."

Although Jenkins' philosophy worked extremely well for him over the course of his career, his ability to consistently be around the plate—especially at hitter-friendly Wrigley Field—led to him surrendering more home runs (271) than any other pitcher in Cubs history.

Jenkins also believed that a pitcher should be able to help himself on offense, suggesting, "Pitching is only one of your baseball abilities. Pitchers should know how to run the bases, how to slide, how to move runners over. When you go up to the plate, you become a batter. All you're doing is just changing positions. If you just stand there, you're a weak sister. But, if you're swinging the bat, you're a dangerous part of the lineup." A good-hitting pitcher throughout his career, Jenkins posted a lifetime batting average of .165, with 13 homers and 85 RBIs, in 896 official at-bats.

After being overshadowed the previous few seasons by star hurlers such as Bob Gibson, Juan Marichal, and Tom Seaver, Jenkins stepped to the forefront in 1971, earning NL Cy Young honors by posting a record of 24-13 that made him the league's winningest pitcher. He also compiled a 2.77 ERA, finished second in the league with 263 strikeouts, and topped the circuit with 325 innings pitched, 30 complete games, and a superb strikeout-to-walk ratio of 7.108. Although somewhat less dominant the following year, Jenkins again performed extremely well, earning his final All-Star selection and a third-place finish in the NL Cy Young balloting by going 20-12, with a 3.20 ERA, 184 strikeouts, 23 complete games, and 289⅓ innings pitched.

With Jenkins subsequently finishing just 14-16 with a 3.89 ERA in 1973, the Cubs elected to trade him to the Texas Rangers for third baseman Bill Madlock and infielder/outfielder Vic Harris following the conclusion of the campaign. While Madlock went on to win two batting titles as a member of the Cubs, Jenkins put together one of the finest seasons of his career for the Rangers in 1974, earning a runner-up finish in the AL Cy Young voting and AL Comeback Player of the Year honors by topping the circuit with 25 victories and 29 complete games, while also ranking among the league leaders with a 2.82 ERA, 6 shutouts, 225 strikeouts, and 328⅓ innings pitched.

Jenkins spent one more year in Texas, going 17-18 with a 3.93 ERA in 1975, before being dealt to the Boston Red Sox for three players at season's end. However, after compiling an overall record of just 22-21 over the course of the next two seasons in Boston, Jenkins returned to Texas for four more years when the Rangers reacquired him for minor league pitcher John Poloni and cash on December 14, 1977. Although Jenkins posted relatively modest numbers during his second tour of duty with the Rangers, going a combined 51-42 from 1978 to 1981, he had one more big year left in his aging right arm, compiling a record of 18-8 and an ERA of 3.04 ERA in the first of those campaigns, before seeing his numbers gradually decline over the course of the next three seasons.

Running afoul of the law during his time in Texas, Jenkins suffered the indignity of being arrested by Canadian police in 1980, when, during a routine customs search in Toronto, authorities discovered 3.0 grams of cocaine, 2.2 grams of hashish, and 1.75 grams of marijuana in his luggage. Subsequently suspended indefinitely by Baseball Commissioner Bowie Kuhn before being reinstated by independent arbiter Raymond Goetz two weeks later due to a missing piece of evidence, Jenkins continued to maintain his innocence through the years, later stating, "It was about two years before my father believed me when I told him I didn't do it."

Granted free agency following the conclusion of the 1981 campaign, Jenkins signed with the Cubs, with whom he spent his final two big league seasons, compiling an overall record of 20-24 during that time, before being released on March 19, 1984. The forty-year-old Jenkins subsequently announced his retirement, ending his career with a record of 284-226, an ERA of 3.34, 267 complete games, 49 shutouts, and 3,192 strikeouts in 4,500⅔ total innings of work. Having surrendered only 997 bases on balls over 19 big-league seasons, Jenkins remains one of only four pitchers in MLB history to record more than 3,000 strikeouts while issuing fewer than 1,000 walks (Curt Schilling, Pedro Martinez, and Greg Maddux are the other three).

Following his retirement, Jenkins continued to play ball professionally in Canada for another two years, before leaving the game for good in 1985. The members of the BBWAA elected him to the Hall of Fame six years later, including his name on 75.4 percent of the ballots they cast in 1991—his third year of eligibility.

Cub Numbers:

Record: 167-132, .559 Win Pct, 3.20 ERA, 154 CG, 29 Shutouts, 6 Saves, 2,673⅔ IP, 2,038 Strikeouts, 1.123 WHIP

Career Numbers:

Record: 284-226, .567 Win Pct, 3.34 ERA, 267 CG, 49 Shutouts, 7 Saves, 4,500⅔ IP, 3,192 Strikeouts,1.142 WHIP

Cub Career Highlights:

Best Season: Although Jenkins also pitched extremely well for the Cubs in each of the previous four seasons, the 1971 campaign would have to be considered the finest of his career. In addition to leading all NL hurlers with 24 wins, 30 complete games, 325 innings pitched, and a magnificent strikeout-to-walk ratio of 7.108 that represents the second-best single-season mark in franchise history, Jenkins finished second in the league with 263 strikeouts, placed third in WHIP (1,049), and ranked ninth in ERA (2.77). Despite tossing a league-leading 325 frames, Jenkins amazingly surrendered only 37 bases on balls the entire year, with his fabulous performance earning him a seventh-place finish in the league MVP voting, NL Cy Young honors, and recognition as *The Sporting News* NL Pitcher of the Year. He also had his best year at the plate, compiling a .243 batting average, while establishing career-high marks in home runs (6), RBIs (20), runs scored (13), and hits (28).

Memorable Moments/Greatest Performances: Jenkins made his Cubs debut a memorable one, earning a 2-0 victory over the Dodgers on April 23, 1966 by throwing 5⅓ scoreless innings of relief, while also collecting 2 hits, including his first big-league homer.

Although Jenkins failed to earn a decision in a game the Cubs eventually lost to Atlanta by a score of 1-0 in 11 innings, he pitched brilliantly against the Braves on June 16, 1968, surrendering just 5 hits and recording 7 strikeouts over 10 shutout innings.

Jenkins hurled another gem a little over five weeks later, allowing only 4 hits and striking out 13, in defeating the Dodgers by a score of 2-1 on July 27, 1968.

Jenkins sandwiched a pair of exceptional performances around a 5-2 loss to Pittsburgh in early July of 1970, surrendering just 4 hits and recording 11 strikeouts during a 5-0 complete-game win over the Cardinals on the first of the month, before yielding only 5 hits and fanning another 11 batters during a 2-0 victory over the Phillies on July 10.

Jenkins again dominated Philadelphia's lineup on May 10, 1971, when he defeated the Phillies by a score of 3-0, allowing just 4 hits and striking out 12 in the process.

Jenkins continued to be a thorn in the side of his former team on July 24, 1971, recording a career-high 14 strikeouts during a complete-Game Two-1 victory over the Phillies.

Jenkins helped his own cause on September 1, 1971, when he homered twice and knocked in 3 runs during a 5-2 complete-game win over the Montreal Expos.

However, Jenkins turned in his finest pitching performance of the 1971 campaign on August 16, when he allowed just 2 hits and recorded 7 strikeouts during a 3-0 win over the Atlanta Braves.

Jenkins nearly tossed what would have been the only no-hitter of his career on July 27, 1972, surrendering only a fourth-inning double to Willie Montanez during a 4-0, one-hit shutout of the Phillies.

Jenkins earned arguably the most satisfying win of his career on April 17, 1973, when he tossed a two-hit shutout against the Mets, out-dueling New York staff ace Tom Seaver by a score of 1-0 in the process.

Although the Cubs ended up losing their July 22, 1973 match-up with the San Francisco Giants by a score of 4-1 in 13 innings, Jenkins turned in a heroic effort, yielding just 4 hits and 2 walks over the first 12 innings, before exiting the contest.

Notable Achievements:

- Won at least 20 games six straight times.
- Compiled ERA under 3.00 three times.
- Struck out more than 200 batters five times, surpassing 250 strikeouts on four occasions.
- Threw more than 300 innings four times, topping 270 innings pitched three other times.
- Threw at least 20 complete games six times, completing 30 of his starts once (30 in 1971).
- Led NL pitchers in: wins once, WHIP once, strikeouts once, complete games three times, innings pitched once, strikeout-to-walk ratio three times, starts three times, and putouts twice.
- Finished second in NL in: wins once, shutouts once, strikeouts four times, innings pitched three times, and complete games once.
- Holds Cubs career records for most strikeouts (2,038) and most starts (347).
- Ranks among Cubs career leaders in: wins (fifth), WHIP (10th), shutouts (fourth), innings pitched (third), pitching appearances (sixth), and strikeout-to-walk ratio (fifth).
- One of only four pitchers in MLB history with more than 3,000 strikeouts (3,192) and fewer than 1,000 walks (997).
- July 1971 NL Player of the Month.
- 1971 *Sporting News* NL Pitcher of the Year.
- 1971 NL Cy Young Award winner.
- Finished in top three of NL Cy Young voting three other times.
- Finished seventh in 1971 NL MVP voting.
- Three-time *Sporting News* All-Star selection (1967, 1971 & 1972).
- Three-time NL All-Star (1967, 1971 & 1972).
- Elected to Baseball Hall of Fame by members of BBWAA in 1991.

7

GABBY HARTNETT

Considered by many baseball historians to be the greatest catcher in National League history prior to the arrival of Johnny Bench, Gabby Hartnett, if nothing else, proved to be easily the senior circuit's preeminent receiver and the Cubs' top position player of the first half of the twentieth century. Spending virtually his entire career in Chicago, Hartnett retired in 1941 holding Major League records for most home runs (236) and highest slugging percentage (.489) by a catcher. In addition to hitting more than 20 homers three times and posting a slugging percentage in excess of .500 on eight separate occasions, the hard-hitting Hartnett batted over .300 six times and knocked in more than 100 runs once, topping 90 RBIs on two other occasions. An excellent defender as well, Hartnett led all NL receivers in putouts four times and assists, double plays, fielding percentage, and caught-stealing percent six times each. Hartnett's outstanding all-around play, which helped lead the Cubs to four NL pennants, earned him one MVP award, two *Sporting News* All-Star selections, six NL All-Star nominations, and a plaque in Cooperstown.

Born in Woonsocket, Rhode Island on December 20, 1900, Charles Leo Hartnett spent his entire childhood in Millville, Massachusetts, where his parents raised him and his thirteen siblings. After finishing the eighth grade at Longfellow Grammar School, the fourteen-year-old Hartnett briefly went to work at the Rubber Shop, before enrolling at the prestigious Dean Academy in nearby Franklin, Massachusetts. All the while, though, Hartnett continued to pursue his dream of playing in the Major Leagues, joining his town's baseball team, while simultaneously playing high school ball.

Following his graduation from Dean Academy, Hartnett took a job with the American Steel and Wire Company in Worcester, which offered

Gabby Hartnett retired with more home runs than
any other catcher in Major League history

him a position in its shipping department, with the understanding that he would also play for the company baseball team. One year later, Hartnett signed with the Worcester Boosters of the Class A Eastern League, with whom he began his professional career at the age of twenty in 1921. Scouted by the New York Giants and Chicago Cubs during his first season at Worcester, Hartnett received an unfavorable report from Giants scout Jesse Burkett, who claimed that the young catcher's smallish hands made him an unlikely candidate to succeed behind home plate at the major league level. However, Chicago scout Jack Doyle felt differently, prompting the Cubs to purchase Hartnett's contract for $2,500 at season's end.

After joining the Cubs in 1922, Hartnett spent his first two seasons in Chicago backing up veteran receiver Bob O'Farrell. During that time, Hartnett ironically acquired the nickname "Gabby" due to the shyness he displayed as a rookie, even though he, in truth, possessed an extremely outgoing personality. Following a difficult rookie campaign in which he batted just .194 in 31 games, Hartnett began to assume a more prominent role in 1923, when, appearing in a total of 85 contests, he hit 8 homers, drove in 39 runs, and batted .268. He then received his big break at O'Farrell's expense in July of 1924, as the latter explained years later:

"In 1924, a foul tip came back, crashed through my mask, and fractured my skull ... Gabby Hartnett had come up to the Cubs in '22 and he was sort of crowding me. But the catcher's job was mine until I got my skull fractured."

Making the most of his opportunity, Hartnett went on to hit 16 homers, knock in 67 runs, and bat .299, in only 111 games, convincing the Cubs to trade O'Farrell to the St. Louis Cardinals early the following year. Hartnett subsequently established himself as the senior circuit's top receiver in 1925 by finishing second in the league with 24 homers, breaking in the process the single-season home run record for catchers. He also drove in 67 runs, batted .289, and led all players at his position in putouts, assists, and double plays.

Plagued by injuries throughout much of the ensuing campaign, Hartnett posted less impressive numbers on offense. However, he performed well in each of the next two seasons, hitting 10 homers, driving in 80 runs, and batting .294 in 1927, before hitting 14 homers, knocking in 57 runs, batting .302, and finishing among the league leaders with a .523 slugging percentage in 1928.

Although the Cubs captured the National League pennant in 1929, they did so without much help from Hartnett, who ended up appearing in only 25 games after mysteriously injuring his arm during spring training. Making a total of only 27 plate appearances over the course of the season, mostly as a pinch-hitter, Hartnett hit just 1 homer and knocked in only 9 runs. However, he rebounded the following year to have the finest statistical season of his career. With the National League using a livelier ball in 1930, offensive numbers soared throughout the league, with Hartnett's statistics proving to be no exception. In addition to breaking his own major league record for catchers by hitting 37 home runs, Hartnett drove in 122 runs, batted .339, compiled an on-base percentage of .404, and posted a slugging percentage of .630. After the senior circuit discontinued its use of the "jack-rabbit" baseball the following year, Hartnett posted far more conventional numbers the next three seasons, averaging 12 home runs and 70 RBIs from 1931 to 1933, while compiling batting averages of .282, .271, and .276.

Nevertheless, Hartnett remained unchallenged for preeminence among National League receivers, with only Philadelphia's Mickey Cochrane and New York's Bill Dickey rivaling him in the junior circuit. In addition to wielding a potent bat, the 6'1", 210-pound Hartnett had arguably the strongest throwing arm of any catcher in the game, with former Cubs manager Joe McCarthy once stating, "Gabby was the greatest throwing catcher that ever gunned a ball to second base. He threw a ball that had the speed of lightning, but was as light as a feather."

McCarthy, who also later managed Bill Dickey in New York, continued, "I rated Gabby the perfect catcher. He was super smart and nobody could throw with him. And he also was an outstanding clutch hitter."

The only weakness in Hartnett's game proved to be his lack of speed, with noted sportswriter Red Smith once writing, "Hartnett was so good that he lasted twenty years in spite of the fact that he couldn't run. All other skills were refined in him."

Noted for his loquacious nature as well, Hartnett became a favorite of the hometown fans, with Chicago's most famous resident, gangster Al Capone, insisting during an exhibition game played between the Cubs and White Sox on September 9, 1931, that Hartnett pose for a picture with him next to the Cubs dugout. After newspapers across the country subsequently published the photo, Hartnett received a telegram from Baseball Commissioner Kenesaw Mountain Landis instructing him to refrain from having his picture taken with Capone in the future. Responding to the Commissioner's edict, Hartnett wrote back, "OK, but if you don't want me to have my picture taken with Al Capone, you tell him."

After earning the first of six straight All-Star selections the previous season by hitting 16 homers, driving in 88 runs, and batting .276, Hartnett clubbed 22 homers, knocked in 90 runs, and batted .299 in 1934. Despite being limited by injuries to only 116 games and 413 official plate appearances the following year, Hartnett ended up winning league MVP honors by leading the Cubs to the NL pennant with one of his finest all-around seasons. In addition to guiding Chicago's pitching staff to the lowest team ERA in the league and finishing first among players at his position in assists, double plays, and fielding percentage, Hartnett hit 13 homers, knocked in 91 runs, and ranked among the league leaders with a .344 batting average, a .404 on-base percentage, and a .545 slugging percentage.

Hartnett again posted solid numbers in 1936, batting .307, with 64 RBIs in only 121 games, before hitting 12 homers, driving in 82 runs, and batting a career-high .354 the following year, en route to earning a runner-up finish in the NL MVP voting. However, after replacing Charlie Grimm as manager midway through the 1938 campaign, Hartnett assumed a part-time role on the playing field for most of the next three seasons, before being released by the Cubs on November 13, 1940. Hartnett then signed with the Giants, with whom he spent his final season in the big leagues, announcing his retirement following the conclusion of the 1941 campaign. In addition to hitting more home runs and compiling a higher slugging percentage than any other catcher in MLB history at the time of his retirement, Hartnett continues to rank among the all-time leaders at his position in double plays (fourth) and caught-stealing percentage (second).

Following his playing days, Hartnett spent five years managing in the minor leagues, before leaving the game for good. He subsequently opened Gabby Hartnett's Recreation Center in the Chicago suburb of Lincolnwood, which eventually grew to include twenty bowling lanes, a barbershop, a soda fountain, a cocktail lounge, and a sporting-goods store. Hartnett continued to enjoy his retirement until 1969, when his health began to deteriorate. After having his spleen removed in 1970, he lived another two years, dying from complications from cirrhosis of the liver on his seventy-second birthday, December 20, 1972.

Cub Numbers:

231 HR; 1,153 RBIs; 847 Runs Scored; 1,867 Hits; 391 Doubles; 64 Triples; 28 Stolen Bases; .297 AVG; .370 OBP; .490 SLG; .860 OPS

Career Numbers:

236 HR; 1,179 RBIs; 867 Runs Scored; 1,912 Hits; 396 Doubles; 64 Triples; 28 Stolen Bases; .297 AVG; .370 OBP; .489 SLG; .858 OPS

Cub Career Highlights:

Best Season: Hartnett performed exceptionally well for the Cubs in 1935, leading them to the NL pennant and capturing league MVP honors by batting .344 and driving in 91 runs, in just 116 games and 413 official at-bats. He also played at an extremely high level two years later, earning a runner-up finish to Triple Crown winner Joe Medwick in the 1937 NL MVP balloting by posting career-high marks in batting average (.354) and on-base percentage (.424), while knocking in 82 runs, in only 110 games and 356 official at-bats. Nevertheless, the 1930 campaign would have to be considered the finest of Hartnett's career, even though the livelier ball employed by the National League in its games that year inflated his numbers somewhat. In addition to batting .339 and compiling an on-base percentage of .404, Hartnett established career-high marks in home runs (37), RBIs (122), runs scored (84), hits (172), slugging percentage (.630), OPS (1.034), games played (141), plate appearances (578), and official at-bats (508). Hartnett's 37 homers stood as the single-season record for catchers until Roy Campanella homered 40 times for the Dodgers in 1953. He also led all NL receivers in putouts, assists, fielding percentage, and base-runners caught stealing, with his 646 putouts representing the highest single-season total of his career.

Memorable Moments/Greatest Performances: Hartnett had his breakout game for the Cubs on April 20, 1923, leading them to a come-from-behind 12-11 victory over Pittsburgh with a pair of late-inning home runs. After contributing to a seven-run, eighth-inning rally with a three-run homer, Hartnett delivered a solo blast in the bottom of the ninth that won the game in walk-off fashion. He finished the contest with 3 hits, 4 RBIs, and 3 runs scored.

Hartnett had another big day at the plate on July 2, 1925, when he led the Cubs to an 11-6 win over St. Louis by going 4-for-5, with a double, a pair of homers, 3 RBIs, and 4 runs scored.

Hartnett turned in the finest performance of his outstanding 1930 campaign on June 25, when he went 4-for-5, with 2 homers, 6 RBIs, and 3 runs scored, during a 13-12 win over the Phillies.

Hartnett proved to be the difference in a 10-7 victory over the Pirates on September 4, 1930, when his 3-run homer in the top of the 10th inning provided the winning margin. He finished the day with 3 hits, 2 home runs, and 6 RBIs.

Although the Cubs lost to St. Louis by a score of 17-13 on July 12, 1931, Hartnett had the first 5-for-5 day of his career, collecting 3 doubles, 2 singles, and scoring 3 times during the defeat.

Hartnett contributed to a 17-4 thrashing of the Phillies on September 10, 1931 by going 4-for-5, with a homer, double, 6 RBIs, and 2 runs scored.

Hartnett once again went 5-for-5 in a losing cause on May 24, 1932, hitting safely in all five of his trips to the plate and scoring twice during an 8-6 loss to the Cardinals.

Hartnett came up just a double shy of hitting for the cycle on June 4, 1935, collecting a homer, triple, and single, driving in 6 runs, and scoring 3 times during a lopsided 10-2 victory over Cincinnati.

Yet, Hartnett experienced the highlight of his career on September 28, 1938, when he delivered arguably the most memorable home run in Chicago Cubs history. With the Cubs and Pirates battling it out for the National League pennant, the two teams met in a pivotal three game series during the season's final week. After the Cubs won the series opener, they came up to bat in the bottom of the ninth inning of Game Two with the score tied at 5-5. With darkness descending on a lightless Wrigley Field, the umpires ruled that, if the Cubs failed to score the winning run, the entire game would have to be replayed the following day. Stepping up to the plate with two men out and no one on base, Hartnett drove a Mace Brown offering into the left-center field bleachers, giving the Cubs a 6-5 walk-off win. Hartnett's blast, which became known as his "Homer in the Gloamin," was later ranked by ESPN as the 47th greatest home run of all time. The Cubs won the following day as well, all but clinching the league championship. Hartnett, who found himself being escorted around the bases by his teammates and the many fans that stormed the playing field, later recalled, "I swung with everything I had, and then I got that feeling, the kind of feeling you get when the blood rushes out of your head and you get dizzy. A lot of people have told me they didn't know the ball was in the bleachers. Well, I did. Maybe I was the only one in the park who did. I knew the moment I hit it.... I don't think I saw third base...and I don't think I walked a step to the plate—I was carried in."

Notable Achievements:

- Hit more than 20 home runs three times, topping 30 homers once (37 in 1930).
- Knocked in more than 100 runs once (122 in 1930).
- Batted over .300 five times, topping the .330-mark on three occasions.
- Surpassed 30 doubles four times.
- Compiled on-base percentage in excess of .400 five times.

- Posted slugging percentage in excess of .500 eight times, topping the .600-mark once (.630 in 1930).
- Finished second in NL in home runs once and third in league batting average twice.
- Led NL catchers in: putouts four times, assists six times, double plays six times, fielding percentage six times, and caught-stealing percent six times.
- Ranks among Cubs career leaders in: home runs (seventh), RBIs (sixth), doubles (sixth), extra-base hits (seventh), total bases (eighth), slugging percentage (tied-10th), OPS (tied-10th), and games played (eighth).
- Ranks among MLB career leaders in double plays turned (fourth) and caught-stealing percent (second) by a catcher.
- 1935 NL MVP.
- Finished second in 1937 NL MVP voting.
- Two-time *Sporting News* All-Star selection (1927 & 1937).
- Six-time NL All-Star (1933, 1934, 1935, 1936, 1937 & 1938).
- Four-time NL champion (1929, 1932, 1935 & 1938).
- Elected to Baseball Hall of Fame by members of BBWAA in 1955.

8

BILLY HERMAN

The National League's top second baseman for nearly a decade, Billy Herman spent parts of 11 seasons in Chicago, establishing himself during that time as one of the senior circuit's finest all-around infielders. An outstanding line-drive hitter who did a superb job of executing the hit-and-run play, Herman batted over .300 seven times as a member of the Cubs, topping the .330-mark on three separate occasions. The right-handed hitting Herman also accumulated more than 200 hits three times, surpassed 50 doubles twice, and scored more than 100 runs five times, earning in the process four top-10 finishes in the NL MVP voting and seven consecutive All-Star selections during his time in the Windy City. An extremely adept fielder as well, Herman led all NL second sackers in putouts six times and assists, double plays, and fielding percentage three times each, recording a total of 466 putouts in 1933 that still stands as the National League's single-season record for players at the position. Herman's exceptional all-around play helped lead the Cubs to three National League pennants, eventually earning him a place in Cooperstown.

Born in New Albany, Indiana, right across the Ohio River from Louisville, Kentucky, on July 7, 1909, William Jennings Bryan Herman never seriously considered a career in baseball as a teenager. Named after three-time Democratic presidential candidate William Jennings Bryan, Herman failed to distinguish himself on the diamond while attending local New Albany High School, recalling years later, "I was a sub on the team—a substitute third baseman and shortstop. I never played regular in high school."

Nevertheless, after dropping out of high school following his junior year to work in a Louisville veneer manufacturing plant, Herman's career path began to take shape when Cap Neal, general manager of the American Association's Louisville Colonels, discovered him while

Courtesy of the Leslie Jones Collection at the Boston Public Library

Billy Herman made the NL All-Star Team
seven straight times while playing for the Cubs

playing for the New Covenant Presbyterian Church team in Louisville. Offered a contract by Neal, Herman later revealed, "I signed for nothing. Would have paid to get a contract with the Louisville Colonels back in 1928 when they signed me. I still wasn't any good."

Yet, in spite of Herman's self-deprecating evaluation, he began to thrive after being shifted from shortstop to second base following his assignment to Vicksburg, a Class-D team in the Cotton State League. Promoted to Louisville in 1929, Herman spent most of the next three seasons in Kentucky, improving his play to such a degree that he posted a .350 batting average through 118 games in 1931, before Chicago purchased his contract for $50,000 on August 4. Starting twenty-five games at second base for the Cubs over the final two months of the campaign, the twenty-two-year-old Herman made an extremely favorable impression on team management, batting .327, driving in 16 runs, and scoring 14 others.

Replacing an injured and aging Rogers Hornsby as Chicago's starting second baseman the following year, Herman went on to have a brilliant rookie season, earning a ninth-place finish in the NL MVP voting and helping the Cubs capture the pennant by batting .314, placing among the league leaders with 102 runs scored, 206 hits, and 42 doubles, and leading all players at his position with 527 assists, while also finishing second with 401 putouts and 102 double plays. Although somewhat less productive at the plate in 1933, finishing the year with a .279 batting average, 82 runs scored, and 173 hits, Herman performed exceptionally well in the field, recording 512 assists and a National League record 466 putouts at second base.

Despite being limited by injuries to just 113 games and 456 official at-bats in 1934, Herman began a string of eight straight seasons (seven as a member of the Cubs) in which he earned a spot on the National League All-Star team. After batting .303 and scoring 79 runs in the first of those campaigns, Herman had perhaps his finest all-around season in 1935, earning a fourth-place finish in the NL MVP balloting by leading the league with 227 hits, 57 doubles, and 24 sacrifice hits, while also knocking in 83 runs, placing among the league leaders with a 341 batting average, 113 runs scored, and 317 total bases, and finishing first among NL second basemen in putouts, assists, double plays, and fielding percentage. He followed that up with another superb all-around performance in 1936, placing third in the league MVP voting after batting .334, driving in a career-high 93 runs, scoring 101 times, collecting 211 hits and 57 doubles, and once again leading all players at his position in putouts and fielding percentage.

Herman, who usually batted second in Chicago's lineup, rarely struck out and excelled at hitting behind the runner when executing the hit-and-run play, with Cubs manager Charlie Grimm stating, "He was a wonderful fielder and as great a hit-and-run batter as I have ever seen. I can't remember anyone who could handle the inside pitch to right field better than Herman."

A smart and instinctive player, the 5'11", 180-pound Herman became expert at positioning himself in the field, moving a few feet in either direction, depending on the batter and the pitch count. In discussing his second baseman's fielding prowess, Charlie Grimm proclaimed, "He's without doubt the best fielding keystone man in the league since I have been in the harness. He can go farther to his right and also to his left than any second sacker I've ever watched. Frankie Frisch, at his best, wasn't the fielder Billy is. Frisch had more power at the plate and speed on the bases, but I'd still pick Herman over him in all-around value."

Meanwhile, Pittsburgh's Hall of Fame outfielder Paul Waner commented, "I'll hit one I think is through there and Herman suddenly comes up through a trapdoor and is standing right in front of the ball."

Herman also developed a reputation through the years as being a hard-nosed player who had little patience for those who did not share his strong work ethic, stating on one occasion, "The only thing we had on our minds was to win. Any way we could, we played to win. And if that wasn't good enough, why you went back home, got a lunch pail, and go to work. If you didn't play hard, you wouldn't have a friend on the club and you wouldn't be there long."

Not the most tolerant of individuals, Herman drew a $200 fine from Baseball Commissioner Kenesaw Mountain Landis for using "vile and unprintable language" during Chicago's ethnically-related verbal assault against Detroit star Hank Greenberg in Game Three of the 1935 World Series. Herman also voted against Mark Koenig receiving more than half a share of the Cubs' 1932 World Series earnings, leading to an extremely contentious fall classic between the Cubs and Yankees—Koenig's former team.

Herman compiled outstanding numbers again in 1937, earning a ninth-place finish in the NL MVP voting by finishing among the league leaders with a .335 batting average, 106 runs scored, 189 hits, 35 doubles, and 11 triples. Although Herman posted a slightly less impressive stat-line for Chicago's 1938 NL championship ball club, concluding the campaign with a .277 batting average, 86 runs scored, 173 hits, and 34 doubles, he had another solid all-around year, leading all players at his position in put-outs and fielding percentage, while placing second in assists and double plays. Herman followed that up with one of his finest seasons in 1939, batting .307, driving in 70 runs, finishing third in the league with 111 runs scored, topping the circuit with a career-high 18 triples, and leading all NL second basemen in putouts, assists, and double plays.

Herman spent one more full season in Chicago, batting .292, knocking in 57 runs, and scoring 77 times in 1940, before being dealt to the Brooklyn Dodgers for two players and $65,000 during the early stages of the ensuing campaign. Following Herman's acquisition, Brooklyn manager Leo Durocher declared, "Herman will help us more than you expect. He'll steady the kid at shortstop [Pee Wee Reese]. He'll take charge of the infield. And he gives us sustained power on attack. Anywhere along the line, right down to the pitcher, we're likely to blast."

Meanwhile, Herman chose not to criticize the Cubs for trading him away, stating, "I've got no squawk against the Chicago club. They treated me great there, and you couldn't ask to work for a better, more considerate organization."

However, years later, Chicago teammate Phil Cavarretta proved to be somewhat less diplomatic when he said, "When we traded Billy, I was sick, believe me. He went over to Brooklyn and won pennants."

Herman actually won just one pennant with the Dodgers, helping them capture the NL flag in 1941 by batting .291 and scoring 77 runs, en route to earning his eighth consecutive All-Star selection and an 11th-place finish in the league MVP balloting. He followed that up with a somewhat subpar performance in 1942, batting just .256 and scoring 76 runs, before having his last big year in 1943, when he earned a fourth-place finish in the MVP voting and the last of his 10 All-Star nominations by batting .330, collecting 193 hits and 41 doubles, scoring 76 times, and driving in a career-high 100 runs. Herman then missed the entire 1944 and 1945 campaigns while serving in the Navy during World War II, before splitting his final two seasons between the Dodgers, Boston Braves, and Pittsburgh Pirates, for whom he spent his last big league season serving as player-manager. After handing in his resignation and retiring as an active player following the conclusion of the 1947 campaign, Herman briefly managed in the minor leagues, before embarking on a lengthy coaching career that saw him serve on the coaching staffs of the Brooklyn Dodgers (1952-57), Milwaukee Braves (1958-59), Boston Red Sox (1960-64), California Angels (1967), and San Diego Padres (1978-79). He also managed the Red Sox for two years and assumed a role in player development as a member of the Oakland Athletics and San Diego Padres organizations.

Despite being elected to the Baseball Hall of Fame by the members of the Veteran's Committee in 1975, Herman never felt totally secure in his abilities on the diamond, stating on one occasion, "Baseball was always kind of a struggle for me. I guess maybe I was doing all right and didn't realize it, but it always seemed like a struggle to me." Herman lived another seventeen years after being inducted into Cooperstown, passing away on September 5, 1992, at the age of eighty-three, following a lengthy battle with cancer.

Cub Numbers:

37 HR; 577 RBIs; 875 Runs Scored; 1,710 Hits; 346 Doubles; 69 Triples; 53 Stolen Bases; .309 AVG; .366 OBP; .417 SLG; .782 OPS

Career Numbers:

47 HR; 839 RBIs; 1,163 Runs Scored; 2,345 Hits; 486 Doubles; 82 Triples; 67 Stolen Bases; .304 AVG; .367 OBP; .407 SLG; .774 OPS

Cub Career Highlights:

Best Season: Herman played his best ball for the Cubs from 1935 to 1937, batting over .330, scoring more than 100 runs, and placing in the top 10 in the NL MVP voting each year. However, even though Herman knocked in 10 more runs and posted a slightly higher OPS the following year, he had his finest all-around season in 1935, when he helped lead the Cubs to the pennant. In addition to hitting 7 homers, driving in 83 runs, placing among the league leaders with career-high marks in batting average (.341), runs scored (113), and total bases (317), he topped the senior circuit with 227 hits, 57 doubles, and 24 sacrifice hits. Herman also led all NL second basemen with 520 assists, 416 putouts, 109 double plays, and a .964 fielding percentage, earning in the process a fourth-place finish in the league MVP balloting.

Memorable Moments/Greatest Performances: Excelling with the glove as well as with the bat, Herman tied a National League record for a nine-inning game on June 28, 1933, when he recorded 11 putouts during a 9-5 win over the Phillies in Philadelphia.

Herman helped lead the Cubs to a 10-6 victory over Cincinnati on August 2, 1933 by going 4-for-5, with a pair of doubles, a stolen base, 2 RBIs, and 2 runs scored.

Herman had a similarly productive afternoon on July 21, 1934, pacing the Cubs to a 14-6 victory over the Phillies by going 4-for-5, with a pair of doubles, 2 RBIs, and 2 runs scored.

Herman again torched Philadelphia's pitching staff on June 13, 1935, going 5-for-6, with a double, 1 RBI, and 4 runs scored, during a 12-6 pasting of the Phillies.

Herman had a big day at the plate against Carl Hubbell and the Giants on June 25, 1935, going 4-for-5, with a homer, 3 RBIs, and 2 runs scored, during a 10-5 Cubs win.

Just six days later, on July 1, 1935, Herman helped pace the Cubs to an 8-4 victory over Cincinnati by going 4-for-5, with a double, 2 triples, and 3 runs scored.

Herman helped the Cubs record a come-from-behind 7-6, 11-inning win over Brooklyn on July 24, 1935 by going 4-for-5, with a homer, 2 RBIs, and 3 runs scored.

Herman tied the Major League record for most hits on opening day by collecting 5 hits during a 12-7 victory over St. Louis on April 14, 1936. He finished the game 5-for-5, with a homer, 3 doubles, 3 RBIs, and 4 runs scored.

Herman had another huge game against St. Louis on June 29, 1937, leading the Cubs to an 11-9 victory over the Cardinals by going 4-for-5, with a grand slam homer, 4 RBIs, and 4 runs scored.

Notable Achievements:

- Batted over .300 seven times, topping the .320-mark on four occasions.
- Scored more than 100 runs five times.
- Surpassed 200 hits three times.

- Finished in double-digits in triples twice.
- Surpassed 30 doubles seven times, topping 50 two-baggers twice.
- Compiled on-base percentage in excess of .400 once (.405 in 1931).
- Led NL in: hits once, doubles once, triples once, sacrifice hits once, games played twice, and plate appearances once.
- Finished second in NL in runs scored once and doubles once.
- Led NL second basemen in: putouts six times, assists three times, double plays three times, and fielding percentage three times.
- Ranks 10th in Cubs history with 346 career doubles.
- Ranks 10th all-time among MLB second basemen with 4,780 career putouts.
- Holds NL single-season record for most putouts by a second baseman (466 in 1933).
- Finished in top 10 of NL MVP voting four times, placing in top five twice.
- Seven-time NL All-Star.
- Three-time NL champion (1932, 1935 & 1938).
- Elected to Baseball Hall of Fame by members of Veteran's Committee in 1975.

9

STAN HACK

A productive hitter and clever base-runner, Stan Hack proved to be the National League's premier leadoff hitter and finest all-around third baseman for much of his sixteen-year career, which he spent entirely with the Cubs. Batting over .300, scoring more than 100 runs, and compiling an on-base percentage in excess of .400 seven times each, while also surpassing 20 steals once, 190 hits four times, and 80 bases on balls on eight separate occasions, Hack annually ranked among the league leaders in each of those offensive categories, topping the senior circuit in hits and steals twice each. An excellent fielder as well, Hack led all players at his position in putouts five times, fielding percentage three times, and assists twice, en route to earning four All-Star selections and two top-10 finishes in the NL MVP voting. Although Hack's stellar all-around play has yet to earn him a place in Cooperstown, the man known as "Smiling Stan" for his pleasant demeanor served as a key member of four pennant-winning ball clubs during his time in Chicago.

Born in Sacramento, California on December 6, 1909, Stanley Camfield Hack attended Sacramento High School, where he starred as an infielder on the school's baseball team. After graduating from high school, Hack took a job working at a bank, although he continued to hone his baseball skills by playing semi-pro ball on weekends. After advancing to the professional level in 1931 as a member of the Pacific Coast League's Sacramento Solons, the left-handed hitting, right-handed throwing Hack compiled a batting average of .352, prompting Cubs president Bill Veeck Sr. to sign him to a contract.

Hack arrived in Chicago the following year, spending most of his rookie season serving as a backup for starting third baseman Woody English, before splitting the 1933 campaign between the Cubs and their top

Courtesy of the Leslie Jones Collection at the Boston Public Library

Stan Hack (left) spent his entire 16-year career in Chicago,
batting over .300 and scoring more than 100 runs
seven times each during that time

minor league affiliate. Joining the Cubs for good in 1934, Hack laid claim
to the team's starting third base job by midseason, finishing the year with
a .289 batting average and 54 runs scored, in 111 games and 402 official
at-bats. He then helped Chicago capture the National League pennant in
1935 by batting .311, driving in 64 runs, scoring 75 times, and finishing
third in the senior circuit with a .406 on-base percentage.

Hack subsequently emerged as a full-fledged star in 1936, beginning
an outstanding six-year run during which he batted over .300 three times
and scored more than 100 runs each season. After batting .298, knocking
in a career-high 78 runs, scoring 102 times, and finishing second in the
league with 17 stolen bases in 1936, Hack batted .297, drove home 63
runs, scored 106 others, and swiped 16 bags the following year, while also
leading all NL third basemen with 151 putouts, 247 assists, and 25 double
plays. Inserted into the leadoff spot in the Cubs' batting order full-time
in 1938 after spending his first few seasons in the Windy City moving all

over the lineup, Hack ended up serving as the offensive catalyst of a Chicago team that went on to win the NL pennant. In addition to topping the senior circuit with 16 stolen bases, Hack ranked among the league leaders with a .320 batting average, a .411 on-base percentage, 109 runs scored, 195 hits, 11 triples, 34 doubles, and 94 bases on balls. He also led all players at his position in putouts (178) and double plays (26), earning in the process his first All-Star selection and a seventh-place finish in the league MVP voting.

Hack continued to excel for the Cubs over the course of the next three seasons, compiling batting averages of .298, .317, and .317, while placing near the top of the league rankings in runs scored each year, with totals of 112, 101, and 111, respectively. After topping the senior circuit with 17 stolen bases in 1939, Hack led the league in hits in each of the next two seasons, accumulating 191 safeties in 1940 and 186 the following year. He also finished second in the NL with a .417 on-base percentage in 1941. Meanwhile, Hack led all NL third basemen in putouts in 1939, before finishing first among players at his position in putouts, assists, and double plays in 1940.

An outstanding contact hitter who used the entire ball field, Hack hit only 57 home runs over the course of his career. However, he amassed 363 doubles and 81 triples, surpassing 30 two-baggers on four separate occasions. Hack also struck out only 466 times, in just over 8,500 total plate appearances. The combination of Hack's keen batting eye and ability to make contact with the ball enabled him to post more walks than strikeouts in every single season. In fact, he compiled a walk-to-strikeout ratio of better than three-to-one on five separate occasions.

Former Cubs teammate and longtime major league scout Len Merullo discussed Hack's hitting style, saying, "He was like Wade Boggs. He hit from foul line to foul line....A line-drive type hitter."

In explaining his tendency to get most of his hits to the opposite field, Hack said, "I watch the ball more than most hitters. I let it get right up on me—maybe I even swing a little late."

Meanwhile, in terms of his defense, Hack took a backseat to no other third baseman of his time. A consistent fielder with good footwork, an accurate arm, and a smooth, easy style, Hack, claimed teammate Phil Cavarretta, turned more bunts into outs than any other third sacker.

Cavarretta also praised Hack for his hitting, stating, "He was especially good when the chips were down; the kind of guy you liked to have at the plate when the big hit was needed."

Clearly the National League's top third baseman by the late-1930s, Hack drew favorable comparisons to Hall of Fame third sacker Pie Traynor from Cubs manager Charlie Grimm, who suggested, "He (Hack) doesn't bat in as many runs...but you must remember that Traynor hit in the clean-up spot with men on the bases in front of him. Stan may never have batted in 100 runs in a season, but what leadoff man ever did? ...In fielding, throwing, place-hitting, and every other department of that third base business, he's the payoff, the greatest of modern times for my money."

In addition to his outstanding playing ability, Hack became well known for his affable nature, which eventually earned him the nickname "Smiling Stan." One of the game's most popular players, Hack had nary an enemy in the sport, with teammate Gabby Hartnett once remarking, "Stan Hack has as many friends in baseball as Leo Durocher has enemies."

Still, not everyone liked "Smiling Stan." After batting an even .300, scoring 91 runs, and drawing 94 bases on balls in 1942, Hack saw his offensive production fall off somewhat the following year, as his relationship with Cubs manager Jimmy Wilson grew increasingly contentious. Although Hack still posted solid numbers, finishing the 1943 season with a .289 batting average, a .384 on-base percentage, and 78 runs scored, he chose to announce his retirement at only thirty-four years of age following the conclusion of the campaign. Subsequently coaxed out of retirement by his old friend Charlie Grimm, who replaced Wilson at the helm just 11 games into the 1944 season, Hack returned to the team shortly thereafter. Appearing in 98 games, Hack ended up compiling a batting average of .282 and scoring 65 runs, which represented his lowest marks since he became a full-time player nearly a decade earlier. Rebounding nicely the following year, Hack had his last big season, helping to lead the Cubs to the NL pennant by placing among the league leaders with a .323 batting average, a .420 on-base percentage, 110 runs scored, 193 hits, and 99 bases on balls.

Hack spent two more years with the Cubs, serving them as a part-time player during that time. He retired following the conclusion of the 1947 campaign with more hits (2,193), doubles (363), total bases (2,889), and games played (1,938) than any other National League third baseman, with the exception of Pie Traynor. Meanwhile, Hack continues to rank among the Cubs all-time leaders in several statistical categories, including hits, doubles, runs scored (1,239), and bases on balls (1,092).

After retiring as an active player, Hack became a minor league manager, piloting three different teams between 1948 and 1953. He then managed the Cubs from 1954 to 1956, leading them to three consecutive losing seasons, before being relieved of his duties. Hack subsequently became a coach for the St. Louis Cardinals, serving in that capacity for two years under manager Fred Hutchinson. He returned to minor league managing in 1959, before finally retiring from baseball in 1966. Hack lived another thirteen years, passing away in Dixon, Illinois on December 15, 1979, just nine days after celebrating his seventieth birthday.

Career Numbers:

57 HR; 642 RBIs; 1,239 Runs Scored; 2,193 Hits; 363 Doubles; 81 Triples; 165 Stolen Bases; .301 AVG; .394 OBP; .397 SLG; .791 OPS

Career Highlights:

Best Season: Although Hack had a big year for the Cubs in 1941, topping the senior circuit with 186 hits and ranking among the league leaders with 111 runs scored, 33 doubles, 99 walks, a .317 batting average, and a .417 on-base percentage, he had his finest all-around season in 1938. En route to earning a seventh-place finish in the NL MVP balloting, Hack helped lead the Cubs to the pennant by placing near the top of the league rankings with a .320 batting average, a .411 on-base percentage, 109 runs scored, 195 hits, 11 triples, 34 doubles, and 94 bases on balls, while also driving in 67 runs, leading the league with 16 stolen bases, and finishing first among players at his position in putouts and double plays.

Memorable Moments/Greatest Performances: Hack helped lead the Cubs to a 15-3 pasting of the Boston Braves on September 11, 1935 by going 4-for-5, with a double, 3 RBIs, and 2 runs scored.

Hack had a big day against New York on May 9, 1939, leading the Cubs to an 11-7 victory over the Giants by collecting 4 hits, 3 RBIs, and 3 runs scored.

Although not known as a home run hitter, Hack experienced a brief power surge in September of 1940. After hitting a pair of homers during a 5-3 loss to the Phillies on September 14, Hack again reached the seats twice just four days later, leading the Cubs to a 6-4 win over the Giants on September 18. Hack's second homer against New York, which broke a 4-4 tie in the top of the ninth inning, proved to be the game's decisive blow. He finished the contest 4-for-4, with 2 RBIs and 2 runs scored.

Hack homered twice in one game for the third and final time in his career the following year, doing so during an 8-7 loss to the Giants on June 11, 1941. He finished that game 4-for-5, with 3 RBIs and 3 runs scored.

Although the Cubs lost their July 30, 1941 matchup with the Phillies by a score of 8-4, Hack had the first 5-for-5 day of his career. He topped that performance, though, on August 9, 1942, when he led the Cubs to a 10-8 win over Cincinnati in 18 innings by reaching base safely in all 9 of his official trips to the plate, collecting 5 hits and 4 walks, while also scoring 4 runs.

Hack had another huge game against the Reds on August 5, 1945, going 4-for-5, with 3 doubles and 4 runs scored, during a 12-5 Cubs victory.

After struggling against Detroit in the 1935 World Series, Hack excelled in each of his next two postseason appearances, batting .471 (8-for-17) against the Yankees in the 1938 fall classic, before posting a mark of .367 (11-for-34) against the Tigers in 1945. Performing particularly well during Chicago's 8-7, 12-inning victory in Game Six of the 1945 Series, Hack helped the Cubs stave off elimination by driving in the winning run with an RBI double in the bottom of the 12th. He finished the day 4-for-5, with 2 walks, 3RBIs, and 1 run scored.

Notable Achievements:

- Batted over .300 seven times, topping the .320-mark on three occasions.
- Scored more than 100 runs seven times.
- Finished in double digits in triples once (11 in 1938).
- Surpassed 30 doubles four times.
- Topped 20 stolen bases once (21 in 1940).
- Compiled on-base percentage in excess of .400 seven times.
- Led NL in: hits twice, stolen bases twice, games played once, and plate appearances three times.
- Finished second in NL in: runs scored three times, stolen bases three times, hits once, and on-base percentage once.

- Led NL third basemen in: putouts five times, assists twice, double plays three times, and fielding percentage twice.
- Holds Cubs career record for most bases on balls (1,092).
- Ranks among Cubs career leaders in: runs scored (seventh), hits (sixth), doubles (seventh), triples (ninth), total bases (10th), on-base percentage (tied-seventh), games played (seventh), plate appearances (sixth), and at-bats (sixth).
- Finished in top 10 of NL MVP voting twice (1938 & 1940).
- Three-time *Sporting News* All-Star selection (1940, 1941 & 1942).
- Four-time NL All-Star (1938, 1939, 1941 & 1943).
- Four-time NL champion (1932, 1935, 1938 & 1945).

10

MARK GRACE

One of the most consistent and reliable players ever to don a Cubs uniform, Mark Grace spent 13 seasons in Chicago, during which time he provided leadership to his teammates, as well as outstanding all-around play at first base. In addition to amassing more hits (1,754) and doubles (364) than any other player during the 1990s, Grace knocked in more than 1,000 runs and compiled a lifetime batting average of .308 as a member of the Cubs, surpassing 90 RBIs three times and batting in excess of .300 on nine separate occasions. An exceptional defensive player as well, Grace won four Gold Gloves for his excellent work around the bag, with his strong all-around play earning him three All-Star selections during his time in the Windy City.

Born in Winston-Salem, North Carolina on June 28, 1964, Mark Eugene Grace lived a somewhat nomadic existence as a youngster, moving several times with his family, before finally settling in Tustin, California. After excelling on the diamond at Tustin High School, Grace enrolled at Saddleback Junior College in Mission Viejo, California, where he spent the next two years starring at first base, prompting the Minnesota Twins to select him in the 15th round of the January 1984 MLB draft. However, Grace chose not to sign with the Twins, instead electing to transfer to San Diego State University for his junior year. After one year at SDSU, Grace decided to forgo his final year of college when the Cubs selected him in the 24th round of the June 1985 amateur draft, with the 622nd overall pick. He subsequently spent the next two-and-a-half years advancing through Chicago's farm system, winning the Midwest League batting title with a mark of .342 while playing for the Class A Peoria Chiefs in 1986, before earning Eastern League MVP honors the following year by hitting 17 homers, driving in 101 runs, and batting .333 for the Double A Pittsfield Cubs.

Summoned to the big leagues during the early stages of the 1988 campaign, Grace had a solid first year in Chicago, earning a runner-up finish to Cincinnati's Chris Sabo in the NL Rookie of the Year voting by hitting 7 homers, knocking in 57 runs, scoring 65 times, and finishing sixth in the league with a .296 batting average and a .371 on-base percentage. Improving upon those numbers the following year, Grace helped the Cubs capture the NL East title by hitting 13 homers, driving in 79 runs, scoring 74 others, placing fourth in the league with a .314 batting average and a .405 on-base percentage, and finishing second among NL first basemen with 126 assists and a .996 fielding percentage.

Grace had another excellent year in 1990, hitting 9 homers, driving in 82 runs, stealing a career-high 15 bases, finishing in the league's top 10 in batting average (.309), hits (182), and doubles (32), and leading all players at his position in assists for the first of three straight times. After a somewhat less productive 1991 campaign in which he scored 87 times but batted just .273 and knocked in only 58 runs, Grace began an outstanding eight-year run, during which he remained one of the senior circuit's most consistent players. Excluding the strike-shortened 1994 season, here are the numbers he posted from 1992 to 1999:

1992: 9 HR, 79 RBIs, 72 Runs Scored, 185 Hits, 37 2B, .307 AVG, .380 OBP, .430 SLG

1993: 14 HR, 98 RBIs, 86 Runs Scored, 193 Hits, 39 2B, .325 AVG, .393 OBP, .475 SLG

1995: 16 HR, 92 RBIs, 97 Runs Scored, 180 Hits, **51** 2B, .326 AVG, .395 OBP, .516 SLG

1996: 9 HR, 75 RBIs, 88 Runs Scored, 181 Hits, 39 2B, .331 AVG, .396 OBP, .455 SLG

1997: 13 HR, 78 RBIs, 87 Runs Scored, 177 Hits, 32 2B, .319 AVG, .409 OBP, .465 SLG

1998: 17 HR, 89 RBIs, 92 Runs Scored, 184 Hits, 39 2B, .309 AVG, .401 OBP, .471 SLG

1999: 16 HR, 91 RBIs, 107 Runs Scored, 183 Hits, 44 2B, .309 AVG, .390 OBP, .481 SLG

Although Grace led the National League just once in a major offensive category during that time, topping the circuit with 51 doubles in 1995, he placed in the league's top five in hits and batting average three times each, and also ranked among the leaders in doubles twice and extra-base hits

Courtesy of Pristine Auction

Mark Grace accumulated more hits and doubles
than any other player in the majors during the 1990s

once. Meanwhile, in addition to leading all NL first sackers in assists three
times, Grace finished first among players at his position in putouts three
times, fielding percentage once, and double plays once, earning in the process Gold Glove honors in four of those eight seasons. He also finished in
the top 20 in the league MVP balloting three times and made the All-Star
team in 1993, 1995, and 1997.

Lacking exceptional home run power, the lefty-swinging Grace, who
stood 6'2" and weighed close to 200 pounds, often found himself being
overshadowed by top sluggers such as Barry Bonds, Mark McGwire, Jeff
Bagwell, and teammate Sammy Sosa. However, very much like his boyhood hero, Keith Hernandez, Grace excelled in the clutch, drove the ball
well to all fields, and did a superb job around first base. A true ballplayer
who saw himself as a "guy who plays baseball for a living," Grace con-
centrated primarily on excelling at the fundamentals of the game, rather
than spending much of his time in the weight room trying to develop his
physique. In describing himself as a player, Grace suggested, "I'm not a
spectacular player. I'm not a flashy player. I don't do dances. I don't wear

fancy sunglasses or fancy earrings. But one thing you can depend on is that I'll be out there playing first base and that I'll be getting a lot of hits."

His description of his own playing style perhaps revealing his distaste for longtime teammate Sammy Sosa, Grace had little in common with the charismatic outfielder, who he later called one of the worst teammates he ever had, suggesting that "Slammin' Sammy" always placed his own personal success above that of the Cubs. Meanwhile, Grace's simplistic approach to his craft and down-to-earth personality, which caused him to spent most of his time away from the game mingling with fans, enjoying the local nightlife, and just being a "regular guy," made him one of the most popular players on the team.

After posting slightly less impressive numbers in 2000, concluding the campaign with 11 homers, 82 RBIs, 75 runs scored, and a .280 batting average, the thirty-six-year-old Grace let it be known that he wished to spend the remainder of his career in Chicago when he became a free agent at season's end. However, he soon found himself headed for Arizona when Cubs general manager Andy MacPhail made no effort to re-sign him, causing Grace to harbor resentment towards MacPhail for years.

Continuing his solid play his first year in Arizona, Grace helped the Diamondbacks capture the National League pennant by hitting 15 homers, driving in 78 runs, scoring 66 times, batting .298, and providing veteran leadership to his younger teammates. He subsequently alienated himself from Chicago management moments after Arizona defeated the New York Yankees in the 2001 World Series by stating during an interview that, although the Cubs apparently no longer considered him good enough to play for them, he had enough left to man first base for the world champion Diamondbacks. With Grace's comment being regarded as a slap in the face to the Cubs organization, he never found himself being treated as well as other former members of the team when he eventually retired from the game.

Grace spent the next two seasons in Arizona serving as a part-time player, before announcing his retirement following the conclusion of the 2003 campaign. He ended his career with 173 home runs, 1,146 RBIs, 1,179 runs scored, 2,445 hits, 511 doubles, a .303 batting average, a .383 on-base percentage, and a .442 slugging percentage. Upon Grace's retirement, the *Chicago Tribune* released the following statement:

> *"For 16 seasons, Mark Grace brought enthusiasm,*
> *humor, and amazing talent to the game of baseball. As a*

Chicago Cub, Mark led his team on the field and in the hearts of its fans from his rookie season in 1988 through the end of the 2000 season. His thirteen seasons playing for the Cubs established him as one of the game's 'good guys' with a throwback style of getting his uniform dirty and having fun on and off the field."

Since ending his playing career, Grace has remained close to the game as a television color commentator for the Diamondbacks and, for a period of time, *Fox Saturday Baseball*, before returning to the field as a coach for the Diamondbacks in 2015. A known smoker and drinker during his playing days, Grace has also run afoul of the law more than once in recent years, having been arrested for drunken driving on two separate occasions. Grace's second conviction, which stemmed from his August 23, 2012 arrest in Scottsdale on suspicion of driving under the influence, driving with a suspended license and without an interlock device, resulted in him serving four months in prison and being placed under supervised probation for two years.

Cub Numbers:

148 HR; 1,004 RBIs; 1,057 Runs Scored; 2,201 Hits; 456 Doubles; 43 Triples;67 Stolen Bases; .308 AVG; .386 OBP; .445 SLG PCT; .832 OPS

Career Numbers:

173 HR; 1,146 RBIs; 1,179 Runs Scored; 2,445 Hits; 511 Doubles; 45 Triples; 70 Stolen Bases; .303 AVG; .383 OBP; .442 SLG PCT; .825 OPS

Cub Career Highlights:

Best Season: Grace had a big year for the Cubs in 1993, batting .325, compiling an OPS of .867, and establishing career-high marks in hits (193) and RBIs (98). He also performed extremely well from 1996 to 1999, batting well in excess of .300 in each of those campaigns, hitting a career-best 17 homers in 1998, and scoring a career-high 107 runs in 1999. However, Grace had his finest all-around season in 1995, when, in addition to hitting 16 homers, driving in 92 runs, scoring 97 times, and batting .326, he established career-high marks in total bases (285), slugging percentage (.516), OPS (.911), and doubles (51), topping the senior circuit in the last category and ranking in the league's top 10 in seven others. Grace's outstanding performance earned him one of his three All-Star selections and a 13th-place finish in the NL MVP balloting, which represented his best showing.

Memorable Moments/Greatest Performances: Grace had a big day at the plate against San Diego on July 5, 1989, leading the Cubs to a 5-3 win over the Padres by going 4-for-4, with a homer, 3 doubles, and 3 RBIs.

Grace provided most of the offensive firepower for the Cubs when they defeated the Dodgers by a score of 3-0 on May 18, 1992, driving in all 3 Chicago runs with a pair of triples.

Although the Cubs lost their May 9, 1993 match-up with the Padres by a score of 5-4, Grace had a huge game, hitting for the cycle and bringing his team to within one run of San Diego by hitting a 3-run homer with two men out in the bottom of the ninth inning.

Grace helped lead the Cubs to a 9-6 win over the Colorado Rockies on April 8, 1996 by going 4-for-4, with 3 doubles, 3 RBIs, and 3 runs scored.

Continuing his assault on San Diego pitching on August 6, 2000, Grace had the only 5-for-5 day of his career during an 8-6 loss to the Padres, finishing the contest with a homer, a pair of doubles, 2 RBIs, and 3 runs scored.

An outstanding clutch performer over the course of his career, Grace delivered a number of memorable game-winning hits for the Cubs through the years, with one of those coming on July 4, 1991, when his leadoff homer in the bottom of the 11th inning (his second of the contest) off Pittsburgh reliever Bill Landrum gave the Cubs a 9-8 victory over the Pirates

Though somewhat less dramatic, Grace delivered a two-out, two-run double in the top of the eighth inning against Colorado on July 20, 1994 that ended up being the decisive blow of a 9-8 win over the Rockies. Grace finished the game 4-for-5, with 3 doubles, 3 RBIs, and 2 runs scored.

Grace again came up big in the clutch against Colorado on May 14, 1998, concluding a 4-for-5 afternoon during which he homered twice, knocked in 3 runs, and scored 3 times with a 2-run homer in the top of the ninth inning that gave the Cubs a 9-7 victory over the Rockies.

Grace gave the Cubs an 11-10 walk-off win over Milwaukee on September 13, 1998, when he topped off a 3-for-6 afternoon by hitting a solo homer off Brewers reliever Alberto Reyes with two men out in the bottom of the 10th inning.

Grace capped off a 4-for-5 performance against Philadelphia on July 26, 2000 during which he drove in a career-high 6 runs by hitting a grand slam homer in the top of the ninth inning that ended up being the decisive blow of a 14-9 win over the Phillies.

Although the Cubs lost the 1989 NLCS to the Giants in five games, Grace performed brilliantly throughout the series, homering once, driving in 8 runs, and collecting 11 hits in 17 official trips to the plate, en route to compiling a batting average of .647.

Notable Achievements:

- Batted over .300 nine times, topping the .320-mark on three occasions.
- Scored more than 100 runs once (107 in 1999).
- Surpassed 30 doubles nine times, topping 40 doubles three times and 50 two-baggers once (51 in 1995).
- Compiled on-base percentage in excess of .400 three times.
- Posted slugging percentage in excess of .500 once (.516 in 1995).
- Led NL in: doubles once; sacrifice flies once; and at-bats once.
- Finished second in NL with 193 hits in 1993.
- Led NL first basemen in: putouts three times; assists three times; fielding percentage once; and double plays once.
- Ranks among Cubs career leaders in: RBIs (eighth), runs scored (ninth), hits (fifth), extra-base hits (eighth), doubles (second), total bases (seventh), bases on balls (fourth), on-base percentage (tied-10th), games played (ninth), plate appearances (seventh), and at-bats (seventh).
- Hit for cycle vs. San Diego Padres on May 9, 1993.
- 1988 *Sporting News* NL Rookie of the Year.
- July 1989 NL Player of the Month.
- Four-time Gold Glove winner (1992, 1993, 1995 & 1996).
- Three-time NL All-Star (1993, 1995 & 1997).

11

HACK WILSON

The holder of one of Major League Baseball's most seemingly unbreakable records, Hack Wilson had a season for the ages in 1930, when he batted .356, hit 56 homers, scored 146 times, and knocked in an all-time record 191 runs. But, while the 1930 campaign proved to be easily the highlight of Wilson's career, the right-handed hitting outfielder had several other outstanding years for the Cubs, establishing himself in the process as one of the greatest sluggers in franchise history. In addition to compiling a batting average well in excess of .300 in five of his six seasons in Chicago, Wilson hit more than 30 home runs four times and topped the 100-RBI mark on five separate occasions, leading the National League in homers four times and RBIs twice. Boasting franchise records for highest career slugging percentage (.590) and OPS (1.002), Wilson also twice posted a slugging percentage in excess of .600. Meanwhile, in spite of his squatty frame, the 5'6", 200-pound outfielder did a creditable job for the Cubs in centerfield, leading all players at his position in putouts, double plays, and fielding percentage once each. Yet, even though Wilson's prolific slugging eventually earned him a place in Cooperstown, his story is a sad one that should serve as a lesson to all.

Born in Ellwood City, Pennsylvania on April 26, 1900, Lewis Robert Wilson suffered through a difficult childhood. The son of alcoholic parents who never married, Lewis spent much of his youth in foster homes after being deserted by his father following the passing of Lewis' mother, who died of appendicitis just seven years after she gave birth to him. Still in grade six at fourteen years of age, Wilson quit school and went to work in a car factory, where he earned $4 a week swinging a sledgehammer. Although only 5'6" tall when he reached adulthood, Wilson weighed 200 pounds, had a large head, size 18 neck, a massive chest and forearms, short legs, skinny ankles, and tiny feet that fit into size 6 shoes. Sportswriter Shirley Povich later observed that he was "built along the lines of a beer keg, and was not wholly unfamiliar with its contents." But, while Povich made light of Wilson's physique more than half a century ago, a modern medical term helps to explain his odd physical appearance. Wilson unfortunately suffered from Fetal Alcohol Syndrome, which is a disease that generates defects and abnormalities in children as a result of a mother's high level of alcohol consumption during pregnancy.

Nicknamed "Hack" due to his resemblance to Russian weightlifter and professional wrestler George Hackenschmidt, who had a similarly-shaped body, Wilson began his career in pro baseball with the Class D League Martinsville Blue Sox in 1921. Despite advancing through the minors the next few seasons by posting batting averages of .356, .366, and .388, Wilson drew little interest from Major League scouts and executives, since most of them considered him too small to succeed at the big-league level. However, New York Giants manager John McGraw felt differently, signing him to a contract during the latter stages of the 1923 campaign.

After appearing in three games with the Giants at the end of 1923, Wilson earned a part-time job in the New York outfield the following year, when he hit 10 home runs, knocked in 57 runs, scored 62 others, and batted .295, in 107 games and 383 official at-bats. But, after Wilson slumped to .239 in 1925, the Giants returned him to the minors at midseason. Upon learning of Wilson's impending departure, Giants outfielder Ross Youngs prophetically told a reporter, "The Giants are going to regret this." Meanwhile, an angry Wilson informed Manager McGraw, "I may not be good enough to play on your ball club, but I'll be back and playing on a better club someday." Subsequently left unprotected in the annual draft of minor league players held on October 10, 1925, Wilson found a new home when the Cubs claimed him off the roster of the Toledo Mud Hens for $5,000.

Arriving in Chicago in 1926, Wilson soon emerged as one of the senior circuit's top sluggers, earning a fifth-place finish in that year's NL MVP voting by leading the league with 21 homers, while also batting .321, scoring 97 runs, and finishing second in the league with 109 RBIs and a .539 slugging percentage. He followed that up with an even stronger performance in 1927, topping the circuit with 30 homers, batting .318, and ranking among the league leaders with 129 RBIs, 119 runs scored, 12 triples, 319 total bases, and a .579 slugging percentage. Wilson also did a good job of patrolling centerfield for the Cubs, leading all players at his position with a career-high 400 putouts.

Before long, Wilson established himself as one of Manager Joe Mc-Carthy's favorite players, endearing himself to his skipper with his hustle and all-out style of play. He also became extremely popular with the home-town fans, pleasing them with his diving, belly-flop catches, prodigious power, and accessibility before and after games. Hitting from a wide-open stance, swinging from his heels, and using long, thin-handled bats that weighed in the neighborhood of 42 ounces, Wilson generated tremendous power with his stocky frame, making headlines in May of 1926 when he hit a long home run that left a large dent in the metal component of the centerfield scoreboard at Wrigley Field. Unfortunately, Wilson made additional news that very same evening when police arrested him during a raid of a nearby speakeasy.

A regular patron at the local bars, Wilson developed a reputation second to none as a drinker. Once asked if he ever played a game while under the influence of alcohol, Wilson replied, "I never played drunk; hung-over, yes...drunk, no." Yet, even when playing with a hangover, Wilson tended to perform well, once telling a writer, "When I see three balls, I just swing at the middle one."

Wilson also became known for his temper, often screaming at umpires when he did not agree with their judgment of the strike zone, and once inciting a riot at Wrigley Field by going into the stands to attack a heck-ling fan. Wilson had another on-field altercation when he charged into the Cincinnati Reds dugout and began pummeling Ray Kolp after the pitcher called him a name associated with his illegitimate birth.

Yet, in spite of his foibles, Wilson became immensely popular in the city of Chicago, further endearing himself to the hometown fans in 1928 by batting .313, driving in 120 runs, and winning his third straight home run title, with 31 round-trippers. Wilson posted even better numbers in 1929, when he helped lead the Cubs to the pennant by batting .345, setting a new NL record by knocking in 159 runs, and placing among the league leaders with 39 homers, 135 runs scored, 355 total bases, and a .618 slugging percentage. However, the season ended disastrously for Wilson, when he lost two fly balls in the sun in the seventh inning of Game Four of the World Series, enabling the Philadelphia Athletics to mount a 10-run rally that turned an 8-0 deficit into a 10-8 victory.

Courtesy of RMYauctions.com

Hack Wilson knocked in a Major League record
191 runs in 1930

Although the Cubs failed to return to the fall classic in 1930, finishing a close second in the NL to the St. Louis Cardinals, Wilson did all he could to make amends for the defensive miscues he committed in the previous year's World Series. In addition to establishing new league marks by hitting 56 homers and driving in 191 runs, Wilson scored 146 times, collected 208 hits, batted .356, posted a .454 on-base percentage, and topped the senior circuit with 105 walks and a .723 slugging percentage.

Unfortunately, Wilson subsequently experienced a precipitous fall from grace, never again coming close to attaining the same level of excellence in future seasons. His troubles began in the spring of 1931, when he reported to training camp some 30 pounds overweight, tipping the scales at close to 230 pounds. Things only got worse when he failed to develop the same rapport with new Cubs manager Rogers Hornsby that he shared with his former skipper, Joe McCarthy. Although McCarthy knew when to tighten the reins on Wilson, he also gave him a considerable amount of freedom, often overlooking his vices, while concealing them from the front office. However, the autocratic Hornsby, who cared about baseball and little else, proved to be much less tolerant than McCarthy. Hornsby also attempted to alter the slugger's hitting style by suggesting that he use a more compact swing. Furthermore, with the National League switching to a heavier ball made with higher stitching in 1931, pitchers gained better control of their fastballs and breaking pitches, causing offensive numbers to drop dramatically throughout the senior circuit. Off to a slow start and burdened by his differences with his new manager, Wilson drank more heavily than ever before. Perhaps remembering the two fly balls he dropped in the World Series, some of the fans even turned on him, adding to his despair.

Wilson finally hit rock-bottom on September 6, when he got into a physical altercation with reporters aboard a train in Cincinnati. Suspended for the rest of the year, Wilson concluded the 1931 campaign with only 13 homers, 61 RBIs, 66 runs scored, and a .261 batting average, in 112 games and 395 official at-bats. Subsequently dealt to the St. Louis Cardinals for pitcher Burleigh Grimes during the offseason, Wilson left Chicago holding franchise records for most home runs (190), highest slugging percentage (.590), and highest OPS (1.002). Some eighty-five years later, he remains the Cubs' all-time leader in each of the last two categories.

Traded by St. Louis to Brooklyn before he appeared in a single game for the Cardinals, Wilson ended up spending three years with the

Dodgers, having his last productive season for them in 1932, when he hit 23 homers, drove in 123 runs, and batted .297. A part-time player in each of the next two seasons, Wilson ended his big-league career with the Philadelphia Phillies in 1934, appearing in seven games with them after being placed on waivers by the Dodgers in early August. Released by the Phillies at season's end, Wilson joined the Albany Senators of the Class A New York-Pennsylvania League, with whom he spent his final year of pro ball, before retiring at only thirty-five years of age following the conclusion of the 1935 campaign.

Wilson's post-playing days were unhappy ones, with the onetime "Toast of Chicago" forced to take on several demeaning jobs due to his lack of education and dependence on alcohol. In 1948, Wilson granted an interview to CBS Radio, during which he warned listeners about the perils of alcohol abuse and pleaded with the nation's youth not to follow in his footsteps. Admitting that he drank his life away, Wilson told listeners, "Talent isn't enough. You need common sense and good advice. If anyone tries to tell you different, tell them the story of Hack Wilson....There are kids, in and out of baseball, who think because they have talent, they have the world by the tail. It isn't so. In life you need things like good advice and common sense. Kids, don't be too big to take advice. Be considerate of others. That's the only way to live. Don't let what happened to me happen to you."

Just a few weeks later, on November 23, 1948, a divorced and penniless Wilson died at only forty-eight years of age from hemorrhaging related to a fall he took in his rented room several days earlier. As a tribute to his former teammate, Cubs manager Charlie Grimm posted a framed excerpt from the CBS interview in the Cubs clubhouse, where it still remains.

Cub Numbers:

190 HR; 769 RBIs; 652 Runs Scored; 1,017 Hits; 185 Doubles; 44 Triples; 34 Stolen Bases; .322 AVG; .412 OBP; .590 SLG; 1.002 OPS

Career Numbers:

244 HR; 1,063 RBIs; 884 Runs Scored; 1,461 Hits; 266 Doubles; 67 Triples; 52 Stolen Bases; .307 AVG; .395 OBP; .545 SLG; .940 OPS

Cub Career Highlights:

Best Season: Aided by a lively ball wound with special Australian wool, Wilson turned in one of the greatest single-season hitting performances in National League history in 1930. In addition to topping the senior circuit with 56 home runs, 191 RBIs, 105 bases on balls, a .723 slugging percentage, and a 1.177 OPS, Wilson ranked among the league leaders with 146 runs scored, 208 hits, 423 total bases, a .356 batting average, and a .454 on-base percentage, establishing career-high marks in each category. Wilson's total of 56 home runs stood as the NL record until 1998, when both Mark McGwire and Sammy Sosa topped it. Meanwhile, his 191 RBIs remain the benchmark in that category. Performing particularly well in August, Wilson hit 13 homers and knocked in 53 runs during the month. Although MLB did not present an official MVP Award in either league that year, the Baseball Writers Association of America unofficially voted Wilson the National League's most "useful" player.

Memorable Moments/Greatest Performances: During his time in Chicago, Wilson put together five hitting streaks of at least 20 games, with the longest of those being a 27-game streak that lasted from June 20 to July 20, 1929.

Wilson exhibited his extraordinary power for the first time as a member of the Cubs on May 23, 1926, when, during a 14-8 victory over the Boston Braves, he became the first player to hit a home run off Wrigley Field's centerfield scoreboard, located at that time at ground level.

Wilson had a big day at the plate on August 24, 1927, leading the Cubs to a 13-1 rout of the Phillies by going 4-for-5, with 2 homers, 4 RBIs, and a career-high 5 runs scored.

Wilson led the Cubs to a 13-0 mauling of the Cincinnati Reds on April 19, 1928 by going 4-for-4, with a pair of homers, a double, 6 RBIs, and 4 runs scored.

Wilson had a huge game against Brooklyn on July 6, 1928, leading the Cubs to a 14-8 victory by going 4-for-5, with a pair of homers, 5 RBIs, and 3 runs scored.

During a 13-6 win over the Cardinals on June 18, 1929, Wilson drove in 6 runs with a pair of homers, one of those being a fifth-inning grand slam that put the Cubs ahead to stay.

Wilson helped lead the Cubs to a lopsided 16-4 victory over Pittsburgh on June 1, 1930 by going 4-for-5, with 2 homers, a double, 5 RBIs, and 4 runs scored.

Wilson had one of his greatest days on June 23, 1930, when he hit for the cycle during a 21-8 win over the Phillies. He finished the game 5-for-6, with 5 RBIs and 4 runs scored.

Wilson turned in another epic performance against the Phillies a little over one month later, on July 26, 1930, when he hit 3 homers, knocked in 5 runs, and scored 4 times during a 16-2 Cubs win.

Yet, the contest for which Wilson is perhaps remembered most is Game Four of the 1929 World Series, when he infamously contributed to a 10-run rally by the Philadelphia Athletics in the bottom of the seventh inning by losing two fly balls in the sun. Wilson committed his second fielding miscue with two men on base, leading to a 3-run inside-the-park home run by A's centerfielder Mule Haas. Wilson's two misplays, which helped the Athletics turn an 8-0 deficit into a 10-8 win that gave them a commanding three-games-to-one lead in the Series, made his .471 batting average in the fall classic a mere afterthought.

Notable Achievements:

- Hit more than 30 home runs four times, topping 50 homers once (56 in 1930).
- Knocked in more than 100 runs five times, surpassing 120 RBIs four times and 150 RBIs twice.
- Batted over .300 five times, topping the .320-mark on three occasions.
- Scored more than 100 runs three times, topping 130 runs scored twice.
- Surpassed 200 hits once (208 in 1930).
- Finished in double digits in triples once (12 in 1927).
- Surpassed 30 doubles five times.
- Topped 100 walks once (105 in 1930).
- Compiled on-base percentage in excess of .400 five times.
- Posted slugging percentage in excess of .500 five times, topping the .600-mark twice and the .700-mark once (.723 in 1930).

- Led NL in: home runs four times; RBIs twice; walks twice; slugging pct. once; and OPS once.
- Finished second in NL in: RBIs twice, slugging percentage once, and OPS once.
- Led NL outfielders in putouts once.
- Led NL center-fielders in: putouts once, double plays once; and fielding percentage once.
- Holds Cubs single-season records for most RBIs (191) and highest OPS (1.177), both in 1930.
- Holds Cubs career records for highest slugging percentage (.590) and OPS (1.002).
- Ranks among Cubs career leaders in: home runs (10th), batting average (eighth), and on-base percentage (second).
- Holds MLB single-season record for most runs batted in (191 in 1930).
- Hit for cycle vs. Philadelphia on June 23, 1930.
- Hit 3 home runs in one game vs. Philadelphia on July 26, 1930.
- Named "unofficial" 1930 NL MVP by members of BBWAA.
- Finished in top 10 of NL MVP voting three times, placing in top five once.
- Two-time *Sporting News* All-Star selection (1929 & 1930).
- 1929 NL champion.
- Elected to Baseball Hall of Fame by members of Veteran's Committee in 1979.

12

KIKI CUYLER

An immensely talented player who excelled in all phases of the game, Kiki Cuyler spent parts of eight seasons in Chicago, joining Hack Wilson and Riggs Stephenson in giving the Cubs the National League's foremost outfield throughout much of that period. After earlier establishing himself as one of the senior circuit's most dynamic players as a member of the Pittsburgh Pirates, Cuyler continued to perform at an extremely high level with the Cubs, helping them capture two National League pennants in his first five years in the Windy City. An outstanding line-drive hitter with occasional home run power, the right-handed swinging Cuyler batted over .330 four times and accumulated more than 100 RBIs and 200 hits two times each during his time in Chicago. Blessed with exceptional running speed, Cuyler also excelled on the base paths, scoring more than 100 runs and leading the league in stolen bases three straight times while playing for the Cubs. Meanwhile, Cuyler's speed, instincts, and strong throwing arm made him equally adept at playing all three outfield positions—something he did at different times during his stay in the Windy City.

Born to German parents in Harrisville, Michigan on August 30, 1898, Hazen Shirley Cuyler attended local Harrisville High School, where he starred in baseball, basketball, football, and track, while simultaneously excelling on the diamond at the semi-pro level. After finishing high school, Cuyler briefly attended the US Military Academy at West Point, before returning to Michigan, where he married his high school sweetheart and took a job working in the auto industry for General Motors. Discovered while playing the outfield for a company baseball team in 1920, Cuyler subsequently signed with the Pittsburgh Pirates, who assigned him to their Bay City affiliate in the Michigan-Ontario League.

Although Cuyler made brief appearances with the Pirates in each of the next three seasons, he didn't arrive in Pittsburgh to stay until 1924, at the relatively advanced age of twenty-five. Performing brilliantly as a rookie, Cuyler batted .354, hit 9 homers, knocked in 85 runs, scored 94 times, and stole 32 bases, in only 117 games and 466 official at-bats. He followed that up with a magnificent sophomore campaign in which he led the Pirates to the 1925 NL pennant and earned a runner-up finish in the league MVP voting by hitting 18 homers, driving in 102 runs, amassing 220 hits, 43 doubles, and 41 stolen bases, compiling a .357 batting average, and topping the senior circuit with 144 runs scored and 26 triples. Cuyler then created a permanent place for himself in the hearts of Pirate fans by driving in the Series-winning run with a two-out, two-run double off Washington's Walter Johnson in the eighth inning of Game Seven of the fall classic.

Unfortunately for Cuyler and the Pirates, the euphoria of that world championship did not last very long. After Cuyler posted excellent numbers again in 1926, the two parties engaged in a bitter contract dispute prior to the start of the ensuing campaign. Things only worsened when ill feelings developed between new Pirates manager Donie Bush and Cuyler after the former asked his right-fielder to move to center and hit second in the lineup, thereby surrendering his preferred third slot in the batting order. Their feud came to a head on August 6, 1927, when Cuyler failed to slide into second base while breaking up a double play, prompting Bush to bench him for the rest of the season and the World Series, which Pittsburgh lost to the Yankees in four straight games. With the Pirates subsequently seeking to rid themselves of Cuyler, the Cubs ended up acquiring the disgruntled star for very little, obtaining him for journeyman infielder Sparky Adams and outfielder Pete Scott on November 28, 1927.

Cuyler's tenure in Chicago began somewhat ominously in the spring of 1928, when he seriously injured his right hand running into an outfield wall while attempting to catch a fly ball during a preseason exhibition game. However, after getting off to a slow start due to the injury, Cuyler caught fire in the season's final two months, batting .338 and scoring 39 runs in his last 49 games, to finish the year with 17 home runs, 79 RBIs, 92 runs scored, a .285 batting average, and a league-leading 37 stolen bases, while also placing first among NL right-fielders with 18 assists. Fully healthy in 1929, Cuyler helped lead the Cubs to the pennant by hitting 15 homers, driving in 102 runs, scoring 111 times, batting .360, and

Courtesy of MEARS Online Auctions

Kiki Cuyler combined with Hack Wilson and
Riggs Stephenson to give the Cubs one of the
greatest offensive outfields in baseball history

topping the senior circuit with 43 steals. Impressed with Cuyler's out-standing all-around play, Cubs Manager Joe McCarthy proclaimed at season's end, "There was never a more valuable team player." Meanwhile,

Boston Braves broadcaster Fred Hoey opined, "Cuyler can hit, run, field and throw with the best of 'em. What a great ballplayer he is."

Although the Cubs failed to repeat as NL champions in 1930, Cuyler continued his exceptional play, finishing the year with 13 home runs, 134 RBIs, 155 runs scored, 228 hits, 50 doubles, 17 triples, a .355 batting average, a major-league leading 37 stolen bases, and a career-high 21 outfield assists. Cuyler's brilliant performance prompted *The Sporting News* to write, "So accustomed are the fans to watching this fellow burn up the bases that it goes almost unnoticed with his constant hitting, running, fielding, and throwing."

Spending most of his time in Chicago hitting third in the Cubs' lineup, ahead of sluggers such as Hack Wilson and Gabby Hartnett, Cuyler proved to be an excellent number three hitter, twice topping 200 hits, and three times compiling an on-base percentage in excess of .400. He also did an outstanding job wherever the Cubs put him in the outfield, with his strong throwing arm making him an ideal right fielder, although he also possessed the quickness and athleticism to patrol centerfield, with syndicated sportswriter John B. Foster commenting, "There is no center fielder who runs farther for long fly hits."

Compared by some to Ty Cobb, Tris Speaker, and Shoeless Joe Jackson, the three greatest outfielders of the Dead Ball Era, Cuyler, suggested Cubs scout Jack Doyle, was the "most graceful player of all time; a fellow who could do more things with a glove than Cobb, who could throw better than Cobb, who could pick up groundballs on his outfield patrol like grounders." Cuyler also developed a reputation for his gentlemanly behavior, both on and off the field. Often described as one of the "gentlemen of baseball," Cuyler neither drank nor smoked, and he rarely argued with umpires or opposing players. He also carried himself with grace and elegance away from the diamond, with sportswriter J.T. Meek calling the 5'10 ½", 180-pound outfielder the "game's fashion plate" and an "exponent of diamond neatness."

Yet, ironically, Cuyler's exceptional all-around ability and proper conduct brought him criticism from others, who claimed that he lacked the drive to reach his full potential. Echoing the sentiments expressed by many throughout Cuyler's playing career, *The Sporting News* wrote years later, "Cuyler had only one flaw that kept him from being rated with the immortals of the game. He lacked the ruthlessness that might have carried him to greater heights and made his record even more brilliant."

Cuyler remained a truly elite player for one more year, driving in 88 runs and placing among the league leaders with 202 hits, 110 runs scored, a .330 batting average, and a .404 on-base percentage in 1931, before injuries and advancing age began to compromise his playing ability. Limited by a broken foot to only 110 games in 1932, Cuyler concluded the campaign with just 77 RBIs, 58 runs scored, and a .291 batting average, although he helped lead the Cubs to the NL pennant by batting .373 and driving in 28 runs in the final 28 games of the regular season. Cuyler then broke his leg during spring training in 1933, causing him to miss half the season. Although the thirty-five-year-old Cuyler had enough left in the tank to knock in 69 runs, score 80 times, lead the league with 42 doubles, and finish third in the circuit with a .338 batting average in 1934, he no longer possessed the exceptional running speed that previously made him one of the game's most feared base runners and top defensive outfielders. Released by the Cubs midway through the ensuing campaign after batting just .268 in 45 games, Cuyler signed with the Cincinnati Reds, with whom he had his last productive season in 1936, driving in 74 runs, scoring 96 times, and batting .326. After assuming a part-time role in Cincinnati the following season, Cuyler ended his career with the Brooklyn Dodgers in 1938, batting .273 and scoring 45 runs in 82 games. He retired from the game with 128 home runs, 1,065 RBIs, 1,305 runs scored, 2,299 hits, and a career batting average of .321—figures good enough to prompt the members of the Veteran's Committee to elect him to the Baseball Hall of Fame in 1968.

Following his playing days, Cuyler spent the next eleven years either managing at the minor league level or coaching in the majors, spending his final year in baseball serving as a member of Joe McCarthy's coaching staff in Boston. Cuyler's life and career in baseball ended on February 11, 1950, nine days after he suffered a heart attack while ice fishing near his home in Harrisville. Only fifty-one years old at the time of his passing, Cuyler died while being transported from a local hospital to another facility in Ann Arbor to treat a blood clot that had formed in his leg.

Cub Numbers:

79 HR; 602 RBIs; 665 Runs Scored; 1,199 Hits; 220 Doubles; 66 Triples;161 Stolen Bases; .325 AVG; .391 OBP; .485 SLG; .876 OPS

Career Numbers:

128 HR; 1,065 RBIs; 1,305 Runs Scored; 2,299 Hits; 394 Doubles; 157 Triples; 328 Stolen Bases; .321 AVG; .386 OBP; .474 SLG; 860 OPS

Cub Career Highlights:

Best Season: Although Cuyler also performed extremely well in both 1929 and 1931, scoring more than 100 runs each year while compiling batting averages of .360 and .330, respectively, he had his finest all-around season for the Cubs in 1930. In addition to hitting 13 homers, amassing 17 triples, leading the league with 37 stolen bases, batting .355, compiling a .428 on-base percentage, and posting a .547 slugging percentage, Cuyler established career-high marks with 134 RBIs, 155 runs scored, 228 hits, 50 doubles, and 21 outfield assists, placing in the league's top five in seven different offensive categories. Particularly effective during a 13-game stretch that began on June 23, Cuyler batted .483 (28-for-58), knocked in 27 runs, and scored 17 times over the course of those 13 contests. Cuyler's magnificent performance nearly allowed the Cubs to overcome the loss of reigning NL MVP Rogers Hornsby, who ended up appearing in only 42 games after breaking his ankle in late May.

Memorable Moments/Greatest Performances: Cuyler helped lead the Cubs to a 12-0 pasting of the Boston Braves on June 18, 1928 by going 4-for-6, with a pair of homers, a double, 4 RBIs, and 4 runs scored.

Cuyler had another big day at the plate against Boston on June 4, 1930, leading the Cubs to an 18-10 win over the Braves by going 5-for-5, with a homer, double, 4 RBIs, and 4 runs scored.

Cuyler began his sizzling stretch of games later that month by collecting 3 hits, driving in 3 runs, and scoring 4 times during a lopsided 21-8 victory over Philadelphia on June 23, 1930.

Four days later, on June 27, 1930, Cuyler delivered arguably his most memorable hit as a member of the Cubs, when he gave them a 7-5 win over the Brooklyn Dodgers by hitting a two-out, two-run walk-off homer off Brooklyn reliever Ray Moss in the bottom of the 10th inning. The blow, which came on Ladies Day before the largest single-game crowd in

Wrigley Field history, ended what team President Bill Veeck Sr. later called the most exciting game he ever witnessed.

Excelling at the plate over the final 28 games of the 1932 campaign, Cuyler put together a string of extraordinary clutch performances against the New York Giants in late August. After collecting 3 hits, driving in 4 runs, hitting an eighth-inning homer, and delivering the game-winning sacrifice fly in the bottom of the ninth inning of a 5-4 Cubs victory over New York on August 28, Cuyler again came up big against the Giants two days later, collecting two hits, knocking in two runs, and hitting a seventh-inning homer off ace left-hander Carl Hubbell, in leading the Cubs to a 4-3 win. However, Cuyler surpassed both those efforts on August 31, when he capped off a 5-hit, 5-RBI day by hitting a 2-out, 3-run walk-off homer in the bottom of the 10th inning that turned an apparent 9-7 loss into a 10-9 victory.

Notable Achievements:

- Batted over .300 five times, topping the .330-mark on four occasions.
- Knocked in more than 100 runs twice, surpassing 130 RBIs once (134 in 1930).
- Scored more than 100 runs three times, topping 150 runs scored once (155 in 1930).
- Surpassed 200 hits twice.
- Finished in double digits in triples twice.
- Surpassed 30 doubles three times, topping 40 two-baggers twice.
- Surpassed 30 stolen bases three times, topping 40 steals once (43 in 1929).
- Compiled on-base percentage in excess of .400 three times.
- Posted slugging percentage in excess of .500 twice.
- Led NL in: doubles once, stolen bases three times, and games played once.
- Finished second in NL in: runs scored once, doubles once, and stolen bases once.
- Led NL center-fielders in assists once.
- Led NL right-fielders in assists once and fielding percentage twice.

- Ranks among Cubs career leaders in: batting average (sixth), on-base percentage (ninth), and OPS (seventh).
- 1934 NL All-Star.
- Two-time NL champion (1929 & 1932).
- Elected to Baseball Hall of Fame by members of Veteran's Committee in 1968.

13

ANDRE DAWSON

Already an established star by the time he arrived in Chicago in 1987, Andre Dawson previously gained general recognition as one of the finest all-around players in the game as a member of the Montreal Expos. Over the course of his first 10 seasons in Montreal, Dawson batted over .300 three times, surpassed 20 home runs seven times, 100 RBIs once, 100 runs scored twice, and 20 stolen bases seven times, and won six Gold Gloves, earning in the process three All-Star selections and a pair of runner-up finishes in the NL MVP voting. Although hampered by knee problems throughout his time in Chicago, Dawson continued to perform at an extremely high level in his six years with the Cubs, topping 20 homers each season, knocking in more than 100 runs three times, batting over .300 twice, and winning two more Gold Gloves, en route to earning another five All-Star nominations and NL MVP honors in 1987, when he became the first player to be named winner of that prestigious award while serving as a member of a last-place team. Yet, Dawson's contributions to the Cubs cannot be measured by statistics alone, since he left his mark on the organization and the fans of Chicago with his courage, determination, and strong sense of decency.

Born in Miami, Florida on July 10, 1954, Andre Nolan Dawson acquired the nickname "The Hawk" at an early age after his uncle told him that he attacked ground balls very much like a hawk. A two-sport star at Miami's Southwest High School, Dawson decided to focus strictly on baseball after he sustained a serious injury on the football field—one that required surgery to repair torn cartilage and ligaments in his left knee. Following a successful four-year stint on the diamond at Florida A&M University, Dawson joined the professional ranks when the Montreal Expos selected him in the 11th round of the 1975 MLB draft.

Advancing rapidly through Montreal's farm system, Dawson spent less than two full seasons in the minor leagues before joining the Expos during the latter stages of the 1976 campaign. Laying claim to the starting centerfield job the following year, Dawson went on to earn NL Rookie of the Year honors by hitting 19 homers, driving in 65 runs, scoring 64 times, stealing 21 bases, and batting .282. After a solid sophomore season, Dawson began an outstanding five-year run during which he established himself as one of the senior circuit's most complete players. In addition to averaging 24 home runs, 88 RBIs, 94 runs scored, and 32 stolen bases from 1979 to 1983, Dawson batted over .300 three times, earned four Gold Gloves and three Silver Sluggers, and finished in the top ten in the NL MVP voting on three separate occasions, placing second in the balloting in both 1981 and 1983. Having perhaps his finest all-around season as a member of the Expos in 1983, Dawson batted .299, stole 25 bases, ranked among the league leaders with 32 homers, 113 RBIs, 104 runs scored, 36 doubles, 10 triples, and a .539 slugging percentage, topped the circuit with 189 hits and 341 total bases, and led all NL center-fielders with a career-high 438 putouts.

Featuring an exceptional blend of power and speed, Dawson excelled in all facets of the game, commenting years later, "I took pride in being a four or five-tool player, and being consistent." Dawson also exhibited a tremendous amount of drive and determination on the ball field, stating, "I am very intense when I am out on the playing field. I play the game as hard as I am capable of playing and try not to let up." Meanwhile, former outfielder and general manager Tom Grieve said of Dawson, "He was a five-tool player; he had excellent speed, one of the greatest arms in the game; he was a Gold Glove caliber defensive player. He had great power."

However, the artificial turf in Montreal's Olympic Stadium began to take its toll on Dawson by the mid-1980s, further damaging his already tender knees, and forcing him to move from centerfield to right in 1984. Unable to appear in more than 139 games in any of the next three seasons, Dawson averaged just 20 homers, 85 RBIs, 68 runs scored, and 15 stolen bases from 1984 to 1986, while posting batting averages of .248, .255, and .284.

A free agent following the conclusion of the 1986 campaign, Dawson narrowed his choice of teams down to a select few, with the Expos and Cubs heading his list. Although Dawson, who had undergone eight knee surgeries by this point, felt a sense of loyalty to the Expos, he ultimately

Courtesy of Pristine Auction

Andre Dawson earned league MVP honors in 1987
even though the Cubs finished last in the NL East

decided that the Cubs represented a more viable option since he wanted to play his home games in a ballpark that had natural grass in the outfield, and in a city that would offer him more national exposure. With his services being undervalued on the open market due to a case of collusion by the owners, Dawson and his agent Dick Moss approached the Cubs with a blank contract during spring training and told them to fill in a suitable amount. "This is no joke," Moss told Chicago General Manager Dallas Green. "Andre really wants to play for the Cubs, and he will do so for any salary that is fair. That is why we left that section of the contract blank. Feel free to fill in your own numbers." With the Cubs subsequently offering Dawson a base salary of $500,000, plus another $200,000 in incentive bonuses, he became a member of the team within twenty-four hours, later writing in his autobiography, "I can't describe for you the feeling of elation I experienced as we walked out of Green's office that afternoon. I had taken back control of my own life."

The deal proved to be an absolute steal for the Cubs. Although they ended up winning only six more games during the regular season than they did one year earlier, concluding the 1987 campaign with a record of 76-85 that left them last in the NL East standings, Dawson earned league MVP honors and the first of his five consecutive All-Star selections as a member of the team by batting .287, scoring 90 runs, and topping the senior circuit with 49 homers, 137 RBIs, and 353 total bases. He followed that up with another strong performance in 1988, placing 15th in the NL MVP voting after hitting 24 homers, driving in 79 runs, scoring 78 times, and finishing among the league leaders with 179 hits, 8 triples, 298 total bases, a .303 batting average, and a .504 slugging percentage.

Despite appearing in only 118 games in 1989, Dawson contributed significantly to Chicago's NL East championship ball club by hitting 21 homers and knocking in 77 runs, in just 416 official at-bats. Playing through pain throughout most of the ensuing campaign, Dawson nevertheless posted excellent numbers, finishing the season with 27 home runs, 100 RBIs, and a .310 batting average, before hitting 31 homers, driving in 104 runs, and batting .272 in 1991.

As Dawson continued to take the field with badly damaged knees that eventually forced him to undergo 12 surgeries, he made a lasting impression on his teammates and coaches, with former Cubs shortstop Shawon Dunston later suggesting, "If Andre didn't have bad knees, he would have finished with 600 home runs and 500 stolen bases." Meanwhile, Don

Zimmer, who managed Dawson in Chicago for three full seasons and part of a fourth, said, "I don't think I ever managed a greater player or human being."

Dawson spent one more year in Chicago, hitting 22 homers, driving in 90 runs, and batting .277 in 1992, before signing with Boston as a free agent at season's end. Serving the Red Sox almost exclusively as a designated hitter over the course of the next two seasons, Dawson totaled 29 home runs and 115 RBIs from 1993 to 1994, before spending his final two seasons with the Florida Marlins, for whom he totaled 10 home runs and 51 RBIs as a back-up outfielder and pinch-hitter. Dawson announced his retirement following the conclusion of the 1996 campaign, ending his career with 438 home runs, 1,591 RBIs, 1,373 runs scored, 2,774 hits, 314 stolen bases, a .279 batting average, a .323 on-base percentage, and a .482 slugging percentage. By surpassing 400 home runs and 300 stolen bases, Dawson joined Willie Mays and Barry Bonds as the only players in MLB history to reach both marks.

Following Dawson's retirement, he failed to gain induction into the Baseball Hall of Fame the first several times his name appeared on the ballot. After the voters chose not to elect Dawson for the fourth straight time in 2005, Ryne Sandberg spoke on behalf of his former teammate at his own induction ceremonies, telling the assembled mass, "No player in baseball history worked harder, suffered more, or did better than Andre Dawson. He's the best I've ever seen. I watched him win an MVP for a last-place team in 1987, and it was the most unbelievable thing I've ever seen in baseball. He did it the right way, the natural way, and he did it in the field and on the bases and in every way, and I hope he will stand up here someday." Although it took Dawson another five years to be admitted to Cooperstown, the members of the BBWAA finally elected him in 2010, in his ninth year of eligibility. The former outfielder received another great honor when Cubs legend Ernie Banks wrote in the foreword of Dawson's autobiography:

> *"There is no one else like Andre Dawson. He is a living example of what a human being should be and can be. Amazingly, the influence he had while he was a Cub is still strongly felt years after he has moved on. In fact, I feel that what he left behind will never leave us. He touched us all—the players, the fans, everyone."*

Cub Numbers:

174 HR; 587 RBIs; 431 Runs Scored; 929 Hits; 149 Doubles; 27 Triples; 57 Stolen Bases; .285 AVG; .327 OBP; .507 SLG PCT; .834 OPS

Career Numbers:

438 HR; 1,591 RBIs; 1,373 Runs Scored; 2,774 Hits; 503 Doubles; 98 Triples; 314 Stolen Bases; .279 AVG; .323 OBP; .483 SLG PCT; .806 OPS

Cub Career Highlights:

Best Season: Although Dawson batted over .300 twice and accumulated more than 100 RBIs two other times for the Cubs, there is little doubt that the 1987 campaign proved to be his finest in Chicago. In addition to batting .287 and scoring 90 runs, Dawson topped the senior circuit with 49 home runs, 137 RBIs, and 353 total bases, ranked among the league leaders with 178 hits and a .568 slugging percentage, and won a Gold Glove for his outstanding defensive work in right field. Dawson's stellar play earned him NL MVP honors, making him the first player to win the award while playing for a last-place team.

Memorable Moments/Greatest Performances: Dawson had his first big day at the plate for the Cubs on April 26, 1987, when he homered twice, knocked in 3 runs, and scored 3 times during a 7-1 victory over his former team, the Montreal Expos.

Dawson turned in an outstanding performance just three days later, hitting for the cycle and going a perfect 5-for-5 during an 8-4 win over the San Francisco Giants at Wrigley Field on April 29, 1987. Dawson punctuated his exceptional all-around effort by throwing out opposing pitcher Roger Mason at first base on an apparent single to right field.

Although the Cubs ended up losing their June 1, 1987 match-up with the Houston Astros by a score of 6-5 in 10 innings, Dawson had a huge game, driving in all 5 of Chicago's runs with a solo homer in the first inning and an eighth-inning grand slam that evened the score at 5-5.

Dawson continued his hot hitting against Houston the very next day, leading the Cubs to a lopsided 13-2 victory over the Astros by going 4-for-5, with 2 homers, a triple, and 7 RBIs.

Just one day after homering twice during a 13-4 loss to Atlanta, Dawson led the Cubs to a 7-5 win over Houston on August 21, 1987 by driving in 3 runs with another pair of homers.

Dawson proved to be the difference in an 8-7 win over the Braves on August 19, 1988, going 4-for-5, with a pair of homers, 5 RBIs, and 3 runs scored. Dawson's final hit of the day—a bases loaded single in the bottom of the ninth inning—drove in the game's winning run.

Dawson again came up big in the clutch against Atlanta on May 8, 1990, when he hit a pair of late-inning home runs that gave the Cubs a hard-fought 10-8 victory over the Braves. After tying the score at 8-8 with a solo shot in the bottom of the ninth, Dawson ended the contest two innings later with a walk-off two-run blast.

However, Dawson turned in his most memorable performance as a member of the Cubs on August 1, 1987, when he led them to a 5-3 win over the Phillies by driving in all 5 runs with 3 homers. Recalling the events that transpired on that hot and humid day at Wrigley, Dawson stated, "I didn't even think I was going to make it past the fifth inning. The fans started getting into it and I hit a third home run. It is just unbelievable considering the circumstances, when you can barely get from the dugout to the outfield [because of the heat]."

Notable Achievements:

- Hit more than 20 home runs six times, topping 30 homers twice and 40 homers once (49 in 1987).
- Knocked in more than 100 runs three times, topping 130 RBIs once (137 in 1987).
- Batted over .300 twice.
- Surpassed 30 doubles once (31 in 1988).
- Posted slugging percentage in excess of .500 three times.
- Led NL in: home runs once, RBIs once, and total bases once.
- Finished second in NL in hits once and total bases once.
- Led NL right-fielders in fielding percentage once and double plays twice.
- Ranks sixth in Cubs history with career slugging percentage of .507.
- Hit for cycle vs. San Francisco on April 29, 1987.

- Hit three home runs in one game vs. Philadelphia on August 1, 1987.
- Two-time NL Player of the Month.
- 1987 NL MVP.
- 1987 *Sporting News* NL Player of the Year.
- 1987 Silver Slugger winner.
- Two-time Gold Glove winner (1987 & 1988).
- 1987 *Sporting News* All-Star selection.
- Five-time NL All-Star (1987, 1988, 1989, 1990 & 1991).
- Elected to Baseball Hall of Fame by members of BBWAA in 2010.

14

SAMMY SOSA

Once an icon in the city of Chicago, Sammy Sosa experienced a precipitous decline in popularity his last few seasons with the Cubs as stories of his selfish and narcissistic nature began to surface, along with allegations of his use of performance enhancing drugs. As a result, the one-time "Toast of Chicago" has spent most of his retirement living in virtual anonymity, shunning the spotlight he so desperately craved during his playing days. Furthermore, with it becoming increasingly apparent that Sosa never would have been able to compile the extraordinary numbers he amassed during his peak years with the Cubs had he not resorted to using steroids, his offensive accomplishments have taken on far less significance, with the members of the BBWAA showing him very little support in the Hall of Fame voting. Nevertheless, even though Sosa's illicit activities prompted me to drop him several notches on this list, I found it impossible to exclude him completely from my rankings since the fact remains that he hit more home runs (545) than any other player in franchise history and also ranks among the leaders in several other offensive categories, including RBIs (1,414), runs scored (1,245), slugging percentage (.569), and OPS (.928). The holder of the top three single-season home run totals in Cubs history, Sosa averaged 58 homers a year from 1998 to 2002, a period during which he became the only player ever to reach the 60-homer plateau on three separate occasions. The slugging outfielder also averaged 141 RBIs and 124 runs scored over the course of those five seasons, earning in the process one NL MVP Award, four other top-10 finishes in the balloting, five consecutive *Sporting News* All-Star selections, and five straight Silver Sluggers. In all, Sosa hit more than 30 home runs in 11 of his 13 seasons with the Cubs, knocked in more than 100 runs nine times, scored more than 100 runs five times, batted over .300 three times, placed in the top 10 in the league MVP voting on seven separate occasions, and earned seven All-Star nominations, making it impossible to put together this list of players without including his name somewhere in the top 50.

Born in San Pedro de Macoris, Dominican Republic on November 12, 1968, Samuel Peralta Sosa suffered through a difficult childhood during which he lost his father at only seven years of age. Growing up in poverty with his mother and six siblings, Sammy lived with his family in an abandoned hospital, helping to make ends meet by selling oranges on the street and shining shoes, while receiving his introduction to baseball by using a branch for a bat, an old milk carton for a glove, and a rolled up sock for a ball.

After competing in several local leagues as a teenager, Sosa had the good fortune to be discovered by Texas Rangers scout Omar Minaya while working out at the Toronto Blue Jays camp in 1985. Subsequently signed by the Rangers as an amateur free agent, the seventeen-year-old Sosa, who Texas' initial scouting report described as "malnourished," spent the next three and a half years in the minors before making his major league debut with the Rangers on June 16, 1989. Appearing in 25 games with Texas over the next six weeks, Sosa homered once, knocked in 3 runs, and batted .238, in 84 official at-bats. Although the Rangers elected to trade Sosa to the Chicago White Sox on July 29, the young outfielder made an extremely favorable impression on Texas skipper Bobby Valentine during his relatively brief stay in the Lone Star State, with the outspoken manager later commenting, "He had great talent; he could hit and run and throw. He was a little raw and undisciplined. He would swing at anything, but you could see he was going to be terrific."

After spending the remainder of the 1989 campaign platooning in centerfield for the White Sox, Sosa earned the starting right-field job the following year, finishing his first full big league season with 15 homers, 70 RBIs, 72 runs scored, and 32 stolen bases, although he also batted just .233 and struck out 150 times. Sosa proved to be less productive in 1991, when, splitting his time between the White Sox and their top minor league affiliate, he hit just 10 homers, knocked in only 33 runs, and batted just .203, prompting the Pale Hose to trade him and pitcher Ken Patterson to the crosstown Cubs for outfielder George Bell on March 30, 1992.

Sharing playing time in centerfield with the switch-hitting Doug Dascenzo his first year at Wrigley, the right-handed swinging Sosa posted

Courtesy of Ben Fenske

Sammy Sosa hit more home runs
than any other player in Cubs history

modest offensive numbers, concluding the 1992 campaign with 8 home runs, 25 RBIs, 41 runs scored, and a .260 batting average, in 67 games and 262 official at bats. Gradually transitioning to right field the following season, Sosa emerged as a top offensive threat, leading the Cubs with 33 homers and 36 stolen bases, while also driving in 93 runs, scoring 92 times, and batting .261. By surpassing 30 home runs and 30 steals in the same season, Sosa became the first player in the long history of the Cubs to accomplish the feat. Meanwhile, his strong throwing arm enabled him to finish second among National League outfielders with 17 assists.

Sosa again performed extremely well in 1994, concluding the strike-shortened campaign with 25 homers, 70 RBIs, 59 runs scored, 22 stolen bases, and a .300 batting average, before earning his first All-Star selection and an eighth-place finish in the MVP voting the following year by finishing second in the league with 36 home runs and 119 RBIs, scoring 89 times, stealing 34 bases, batting .268, and leading all NL right-fielders with 13 assists. Although Sosa failed to earn a spot on the National League All-Star squad in either of the next two seasons, he remained one of the senior circuit's top sluggers, totaling 76 home runs and 219 RBIs from 1996 to 1997, while compiling batting averages of .273 and .251. Sosa also ranked among the league leaders in outfield assists each year, finishing first among NL right-fielders with 16 assists in 1997.

After bulking up to 225 pounds during the subsequent off-season, the six-foot Sosa, who began his Major League career some 60 pounds lighter, embarked on an extraordinarily successful five-year run during which he established himself as one of the game's great sluggers, posting the following eye-popping numbers:

1998: 66 HR; **158** RBIs; **134** Runs Scored; .308 AVG; .377 OBP; .647 SLG; 1.024 OPS

1999: 63 HR; 141 RBIs; 114 Runs Scored; .288 AVG; .367 OBP; .635 SLG; 1.002 OPS

2000: **50** HR; 138 RBIs; 106 Runs Scored; .320 AVG; .406 OBP; .634 SLG; 1.040 OPS

2001: 64 HR; **160** RBIs; **146** Runs Scored; .328 AVG; .437 OBP; .737 SLG; 1.174 OPS

2002: **49** HR; 108 RBIs; **122** Runs Scored; .288 AVG; .399 OBP; .594 SLG; .993 OPS

In addition to leading the league in home runs twice, RBIs twice, and runs scored three times during the period, Sosa topped the senior circuit in total bases in three of those five seasons, twice amassing more than 400 total bases. He also finished second in homers three times, RBIs once, total bases once, bases on balls once, slugging percentage twice, and OPS once, with his prolific slugging earning him All-Star and Silver Slugger honors each year, five consecutive top-10 finishes in the NL MVP voting, and recognition as the league's Most Valuable Player in 1998, when he helped lead the Cubs into the playoffs as a wild card.

Engaged in an epic home run race with St. Louis slugger Mark McGwire throughout much of the 1998 campaign, Sosa drew praise from Philadelphia back-up catcher Mark Parent, who noted, "He's not missing mistakes. That's the big thing for all good hitters: Mark [McGwire], [Ken] Griffey, and those guys. They don't swing at bad balls, and they hammer mistakes. They make you pay for every mistake, and that's what Sammy's doing."

Cardinals manager Tony La Russa gave Sosa his just due during the latter stages of the 1998 season by suggesting, "It hurts me to say this because I've pulled for my man [McGwire] as hard as I can, but I think Sosa is the MVP. He has had a great year and the Cubs are in the hunt with a week to go in the season. I think that tips it to Sosa."

Meanwhile, Chicago teammate Mark Grace marveled, "He's beyond description. I don't know the right words to describe how great a season he's had. You say MVP type season, but I don't know if that's enough to describe it."

Sosa grew increasingly popular over the course of that 1998 campaign, with his signature post-home run ritual of hopping at home plate, blowing a kiss, and touching his heart becoming a familiar sight to the hometown fans. Sosa also became a favorite of the media, which continued to heap adulation and praise on both him and McGwire as the two inflated sluggers drew inexorably closer to Roger Maris' single-season home run record.

Yet, behind the disingenuous smile that Sosa displayed to the general public laid a dark heart that cared little for the feelings of others. Disliked by most of his teammates, who he agitated with his constant blaring of salsa music at ear-piercing levels in the Chicago clubhouse, Sosa treated those around him in an arrogant and dismissive manner. Meanwhile, he became a constant source of aggravation to his managers, who incurred his wrath by suggesting that he make an effort to reduce his inordinately high strikeout totals and work more on his base-running and defense, which gradually deteriorated as he shifted his focus almost exclusively on hitting home runs.

After forcing manager Don Baylor out of town midway through the 2002 season by lambasting him in the local newspapers, Sosa became embroiled in another controversy the following year when he drew a seven-game suspension from Major League Baseball for using a corked bat in a game. His playing time further reduced by a series of minor injuries, Sosa posted a less impressive stat-line in 2003, although he still managed to hit 40 homers, drive in 103 runs, score 99 times, and bat .279. Sosa again missed significant playing time in 2004 after freakishly injuring his back while sneezing. Suffering from chronic back spasms the rest of the year, he concluded the campaign with only 35 homers, 80 RBIs, 69 runs scored, and a .253 batting average. Meanwhile, as had been the case with Don Baylor, Sosa's relationship with Dusty Baker grew increasingly contentious during their time together, with the Cubs' manager benching the star outfielder for the final game of the 2004 season when Sosa showed up to the ballpark late. Informed of Baker's decision, Sosa cleaned out his locker and walked out of Wrigley Field, doing so for the last time as a member of the Cubs, who traded him to the Baltimore Orioles for Jerry Hairston,

Mike Fontenot, and minor league pitcher Dave Crouthers prior to the start of the ensuing campaign.

The thirty-six-year-old Sosa ended up spending just one season in Baltimore, hitting 14 homers, driving in 45 runs, and batting .221 in a part-time role, before sitting out the entire 2006 campaign after becoming a free agent. He returned to the playing field for one final season, though, eventually signing with the Texas Rangers, for whom he hit 21 homers, knocked in 92 runs, and batted .252 in 2007. Failing to receive any substantial offers at season's end, Sosa retired from the game, ending his career with 609 home runs, 1,667 RBIs, 1,475 runs scored, 2,408 hits, a .273 lifetime batting average, a .344 on-base percentage, and a .534 slugging percentage.

However, controversy continued to follow Sosa even in retirement. After vehemently denying during a 2005 congressional hearing that he had ever used steroids, telling the members of Congress in attendance, "I have never taken illegal performance-enhancing drugs. I have never injected myself or had anyone inject me with anything," Sosa again found himself in the midst of a drug-use scandal in 2009, when *The New York Times* reported that a supposedly anonymous drug test conducted by Major League Baseball in 2003 revealed that he had tested positive for the use of some type of performance-enhancing drug. Although Congress elected not to prosecute Sosa for the perjury he committed during his 2005 testimony, he remains guilty in the court of public opinion, with his nefarious behavior and fraudulent numbers almost certain to deny him a place in Cooperstown anytime in the foreseeable future.

Cub Numbers:

545 HR; 1,414 RBIs; 1,245 Runs Scored; 1,985 Hits; 296 Doubles; 32 Triples; 181 Stolen Bases; .284 AVG; .358 OBP; .569 SLG PCT; .928 OPS

Career Numbers:

609 HR; 1,667 RBIs; 1,475 Runs Scored; 2,408 Hits; 379 Doubles; 45 Triples; 234 Stolen Bases; .273 AVG; .344 OBP; .534 SLG PCT; .878 OPS

Cub Career Highlights:

Best Season: En route to earning NL MVP and *Sporting News* Major League Player of the Year honors in 1998, Sosa compiled extraordinary numbers, finishing the season with 66 home runs, 158 RBIs, 134 runs scored, 198 hits, a .308 batting average, and an OPS of 1.024. Meanwhile, his 416 total bases represented the highest single-season mark since Stan Musial amassed 429 total bases for the Cardinals in 1948. Particularly dominant during the month of June, Sosa emerged as a challenger to Mark McGwire for the home run title by hitting 20 homers, driving in 47 runs, and posting a .842 slugging percentage. However, Sosa compiled even better numbers in 2001, when, in addition to hitting 64 home runs, he established career-high marks in RBIs (160), runs scored (146), total bases (425), bases on balls (116), batting average (.328), on-base percentage (.437), slugging percentage (.737), and OPS (1.174), earning in the process a runner-up finish to Barry Bonds in the league MVP voting.

Memorable Moments/Greatest Performances: Sosa had his breakout game for the Cubs on April 23, 1993, when he collected 3 hits, 2 home runs, and 5 RBIs during a 7-4 win over Cincinnati.

Although the Cubs lost their May 4, 1993 match-up with the Colorado Rockies by a score of 14-13 in 11 innings, Sosa had another huge game, going 5-for-6, with a pair of homers and 5 RBIs.

Gaining a measure of revenge against Colorado some two months later, Sosa led the Cubs to an 11-8 victory over the Rockies on July 2, 1993 by going 6-for-6, with 2 RBIs and 2 runs scored.

Sosa had a big day at the plate against San Diego on May 16, 1997, pacing the Cubs to a 16-7 win over the Padres by going 4-for-4, with a homer, triple, 6 RBIs, and 2 runs scored.

Sosa hit a number of memorable game-winning home runs during his time in Chicago, with one of those coming on April 17, 1996, when his two-run blast off Cincinnati reliever Johnny Ruffin (his second of the contest) in the bottom of the 10th inning gave the Cubs an 8-6 walk-off win over the Reds.

Sosa again came up big in the clutch less than three weeks later, on May 5, 1996, when his solo shot off New York right-hander Jerry DiPoto in the bottom of the ninth gave the Cubs a 5-4 win over the Mets in walkoff fashion. Sosa finished the game with 3 hits, 2 homers, and 3 RBIs.

Sosa provided further heroics on July 27, 1998, when his grand slam homer in the top of the eighth inning gave the Cubs a 6-2 victory over the Arizona Diamondbacks. He finished the day with 2 home runs and 6 RBIs.

Sosa hit another game-winning grand slam in the top of the eighth inning on September 16, 1998, doing so during a 6-3 victory over the San Diego Padres in which he collected 3 hits and 6 RBIs.

Sosa put his name in the record book on September 18, 1999, when, during a 7-4 loss to the Milwaukee Brewers in 14 innings, he became the first player in MLB history to reach the 60-homer mark in back-to-back seasons.

Sosa hit 3 home runs in one game six times during his career, doing so for the first time on June 5, 1996, when he led the Cubs to a 9-6 win over the Phillies by reaching the seats three times and driving in 5 runs.

Sosa accomplished the feat again on June 15, 1998, when his 3 solo blasts paced the Cubs to a 6-5 victory over the Milwaukee Brewers.

Although the Cubs lost their August 9, 2001 match-up with the Colorado Rockies by a score of 14-5, Sosa again delivered 3 solo blasts during the contest.

Sosa again went deep three times less than two weeks later, doing so during a 16-3 win over the Brewers on August 22, 2001 in which he knocked in 6 of the Cubs' runs.

Sosa accomplished the feat for a third time that season, when, during a 7-6 loss to the Houston Astros on September 23, 2001, he hit a pair of solo homers and a two-run shot.

However, Sosa had the greatest day of his career on August 10, 2002, when he led the Cubs to a 15-1 mauling of Colorado by going deep three times with two men on base, driving in 9 runs in the process.

Notable Achievements:

- Hit more than 30 home runs 11 times, topping 40 homers seven times, 50 homers four times, and 60 homers three times.
- Knocked in more than 100 runs nine times, surpassing 130 RBIs on four occasions.
- Scored more than 100 runs five times, topping 120 runs scored on three occasions.
- Batted over .300 four times, topping the .320-mark twice.
- Surpassed 30 doubles three times.
- Stole more than 20 bases four times, topping 30 steals twice.

- Drew more than 100 bases on balls twice.
- Compiled on-base percentage in excess of .400 twice.
- Posted slugging percentage in excess of .500 ten times, topping the .600-mark four times and the .700-mark once (.737 in 2001).
- Compiled OPS in excess of 1.000 four times.
- Led NL in: home runs twice, RBIs twice, runs scored three times, total bases three times, and games played three times.
- Finished second in NL in: home runs four times, RBIs twice, total bases once, bases on balls once, slugging percentage twice, and OPS once.
- Led NL right-fielders in: putouts twice, assists twice, and double plays once.
- Holds Cubs single-season records for: most home runs (66 in 1998), most total bases (425 in 2001), most extra-base hits (103 in 2001), and highest slugging percentage (.737 in 2001).
- Holds Cubs career record for most home runs (545).
- Ranks among Cubs career leaders in: RBIs (third), runs scored (sixth), hits (ninth), extra-base hits (third), total bases (fourth), bases on balls (sixth), slugging percentage (second), OPS (second), games played (10th), plate appearances (eighth), and at-bats (eighth).
- Ranks eighth in MLB history with 609 career home runs.
- Hit three home runs in one game six times.
- Five-time NL Player of the Month.
- Six-time Silver Slugger winner (1995, 1998, 1999, 2000, 2001 & 2002).
- 1998 Sporting News Major League Player of the Year.
- 1998 Sports Illustrated Co-Sportsman of the Year.
- 1998 Roberto Clemente Award winner.
- 1998 NL MVP.
- Finished second in 2001 NL MVP voting.
- Finished in top 10 in NL MVP voting five other times.
- Six-time Sporting News All-Star selection (1995, 1998, 1999, 2000, 2001 & 2002).
- Seven-time NL All-Star (1995, 1998, 1999, 2000, 2001, 2002 & 2004).

15

FRANK CHANCE

His name immortalized in the Franklin P. Adams poem entitled *Baseball's Sad Lexicon*, Frank Chance spent virtually his entire seventeen-year playing career in Chicago, serving as the Cubs' starting first baseman alongside infield mates Joe Tinker and Johnny Evers for eight full seasons. After originally being signed as a catcher/outfielder, Chance gradually shifted to first base, where he found a home as a member of arguably the most famous infield in baseball history. Part of the legendary double play combination of "Tinker-to-Evers-to-Chance," the right-handed throwing Chance did a solid job both in the field and at the bat, annually placing among the top players at his position in putouts, assists, and double plays, while compiling a lifetime batting average of .296 and a career on-base percentage of .394. Chance also excelled on the base paths, stealing more than 30 bases five times, en route to leading the league in that category twice. Renowned for his leadership ability, Chance also spent much of his time in Chicago managing the Cubs, leading them to four National League pennants and two world championships.

Born in Fresno, California on September 9, 1876, Frank Leroy Chance attended local Fresno High School, before enrolling at the University of California, where he initially intended to pursue a career in dentistry. However, Chance's plans changed shortly after he transferred to Washington College in Irvington, California, when he caught the attention of Chicago Orphans (the Chicago franchise officially became known as the Cubs in 1902) outfielder Bill Lange while playing in an independent league in the summer of 1897. After Lange convinced Chicago management to offer Chance a contract by stating, "Here's the most promising player I ever saw. Someday he'll be a wonder," the twenty-one-year-old catcher/outfielder signed with the Orphans for $40 a month, choosing in the process a baseball uniform over a dentist's smock.

After joining the Orphans in the spring of 1898, Chance spent most of the campaign serving as a backup behind the plate and in the outfield, batting .279, hitting one homer, driving in 14 runs, and scoring 32 times, in 53 games and 147 official at-bats. Continuing to fill a similar role in each of the next three seasons, Chance posted decent offensive numbers, displaying very little power at the plate, but compiling respectable batting averages of .286, .295, and .278. Chance also began to exhibit his base-stealing prowess in the last of those campaigns, stealing 27 bases in only 69 games in 1901.

Unable to garner more significant playing time his first few years in Chicago due to a series of broken fingers and other hand injuries sustained while trying to catch foul tips, Chance finally saw a bit more action in 1902 after Cubs manager Frank Selee moved him to first base during the season. Appearing in 75 games and accumulating 240 official at-bats, the right-handed hitting Chance finished the year with 1 home run, 31 RBIs, 39 runs scored, 27 steals, and a .288 batting average. Inserted at first base full-time the following year, Chance had his finest season to-date, concluding the 1903 campaign with 2 homers, 81 RBIs, 83 runs scored, a .327 batting average, and a league-leading 67 stolen bases.

After hitting a career-high 6 homers, driving in 49 runs, scoring 89 times, stealing 42 bases, and batting .310 in 1904, Chance saw his role continue to expand the following year when he replaced Selee as Cubs manager after the latter contracted tuberculosis. Excelling in his dual role, Chance knocked in 70 runs, scored 92 times, stole 38 bases, batted .316, and topped the senior circuit with a .450 on-base percentage, while also leading the Cubs to a record of 92-61. He followed that up by driving in 71 runs, batting .319, and leading the league with 103 runs scored and 57 stolen bases in 1906, prompting St. Louis Cardinals infielder Danny Shay to proclaim, "Chance is one great artist and, to my mind, ranks with [Napoleon] Lajoie and [Honus] Wagner. He is everything they are—a great hitter, splendid fielder, fast base-runner, and has a head full of brains." Meanwhile, the Cubs romped to the National League pennant under Chance's direction, compiling a regular-season record of 116-36 that left them a full 20 games ahead of their closest competition. Unfortunately, the Cubs' superb play failed to carry over to the postseason, since they ended up losing the World Series to the crosstown Chicago White Sox in six games.

Chance remained the Cubs' full-time starting first baseman another two years, posting solid offensive numbers in 1907 and 1908, while guiding his team to consecutive world championships. However, he gradually began to phase himself out of the starting lineup in 1909 after suffering a series of beanings through the years that ended up leaving him completely deaf in one ear, and with only limited hearing in the other.

Yet, even as Chance became less of a factor on the playing field, his influence as a manager continued to grow. Having earlier developed a reputation as one of the game's fiercest competitors, Chance became known for his poor sportsmanship and shabby treatment of the opposition. Once inciting a riot at the Polo Grounds by physically assaulting Giants pitcher Joe McGinnity, Chance regularly responded to the taunts of Brooklyn fans by tossing beer bottles at them. In addressing Chance's hard-nosed approach to his craft, Giants Hall of Fame pitcher Christy Mathewson wrote in his 1912 book, *Pitching in a Pinch*, "If Frank Chance has to choose between accepting a pair of spikes in a vital part of his anatomy and getting a putout, or dodging the spikes and losing the putout, he always takes the putout." Spending several off-seasons working as a prizefighter, Chance, who stood six feet tall and weighed close to 200 pounds, received praise from former heavyweight boxing champions John L. Sullivan and James J. Corbett, both of whom called him "the greatest amateur brawler of all time." Employing the same aggressive approach to managing, Chance ruled the Cubs with an iron hand, once forcing outfielder Solly Hofman to postpone his wedding until the end of the season to ensure that his marital bliss did not adversely affect his performance on the field. Chance also reportedly fined his players for shaking hands with members of the opposing team, once remarking, "You do things my way or you meet me after the game." Although most of Chance's players disliked him, they also respected his baseball acumen and leadership ability, which eventually earned him the nickname "The Peerless Leader."

Chance also became famous for the role he played in Chicago's dynamic double play combination of "Tinker-to-Evers-to-Chance," which twenty-eight-year-old *New York Evening Mail* newspaper columnist Franklin P. Adams immortalized in his 1910 poem entitled *Baseball's Sad Lexicon*. Frustrated over the inability of his beloved Giants to overcome the powerful Cubs, who predicated much of their success on their extraordinary pitching and the outstanding defensive work of their infield, Adams expressed his sentiments by writing:

Frank Chance led the Cubs to four pennants and two world championships as the team's player/manager

These are the saddest of possible words:

> *"Tinker to Evers to Chance."*
> *Trio of bear cubs, and fleeter than birds,*
> *Tinker and Evers and Chance.*
> *Ruthlessly pricking our gonfalon bubble,*
> *Making a Giant hit into a double –*
> *Words that are heavy with nothing but trouble:*
> *"Tinker to Evers to Chance."*

Although the trio of Cubs infielders never actually led the National League in double plays, Adams' poem gave them a permanent place in baseball lore, leading to their eventual induction into the Baseball Hall of Fame by the members of the Old Timers Committee in 1946.

After batting .298, driving in 36 runs, scoring 54 times, and stealing 16 bases in a part-time role in 1910, Chance relegated himself to backup duty his final two years in Chicago, before undergoing brain surgery following the conclusion of the 1912 campaign to correct blood clots that had formed as the result of multiple beanings. While in the hospital, though, Chance engaged in a heated argument with Cubs owner Charles Murphy when he criticized Murphy for releasing several good players in order to save the team money. Promptly released by Murphy as well, Chance subsequently signed a three-year contract to manage the Yankees after he made a miraculous recovery from his brain injuries. Chance left Chicago having led the Cubs to an overall record of 768-389 in his eight seasons as manager, giving him an outstanding .664 winning percentage—easily the best in franchise history.

Chance spent the next two years managing the Yankees, while also appearing in a total of 13 games. However, he handed in his resignation during the latter stages of the 1914 campaign after expressing his dissatisfaction with the talent Yankees scout Arthur Irwin gave him. Returning to his home in California, Chance operated an orange grove and briefly managed the Los Angeles team of the Pacific Coast League, before returning to the Major Leagues in 1923 for a short stint as manager of the Boston Red Sox. After accepting an offer to manage the Chicago White Sox at season's end, Chance found himself unable to fulfill the terms of his contract when his health took a sudden turn for the worse. Plagued by chronic headaches for more than a decade, Chance found his health further compromised by heart disease brought on by severe spasms of bronchial asthma. After falling ill for several months, Chance passed away at only forty-eight years of age, on September 15, 1924. Following his passing, fellow Hall of Fame manager John McGraw said of his former rival, "He was a great player—I think one of the best first basemen ever in the game—but, in addition, he was a great leader because he asked no man to take any chance that he would not take himself, and because he had the power to instill enthusiasm even in a losing cause.

Career Numbers:

20 HR; 596 RBIs; 798 Runs Scored; 1,274 Hits; 200 Doubles; 79 Triples; 403 Stolen Bases; .296 AVG; .394 OBP; .394 SLG; .788 OPS

Cub Career Highlights:

Best Season: Chance had his breakout year for the Cubs in 1903, scoring 83 runs and establishing career-high marks in RBIs (81), batting average (.327), and stolen bases (67), leading the league in the last category. He also performed extremely well in 1905, driving in 70 runs, scoring 92 times, stealing 38 bases, batting .316, topping the circuit with a .450 on-base percentage, and posting a career-best .883 OPS. Nevertheless, the

1906 campaign would have to be considered Chance's finest all-around season. In addition to knocking in 71 runs, batting .319, and leading the league with 103 runs scored and 57 stolen bases, Chance guided the Cubs to a regular season record of 116-36, giving them the highest single-season winning percentage (.763) in major league history.

Memorable Moments/Greatest Performances: Chance displayed his outstanding base-running ability during a 1906 contest against Cincinnati, when he broke a late-inning tie with the Reds by stealing home all the way from second base, after swiping second on the previous pitch.

Although just a part-time player by 1911, Chance showed that he still had something left in the tank on April 20, leading the Cubs to a 9-5 victory over the Cardinals by going 3-for-4, with a triple, 4 RBIs, and 2 runs scored.

A solid postseason performer over the course of his career, Chance compiled a lifetime batting average of .300 in World Series play, stealing 10 bases in only 20 games. Excelling in particular against Detroit in the 1908 fall classic, Chance led the Cubs to a five-game victory over the Tigers by batting .421, scoring 4 runs, and stealing 5 bases. He also batted .353 and knocked in 4 runs during Chicago's five-game loss to the Philadelphia Athletics in the 1910 Series.

Notable Achievements:

- Batted over .300 four times, topping the .320-mark once (.327 in 1903).
- Scored more than 100 runs once (103 in 1906).
- Finished in double digits in triples four times.
- Stole more than 20 bases nine times, topping 50 steals twice and 60 thefts once (67 in 1903).
- Compiled on-base percentage in excess of .400 five times.
- Led NL in: runs scored once, stolen bases twice, and on-base percentage once.
- Led NL first basemen with .992 fielding percentage in 1907.
- Holds Cubs career record for most stolen bases (402).
- Tied for seventh in Cubs history with .394 career on-base percentage.
- Four-time NL champion (1906, 1907, 1908 & 1910).

- Two-time world champion (1907 & 1908).
- Elected to Baseball Hall of Fame by members of Old Timers Committee in 1946.

16

PHIL CAVARRETTA

A native Chicagoan, Phil Cavarretta ended up spending more seasons with his beloved Cubs than any other player in franchise history. Splitting his time between first base and the outfield, Cavarretta spent parts of 20 seasons with the Cubs, before moving across town, where he joined the White Sox for his final two campaigns. A fierce competitor of whom *Baseball Digest* sportswriter Herb Graffis said in 1949, "Phil Cavarretta would cut your heart out for a run the Cubs need," Cavarretta gave his heart and soul to his hometown team, helping them advance to the World Series three times and earning three All-Star nominations and one league MVP award in the process. En route to compiling a lifetime batting average of .293, the left-handed hitting Cavarretta batted in excess of .300 five times, posting a league-leading mark of .355 in his MVP campaign of 1945. Ranking among the franchise's all-time leaders in several statistical categories, Cavarretta also compiled an on-base percentage in excess of .400 three times, scored more than 100 runs once, and finished in double digits in triples on four separate occasions.

Born in Chicago, Illinois on July 19, 1916, Philip Joseph Cavarretta went to high school in the shadow of Wrigley Field, attending nearby Lane Technical High School. Excelling on the diamond at Lane Tech, Cavarretta established himself as a local sensation as both a pitcher and a hitter, prompting the Cubs to sign him as an amateur free agent prior to his eighteenth birthday. Following his graduation, Cavarretta spent most of the 1934 campaign with Chicago's minor league affiliate in Peoria, Illinois, where he hit for the cycle in his very first game as a professional. After joining the Cubs in mid-September, Cavarretta acquitted himself extremely well during the season's final two weeks, batting .381, with 1 homer and 6 RBIs, in only 21 official at-bats.

With Chicago player-manager Charlie Grimm choosing to focus more on his managerial duties in 1935, he assigned the starting first-base job to Cavarretta, who rewarded his skipper for the faith he placed in him by hitting 8 homers, driving in 82 runs, scoring 85 times, batting .275, and placing among the league leaders with 12 triples. After a somewhat less productive 1936 campaign in which he hit 9 homers, batted .273, knocked in 56 runs, and scored 55 others, Cavarretta assumed more of a part-time role the following year, when, splitting his time between first base and the outfield, he hit 5 homers, drove in 56 runs, scored 43 times, and batted .286.

Cavarretta continued to function primarily as a part-time player the next four seasons, finding his playing time further reduced by a series of injuries he sustained. After appearing in only 22 games in 1939 due to a broken ankle, Cavarretta broke his ankle again the following year, limiting him to just 65 games. Playing the outfield mostly in 1941, a healthy Cavarretta batted .286, with 6 home runs, 40 RBIs, and 46 runs scored, in 107 games and 346 official at-bats. Returning to the everyday starting lineup in 1942, Cavarretta posted modest offensive numbers, finishing the season with 3 homers, 54 RBIs, 59 runs scored, and a .270 batting average, while splitting his playing time almost equally between first base and centerfield.

Ruled exempt from military duty during World War II due to an ear problem, Cavarretta remained behind while many of the game's top players entered the service, enabling him to compile the best numbers of his career over the course of the next three seasons. Playing first base almost exclusively during that time, Cavarretta hit 8 homers, knocked in 73 runs, scored 93 times, batted .291, and posted a .382 on-base percentage in 1943, before earning the first of his three All-Star selections the following year by hitting 5 homers, driving in 82 runs, topping the senior circuit with 197 hits, and placing among the league leaders with a .321 batting average, 106 runs scored, 15 triples, and 35 doubles. Cavarretta then led the Cubs to the pennant in 1945, capturing NL MVP honors in the process, by hitting 6 homers, knocking in 97 runs, scoring 94 times, and leading the league with a .355 batting average and a .449 on-base percentage.

Earning the favor of his teammates with his tremendous hustle and fierce competitive spirit, Cavarretta drew praise from Chicago manager Charlie Grimm, who suggested that he "must have been the inspiration for whoever coined the phrase, 'He came to play.'"

Meanwhile, teammate Roy Smalley stated, "I liked Cavarretta a lot. Phil was as generous as can be. He expected you to give 120%, as he did—and sorry if you don't like that."

Popular with the local fans as well, Cavarretta, said Paul Schramka, was "tough…a good baseball man. He hated to lose—a great competitor. After the game, the players would get changed, and he'd complain, 'You can't wait to get outta here!' So they'd wait until he started dressing."

Although Cavarretta never again reached such heights after the war, he remained an extremely effective player the next several seasons as he resumed his practice of shuttling back and forth between first base and the outfield. Performing particularly well in 1946, Cavarretta earned his second All-Star nomination and a 10th-place finish in the NL MVP voting by driving in 78 runs, scoring 89 times, batting .294, and finishing third in the league with a .401 on-base percentage. He followed that up by batting .314 and earning his final All-Star selection in 1947, before gradually transitioning into a back-up role over the course of the next few seasons. After compiling batting averages of .278, .294, .273, and .311 as a part-time player from 1948 to 1951, Cavarretta became strictly a back-up in 1952—his first full season as Cubs' manager.

After replacing Frankie Frisch at the helm midway through the 1951 campaign, Cavarretta continued to manage the Cubs until the spring of 1954, when he incurred the wrath of team owner Phil Wrigley by telling him that he did not think the Cubs had the ability to remain competitive that year. Claiming that Cavarretta's words revealed a "defeatist attitude," Wrigley promptly relieved him of his duties, replacing him with another longtime member of the organization, Stan Hack. Refusing to accept a minor league managing assignment, Cavarretta instead signed with the crosstown Chicago White Sox, with whom he spent the remainder of his playing career serving as a back-up, before announcing his retirement early the following year after being released by the club on May 9, 1955. Following his playing days, Cavarretta remained in baseball another two decades, serving at different times as a coach, scout, and minor league manager until 1978, when he left the game after spending the previous six seasons coaching batters in the New York Mets' farm system. Cavarretta subsequently lived until the ripe old age of 94, passing away on December 18, 2010, after suffering a stroke one week earlier.

Cub Numbers:

92 HR; 896 RBIs; 968 Runs Scored; 1,927 Hits; 341 Doubles; 99 Triples; 61 Stolen Bases; .292 AVG; .371 OBP; .416 SLG; .787 OPS

Career Numbers:

95 HR; 920 RBIs; 990 Runs Scored; 1,977 Hits; 347 Doubles; 99 Triples; 65 Stolen Bases; .293 AVG; .372 OBP; .416 SLG; .788 OPS

Cub Career Highlights:

Best Season: Cavarretta had an outstanding year for the Cubs in 1944, driving in 82 runs, batting .321, and establishing career-high marks with 106 runs scored, 15 triples, 35 doubles, and a league-leading 197 hits. Nevertheless, the 1945 campaign is generally considered to be his signature season. In addition to leading the NL with a .355 batting average and a .449 on-base percentage, Cavarretta knocked in a career-high 97 runs, scored 94 times, collected 177 hits, and finished in the league's top five with 10 triples, 34 doubles, a .500 slugging percentage, and a .949 OPS, establishing career-best marks in each of the last two categories as well, en route to earning NL MVP honors.

Memorable Moments/Greatest Performances: Cavarretta made his Wrigley Field debut a memorable one, hitting his first big league home run in his first at-bat in his home ballpark, to give the Cubs a 1-0 win over Cincinnati on September 26, 1934.

Cavarretta turned in an outstanding effort on August 21, 1935, when he helped lead the Cubs to a lopsided 19-5 victory over Philadelphia by going 5-for-6, with 4 RBIs and 2 runs scored.

Primarily a gap-to-gap hitter, Cavarretta flexed his muscles on August 30, 1936, when he hit 2 home runs in one game for the only time in his career, reaching the seats twice during an 8-6 loss to the New York Giants.

Cavarretta had a big day at the plate on June 9, 1940, going 4-for-5, with 4 RBIs and 2 runs scored, during a 15-8 home win over Boston.

Although the Cubs ended up losing their August 17, 1941 matchup with the Cincinnati Reds by a score of 6-3, Cavarretta had the only 5-for-5 day of his career, collecting a double and 4 singles during the defeat.

Cavarretta gave the Cubs a 12-9, extra-inning win over the Reds on September 1, 1943, when he homered with 2 men on base and 1 man out in

Courtesy of MEARS Online Auctions

Phil Cavarretta captured NL MVP honors in 1945,
when he led the Cubs to the pennant by topping
the senior circuit with a .355 batting average

the top of the 10th. The first baseman's 3-run blast put the finishing touches on a 4-for-5, 5-RBI performance.

After collecting 4 hits and scoring 3 runs the previous day, Cavarretta continued his hot-hitting against Philadelphia on September 26, 1944, leading the Cubs to a 15-0 mauling of the Phillies by going 4-for-5, with a pair of triples, 4 RBIs, and 2 runs scored.

Cavarretta had the most productive day of his career on July 3, 1945, when he collected 5 hits, knocked in 5 runs, and scored 5 times during a 24-2 rout of the Boston Braves.

Cavarretta had another huge game just five days later, when he led the Cubs to a 12-6 win over the Phillies on July 8 by going 4-for-5, with a triple, 4 RBIs, and 2 runs scored.

Cavarretta continued to excel the following month, leading the Cubs to an 11-5 victory over Cincinnati on August 3, 1945 by going 3-for-4, with a homer, 5 RBIs, and 3 runs scored.

Cavarretta again torched Cincinnati's pitching staff two days later, when he went 5-for-6, with a triple and 5 RBIs, during a 12-5 win over the Reds on August 5.

Cavarretta came up just a home run short of the hitting for the cycle on July 10, 1949, when he collected a single, double, 2 triples, and 5 RBIs during an 8-6 victory over the Pittsburgh Pirates.

Although the Cubs came up short both times, Cavarretta performed magnificently in both the 1938 and 1945 World Series. After batting .462 against the Yankees in the 1938 Fall Classic, Cavarretta nearly led the Cubs to their first world championship in thirty-seven years in 1945 by homering once, knocking in 5 runs, scoring 7 times, and batting .423 during their seven-game loss to Detroit.

Yet, Cavarretta got arguably the biggest hit of his career on September 25, 1935, when he delivered the decisive blow in the opener of a crucial five-game series between the first-place Cubs and second-place Cardinals. With the Cubs holding a slim three-game lead over the Cards with just those five regular-season contests remaining, they needed to win just twice to clinch the National League pennant. Cavarretta helped the Cubs move one step closer to reaching that goal when he homered off St. Louis starter Paul Dean in the second inning of the series opener. With Chicago's Lon Warneke shutting out the Cardinals on just 2 hits, Cavarretta's homer stood up as the game's only run, clinching at least a tie for the pennant. After a rainout the next day, the Cubs beat Dizzy Dean and the demoralized Cardinals by a score of 6-2 in game two of the series, eliminating St. Louis from contention.

Notable Achievements:

- Batted over .300 four times, topping the .350-mark once (.355 in 1945).
- Scored more than 100 runs once (106 in 1944).
- Finished in double digits in triples four times.
- Surpassed 30 doubles twice.
- Compiled on-base percentage in excess of .400 twice.
- Posted slugging percentage in excess of .500 once (.500 in 1945).
- Led NL in: batting average once, hits once, and on-base percentage once.
- Finished second in NL in triples once and OPS once.
- Led NL first basemen in double plays once.
- Ranks among Cubs career leaders in: RBIs (10th), runs scored (10th), hits (10th), extra-base hits (10th), triples (fifth), bases on balls (seventh), games played (sixth), plate appearances (10th), and at-bats (10th).
- 1945 NL MVP.
- 1945 *Sporting News* All-Star selection.
- Three-time NL All-Star (1944, 1946 & 1947).
- Three-time NL champion (1935, 1938 & 1945).

17

ARAMIS RAMIREZ

Acquired by the Cubs in one of the best trades Jim Hendry ever made as General Manager of the team, Aramis Ramirez spent eight-and-a-half seasons in Chicago, during which time he established himself as one of the most potent batsmen in franchise history. Appearing in more games at third base for the Cubs than anyone else, with the exception of Ron Santo and Stan Hack, Ramirez hit at least 25 home runs in seven of his eight full seasons in the Windy City, with his 239 homers as a member of the ball club representing the sixth-highest total in team annals. Despite being plagued by injuries much of his time in Chicago, Ramirez also knocked in more than 100 runs four times and batted over .300 on five separate occasions, earning in the process two All-Star selections and a pair of top-10 finishes in the NL MVP voting. Ramirez's strong hitting and solid play at third helped the Cubs capture three NL Central titles and earn a berth in the 2003 NLCS, where they came within one game of advancing to the World Series for the first time in fifty-eight years.

Born in Santo Domingo, Distrito Nacional, Dominican Republic on June 25, 1978, Aramis Nin Ramirez went to high school at Aida Cartagena Portalatin, which he continued to attend after signing with the Pittsburgh Pirates as an amateur free agent at only sixteen years of age in 1994. Following his graduation, Ramirez traveled to the United States, where he spent most of the next five seasons advancing through Pittsburgh's farm system, although he also appeared in a total of 163 games with the Pirates during that time. Arriving in the big leagues to stay in 2001, Ramirez earned the starting third base job for the Pirates, concluding his first full season with 34 home runs, 112 RBIs, 83 runs scored, and a batting average of an even .300, while committing 25 errors at the hot corner. However, after his offensive numbers slipped to 18 homers, 71 RBIs, 51 runs scored, and a .234 batting average the following year, the Pirates elected to include him in a trade they completed with the Cubs on July 23, 2003 that sent Ramirez and veteran outfielder Kenny Lofton to Chicago, in exchange for utility infielders Jose Hernandez and Bobby Hill and minor league pitcher Matt Bruback,

Making an immediate impact in the middle of the Cubs' lineup, Ramirez hit 15 homers, knocked in 39 runs, and batted .259 over the final 63 games of the 2003 campaign, to finish the season with 27 home runs, 106 RBIs, and a composite batting average of .272, although he also committed a league-leading 33 errors at third. Ramirez followed that up by hitting 36 homers, driving in 103 runs, scoring 99 times, batting .318, and reducing his error total to just 10 in 2004, with his outstanding all-around performance earning him a 10th-place finish in the NL MVP voting. Despite spending the final five weeks of the ensuing campaign on the disabled list after straining a muscle in his quadriceps on August 24, Ramirez had another big year, earning his first All-Star nomination by hitting 31 homers, knocking in 92 runs, and batting .302.

Yet, in spite of the excellent offensive numbers Ramirez compiled over the course of his first two-and-a-half seasons in Chicago, he went mostly unappreciated by Cubs fans, many of whom considered him to be lazy and criticized him for his dispassionate play and subpar defense. It should be noted, though, that Ramirez worked hard at improving himself as a defender, eventually turning himself into an adequate fielder and increasing his range at third. However, it was on offense that the right-handed hitting Ramirez truly excelled, consistently finishing somewhere in the vicinity of 30 home runs and 100 RBIs. And, unlike most power hitters of his era, Ramirez did not strike out a great deal, fanning more than 70 times only twice as a member of the Cubs.

Healthy again in 2006, Ramirez had one of his finest all-around seasons, establishing career-high marks in home runs (38) and RBIs (119), while also scoring 93 times, batting .291, and leading all NL third sackers with a .965 fielding percentage. He followed that up by hitting 26 homers, driving in 101 runs, and batting .310 in 2007, despite missing 30 games due to injury. Ramirez then earned All-Star honors and a 10th-place finish in the league MVP voting for the second time in 2008 by hitting 27 homers, knocking in 111 runs, scoring 97 times, and batting .289.

Although Ramirez performed well when healthy in 2009, hitting 15 homers, driving in 65 runs, and batting .317, he ended up missing half of the campaign with a dislocated shoulder. Plagued by a series of nagging injuries the following year, Ramirez appeared in only 124 games, finishing the season with 25 home runs, 83 RBIs, and a batting average of just .241. He rebounded in 2011, though, earning his lone Silver Slugger by reaching the seats 26 times, knocking in 93 runs, and raising his batting average 65 points, to .306.

With Ramirez becoming a free agent following the conclusion of the 2011 campaign, the Cubs chose not to actively pursue the thirty-three-year-old third baseman, leaving him to sign a multi-year deal with the Milwaukee Brewers. On his way out the door, though, Ramirez found himself being criticized by Cubs' color man, Bob Brenly, who, among other things, accused him of being a bad influence on younger players, a below-average defender, and a poor base-runner. When asked about the criticism directed at him, Ramirez responded, "You talking about Bob Brenly? I ain't going to get into a war with Brenly or any other guy. Brenly played the game. He knows how it is. And, if you want, you can put my numbers right next to his and see who did better in their career."

Ramirez ended up spending parts of the next four seasons in Milwaukee, having his best year for the Brewers in 2012, when he earned a ninth-place finish in the NL MVP voting by hitting 27 homers, driving in 105 runs, scoring 92 times, batting .300, and leading the league with 50 doubles. Ramirez continued to man third base for the Brewers until midway through the 2015 campaign, when his original team, the Pittsburgh Pirates, reacquired him for minor league pitcher Yhonathan Barrios. A free agent again at season's end, the thirty-seven-year-old Ramirez elected to announce his retirement, ending his career with 386 home runs, 1,417 RBIs, 1,098 runs scored, 2,303 hits, a .283 batting average, a .341 on-base percentage, and a .492 slugging percentage. Upon making his announcement, Ramirez stated that he hoped to remain involved in baseball in some capacity in the future.

Cub Numbers:

239 HR; 806 RBIs; 651 Runs Scored; 1,246 Hits; 256 Doubles; 14 Triples; 8 Stolen Bases; .294 AVG; .356 OBP; .531 SLG PCT; .887 OPS

Aramis Ramirez surpassed 25 home runs in
seven of his eight full seasons with the Cubs

Courtesy of Jauerback

Career Numbers:

386 HR; 1,417 RBIs; 1,098 Runs Scored; 2,303 Hits; 495 Doubles; 24 Triples; 29 Stolen Bases; .283 AVG; .341 OBP; .492 SLG PCT; .833 OPS

Cub Career Highlights:

Best Season: Although Ramirez batted .291, scored 93 runs, and posted career-high marks in home runs (38), RBIs (119), triples (4), and total bases (333) in 2006, he actually compiled slightly better overall numbers two years earlier. En route to earning the first of his two top-10 finishes in the NL MVP voting as a member of the Cubs in 2004, Ramirez hit 36 homers, knocked in 103 runs, scored 99 times, batted .318, and posted an OPS of .951, reaching career highs in each of the last three categories. Meanwhile, he committed only 10 errors in the field and compiled a fielding percentage of .969, which represented the second-highest mark he posted during his time in Chicago.

Memorable Moments/Greatest Performances: Ramirez had a big day at the plate against his former team on September 21, 2003, leading the Cubs to a 4-1 victory over the Pirates by going 3-for-4, with a pair of homers and 3 RBIs.

Later that year, in Game Four of the 2003 NLCS, Ramirez helped the Cubs grab a commanding three-games-to-one lead against the Florida Marlins in the series by driving in 6 runs during an 8-3 Chicago win. Ramirez finished the contest with 3 hits and 2 home runs, including a first-inning grand slam against Dontrelle Willis—the first ever bases loaded homer by a member of the Cubs in postseason play. Unfortunately, the Marlins came back to win the next three games, thereby denying the Cubs their first World Series appearance since 1945.

Just two days after collecting 3 hits and homering twice during an 8-3 victory over the Pittsburgh Pirates, Ramirez helped lead the Cubs to a come-from-behind 11-10 win over Cincinnati on April 16, 2004 by going 4-for-4, with a homer, 2 doubles, and 5 RBIs.

Ramirez scored a career-high 4 runs during a lopsided 16-6 victory over the Arizona Diamondbacks on April 4, 2005, also driving in 4 runs with 3 hits, including a homer and a double.

Ramirez proved to be a one-man wrecking crew on July 19, 2005, leading the Cubs to a 7-3 win over Cincinnati by knocking in 5 runs with a double and a pair of homers.

Ramirez led the Cubs to an 11-6 win over the Phillies on September 18, 2006 by going 4-for-5, with 2 home runs and a career-high 7 RBIs.

Ramirez continued to torment his former team on September 21, 2007, when he homered twice and knocked in 6 runs during a 13-8 victory over the Pirates at Wrigley Field. One of Ramirez's blasts, which traveled an estimated 495 feet, proved to be the longest home run hit the entire year.

Ramirez had a similarly productive afternoon against Washington on August 23, 2008, leading the Cubs to a 9-2 pasting of the Nationals by driving in 6 runs with 3 hits, including a pair of homers.

Exactly three years later, on August 23, 2011, Ramirez had the only 5-for-5 day of his career, hitting safely in all 5 of his trips to the plate during a 5-4 loss to the Braves.

Ramirez's potent bat provided Cubs fans with many thrills through the years, with one of the most exhilarating moments taking place on June 29, 2007, when his two-out, two-run homer in the bottom of the ninth inning completed a three-run rally that gave the Cubs a memorable 6-5 come-from-behind victory over the Milwaukee Brewers.

Ramirez delivered a pair of clutch late-inning homers against the Chicago White Sox on June 20, 2008 that helped the Cubs defeat their cross-town rivals by a score of 4-3. After tying the game at 3-3 with a solo blast in the bottom of the seventh inning, Ramirez homered again two frames later, to give the Cubs the victory in walk-off fashion.

Ramirez again came up big in the clutch on August 28, 2008, when his grand slam homer in the bottom of the eighth inning turned a 4-2 deficit to the Philadelphia Phillies into a 6-4 Cubs' win.

Ramirez provided further heroics on April 18, 2009, when his two-out, two-run homer in the bottom of the 11th inning gave the Cubs a 7-5 victory over the St. Louis Cardinals.

Ramirez hit 3 home runs in one game three times as a member of the Cubs, accomplishing the feat for the first time on July 30, 2004, when his 3 solo blasts provided the margin of victory in a 10-7 win over the Phillies. Ramirez again reached the seats three times in one game later in the year, doing so during a 5-4 victory over the Cincinnati Reds in which he also doubled and knocked in 5 runs. However, Ramirez had his biggest day at the plate on July 20, 2010, when he homered three times and drove in a career-high 7 runs, in leading the Cubs to a 14-7 win over the Houston Astros.

Notable Achievements:

- Hit more than 20 home runs seven times, topping 30 homers on three occasions.
- Knocked in more than 100 runs four times.
- Batted over .300 five times.
- Surpassed 30 doubles six times, topping 40 two-baggers once (44 in 2008).
- Posted slugging percentage in excess of .500 seven times.
- Led NL third basemen in assists once and fielding percentage once.
- Ranks among Cubs career leaders in: home runs (sixth), slugging percentage (third), and OPS (fifth).
- Hit three home runs in one game three times (July 30, 2004 vs. Philadelphia; September 16, 2004 vs. Cincinnati; July 20, 2010 vs. Houston).
- Finished in top 10 in NL MVP voting twice (2004 & 2008).
- 2008 NL Hank Aaron Award winner.
- 2011 Silver Slugger winner.
- 2011 *Sporting News* All-Star selection.
- Two-time NL All-Star (2005 & 2008).

18

JOHNNY EVERS

Standing 5'9" tall and weighing only 125 pounds, Johnny Evers lacked the physical gifts generally associated with professional athletes. Bereft of power, Evers hit just 12 homers and knocked in only 538 runs over the course of his major-league career, which he spent mostly with the Cubs. However, using his intelligence to gain every possible advantage over his opponents, Evers eventually established himself as one of the Dead Ball Era's premier middle infielders, developing a reputation for being one of the period's smartest players. An outstanding bunter, accomplished base stealer, and pesky left-handed hitter who typically posted one of the National League's best walks-to-strikeouts ratios, Evers ended up compiling a lifetime batting average of .270, posting a career on-base percentage of .356, scoring 919 runs, and stealing 324 bases. Having most of his finest seasons for the Cubs between 1902 and 1913, Evers batted over .300 twice, compiled an on-base percentage in excess of .400 three times, and stole more than 40 bases twice, in helping to lead them to four NL pennants and two world championships. Meanwhile, the plucky second baseman did an excellent job of serving as the middle man for Chicago's famous double play combination of "Tinker-to-Evers-to-Chance," leading all NL second sackers in assists and putouts twice each, while annually placing among the top players at his position in double plays.

Born in Troy, New York on July 21, 1881, John Joseph Evers honed his baseball skills on the local sandlots, before making his professional debut as a shortstop with the Troy Trojans of the Class-B New York State League in 1902. Performing well for the Trojans, Evers batted .285 and hit 10 home runs, prior to being acquired by the Cubs during the latter stages of the campaign after Chicago manager Frank Selee discovered him during an exhibition game between the two clubs.

Moved to second base by Selee upon his arrival in the Windy City, Evers appeared in a total of 26 games for the Cubs in the season's final month, scoring 7 runs and compiling a batting average of .222 in 90 official at-bats. Assuming the starting second base job the following year, Evers had a solid rookie season, concluding the 1903 campaign with a .293 batting average, 52 RBIs, 70 runs scored, and 25 stolen bases, while finishing third among players at his position in fielding percentage. Despite seeing his offensive production fall off to 47 RBIs, 49 runs scored, and a .265 batting average the following year, Evers emerged as arguably the senior circuit's best all-around second baseman, leading all players at his position with 381 putouts and 518 assists, although he also committed a league-leading 54 errors.

After suffering through an injury-marred 1905 campaign in which he appeared in only 99 games, Evers missed just one contest in 1906, helping the Cubs claim the first of their three straight National League pennants by batting .255, driving in 51 runs, scoring 65 times, and stealing a career-high 49 bases, while also finishing first among NL second basemen with 344 putouts. Evers posted extremely similar numbers for Chicago's world championship ball club the following year, batting .250, knocking in 51 runs, scoring 66 times, finishing second in the league with 46 stolen bases, amassing 346 putouts in the field, and leading all NL second sackers with 500 assists. Evers' strong all-around play prompted Cubs' player-manager Frank Chance to comment, "I doubt if any second baseman has had so great an influence on the work of a club as a whole, or has been so important a factor in its success, as Evers has been with the Chicago Nationals."

As Evers began to establish himself as one of the Cubs' most indispensable players, he also developed a reputation as one of the game's shrewdest competitors. Obsessed with excelling in the more subtle aspects of his chosen profession, Evers compensated for his lack of size by frequently out-thinking his opponents. After failing to draw more than 40 bases on balls in any of his first five seasons, Evers evolved into one of the senior circuit's most patient hitters, finishing in the league's top three in walks three straight times between 1908 and 1910, including earning a free trip to first base a career-high 108 times in the last of those campaigns. In explaining his approach at the plate years later, Evers stated:

> *"I am convinced that, in my own career, I could usually have hit 30 points higher if I had made a specialty of hitting. Some lumbering bonehead who does make a specialty*

of hitting, and nothing else, may forge well across the .300
line and everybody says, 'What a grand hitter.' The fact is,
the bonehead may have been playing rotten baseball when
he got that average, and someone else who didn't look
to be in his class might be the better hitter of the two. Of
course, there are plenty of times when there is nothing like
the old bingle. But there are plenty of other times when
the batter at the plate should focus his attention on trying
to fool the pitcher. In my own case, I have frequently faced
the pitcher when I had no desire whatever to hit. I wanted
to get a base on balls."

Evers also became known for his quick temper, fiery disposition, and lack of tolerance for others—particularly umpires, for whom he expressed his disdain on one occasion by saying, "My favorite umpire is a dead one." Although Evers originally acquired the nickname "The Human Crab" due to his unorthodox method of fielding ground balls, the moniker eventually became more closely associated with his temperament, since he always seemed to be complaining about something. Whether interacting with teammates, opponents, or umpires, Evers frequently found himself quarreling with others, prompting Cleveland Indians manager Joe Birmingham to observe, "They claim he is a crab, and perhaps they are right." But Birmingham quickly added, "But I would like to have twenty-five such crabs playing for me. If I did, I would have no doubts over the pennant. They would win hands down."

Evers, in fact, ended up engaging in a legendary dispute with his keystone partner, Joe Tinker, with whom he did not communicate off the field for decades. Although some commentators dated their mutual animosity to a highly-publicized on-field brawl in 1905, Evers suggested otherwise years later. "One day early in 1907, he threw me a hard ball; it wasn't any farther than from here to there," claimed Evers, pointing to a lamp some ten feet away from where he sat. "It was a real hard ball, like a catcher throwing to second." With Tinker's toss having bent back one of the fingers on his right hand, Evers later recalled, "I yelled to him, 'You so-and-so.' He laughed. That's the last word we had for, well, I just don't know how long." Yet, in spite of their personal disdain for one another, Evers and Tinker continued to function well together on the field, with Evers commenting, "Tinker and myself hated each other, but we loved the Cubs. We wouldn't fight for each other, but we'd come close to killing people for our team. That was one of the answers to the Cubs' success."

Evers continued his strong all-around play in 1908, helping the Cubs capture their third consecutive pennant by batting an even .300, scoring 83 runs, and stealing 36 bases, even though injuries limited him to only 126 games. Although the Cubs failed to repeat as NL champions the following year, finishing 6 ½ games behind the first-place Pittsburgh Pirates despite winning 104 games themselves, Evers had another solid season, batting .263 and scoring a career-high 88 runs. He then helped the Cubs return to the top of the NL standings in 1910 by batting .263, scoring 87 runs, and placing among the league leaders with 108 walks and a .413 on-base percentage. However, a broken leg forced him to miss the final month of the campaign, preventing him from taking part in the World Series, which the Cubs lost to Philadelphia in five games.

Evers' volatile disposition finally got the better of him in 1911, when he suffered a nervous breakdown after losing most of his savings in a failed business venture. Appearing in only 46 games over the course of the campaign, Evers batted just .226, knocked in only 7 runs, and scored just 29 others. However, he returned with a vengeance in 1912 to have the finest statistical season of his career. In addition to driving in 63 runs, scoring 73 times, and collecting 11 triples, Evers finished fourth in the league with a .341 batting average and placed second in the circuit with a .431 on-base percentage. After being named Chicago's player-manager following the release of Frank Chance at season's end, Evers had another solid year in 1913, earning a 10th-place finish in the league MVP voting by scoring 81 runs and batting .285. Nevertheless, team ownership elected to part ways with him shortly thereafter, trading him to the Boston Braves for veteran infielder Bill Sweeney and cash prior to the start of the 1914 campaign.

The swap of players proved to be an ill-advised move by the Cubs, with whom Sweeney spent just one season. Meanwhile, Evers helped lead the Braves to the NL pennant in his first year in Boston, earning league MVP honors by scoring 81 runs, batting .279, compiling a .390 on-base percentage, and leading all NL shortstops in fielding percentage for the only time in his career. He then compiled a .438 batting average during Boston's stunning four-game sweep of the Philadelphia Athletics in the World Series.

The 1914 campaign ended up being Evers' last as a full-time player. Limited to only 83 games the following year by injuries and suspensions incurred from arguing with umpires, Evers nearly missed additional playing time after expressing concerns that he might be on the verge of another

Courtesy of the Bain Collection at the Library of Congress

Johnny Evers stole more than 20 bases seven times
as a member of the Cubs

nervous breakdown. After Evers batted just .216 in 71 games in 1916, the Braves placed him on waivers when he got off to a slow start the following year. Evers subsequently signed with the Philadelphia Phillies, with whom he essentially ended his playing career in 1917, although he also appeared in two more games as a player-coach during the 1920s.

Following his playing days, Evers spent one year in New York serving as a coach for the Giants, before returning to Chicago in 1921 to manage the Cubs. However, after Evers led them to a record of just 41-55 through early August, he suffered the indignity of being fired by his former team. He subsequently joined the Chicago White Sox, with whom he spent the next three years serving first as a coach, and then as manager, before being replaced at the end of the 1924 season. Evers later became a coach for the Boston Braves, remaining in that post from 1929 to 1932, before spending the next two years scouting for the organization. After leaving baseball, Evers ran a sporting-goods store in Albany, New York, which remained in family hands until it closed its doors for good during the 1990s. Evers suffered a stroke in August 1942 that debilitated him for the rest of his life. The entire right side of his body paralyzed, Evers remained bedridden or confined to a wheelchair for most of the next five years, before dying of a cerebral hemorrhage at the age of sixty-five on March 28, 1947, just one year after being inducted into the National Baseball Hall of Fame.

Cub Numbers:

9 HR; 446 RBIs; 742 Runs Scored; 1,340 Hits; 183 Doubles; 64 Triples; 291 Stolen Bases; .276 AVG; .354 OBP; .345 SLG; .700 OPS

Career Numbers:

12 HR; 538 RBIs; 919 Runs Scored; 1,659 Hits; 216 Doubles; 70 Triples; 324 Stolen Bases; .270 AVG; .356 OBP; .334 SLG; .690 OPS

Cub Career Highlights:

Best Season: Although the Cubs failed to win the pennant in 1912, finishing third in the National League, 11 ½ games behind the first-place New York Giants, Evers had easily his finest season, establishing career-high marks in RBIs (63), hits (163), triples (11), batting average (.341), on-base percentage (.431), and slugging percentage (.441).

Memorable Moments/Greatest Performances: Evers didn't hit his first home run in the majors until his third full season with the Cubs, celebrating his twenty-fourth birthday by reaching the seats during a 3-2 win over the Boston Braves on July 21, 1905.

Evers helped lead the Cubs to a 9-0 victory over the St. Louis Cardinals on September 6, 1911 by going 4-for-5, with an RBI, 2 runs scored, and a stolen base.

Evers had a similarly productive afternoon against St. Louis on May 25, 1913, when he went 4-for-5, with 2 RBIs, 1 run scored, and a stolen base, during a 9-2 win over the Cardinals.

Evers had a perfect day at the plate on June 30, 1913, helping the Cubs record a lopsided 12-2 victory over Pittsburgh by going 3-for-3, with a pair of walks, a double, 1 RBI, and 4 runs scored.

Evers had another big game just five days later, hitting one of his 12 career homers, driving in 3 runs, and scoring twice during a 12-6 win over Cincinnati on July 5, 1913.

Displaying a fondness for Pittsburgh pitching, Evers had his second perfect day of the year against the Pirates' pitching staff on September 25,

1913, when he helped lead the Cubs to a 7-1 victory over the Bucs by going 4-for-4, with 2 doubles and 3 runs scored.

Yet, the game for which Evers will always be remembered most took place at the Polo Grounds during the latter stages of the 1908 campaign. With the Giants and Cubs engaged in an extremely tight pennant race, the New Yorkers seemingly recorded a significant victory over the two-time defending league champions when Al Bridwell singled in the bottom of the ninth inning to bring home Moose McCormick with the apparent winning run. However, with the always alert Evers noticing that Fred Merkle, the Giants runner at first base, failed to touch second base following Bridwell's hit, instead heading for the clubhouse in center field, the Chicago second sacker called for the ball and prevailed upon umpire Hank O'Day to call Merkle out at second on a force play. O'Day's correct call nullified New York's game-winning run, setting off a near riot at the Polo Grounds that prevented the two teams from continuing the contest. When the Giants and Cubs finished the season deadlocked, they had to replay the game, which the Cubs won, claiming in the process their third straight flag.

Notable Achievements:

- Batted over .300 twice, topping the .340-mark once (.341 in 1912).
- Finished in double digits in triples once (11 in 1912).
- Stole more than 20 bases seven times, topping 40 steals twice.
- Drew more than 100 bases on balls once (108 in 1910).
- Compiled on-base percentage in excess of .400 three times.
- Finished second in NL in: on-base percentage twice, stolen bases once, and bases on balls once.
- Led NL second basemen in assists twice and putouts twice.
- Ranks among Cubs career leaders in stolen bases (seventh) and sacrifice hits (fourth).
- Four-time NL champion (1906, 1907, 1908 & 1910).
- Two-time world champion (1907 & 1908).
- Elected to Baseball Hall of Fame by members of Old Timers Committee in 1946.

19

JOE TINKER

Known for his strong defense, quickness afoot, clutch hitting, and ability to execute the hit-and-run play, Joe Tinker helped lead the Cubs to four pennants and two world championships during his 11 seasons in Chicago. Serving as the anchor of the Cubs' defense from 1902 to 1912, Tinker led all NL shortstops in assists three times, putouts twice, double plays twice, and fielding percentage four times, en route to earning two top-10 finishes in the league MVP voting. A solid offensive performer as well, Tinker finished in double digits in triple four times and stole more than 30 bases five times, concluding his career with 114 three-baggers and 336 steals. However, Tinker will always be remembered most for being the centerpiece of the most famous infield of his day—one that served as the focal point of arguably the greatest team of the Dead Ball Era.

Born in Muscotah, Kansas on July 27, 1880, Joseph Bert Tinker moved with his family to Kansas City, Kansas at the age of two. After spending several years playing for school and local semi-pro teams, Tinker began his professional career in 1900 when Billy Hulen, a teammate of his with the Coffeyville, Kansas squad, recommended him to George Tebeau, the manager of the Denver Grizzlies of the Western League. Transitioning from second base to third over the course of the next two seasons while advancing to Portland of the Pacific Northwest League, Tinker eventually joined the Chicago Cubs when they purchased his contract prior to the start of the 1902 campaign.

After reluctantly agreeing to switch from his preferred position of third base upon his arrival in Chicago, Tinker became the Cubs starting shortstop in 1902. However, while he posted decent offensive numbers as a rookie, concluding the campaign with 54 RBIs, 55 runs scored, a .261 batting average, and 27 stolen bases, Tinker struggled terribly in the field, committing a league-leading 74 errors. Tinker's defensive woes continued the following year, when he made another 67 miscues, although he increased his offensive production considerably, finishing the season with 70 RBIs, 67 runs scored, a .291 batting average, and another 27 steals.

Tinker failed to distinguish himself at the plate in any of the next four seasons, driving in more than 45 runs and scoring more than 55 times just twice each, while posting batting averages of .221, .247, .233, and .221. Nevertheless, he proved to be an adept base runner, swiping more than 30 bases three times, including amassing a career-high 41 steals in 1904. More importantly, Tinker improved dramatically in the field, gradually developing into one of the senior circuit's top defensive shortstops. In fact, after Tinker led all players at his position in fielding percentage for the first of four times in 1906, F. C. Lane wrote in *Baseball Magazine*:

> *"It is impossible to speak of the great deeds which made the Cubs of 1906 the most formidable team in the history of the game without due mention of their peerless shortstop, Joe Tinker. The shadow of Hans Wagner has long obscured the deeds of the short-field men, and the great Dutchman will go down in history as the most incomparable shortstop who ever played the game. But it is hardly fair to make comparisons where Wagner is concerned. Admit that he is in a class by himself, a most obvious statement, and then state what is equally obvious, that the head of the shortstop department outside the Flying Dutchman clearly belongs to the Chicago star."*

Equally significant is the fact that Tinker and Cubs second baseman Johnny Evers developed a symbiotic on-field relationship that prompted Lane to call them the "Siamese twins of baseball" because "they play the bag as if they were one man, not two." Tinker and Evers managed to function as one in spite of the personal enmity they felt for each other, which Tinker attempted to downplay by stating, "They (the press) make a great deal of such differences among ball players, but this is pure exaggeration. You cannot expect to be on intimate terms with everybody on your club, and there is no reason why you should be, so long as you are playing the game." Tinker and Evers finally ended their thirty-three-year-old feud in 1938 when, unbeknownst to one another, they both received invitations to help broadcast the World Series between the Cubs and Yankees. After a moment of strained silence, the former keystone partners embraced each other in the broadcast booth.

After Tinker posted modest offensive numbers in each of the previous two pennant-winning campaigns, he helped lead the Cubs to their third consecutive league championship in 1908 by batting .266, scoring 67 runs, and finishing first on the team with 6 home runs, 68 RBIs, 146 hits, 14 triples, and a .391 slugging percentage, while also leading all NL shortstops in assists and fielding percentage. Making an extremely favorable impression on Christy Mathewson, against whom he posted a lifetime batting average of .291 (nearly 30 points higher than his career major-league mark of .262), the right-handed hitting Tinker drew praise from the Hall of Fame pitcher in the latter's 1912 book entitled *Pitching in a Pinch*. Mentioning Tinker in the opening paragraph, Mathewson described his tormentor as "the worst man I have to face in the National League." Mathewson went on to explain that Tinker had a short, chopping swing when he first entered the league, making him susceptible to slow curves on the outer half of the plate. However, he added that Tinker later made an adjustment in which he began using a long bat and took to standing far back in the batter's box, enabling him to reach out over the plate and drive outside pitches to the opposite field for hits. Mathewson wrote, "Ever since the day he adopted the new 'pole' he has been a thorn in my side and has broken up many a game. That old low curve is his favorite now, and he reaches for it with the same cordiality as is displayed by an actor reaching for his pay envelope. The only thing to do is to keep them close and try to outguess him, but Tinker is a hard man to beat at the game of wits."

Tinker continued to improve offensively over the course of the next four seasons, batting .288 and driving in 69 runs for the pennant-winning Cubs in 1910, before posting a mark of .278, knocking in another 69 runs, and scoring 61 times the following year. He then had his most productive offensive season in 1912, earning a fourth-place finish in the Chalmers Award (league MVP) balloting by batting .282 and posting career-high marks in RBIs (75) and runs scored (80).

Ironically, the 1912 campaign proved to be Tinker's last season as the Cubs' starting shortstop. With Johnny Evers being appointed manager of the team during the subsequent offseason, Tinker asked to be sent elsewhere, prompting the Cubs to include him in an eight-player trade they completed with the Cincinnati Reds on December 15, 1912. Tinker ended up spending just one season in Cincinnati, batting a career-high .317 while serving as the team's player-manager, before jumping to the Chicago Whales of the short-lived Federal League prior to the start of the

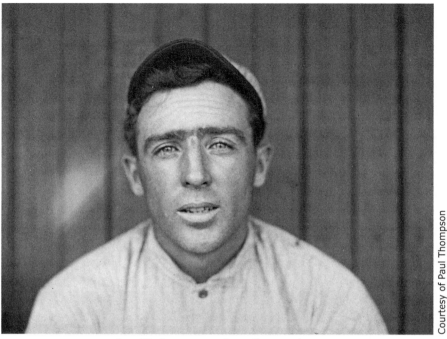

Courtesy of Paul Thompson

Joe Tinker served as the anchor
of the Cubs' infield for 11 seasons

1914 campaign. After leading the Whales to the Federal League pennant in 1915, Tinker returned to the Cubs the following year when the league folded. With Evers having been dealt to the Boston Braves two years earlier, Tinker took over as Cubs manager, also appearing in seven games in the field before being relieved of his duties at season's end. He ended his playing career with Columbus of the American Association in 1917, announcing his retirement after appearing in 22 games for a team in which he had purchased partial ownership.

Tinker subsequently settled in Orlando, Florida, where he built a small fortune developing real estate, before losing most of his savings during the Great Depression. Tinker later experienced serious health problems, nearly dying of complications stemming from diabetes mellitus and Bright's disease in 1936 and 1944, before becoming a scout for the Braves. After being inducted into the Baseball Hall of Fame the previous year, Tinker developed an infection related to diabetes that necessitated the amputation of a toe in 1947. He later had his left leg amputated as well, before passing away on his sixty-eighth birthday, on July 27, 1948.

Although many questions have since arisen regarding the legitimacy of Tinker's Hall of Fame qualifications, author Gil Bogen wrote in his 2003 book entitled, *Tinker, Evers and Chance: A Triple Biography*, "His ability to hit in the clutch, especially against Christy Mathewson, coupled with his non-paralleled play at shortstop, made Joe Tinker a great player."

Cub Numbers:

28 HR; 673 RBIs; 670 Runs Scored; 1,439 Hits; 220 Doubles; 93 Triples; 304 Stolen Bases; .259 AVG; .303 OBP; .347 SLG; .651 OPS

Career Numbers:

31 HR; 785 RBIs; 774 Runs Scored; 1,690 Hits; 263 Doubles; 114 Triples; 336 Stolen Bases; .262 AVG; .308 OBP; .353 SLG; .661 OPS

Cub Career Highlights:

Best Season: It could certainly be argued that Tinker played his best ball for the Cubs in his final two seasons in Chicago. In addition to leading all NL shortstops in every major fielding category except double plays in 1911, Tinker knocked in 69 runs, scored 61 times, stole 30 bases, and batted .278. He followed that up with perhaps his finest statistical season, concluding the 1912 campaign with career-high marks in RBIs (75), runs scored (80), and hits (155), while also batting .282 and stealing 25 bases, en route to earning a fourth-place finish in the NL MVP voting. Nevertheless, the feeling here is that Tinker had his finest all-around season in 1908, when he held the pennant-winning Cubs together during a rash of injuries that forced several of his teammates to miss a significant amount of playing time. Starting all 157 games at shortstop, Tinker batted .266, scored 67 runs, stole 30 bases, and led the team with 6 home runs, 68 RBIs, 146 hits, 14 triples, and a .391 slugging percentage, placing in the league's top five in homers and RBIs for the only time in his career. Tinker also led all NL shortstops with 570 assists and a .958 fielding percentage, establishing in the process career-high marks in both categories.

Memorable Moments/Greatest Performances: Tinker experienced one of his more inglorious moments on the playing field on September 14, 1905, when he engaged teammate Johnny Evers in a fistfight in the middle of the diamond after the latter had taken a cab to the stadium, leaving his teammates behind in the hotel lobby. While Evers claimed otherwise, Tinker identified the incident as the cause for the lengthy feud between the two men.

Although Evers received much of the credit for pointing out Fred Merkle's base-running blunder to umpire Hank O'Day in the disputed 1-1 tie played between the Cubs and Giants on September 23, 1908, Tinker gave the Cubs their only run of the game with an inside-the-park homer against Christy Mathewson. Tinker continued to be a thorn in the side of Mathewson in the makeup game played between the two teams some two weeks later, sparking a four-run Chicago rally in the top of the third inning by delivering a leadoff triple. The Cubs went on to win the contest by a score of 4-2, clinching in the process their third straight National League pennant.

Tinker subsequently came up big for the Cubs in the 1908 World Series, breaking a scoreless tie in the bottom of the eighth inning of Game Two by hitting a two-run homer off Detroit starter "Wild" Bill Donovan. The Cubs ended up pushing across 4 more runs, en route to recording a 6-1 victory over the Tigers that gave them a 2-0 Series lead. Tinker's blast— the first World Series home run hit by a member of the Cubs—was the first homer hit by anyone in the fall classic since 1903.

Tinker had one of the biggest offensive days of his career on August 7, 1911, when he went 4-for-4, with a double, triple, 4 RBIs, and 3 runs scored, during an 8-6 win over the Giants.

However, Tinker accomplished his greatest feat on July 28, 1910, when he stole home twice during a 3-0 victory over the St. Louis Cardinals.

Notable Achievements:

- Finished in double digits in triples four times.
- Stole more than 20 bases 11 times, topping 30 steals four times and 40 thefts once (41 in 1904).
- Led NL with 157 games played in 1908.
- Finished third in NL with 13 triples in 1904.
- Finished second in NL in sacrifice hits three times.
- Led NL shortstops in: assists three times, putouts twice, fielding percentage four times, and double plays twice.

- Ranks among Cubs career leaders in: triples (sixth), stolen bases (fifth), and sacrifice hits (second).
- Finished fourth in 1912 NL MVP voting.
- Four-time NL champion (1906, 1907, 1908 & 1910).
- Two-time world champion (1907 & 1908).
- Elected to Baseball Hall of Fame by members of Old Timers Committee in 1946.

20

ED REULBACH

One of the most overlooked and underappreciated pitchers of his time, Ed Reulbach teamed up with Mordecai Brown to give the Cubs arguably the National League's most formidable pitching duo of the Dead Ball Era. Described as "one of the greatest pitchers that the National League ever produced, and one of the finest, clean-cut gentlemen who ever wore a big league uniform" in an early edition of *Baseball Magazine*, Reulbach helped lead the Cubs to four pennants and two world championships between 1906 and 1910 by compiling an overall record of 91-33 during that five-year period. The 6'1", 190-pound right-hander proved to be one of the most difficult pitchers for opposing hitters to solve, using what many people considered to be the finest curve ball in the game to toss two one-hitters, six two-hitters, and 13 three-hitters over the course of his career. In addition to posting the best hits-to-innings pitched ratio of any NL hurler twice and topping the senior circuit in winning percentage three times, Reulbach annually placed among the league leaders in wins and ERA, surpassing 20 wins once and 17 victories four other times, while compiling an ERA under 2.00 on four separate occasions. Posting an overall record of 136-65 and an ERA of 2.24 in his nine seasons in Chicago, Reulbach clearly ranks as one of the finest pitchers in Cubs history.

Born in Detroit, Michigan on December 1, 1882, Edward Marvin Reulbach spent much of his youth in St. Louis, Missouri, where he attended Manual Training High School. After beginning his minor league career one year earlier with Sedalia of the Missouri Valley League, Reulbach enrolled at the University of Notre Dame in the fall of 1901. Declared ineligible for the 1902 college baseball season due to his status as a freshman, Reulbach continued to develop his pitching skills at Sedalia, before advancing to Montpelier of Vermont's outlaw Northern League in

1904. Electing to forego his senior year at Notre Dame and enroll in medical school at the University of Vermont in order to be closer to his future bride, who lived in Montpelier, Reulbach went on to star for the UVM baseball team, batting cleanup and playing left field on those days he didn't pitch. With local newspapers calling him the "greatest of all college pitchers," Reulbach received an offer from the Chicago Cubs on May 12, 1905 that "would take the breath away from an average person," according to the *Burlington Free Press*.

After making his major-league debut with the Cubs a few days later, Reulbach went on to have an outstanding rookie season, concluding the 1905 campaign with a record of 18-14, 152 strikeouts, 5 shutouts, 28 complete games, and 291 ⅔ innings pitched, while placing second in the league with a 1.42 ERA and a 0.963 WHIP. He followed that up with an equally impressive sophomore season in which he helped the Cubs capture the first of their three straight pennants by compiling a record of 19-4 that gave him a league-leading .826 winning percentage. Reulbach also threw 20 complete games and finished among the league leaders with 6 shutouts, a 1.65 ERA, and a 1.014 WHIP. Particularly effective during the season's second half, Reulbach began a personal 17-game winning streak that lasted until June 29, 1907, when he lost a 2-1 decision to Pittsburgh's Deacon Phillippe.

Reulbach continued to excel in each of the next two pennant-winning campaigns, compiling a record of 17-4 and an ERA of 1.69 in 1907, before going 24-7, with a 2.03 ERA, 25 complete games, and 7 shutouts the following year. Although the Cubs failed to capture the league championship again in 1909, Reulbach had another outstanding year, posting 19 victories, a 1.78 ERA, 23 complete games, and 6 shutouts.

Employing a high leg kick similar to the one used decades later by San Francisco Giants great Juan Marichal, Reulbach did an exceptional job of hiding the ball during his wind-up. He also threw arguably the best curveball in either league, rivaling teammate Mordecai Brown in the ability to exasperate opposing batters with that particular offering. If Reulbach exhibited any flaws at all in his game over the course of his first several seasons in Chicago, it would be that he occasionally displayed a lack of control on the mound. However, following the conclusion of his playing career, Reulbach revealed that he had a weak left eye that not only interfered with his ability to field balls hit to his left, but that also affected his control at times. Speaking with noted sportswriter Hugh Fullerton in 1920,

Reulbach explained, "There were times when the weak eye was worse than usual, especially on hot, gray days, or when the dust was blowing from the field. Lots of times the sweat and heat would affect the good eye and I'd have to figure out where the plate was." Reulbach went on to say that he never revealed his problem to his teammates, although outfielder Jimmy Sheckard once caught him wearing glasses while reading. But Reulbach added that "Sheck was a good old scout and kept quiet about it."

Reulbach's exceptional five-year run ended in 1910, when, burdened by concerns over his ailing son, who experienced an attack of diphtheria, he finished just 12-8 with a 3.12 ERA. After rebounding somewhat the following year to win 16 games and compile a 2.96 ERA, Reulbach suffered through a subpar 1912 campaign during which he went 10-6 with an inordinately high 3.78 ERA. Off to a slow start again in 1913, Reulbach found himself headed to Brooklyn in July when the Cubs practically gave him away for cash and a mediocre pitcher named Eddie Stack.

After compiling an overall record of 18-24 with the Dodgers over the course of the next year-and-a-half, Reulbach decided to jump to the rival Federal League prior to the start of the 1915 campaign. Spending just one year in that short-lived circuit, the thirty-two-year-old right-hander had his last big season, going 21-10 with a 2.23 ERA for the Newark Peppers, before joining the Boston Braves when the league folded at season's end. Reulbach subsequently spent his final two big league seasons pitching mostly in relief for the Braves, before ending his playing career with Providence in the International League in 1917.

Following his playing days, Reulbach entered into a dark period in his life that saw him spend a fortune trying to save the life of his constantly ill son, who ended up dying in 1931. An article in the *Chicago Tribune* the following year referred to the fifty-year-old Reulbach as a "sad and lonely man." Nevertheless, Reulbach, one of the Founding Directors of the Baseball Fraternity (which later morphed into the Player's Union), never stopped thinking about baseball. Described by Cubs teammate Johnny Evers as someone who was "always five years ahead of his time in baseball thought," Reulbach copyrighted in 1945 the "Leadership Development Plan," which suggested that the position of captain be rotated among all nine players, one inning at a time, as a means of developing leadership qualities. Reulbach lived another sixteen years, passing away at the age of seventy-eight, on July 17, 1961, the same day that Ty Cobb died.

Cub Numbers:

Record: 136-65, .677 Win Pct., 2.24 ERA, 149 CG, 31 Shutouts, 9 Saves, 1,864⅔ IP, 799 Strikeouts, 1.131 WHIP

Career Numbers:

Record: 182-106, .632 Win Pct., 2.28 ERA, 201 CG, 40 Shutouts, 13 Saves, 2,632⅓ IP, 1,137 Strikeouts, 1.143 WHIP

Cub Career Highlights:

Best Season: It could certainly be argued that Reulbach had his finest season in 1908, when, in addition to posting career-high marks in wins (24), shutouts (7), and innings pitched (297⅔), he compiled an ERA of 2.03, a WHIP of 1.119, and tossed 25 complete games. However, Reulbach performed slightly better two years earlier, concluding the 1906 campaign with a record of 19-4 that gave him a league-leading and career-best winning percentage of .826. He also finished among the NL leaders with 6 shutouts, an ERA of 1.65, and a WHIP of 1.014. Meanwhile, Reulbach—one of the few pitchers in MLB history to go his entire career without allowing more hits than innings pitched in any single season—yielded only 5.33 hits per nine innings pitched over the course of the campaign, which remains the third-lowest ratio of all time.

Memorable Moments/Greatest Performances: After compiling a 17-game winning streak that lasted from 1906 until well into the 1907 campaign, Reulbach put together another lengthy streak in 1909, winning 14 straight times before finally tasting defeat. The second skein, which began on May 30 and ended on August 14, made Reulbach the only twentieth-century NL pitcher to win as many as 14 consecutive games twice. Rated by *Baseball Magazine* in a November 1913 article as the most impressive streak in history, to that point, Reulbach's 14-game streak included five shutouts and five one-run efforts, with the right-hander surrendering a total of only 14 runs while going undefeated.

Reulbach also gained a significant amount of notoriety by setting a National League record (since broken) by throwing 44 consecutive scoreless innings during the latter stages of the 1908 season.

Reulbach turned in one of the most memorable performances of his career on August 24, 1905, when he allowed just one run over 20 innings, in defeating the Philadelphia Phillies by a score of 2-1.

Courtesy of the Bain Collection at the Library of Congress

Ed Reulbach combined with Mordecai Brown to give
the Cubs one of the National League's most formidable
pitching duos of the Dead Ball Era

Excelling for the Cubs in both the 1906 and 1907 World Series, Reulbach pitched brilliantly in Game Two of the 1906 fall classic, allowing just one hit—a seventh-inning single to Chicago third baseman Jiggs Donahue—in defeating the White Sox by a score of 7-1. Equally impressive in the following year's fall classic, Reulbach worked three scoreless relief innings in Game One, before returning to the mound two days later to record a complete-game, 5-1 victory over the Detroit Tigers. Reulbach finished the series with a record of 1-0 and an ERA of 0.75, having surrendered just 6 hits and 1 run in 12 total innings of work.

Yet, Reulbach accomplished the greatest feat of his career on September 26, 1908, when he became the only pitcher in MLB history to toss two complete-game shutouts on the same day, blanking Brooklyn by scores of 5-0 and 3-0. After allowing just 5 hits in Game One of the doubleheader, Reulbach turned in an even more dominant performance in Game Two, yielding only 3 hits and a walk in a contest he needed only 1 hour and 12 minutes to complete.

Notable Achievements:

- Won 24 games in 1908, surpassing 17 victories four other times.
- Posted winning percentage in excess of .700 three times, topping the .800-mark twice.
- Compiled ERA below 2.00 four times.
- Posted WHIP under 1.000 once (0.963 in 1905).
- Threw more than 250 innings three times.
- Tossed more than 20 complete games four times.
- Led NL pitchers in winning percentage three times and fewest hits allowed per nine innings pitched twice.
- Finished second in NL in ERA once and WHIP once.
- Holds Cubs single-season record for fewest hits allowed per nine innings pitched (5.326 in 1906).
- Ranks among Cubs career leaders in: ERA (seventh), winning percentage (seventh), shutouts (third), and fewest hits allowed per nine innings pitched (fifth).
- Four-time NL champion (1906, 1907, 1908 & 1910).
- Two-time world champion (1907 & 1908).

21

CHARLIE ROOT

Although he is remembered most for the role he played in one of baseball's most enduring legends—Babe Ruth's "called shot" in Game Three of the 1932 World Series—Charlie Root proved to be one of the most consistent and reliable pitchers of his era. Averaging nearly 18 wins and 252 innings pitched from 1926 to 1933, Root surpassed 20 victories once and 17 wins three other times over the course of those eight seasons, en route to compiling a total of 201 victories as a member of the Cubs that remains a franchise record. The hard-throwing right-hander, who spent 16 of his 17 big-league seasons in the Windy City, also threw more than 20 complete games three times and tossed more than 300 innings once, establishing himself in the process as the workhorse of Chicago's pitching staff. And, after Root assumed a less prominent role on the team during the latter stages of his career, he continued to contribute to the success of the ball club as a spot-starter/long reliever by posting double-digit wins two more times. In all, Root won at least 15 games on eight separate occasions, contributing mightily to four pennant-winning Cubs teams.

Born in Middletown, Ohio on March 17, 1899, Charles Henry Root left school at the age of thirteen after being reprimanded by one of his teachers for his disruptive behavior. Looking back at the incident years later, Root recalled, "I quit school. And I never spent another day in the classroom." After spending the next five years working at various jobs while spending most of his free time playing baseball on vacant lots, Root took a job as a patternmaker at Armco, for whose factory team he pitched and played shortstop. Before long, Root advanced to the semi-pro level, joining the Middletown Eagles in 1919, before accepting a position with Hamilton Engine Works, which offered him a job paying $50 a week, plus another $35 per game to pitch for its team in the Southern Ohio industrial league. Discovered by St. Louis Browns scout Carl Weilman while pitching in Hamilton, Root signed with the Browns, in whose organization he began his professional career in 1921.

Root spent the next two seasons pitching for the Terre Haute Tots in the Class B Illinois-Indiana-Iowa League, posting 16 victories in 1922, before earning a spot on the St. Louis roster the following spring. However, after Root struggled on the mound in 1923, going 0-4 with a 5.70 ERA, the Browns returned him to the minor leagues, with the right-hander later commenting, "I was glad to go. Those fellows just murdered my fast one, and they were the best I had in the bag."

After being dealt to the Los Angeles Angels of the Pacific Coast League during the subsequent offseason, Root became a far more effective pitcher under the tutelage of veteran hurler Doc Crandall, who taught him a hard curveball and helped him develop a changeup. Posting a total of 46 victories over the course of the next two seasons, Root earned a return trip to the Major Leagues as a member of the Cubs, who purchased his contract following the conclusion of the 1924 campaign.

Arriving in Chicago at the somewhat advanced age of twenty-seven, Root immediately established himself as the ace of Manager Joe McCarthy's pitching staff, finishing the 1926 season with a team-leading 2.82 ERA, 127 strikeouts, 21 complete games, 271⅓ innings pitched, and record of 18-17 that would have been considerably better had he received more run support (in 13 of his losses, the Cubs scored 2 runs or less). Although Root's ERA rose to 3.76 the following year, he posted the best overall numbers of his career, topping the senior circuit with 26 wins (against 15 losses), 309 innings pitched, and 48 mound appearances, while also ranking among the league leaders with 21 complete games, 4 shutouts, and 145 strikeouts. Root's exceptional performance earned him widespread acclaim, with the *New York Times* hailing him as "the best pitcher in the league" and "the sensation of the Major Leagues."

Perhaps allowing his success to go to his head, the 5'10 ½", 190-pound Root reported to camp some fifteen pounds overweight the following spring, after which he suffered through a disappointing 1928 season. Battling his waistline all year, Root finished just 14-18, with a 3.57 ERA, 13 complete games, and 237 innings pitched. However, he rebounded in 1929, when, relying mostly on his fastball and curve, he helped lead the Cubs to the National League pennant by going 19-6, with a 3.47 ERA, 4 shutouts, 19 complete games, and 272 innings pitched. Particularly effective down the stretch, Root tossed five complete games during the month of September, winning four.

Known for his multiple deliveries to home plate, Root had the ability to deliver his outstanding fastball and curve from various angles, switching from an overhand to either a three-quarters or side-arm motion, depending on the batter and pitch count. Root also liked to intimidate opposing batters with his high hard one, earning the nickname "Chinski" by frequently coming up and in to hitters. A hard-nosed player, "Root," wrote Joseph E. Bennett in *Baseball Legends: The Charlie Root Story*, "was one of the fiercest competitors the game ever knew... his cigar-chomping, no-nonsense visage was one of the most intimidating tools in his baseball arsenal."

Root continued to perform well for the Cubs over the course of the next three seasons, compiling an overall record of 48-38 from 1930 to 1932, while also averaging 15 complete games and 227 innings pitched during that time. However, after helping Chicago capture the National League pennant in 1932 by winning 15 games, Root faltered against the Yankees in Game Three of the World Series, surrendering 6 runs on 6 hits, in just 4⅓ innings of work, including a pair of homers to Babe Ruth, the second of which has gone down in history as the legendary slugger's "called shot." But, while some accounts support the contention that Ruth actually "called his shot," the general consensus seems to be that "The Babe" never really predicted his home run. Root, for one, vehemently denied that Ruth did so, suggesting that, if he had tried to show him up by gesturing to the outfield, "I'd have put one in his ear and knocked him on his ass."

Root remained a regular member of Chicago's starting rotation just one more year, compiling a record of 15-10, ranking among the league leaders with a 2.60 ERA, and tossing 20 complete games and 242⅓ innings in 1933, before he discovered that he no longer had the ability to start every fourth or fifth day. Having lost much of the velocity on his fastball, the thirty-five-year-old Root developed an effective hard knuckleball to complement his breaking pitches and transformed himself into a wily, cerebral hurler to whom the local newspapers referred as the "grand-pappy" of the Cubs staff. Moving to the bullpen in 1934, Root subsequently became invaluable to the Cubs as a spot-starter/long reliever, averaging 8 wins, 35 appearances, and 140 innings pitched over the course of the next eight seasons, including posting a mark of 15-8 and throwing 11 complete games and 201⅓ innings for Chicago's 1935 NL championship ball club. Root remained with the Cubs until 1941, when, after he went 8-7 with an inordinately high 5.40 ERA, the team released him at season's end. In addition to winning more games than any other pitcher in Cubs history, Root holds franchise records for most innings pitched (3,137⅓) and most pitching appearances (605).

After leaving the Cubs, Root spent another eight years pitching in the minor leagues, serving as a player-manager in four of those. He finally retired at forty-nine years of age following the conclusion of the 1948 campaign, ending his minor-league career with another 111 victories. Following his playing days, Root became a successful pitching coach, serving on the staffs of the Cubs and Milwaukee Braves, with whom he won a world championship in 1957. Leaving the game for good in 1960, Root retired with his wife to their 1,000-acre Diamond-R Ranch in Paicines, California, where he became a successful cattle rancher. He lived another 10 years, passing away at seventy-one years of age, on November 5, 1970, following an extended illness. Taking Babe Ruth's alleged "called shot" with him to his grave, Root, according to his daughter Della, told her two days before his death, "I gave my life to baseball, and I'll only be remembered for something that never happened."

Cub Numbers:

Record: 201-156, .563 Win Pct., 3.55 ERA, 177 CG, 21 Shutouts, 42 Saves, 3,137⅓ IP, 1,432 Strikeouts, 1.292 WHIP

Career Numbers:

Record: 201-160, .557 Win Pct., 3.59 ERA, 177 CG, 21 Shutouts, 42 Saves, 3,197⅓ IP, 1,459 Strikeouts, 1.295 WHIP

Cub Career Highlights:

Best Season: Even though Root finished just one game above .500 with a record of 18-17 in 1926, it could be argued that he pitched his best ball for the Cubs that year. In addition to finishing second in the NL with a 2.82 ERA and 127 strikeouts, he ranked among the league leaders with 21 complete games, 271⅓ innings pitched, and a WHIP of 1.213. Root also performed extremely well in 1929 and 1933, helping the Cubs capture the NL pennant in the first of those campaigns by finishing second

Courtesy of RMYauctions.com

Charlie Root won more games than any other pitcher
in Cubs history

in the league with 19 wins, 4 shutouts, 19 complete games, and 272 innings pitched, while also ranking among the leaders with a 3.47 ERA and 124 strikeouts. Meanwhile, Root's 2.60 ERA and 1.209 WHIP in 1933 both represented career-best marks. Nevertheless, the 1927 campaign is generally considered to be Root's finest season. Although he failed to finish among the league leaders in either ERA (3.76) or WHIP (1.337), Root topped the senior circuit in wins (26), innings pitched (309), and mound appearances (48), placed second in shutouts (4), strikeouts (145), and starts (36), and finished sixth in complete games (21), earning in the process a fourth-place finish in the NL MVP voting.

Memorable Moments/Greatest Performances: Root turned in one of the most dominant performances of his career on July 8, 1927, winning a 1-0 pitcher's duel with Pittsburgh's Lee Meadows by tossing a one-hitter. The Pirates got their only hit off Root with two men out in the bottom of the eighth inning, when catcher Johnny Gooch singled to left field. Root also walked 3 batters and recorded 2 strikeouts during the contest.

Root tossed consecutive shutouts in August, 1927, allowing just 5 hits and recording 9 strikeouts during a 3-0 whitewashing of Brooklyn on August 16, after blanking Cincinnati, 2-0, just 5 days earlier. Root also singled home 2 of Chicago's 3 runs in the second contest.

Root continued to excel on the mound later in the month, yielding just a double and a pair of singles during an 8-0 shutout of Philadelphia on August 25, 1927.

Root again throttled Brooklyn's lineup on June 6, 1930, surrendering just a pair of harmless fourth-inning singles, in earning a 13-0 complete-game victory over the Dodgers.

Root hurled another gem some two months later, when he scattered 3 singles during a 6-0 win over the Boston Braves on August 10, 1930.

Root tossed the second two-hitter of his career on June 14, 1933, allowing just a first-inning single to third baseman Sparky Adams and a fifth-inning single to right-fielder Wally Roettger during a 7-0 blanking of the Cincinnati Reds.

Root experienced one of his finest moments on April 21, 1934, when he out-dueled St. Louis right-hander Tex Carleton by a score of 2-1, driving in Chicago's first run of the game with a solo homer in the top of the third inning.

Yet, the most memorable moment of Root's career undoubtedly occurred on October 1, 1932, in the third game of that year's World Series. The Yankees, who already held a two-games-to-none lead over the Cubs in the fall classic, entered the contest harboring ill feelings towards their National League counterparts after learning in the local newspapers that they had voted former New York teammate Mark Koenig only half a share of their World Series earnings, even though the shortstop compiled a batting average of .353 over the season's final 33 games after he arrived in Chicago in early August. With the Yankees (and Ruth in particular) subsequently deriding the Cubs as "cheap" and "penny-pinching," the scene at Wrigley Field proved to be an extremely contentious one, with Chicago players heckling Ruth each time he stepped into the batter's box. Ruth, whose 3-run homer off Root in the first inning had given the Yankees an early 3-0 lead, stepped up to the plate again with the score tied at 4-4 in the top of the fifth. Cubs' infielder Woody English later described the events that subsequently transpired:

"I was playing third base. I was right close to it. Ruth's got two strikes on him. The guys are yelling at him from our dugout. He's looking right in our dugout, and he holds up two fingers. He said, 'That's only two strikes.' But the press box was way back on top of Wrigley Field, and, to the people in the press, it looked like he pointed to center field. But he was looking right into our dugout and holding two fingers up. That is the true story. I've been asked that question 500 times."

Although English likely gave an accurate account of the incident, the fact remains that Ruth drove Root's next offering deep into the center-field bleachers, providing fodder for the media to further glorify the accomplishments of the game's most legendary player. Lou Gehrig followed with a home run of his own, giving the Yankees a 2-run lead in a game they eventually won by a score of 7-5, and leaving the Cubs thoroughly demoralized. Reflecting back on the Series, English admitted, "The Yankees had just too much power for us. It was discouraging."

Notable Achievements:

- Won more than 20 games once (26 in 1927).
- Surpassed 15 victories seven other times, winning 19 games once (1929).
- Posted winning percentage in excess of .700 twice.
- Compiled ERA below 3.00 three times.
- Threw more than 300 innings once, tossing more than 250 innings three other times.
- Threw more than 20 complete games three times.
- Led NL pitchers in: wins once, winning percentage once, shutouts once, innings pitched once, and pitching appearances once.
- Finished second in NL in: wins once, winning percentage once, ERA twice, strikeouts twice, shutouts twice, complete games once, and innings pitched once.
- Holds Cubs career records for most: wins (201), innings pitched (3,137⅓), and pitching appearances (605).
- Ranks among Cubs career leaders in: strikeouts (fourth), shutouts (tied-10th), complete games (tied-seventh), and games started (tied-third).

- Finished fourth in 1927 NL MVP voting.
- 1927 *Sporting News* All-Star selection.
- Four-time NL champion (1929, 1932, 1935 & 1938).

22

RIGGS STEPHENSON

One of the best pure hitters to ever don a Cubs uniform, Riggs Stephenson spent nine years in Chicago, during which time he compiled a lifetime batting average of .336 that ranks as the highest in franchise history. Affectionately known to his teammates as "Old Hoss" because of his reliability with the bat and hard-working nature, Stephenson excelled at the plate even though he spent his entire time in the Windy City being plagued by injuries and a bum shoulder he damaged while playing football in college. Teaming up with Hack Wilson and Kiki Cuyler to form one of the best hitting outfields in the history of the senior circuit, Stephenson batted over .330 four times as a member of the team, topping the .360-mark on two separate occasions. He also knocked in more than 100 runs once, scored more than 100 runs once, and amassed more than 40 doubles twice, helping to lead the Cubs to two National League pennants in the process.

Born in Akron, Alabama on January 5, 1898, Jackson Riggs Stephenson received his introduction to baseball from his older brother Samuel Gardner, who spent two years pitching in the minor leagues. After moving with his family some 150 miles northeast to the town of Guntersville, Stephenson got his start in organized ball playing the infield for his local town team, while also attending Marshall County High School. Enrolling at the University of Alabama following his graduation, Stephenson soon established himself as a two-sport star with the Crimson Tide, excelling on both the gridiron as a quarterback and on the diamond as a second baseman. However, his football playing days came to an end in his senior year, when he suffered an injury to his shoulder that left him with a below-average throwing arm.

No longer able to make long throws, Stephenson decided to pursue a career in baseball, procuring a tryout with the Cleveland Indians with the assistance of his college football coach, Ken Scott, who had connections with the ball club. Making a favorable impression on all those in attendance at 1921 spring training, Stephenson drew praise from sportswriter Wilbur Wood, who said of the twenty-three-year-old rookie, "The very first day he stepped on the diamond, he looked like a polished big league workman." After making the Cleveland roster, Stephenson spent most of his rookie season serving as a back-up second baseman, doing an outstanding job at the plate but struggling in the field. Although the right-handed hitting Stephenson batted .330, drove in 34 runs, and scored 45 times, in only 206 official at-bats, he also committed 17 errors in just 52 starts at second. Finding it particularly difficult to turn two on the double play due to his suspect arm, Stephenson continued to try the patience of Indians player-manager Tris Speaker over the course of the next three seasons, preventing him from ever earning a starting job. Nevertheless, he remained a threat at the plate, compiling batting averages of .339, .319, and .371 from 1922 to 1924.

After spending most of 1925 in the minor leagues learning to play the outfield, Stephenson received his big break early the following year, when Cleveland traded him to the Chicago Cubs. Inserted in left field upon his arrival in the Windy City, Stephenson appeared in 82 games over the final four months of the campaign, batting .338, hitting 3 homers, driving in 44 runs, and scoring 40 times, in 281 official at-bats. Starting almost every game in left for the Cubs in 1927, Stephenson emerged as one of the senior circuit's best hitters, leading the league with 46 doubles and ranking among the leaders with 199 hits, 101 runs scored, a .344 batting average, and a .415 on-base percentage. He followed that up with another excellent year in 1928, driving in 90 runs, scoring 75 times, batting .324, and compiling a .407 on-base percentage. Stephenson also acquitted himself quite well in the outfield, leading all NL left-fielders in putouts in 1928, after leading all players at his position in assists and double plays the previous season.

A classic line-drive hitter who sprayed the ball to all fields, the 5'10", 185-pound Stephenson did not possess a great deal of power at the plate, finishing in double digits in home runs just once his entire career. However, he proved to be a model of consistency, batting at least .319 in each of his first eight seasons with the Cubs. In discussing Stephenson's hitting ability in the book, *Wrigleyville: A Magical History Tour of the Chicago Cubs*, former teammate Woody English said, "I'll tell you something about

Riggs Stephenson. If the winning run was in scoring position where they couldn't walk him in the ninth inning, we'd put our gloves in our pockets and go up the runway to the clubhouse. That's what we thought of Riggs Stephenson. He would drive that winning run in time after time."

Yet, while English referred to Stephenson as "one great ballplayer" in that same work, he had less complimentary things to say about his former teammate's defense, stating, "Well, one thing about him, he couldn't run very good, and he couldn't throw. When I'd play shortstop, I had to go farther out to Stephie. He was muscle-bound. He had been an All-American football player."

Stephenson, himself, once discussed his defensive shortcomings, admitting, "My arm wasn't strong enough to play right field. You gotta have the best arm on the team in right field. I was lucky to get to Chicago. They needed a left fielder. Maybe my throwing arm wasn't even average. I was accurate, but I couldn't throw long distances."

Nevertheless, Stephenson eventually turned himself into a serviceable outfielder whose hitting skills more than compensated for any defensive deficiencies he displayed in left. Popular with the local scribes, Stephenson received praise from Henry L. Farrell, who wrote, "Stephenson is one of the immensely valuable players who doesn't command the spotlight. The Chicago fans know how valuable he is, but the customers in other cities know more about Gabby Hartnett, Hack Wilson, and others." Content to assume a supporting role on the ball club, "Stephenson," wrote Cubs reporter Edward Burns, "is the Cubs' most vicious batsman and mildest citizen." A true gentleman, who, unlike most of the other players of his time, attended college, Stephenson always conducted himself with an air of Southern aristocracy. Neither a drinker nor a smoker, he chose not to frequent the many speakeasies on Chicago's North Side that most of his teammates visited regularly.

Stephenson, though, built his reputation primarily on his excellent hitting, which peaked in 1929, when he helped lead the Cubs to their first pennant in more than a decade by hitting 17 home runs, knocking in 110 runs, scoring 91 times, batting .362, and compiling an OPS of 1.007. By driving in 110 runs, Stephenson joined Hack Wilson and Kiki Cuyler as a member of the only outfield trio in National League history to top the 100-RBI mark in the same season.

Plagued by injuries in each of the next two seasons, Stephenson failed to approach the same level of offensive production. Nevertheless, he continued to post outstanding numbers, concluding the 1930 campaign with a .367 batting average and 68 RBIs, in only 109 games, before batting .319 and driving in 52 runs the following year, despite missing nearly half the season with a broken ankle. Healthy again in 1932, the thirty-four-year-old Stephenson had his last big year for the Cubs, helping them capture the NL flag and earning a fifth-place finish in the league MVP voting by batting .324, driving in 85 runs, scoring 86 times, and collecting 189 hits and a career-high 49 doubles. Relegated to part-time duty the following season, Stephenson compiled a batting average of .329 in just under 100 games, before assuming a backup role in 1934. Released by the Cubs on October 30, 1934, Stephenson failed to garner interest from any other team, forcing him to end his major league career with a batting average of .336, which represents the highest mark ever posted by an eligible player who has failed to gain admittance to Cooperstown.

After leaving the Cubs, Stephenson spent another five years playing and managing in the minor leagues, before finally retiring following the conclusion of the 1939 campaign. He subsequently returned to Alabama, where he ran a car dealership in Tuscaloosa for many years. Stephenson lived until November 15, 1985, when he died of natural causes at the age of eighty-seven.

Cub Numbers:

49 HR; 589 RBIs; 533 Runs Scored; 1,167 Hits; 237 Doubles; 40 Triples; 39 Stolen Bases; .336 AVG; .408 OBP; .469 SLG; .877 OPS

Career Numbers:

63 HR; 773 RBIs; 714 Runs Scored; 1,515 Hits; 321 Doubles; 54 Triples; 53 Stolen Bases; .336 AVG; .407 OBP; .473 SLG; .880 OPS

Cub Career Highlights:

Best Season: Stephenson had a big year in 1927, driving in 82 runs, batting .344, collecting 46 doubles, and establishing career-high marks in hits (199), triples (9), and runs scored (101). Nevertheless, he played his best ball for the Cubs in 1929, helping them capture the NL pennant by batting .362, scoring 91 runs, accumulating 179 hits and 36 doubles, and

Courtesy of MEARS Online Auctions

Riggs Stephenson's .336 career batting average as a member of
the Cubs ranks as the best in franchise history

posting career-high marks in home runs (17), RBIs (110), on-base percentage (.445), and slugging percentage (.562).

Memorable Moments/Greatest Performances: Stephenson helped pace the Cubs to a lopsided 9-0 victory over Philadelphia on August 24, 1926 by going 4-for-5, with a pair of doubles, 4 RBIs, and 1 run scored.

Although Stephenson garnered just two official plate appearances during a 10-2 win over the Phillies on September 24, 1927, walking once and delivering two sacrifice flies during the contest, he made the most of those two at-bats, finishing the game with a homer, single, and 5 RBIs.

Stephenson celebrated Independence Day in 1928 by going 5-for-6, with a homer, double, 3 RBIs, and 3 runs scored, during a 16-9 victory over St. Louis at Sportsman's Park on July 4.

Stephenson had an extremely productive day against Brooklyn on May 7, 1929, leading the Cubs to a 9-4 win over the Dodgers by driving in 4 runs with a homer and single, while also scoring 4 times.

Although not known for his home run hitting prowess, Stephenson flexed his muscles on July 1, 1929, homering twice and knocking in a career-high 7 runs during an 11-11 tie with the Cardinals that the umpires called after six innings due to rain.

Stephenson contributed to an 18-10 pasting of the Boston Braves on June 4, 1930 by going 5-for-6, with a pair of doubles, 4 RBIs, and 4 runs scored.

Stephenson delivered what proved to be the winning run of a 10-8, 11-inning win over Philadelphia on August 6, 1932 with an RBI single in the top of the 11th. He finished the afternoon with 4 hits, 4 RBIs, and 3 runs scored.

Even though the Yankees swept the Cubs in the 1932 World Series in four straight games, Stephenson performed admirably for the losing team, batting .444, with 8 hits in 18 at-bats, 4 RBIs, and 2 runs scored.

Notable Achievements:

- Batted over .300 eight times, topping the .360-mark twice.
- Knocked in more than 100 runs once (110 in 1929).
- Scored more than 100 runs once (101 in 1927).
- Surpassed 30 doubles four times, topping 40 two-baggers twice.

- Compiled on-base percentage in excess of .400 six times.
- Posted slugging percentage in excess of .500 once (.562 in 1929).
- Led NL with 46 doubles in 1927.
- Led NL left-fielders in: putouts once, assists once, double plays once, and fielding percentage once.
- Holds Cubs record (tied with Bill Madlock) for highest career batting average (.336).
- Ranks among Cubs career leaders in on-base percentage (third) and OPS (sixth)
- Finished fifth in 1932 NL MVP voting.
- Two-time NL champion (1929 & 1932).

23

HIPPO VAUGHN

The greatest left-handed pitcher in the rich history of the Cubs, Hippo Vaughn spent nine seasons in Chicago, starring on the mound in seven of those. After being cast aside by two American League teams, Vaughn compiled an overall record of 143-93 for the Cubs from 1914 to 1920, establishing himself in the process as the senior circuit's finest southpaw. Over the course of those seven seasons, Vaughn surpassed 20 victories five times, compiled an ERA under 2.00 twice, threw more than 20 complete games six times, and tossed more than 300 innings twice. Furthermore, the burly left-hander led the Cubs to the National League pennant in 1918 by capturing the pitcher's version of the Triple Crown, leading all NL hurlers with 22 wins, a 1.74 ERA, and 148 strikeouts. Vaughn continued his outstanding pitching in each of the next two seasons, before ending his big-league career by mysteriously leaving the Cubs midway through the 1921 campaign.

Born in Weatherford, Texas on April 9, 1888, James Leslie Vaughn attended local Weatherford High School, before beginning his professional career with Temple in the Texas League in 1906. Advancing to Hot Springs in the Arkansas State League by 1908, Vaughn compiled a record of 9-1 during the first half of the campaign, earning him a brief trial with the New York Highlanders. However, after appearing in just two games with the team that eventually came to be known as the Yankees, the twenty-year-old southpaw ended up finishing the season with Scranton of the New York State League.

After tossing a pair of no-hitters while splitting the following year between two different minor league teams, Vaughn returned to New York in 1910, making such a strong impression on manager George Stallings during spring training that the Highlanders skipper gave him the

Hippo Vaughn won more than 20 games
five times as a member of the Cubs

opening day assignment. Vaughn went on to have a strong rookie season for the second-place Highlanders, finishing the year with a record of 13-11, an ERA of 1.83, and 18 complete games. But, after he performed erratically over the course of the next year-and-a-half, New York placed him on waivers midway through the 1912 campaign. Subsequently claimed by the Washington Senators, Vaughn spent two months in the nation's capital, before being dealt to Kansas City of the American Association on August 23, 1912. Vaughn then spent nearly one whole year back in the minors, before finally being rescued by the Cubs on August 9, 1913, when they acquired him from Kansas City for journeyman pitcher Lew Richie.

Making an immediate impact upon his arrival in the Windy City, Vaughn compiled a record of 5-1 and an ERA of 1.45 during the final two months of the 1913 campaign, while completing five of his six starts and tossing two shutouts. The twenty-six-year-old left-hander emerged as a full-fledged star the following year, when he finished 21-13, with a 2.05 ERA, 165 strikeouts, 4 shutouts, 23 complete games, and 293⅔ innings pitched. Continuing his ascension into stardom in 1915, Vaughn concluded his second full season in Chicago with a record of 20-12, an ERA of 2.87, 18 complete games, another 4 shutouts, and 148 strikeouts in 269⅔ innings of work. Although Vaughn's record slipped to 17-15 the following year, he remained one of the senior circuit's top pitchers, compiling an ERA of 2.20 and ranking among the league leaders with 144 strikeouts, 21 complete games, and 294 innings pitched.

Known affectionately to his teammates as "Hippo," the 6'4", 220-pound Vaughn acquired that nickname not because of his weight or likeness to a hippopotamus, but, rather, for the ungainly way he carried his stout frame when he ran. But, while that moniker might seem cruel to some, Vaughn actually embraced it, passing it on to his young son, who he nicknamed "Little Hippo." Meanwhile, before ballooning to almost 300 pounds during the latter stages of his career, Vaughn proved to be quite an imposing figure on the mound, intimidating many of the small-framed players who competed during the Dead Ball Era. A hard thrower with good control, Vaughn used his intelligence, as well as his size, to navigate his way past opposing lineups. Grover Cleveland Alexander, who spent parts of four seasons anchoring Chicago's starting rotation along with Vaughn, said of his former teammate, "Big Jim Vaughn used to pitch the particular kind of ball a batter liked best just to show him that he couldn't hit it. Nothing pleased him better than to strike a man out pitching to his strength." However, Vaughn presented a more complex pitching philosophy to F. C. Lane, telling the *Baseball Magazine* writer that he only did this occasionally, preferring instead to pitch to a hitter's weakness. In discussing his approach to his craft with Lane, Vaughn suggested, "That isn't to say, of course, that every ball pitched is to the batter's weakness. If this were so, the batter would always know what was coming and, in time, would break himself of that weakness. But it does follow that, in the main, the pitcher tries to give the batter balls that he is known to have difficulty in meeting."

After winning 17 games the previous year, Vaughn surpassed 20 victories for the third time in four seasons in 1917, concluding the campaign with a record of 23-13 that placed him third in the league in wins. He also finished among the NL leaders with a 2.01 ERA, 5 shutouts, 27 complete games, 295 ⅔ innings pitched, and a career-high 195 strikeouts. Vaughn topped that performance, though, in 1918, when he led all NL hurlers in virtually every major statistical category for pitchers. Although the nation's involvement in World War I brought the regular season to a premature end on September 2, Vaughn posted a league-leading 22 wins (against 10 losses) and also finished first in the senior circuit with a 1.74 ERA, 148 strikeouts, 8 shutouts, 27 complete games, 290⅓ innings pitched, and a WHIP of 1.006. His extraordinary performance led the Cubs to the National League pennant and a berth in the World Series, where they ended up losing to the Boston Red Sox in six games.

Vaughn had another exceptional year in 1919, going 21-14, to finish second in the league in wins. He also placed second in the circuit with a 1.79 ERA, finished third with 25 complete games, and led the league for the second straight season in strikeouts (141) and innings pitched (306⅔). Vaughn followed that up with a somewhat less impressive 1920 campaign in which he finished just three games over .500, with a record of 19-16. Nevertheless, he still managed to place among the league leaders in ERA (2.54), strikeouts (131), shutouts (4), complete games (24), and innings pitched (301).

However, the 1920 season proved to be Vaughn's last full year in the Major Leagues. With his performance the following year being adversely affected either by a sore arm or poor conditioning (no one has ever been able to determine the true cause), Vaughn struggled terribly on the mound during the season's first half, compiling a record of just 3-11 and an unseemly 6.01 ERA through early July. Choosing to leave the Cubs two days after being removed from a contest against the New York Giants on July 9, Vaughn never pitched another game in the majors. Although the reason for Vaughn's departure remains a mystery to this day, different theories have been presented through the years, with some suggesting that his poor performance prompted his disappearance, and others speculating that he had grown tired of playing under Cubs manager Johnny Evers. Whatever the cause, team management ended up suspending him for what the *Chicago Tribune* described as "failure to keep in fighting trim." Meanwhile, Vaughn signed a contract to play for Beloit in the independent Midwest League, beginning a lengthy stint in minor-league and semi-pro ball that lasted until 1937, when he finally hung up his cleats at age forty-nine. Following the conclusion of his playing career, Vaughn became an assembler for a refrigeration products company. He spent the remainder of his life in Chicago, passing away at the age of seventy-eight, on May 29, 1966. Some ninety-five years after he threw his last pitch for the Cubs, Vaughn remains the franchise's all-time leader in wins by a left-handed pitcher, having posted a total of 151 victories as a member of the team.

Cub Numbers:

Record: 151-105; .590 Win Pct.; 2.33 ERA; 177 CG; 35 Shutouts; 4 Saves; 2,216⅓ IP; 1,138 Strikeouts; 1.169 WHIP

Career Numbers:

Record: 178-137; .565 Win Pct.; 2.49 ERA; 215 CG; 41 Shutouts; 5 Saves; 2,730 IP; 1,416 Strikeouts; 1.201 WHIP

Cub Career Highlights:

Best Season: Vaughn performed brilliantly for the Cubs in 1917, establishing career-high marks in wins (23), strikeouts (195), and complete games (27), while also finishing among the league leaders in ERA (2.01), shutouts (5), and innings pitched (295⅔). Nevertheless, there is little doubt that he had the finest season of his career the following year, when he led all NL hurlers in nine different statistical categories, en route to capturing the pitcher's version of the Triple Crown. In addition to finishing first in the senior circuit with 22 wins, a 1.74 ERA, and 148 strikeouts, Vaughn tossed a league-leading 8 shutouts, which remained the National League record for southpaws until Carl Hubbell threw 10 for the Giants in 1933.

Memorable Moments/Greatest Performances: Vaughn turned in his first dominant performance for the Cubs on September 13, 1913, when he defeated Brooklyn by a score of 4-0, surrendering just 2 hits and 3 walks during the contest, while recording 10 strikeouts.

Vaughn hurled another gem against Brooklyn almost exactly two years later, when, on September 16, 1915, he went the distance in winning a 12-inning, 1-0 pitcher's duel with Jeff Pfeffer. Vaughn yielded only 4 hits, did not walk anyone, and struck out 7 during the game.

Vaughn continued his domination of Brooklyn on August 8, 1917, surrendering just 2 hits and 1 walk, while striking out 7, in earning a 2-0 victory over the team known at that time as the Robins.

Vaughn defeated the Giants almost singlehandedly on July 6, 1918, working 12 scoreless innings and driving in the game's only run with a walk-off single in the bottom of the 12th.

Vaughn won another 1-0 pitcher's duel on July 25, 1919, doing so without the need for extra innings, when he allowed just a pair of singles and 3 walks, in defeating the St. Louis Cardinals.

Vaughn tossed four one-hitters during his career, accomplishing the feat for the first time on May 14, 1914, when he allowed just 1 single and 4 walks during a 5-0 win over Brooklyn. Vaughn threw his second one-hitter on April 24, 1918, when he surrendered just a pair of walks and a single to Cardinals great Rogers Hornsby during a 2-0 victory over St. Louis. Vaughn turned in a similarly dominant performance later that season, yielding only 2 walks and a single to former Cubs teammate Heinie Zimmerman during a 5-0 shutout of the Giants. Vaughn tossed his final one-hitter on June 30, 1920, allowing just a pair of walks and a single to Pittsburgh third baseman Possum Whitted, in defeating the Pirates by a score of 1-0.

Although Vaughn ended up losing two of his three starts against Boston in the 1918 World Series, he performed brilliantly against the Red Sox. After losing a 1-0 pitcher's duel to Babe Ruth in the Series opener, Vaughn suffered another heartbreaking loss in Game Three, dropping a 2-1 decision to Carl Mays. Returning to the mound in Game Five, Vaughn kept Chicago's hopes alive for one more day by shutting out the Red Sox, 3-0. Vaughn finished the Series with a record of 1-2, an ERA of 1.00, 3 complete games, and 17 strikeouts in 27 total innings of work.

Nevertheless, the game for which Vaughn is best remembered took place on May 2, 1917, when he combined with Cincinnati's Fred Toney for MLB's only nine-inning double no-hit game. Unfortunately, after both pitchers worked nine hitless innings, the Reds pushed across a run in the top of the 10th on a one-out single, an error, a stolen base, and a fielder's choice at home plate. With Toney subsequently retiring the Cubs in order in the bottom of the frame, Vaughn lost another heartbreaking 1-0 decision.

Notable Achievements:

- Won at least 20 games five times, topping 17 victories on two other occasions.

- Compiled ERA below 2.00 three times, posting mark under 2.50 on three other occasions.
- Threw more than 300 innings twice, tossing more than 275 innings four other times.
- Threw more than 20 complete games six times.
- Led NL pitchers in: wins once, ERA once, WHIP once, strikeouts twice, shutouts once, innings pitched twice, fewest hits allowed per nine innings pitched once, and games started twice.
- Finished second in NL in: wins once, strikeouts twice, and complete games once.
- Ranks among Cubs career leaders in: wins (eighth), strikeouts (eighth), shutouts (second), complete games (tied-seventh), innings pitched (eighth), and games started (ninth).
- 1918 NL Pitching Triple Crown winner.
- 1918 NL champion.

24

GROVER CLEVELAND ALEXANDER

Rivaling Walter Johnson and Christy Mathewson as the greatest pitcher of the Dead Ball Era, Grover Cleveland Alexander established himself as the National League's preeminent hurler prior to joining the Cubs in 1918. In his previous seven seasons with the Philadelphia Phillies, the man affectionately known to his teammates as "Old Pete" won more than 20 games six times, surpassing 30 victories on three separate occasions. Alexander also compiled an ERA under 2.00 three times, threw more than 30 complete games five times, tossed more than 10 shutouts twice, and recorded more than 200 strikeouts four times while anchoring Philadelphia's pitching staff, en route to winning three pitcher's Triple Crowns. Although Alexander never quite reached the same level of dominance during his lengthy stay in Chicago, he remained an extremely effective pitcher, winning more than 20 games twice, compiling an ERA under 2.00 three times, and winning a fourth Triple Crown, before spending virtually all of his final four seasons with the St. Louis Cardinals. By the time Alexander ended his career in 1930, he had compiled 373 victories, tying him with Christy Mathewson for the third-highest total in MLB history. Meanwhile, his 90 shutouts place him second only to Walter Johnson in baseball annals. Alexander accomplished all he did even though he spent much of his career suffering from epilepsy and battling alcoholism.

Born in the farming community of Elba, Nebraska on February 26, 1887, Grover Cleveland Alexander owed his name to United States President Grover Cleveland, who was in his first term of office at the time. One of 13 children, Alexander attended nearby St. Paul High School, before discontinuing his education to become a telephone lineman so that he could play baseball on weekends.

After playing for several semi-pro teams, Alexander signed his first professional contract with Galesburg of the Illinois-Missouri League in 1909. Performing extremely well in his first year of pro ball, the twenty-two-year-old right-hander compiled a record of 15-8, before his season ended prematurely when he fell unconscious for two days after being struck in the head by the opposing shortstop's throw while trying to break up a double play. Awakening with double vision, Alexander found himself unable to pitch until the following year, by which time his contract had been sold to the Syracuse Chiefs of the New York State League. Although Alexander's condition improved sufficiently to allow him to win 29 games for the Chiefs in 1910, it is believed that the long term effects of the incident may well have caused the epilepsy that haunted him the rest of his life.

After having his contract purchased by the Philadelphia Phillies for $750 prior to the start of the 1911 campaign, Alexander proved to be a huge bargain, establishing a rookie record by posting a league-leading 28 victories (against 13 losses). He also finished among the NL leaders with 227 strikeouts and a 2.57 ERA, while topping the circuit with 31 complete games, 367 innings pitched, and 7 shutouts, en route to earning a third-place finish in the league MVP voting. Alexander followed up his extraordinary first-year performance with three more outstanding seasons, compiling a total of 68 wins from 1912 to 1914, before beginning arguably the most dominant three-year stretch of any pitcher in MLB history. Posting an overall record of 94-35 between 1915 and 1917, Alexander won more than 30 games and captured the pitcher's version of the Triple Crown each year, compiling the following numbers over the course of those three seasons:

> 1915: **31**-10, **1.22** ERA, **241** Strikeouts, **0.842** WHIP, **12** Shutouts, **36** CG, **376** IP
>
> 1916: **33**-12, **1.55** ERA, **167** Strikeouts, **0.959** WHIP, **16** Shutouts, **38** CG, **389** IP
>
> 1917: **30**-13, **1.83** ERA, **200** Strikeouts, 1.010 WHIP, **8** Shutouts, **34** CG, **388** IP

In addition to topping the senior circuit in virtually every major statistical category for pitchers all three seasons, Alexander led the Phillies to their first National League pennant in 1915. Meanwhile, his 16 shutouts the following year remain a single-season MLB record.

Although Alexander had outstanding movement on his pitches, which included a live fastball that moved in on right-handed batters and a sharp-breaking curveball, the secret of his success lay primarily with his exceptional control. Employing a seemingly effortless pitching motion, a minimal wind-up, a short stride, and a three-quarters overhand delivery to home plate, Alexander appeared to be able to spot the ball to any place he so desired, with legendary sportswriter Grantland Rice once commenting, "He [Alexander] could pitch into a tin can. His control was always remarkable—the finest I have ever seen."

Meanwhile, in describing Alexander's smooth delivery to the plate, one teammate said, "He looked like he was hardly working at all, like he was throwing batting practice."

Johnny Evers, who spent several seasons hitting against Alexander before briefly managing him in Chicago following the conclusion of his playing career, expressed the sense of helplessness he felt every time he stepped into the batter's box against "Old Pete," revealing, "He made me want to throw my bat away when I went to the plate. He fed me pitches I couldn't hit. If I let them go, they were strikes. He made you hit bad balls. He could throw into a tin can all day long."

Yet, in spite of the brilliance Alexander displayed on the mound during his time in Philadelphia, Phillies owner William Baker elected to trade him to the Cubs for two nondescript players and $55,000 prior to the start of the 1918 campaign. Although Baker claimed that he made the move because he needed the money, he actually parted ways with his team's best player because he feared that the nation's involvement in World War I would inevitably result in Alexander joining the military.

Baker proved to be prophetic. After winning two of his first three decisions for the Cubs, Alexander enlisted in the U.S. Army early in 1918. He spent the remainder of the year serving as an artillery officer in France, during which time he experienced a series of events that traumatized him for the rest of his life, both physically and mentally. Spending seven weeks at the front under constant bombardment, Alexander subsequently suffered from shell shock, deafness in his left ear, muscle damage to his pitching arm, and increasingly worse seizures. He also caught shrapnel in his right ear, which may have led to his bout with cancer years later.

Always a heavy drinker, Alexander hit the bottle particularly hard after the War, often as a means of concealing his epilepsy from others.

In spite of all the difficulties he encountered, Alexander somehow managed to pull himself together after he returned to the Cubs on May 11, 1919. After losing his first five decisions, the thirty-two-year-old right-hander went on to finish the season with a record of 16-11, while leading all NL hurlers with 9 shutouts and a 1.72 ERA, which remains the lowest mark posted by any Cubs starting pitcher since the team began playing its home games in Wrigley Field. Alexander followed that up with a magnificent 1920 campaign in which he led the league with 27 wins (against 14 losses), a 1.91 ERA, 173 strikeouts, 33 complete games, and 363⅓ innings pitched, winning in the process his fourth Triple Crown.

No longer able to throw the ball with the same velocity in the years that followed, Alexander developed into more of a finesse pitcher who relied primarily on guile, changing speeds, pitch location, and his extraordinary control to retire opposing batters. Further hampered by an ever-increasing dependency on alcohol, Alexander, it was said, "drank to relive the past, forget the present, and forestall the future." Ungainly even as a youth, with a uniform that never seemed to fit properly and a cap that always looked a size too small, Alexander appeared even more out of place on a baseball diamond during the latter stages of his career. Yet, even though he never again demonstrated the same level of dominance he displayed earlier in his career, "Old Pete" continued to pitch effectively, winning a total of 80 games between 1921 and 1925 for mediocre Cubs teams. Performing particularly well in 1923, Alexander, at the age of thirty-six, finished 22-12, with a 3.19 ERA, 26 complete games, 305 innings pitched, and a league-leading 1.108 WHIP.

Following a last-place finish in 1925, the Cubs hired Joe McCarthy to be their new manager. With the straight-laced McCarthy showing little patience for Alexander, whose drunken and insubordinate behavior he considered to be detrimental to the team, the Cubs sold the veteran right-hander to the St. Louis Cardinals for the waiver price at midseason. Thriving in his new surroundings, Alexander helped the Cardinals capture the NL pennant by winning 9 games over the season's final three months. He then performed brilliantly in the World Series, leading St. Louis to an upset seven-game victory over the Yankees by earning complete-game wins in Games Two and Six, before making an unexpected appearance in the decisive seventh contest.

Despite being plagued by epilepsy and alcoholism for much of his career, Grover Cleveland Alexander established himself as one of the greatest pitchers in baseball history

With the Cardinals ahead by a score of 3-2, the bases loaded, two men out in the bottom of the seventh inning, and Yankee slugger Tony Lazzeri due to hit, Alexander entered the game (according to legend) with a huge hangover he acquired the previous evening after pitching his team to victory. Alexander struck out Lazzeri on four knee-high pitches and then threw two more hitless innings to wrap up the world championship for his team. The thirty-nine-year-old pitcher's performance remains one of the most memorable in the history of the fall classic.

Alexander had two more good years for the Cardinals, winning 21 games in 1927 and another 16 the following year, before his skills finally left him. After posting only 9 victories in 1929, Alexander found himself headed back to Philadelphia when St. Louis traded him to the Phillies at season's end. The forty-two-year-old hurler subsequently ended his major-league career in the same place it began, making his final mound appearance on May 28, 1930, before being released by the Phillies a few days later after getting off to a 0-3 start.

Although Alexander experienced one more brief moment of glory when he gained induction into the Baseball Hall of Fame in 1938, his remaining days proved to be extremely unhappy ones. After leaving the majors, Alexander pitched in demeaning circumstances with touring teams for another 10 years. Unable to cure his drinking problem even though he visited numerous sanitariums in an effort to do so, Alexander roamed the country, staying in cheap hotels and falling in and out of poverty, while taking on several odd jobs. After suffering a heart attack in 1946, Alexander injured himself while falling down a flight of stairs during an epileptic seizure the following year. The doctors discovered cancer on his right ear, which subsequently had to be removed. Three years later, Alexander attended Game Three of the 1950 World Series at Yankee Stadium, where he saw the Phillies lose to the Yankees. He died less than a month later, on November 4, 1950 in St. Paul, Nebraska, at the age of sixty-three.

Following Alexander's passing, Grantland Rice called the winner of 373 big-league games the "most cunning, the smartest, and the best control pitcher that baseball had ever seen," adding, "Above everything else, Alex had one terrific feature to his pitching—he knew just what the batter didn't want—and he put it there to the half-inch."

Cub Numbers:

Record: 128-83; .607 Win Pct.; 2.84 ERA; 158 CG; 24 Shutouts; 10 Saves; 1,884⅓ IP; 614 Strikeouts; 1.161 WHIP

Career Numbers:

Record: 373-208; .642 Win Pct.; 2.56 ERA; 437 CG; 90 Shutouts; 32 Saves; 5,190 IP; 2,198 Strikeouts; 1.121 WHIP

Cub Career Highlights:

Best Season: Although Alexander also pitched extremely well for the Cubs in both 1919 and 1923, he clearly had his best season for them in 1920. In addition to winning his fourth and final Triple Crown by leading all NL hurlers with 27 victories, a 1.91 ERA, and 173 strikeouts, Alexander finished among the league leaders with 7 shutouts and a WHIP of 1.112, while also topping the circuit with 33 complete games, 363⅓ innings pitched, and 40 starts.

Memorable Moments/Greatest Performances: En route to posting a league-leading 9 shutouts and 1.72 ERA in 1919, Alexander put together a pair of impressive 29 consecutive scoreless innings streaks, with one skein lasting from July 15 to August 2, and the other extending from August 6 to August 19.

Although the first of those aforementioned streaks came to an end on August 2, Alexander performed heroically for the Cubs that day, losing a heartbreaking 14-inning, 2-1 decision to his former team, the Philadelphia Phillies. Working all 14 innings, Alexander recorded 15 strikeouts and yielded 9 hits, before allowing the game-winning run to cross the plate in the final frame.

Alexander topped that performance, though, on October 1, 1920, when he worked a career-high 17 innings, en route to earning a well-deserved 3-2 victory over the St. Louis Cardinals.

Nevertheless, even though he recorded just one strikeout during the contest, Alexander turned in what would have to be considered his most dominant performance as a member of the Cubs on May 25, 1923, when he surrendered just 2 harmless singles and no walks during a 4-0 win over the Cincinnati Reds.

Notable Achievements:

- Won more than 20 games twice, surpassing 15 victories four other times.
- Posted winning percentage in excess of .700 once (.706 in 1924).
- Compiled ERA under 2.00 three times.
- Posted WHIP under 1.000 twice.
- Threw more than 300 innings twice.
- Surpassed 20 complete games six times, completing more than 30 of his starts once (33 in 1920).
- Threw 9 shutouts in 1919.
- Led NL pitchers in: wins once, ERA twice, WHIP once, strikeouts once, complete games once, innings pitched once, shutouts twice, fewest hits allowed per nine inning pitched once, games started once, and assists once.
- Ranks among Cubs career leaders in shutouts (seventh) and complete games (10th).
- Ranks among MLB career leaders in: wins (tied-third), shutouts (second), innings pitched (10th), and complete games (13th).
- 1920 NL Pitching Triple Crown winner.
- Number 12 on *The Sporting News'* 1999 list of Baseball's 100 Greatest Players.
- Elected to Baseball Hall of Fame by members of BBWAA in 1938.

25

LON WARNEKE

One of the National League's best pitchers for nearly a decade, Lon Warneke spent most of his peak seasons in Chicago being overshadowed by the senior circuit's top two hurlers, Carl Hubbell and Dizzy Dean. Nevertheless, Warneke matched those Hall of Fame pitchers in terms of consistency, winning at least 16 games eight times between 1932 and 1941, including posting more than 20 victories on three separate occasions. Splitting his career between the Cubs and Cardinals, Warneke spent parts of 10 seasons in the Windy City, serving as the ace of Chicago's pitching staff from 1932 to 1936, during which time he averaged 20 wins, 21 complete games, and 272 innings pitched per season. In addition to annually finishing among the NL leaders in each of those three categories, Warneke consistently placed near the top of the league rankings in ERA, shutouts, and strikeouts. An excellent hitting pitcher as well, Warneke compiled a lifetime batting average of .223, topping the .300-mark in three different seasons. Meanwhile, Warneke's stellar defense enabled him to go nine seasons without committing an error, with the hard-throwing right-hander setting an MLB record at one point by flawlessly handling 227 consecutive chances in the field.

Born in the farming community of Mount Ida, Arkansas on March 28, 1909, Lon Warneke attended Mount Ida High School, where he spent his final two seasons playing baseball, gradually transitioning from first base to the pitcher's mound during that time. After moving to Houston, Texas to live with his sister and brother-in-law following his graduation, Warneke took a job as a bicycling messenger for Western Union, although he continued to hone his pitching skills at the semi-pro level. The nineteen-year-old Warneke began his professional career with Class-D Laurel of the Cotton States League in 1928, before joining Alexandria in that same circuit the following year. Making a favorable impression on Major League scouts by compiling a record of 16-10 for Alexandria in 1929, Warneke subsequently signed with the Cubs, who assigned him to their Reading (Pennsylvania) affiliate in the Class AA International League in 1930.

After appearing in one game with the Cubs in 1930, Warneke arrived in Chicago to stay the following year, when, working primarily in relief, he went 2-4 with a 3.22 ERA. Struggling with his control as a rookie, Warneke walked 37 batters in only 64⅓ innings of work, before he corrected a flaw in his delivery to home plate that enabled him to gain better control of his blazing fastball and sharp-breaking curve. Instead of keeping his eyes focused on home plate just prior to releasing the ball, Warneke tended to look down at his feet, preventing him from picking up the catcher's mitt. However, after working with veteran backup receiver Zack Taylor, Warneke altered his delivery, turning him into one of the league's finest control pitchers.

Joining Chicago's starting rotation in 1932, Warneke soon emerged as the National League's best pitcher, winning his first five decisions before suffering his first defeat. After posting his fourteenth victory of the year on July 19, Warneke received praise from Brooklyn outfielder Lefty O'Doul, who commented, "He (Warneke) has shown me as much stuff as any other pitcher I've hit against this year…He has more than enough to make him a consistent winner. Now he's pitching over the corners of the plate, and it's hard to clout the ball solidly against him." Some two weeks later, *The Sporting News* wrote of Warneke, "He's just a great pitcher, such as pops up once in a lifetime." Meanwhile, Sports Editor Bill Reed wrote in the July 20, 1932 edition of *The Reading Eagle,* "Brooklyn players recently held a discussion over the pitching merits of Lon Warneke, and all of them agreed that he was just about the best hurler in the National League this year. 'Not many pitchers in our league will win as many as 20 games this season,' said Bill Clark, star southpaw of the [Brooklyn] Robins, 'but I think Warneke will reach that total. He may be the only one to win that many games.'"

Warneke ended up posting a league-leading 22 victories, finishing the year with a record of 22-6 that gave him the circuit's best winning percentage (.786). He also led all NL hurlers with a 2.37 ERA and 4 shutouts, placed second with 25 complete games, and finished third with 277 innings pitched, earning in the process a runner-up finish to Philadelphia's Chuck Klein in the league MVP balloting. He followed that up with another brilliant performance in 1933, earning the first of his five All-Star selections by going 18-13, leading the league with 26 complete games, and placing among the leaders with a 2.00 ERA, 133 strikeouts, 4 shutouts, and 287⅓ innings pitched. Plagued by poor run support the entire year, the usually mild-mannered Warneke lost his temper after dropping a 2-1, 11-inning decision to the Braves on June 4, taking a bat and destroying the Boston clubhouse—an act that ended up costing him $25 in damages.

Warneke again pitched extremely well for the Cubs in 1934, earning his second consecutive All-Star nomination by going 22-10, with a 3.21 ERA, 23 complete games, and a career-high 143 strikeouts and 291⅓ innings pitched. He reached 20 wins for the third and final time the following year, helping the Cubs capture the NL pennant by going 20-13, with a 3.06 ERA, 20 complete games, and 261⅔ innings pitched. Warneke subsequently performed magnificently against the Tigers in the World Series, giving the Cubs their only two wins of the fall classic by surrendering just one run to Detroit's powerful lineup over 16⅔ innings of work.

Although Warneke had excellent control and threw extremely hard his first few years in the league, he also relied heavily on his intelligence to establish himself as one of the National League's top hurlers. A master at the art of shaking off his catcher to confuse opposing hitters, Warneke often rejected his receiver's initial sign, before accepting it on the second series of signals as a means of disconcerting the batter. Legendary GM Branch Rickey, who considered this strategy an important part of pitching, later called Warneke the greatest "shaker-offer" he ever saw. Warneke also frequently helped his own cause with his solid hitting and exceptional fielding, having his best season at the plate in 1933, when he hit 2 homers, drove in 13 runs, and batted an even .300.

Warneke spent one more year in Chicago, posting 16 victories, a 3.45 ERA, and a league-high 4 shutouts in 1936, before being dealt to the St. Louis Cardinals at season's end for hard-hitting first baseman Ripper Collins and pitcher Roy Parmelee. Years after Warneke left the Cubs, former teammate Phil Cavarretta said of him, "To me, during the years I saw him pitch with the Cubs (and later with the Cardinals), he was one of the best pitchers I've ever seen; he'd win 18, 19, 20 games for you. His best pitch was an overhand curveball. He had a good change and a good fastball—his fastball had good movement."

Even though Warneke never again won 20 games after he left Chicago, he remained an extremely effective pitcher during his time in St. Louis, compiling an overall record of 83-49 for the Cardinals from 1937 to 1942, en route to earning two more All-Star selections. Nicknamed "The Arkansas Hummingbird" by *St. Louis Post-Dispatch* sportswriter Roy Stockton for his darting fastball, Warneke had his finest season for the Cardinals in 1941, when he went 17-9, with a 3.15 ERA and 4 shutouts. Warneke also began his string of six straight seasons in which he did not commit a single error while pitching for the Redbirds, with his record-setting streak (since broken) covering 163 games and 227 consecutive chances.

In spite of the success Warneke experienced the previous season, the Cardinals elected to sell him back to the Cubs for $7,500 midway through the 1942 campaign. Although the thirty-three-year-old right-hander won only 5 of his 12 decisions over the course of the season's final three months, he pitched effectively for the Cubs down the stretch, compiling a 2.27 ERA and tossing 8 complete games. After assuming the role of a spot-starter the following year, Warneke enlisted in the U.S. Army in January 1944. He subsequently missed virtually all of the next two seasons, before returning to the Cubs during the latter stages of the 1945 campaign, when, appearing in 9 games, he lost his only decision. Warneke announced his retirement at season's end, concluding his career with a record of 192-121, an ERA of 3.18, 192 complete games, 30 shutouts, and 1,140 strikeouts in 2,782⅓ total innings of work.

Following his playing days, Warneke embarked on a career in umpiring, getting his start as an official in the Pacific Coast League in 1946, before being promoted to the National League 3 years later. Warneke continued to serve as an arbiter until 1955, when he retired to his home in Hot Springs, Arkansas, where he ended up spending 10 years serving as Garland County judge. After retiring from that post in 1972, Warneke lived another four years, dying of a heart attack at his home in Hot Springs at the age of sixty-seven, on June 23, 1976.

Cub Numbers:

Record: 109-72; .602 Win Pct.; 2.84 ERA; 122 CG; 17 Shutouts; 12 Saves; 1,624⅔ IP; 706 Strikeouts; 1.208 WHIP

Lon Warneke averaged 20 wins per season
for the Cubs from 1932 to 1936

Courtesy of MEARS Online Auctions

Career Numbers:

Record: 192-121; .613 Win Pct.; 3.18 ERA; 192 CG; 30 Shutouts; 14 Saves; 2,782⅓ IP; 1,140 Strikeouts; 1.214 WHIP

Cub Career Highlights:

Best Season: Although Warneke posted 18 victories, compiled a career-best 2.00 ERA, led all NL hurlers with 26 complete games, and ranked among the league leaders with 4 shutouts, 133 strikeouts, and 287⅓ innings pitched in 1933, he had his finest season for the Cubs one year earlier. In addition to leading the league with 22 wins, a .786 winning percentage, a 2.37 ERA, and 4 shutouts in 1932, Warneke placed in the league's top five with 25 complete games, 277 innings pitched, and a career-best WHIP of 1.123, earning in the process a runner-up finish in the NL MVP voting.

Memorable Moments/Greatest Performances: An excellent hitting pitcher over the course of his career, Warneke turned in his finest batting performance on May 12, 1935, when he went 4-for-4, with 2 RBIs, during a 4-1 complete-game win over the Boston Braves.

Warneke performed brilliantly against St. Louis on September 4, 1932, yielding just 3 hits, 1 walk, and striking out 6, in defeating the Cardinals by a score of 3-0.

Warneke tossed another three-hit shutout on May 2, 1933, when he allowed just 3 harmless singles during an 11-0 whitewashing of the Giants.

Warneke began the 1934 campaign in style, surrendering just 1 hit and 2 walks during a 6-0 opening day shutout of the Cincinnati Reds in which he recorded a career-high 13 strikeouts. The Reds got their only safety of the game with one man out in the bottom of the ninth inning, when leadoff batter Adam Comorosky singled to centerfield.

Warneke followed that up with another gem just five days later, allowing only 1 hit during a complete-game 15-2 victory over the Cardinals on April 22, 1934.

Warneke out-pitched Carl Hubbell on August 29, 1934, when he surrendered just 3 hits during a 1-0 victory over Hubbell and the Giants.

Warneke made his 20th win of the 1935 campaign a memorable one, yielding just 2 hits during a 1-0 victory over the Cardinals on September 25 that clinched at least a tie for the pennant.

Warneke again dominated St. Louis on September 18, 1936, surrendering just 3 hits, 1 walk, and recording 8 strikeouts during a 3-0 win over the Cardinals.

Warneke turned in the finest performance of his second tour of duty with the Cubs on August 23, 1942, when he allowed just 2 hits during a 3-0 whitewashing of the Cincinnati Reds.

Although the Cubs ended up losing the 1935 World Series to Detroit in six games, Warneke dominated Tiger batsmen, winning both his starts, while surrendering just 9 hits and 1 run over $16\frac{2}{3}$ innings, en route to compiling an ERA of 0.54. Particularly effective in Game One, Warneke gave the Cubs an early 1-0 Series lead by surrendering just 4 hits during a 3-0 Chicago victory.

Notable Achievements:

- Won at least 20 games three times, surpassing 16 victories on two other occasions.
- Posted winning percentage in excess of .700 once (.786 in 1932).
- Compiled ERA below 2.50 three times.
- Threw more than 250 innings four times.
- Tossed more than 20 complete games four times.
- Led NL pitchers in: wins once, winning percentage once, ERA once, shutouts twice, complete games once, and fielding percentage three times.
- Finished second in NL in: ERA once, WHIP once, and complete games once.
- Finished second in 1932 NL MVP voting.
- 1932 *Sporting News* All-Star selection.
- Three-time NL All-Star (1933, 1934 & 1936).
- Two-time NL champion (1932 & 1935).

26

BILL NICHOLSON

Just the third player in MLB history to lead his league in home runs and RBIs in back-to-back seasons, Bill "Swish" Nicholson proved to be one of the National League's top sluggers for much of the 1940s, a period during which he established himself as easily the Cubs' most popular player. A powerful left-handed batter with a natural home-run swing, Nicholson spent 10 seasons in Chicago, leading the Cubs in homers in eight of those. In addition to hitting more than 20 home runs six times, Nicholson knocked in more than 100 runs twice and batted over .300 once, earning in the process four All-Star selections and two top-five finishes in the NL MVP voting. A solid outfielder as well, Nicholson led all NL right-fielders in putouts four times, while also leading all players at his position in assists and fielding percentage two times each. Had Nicholson not experienced his greatest success during World War II, he likely would be better remembered today as one of the elite sluggers of his era.

Born on his family's farm in Chestertown, Maryland on December 11, 1914, William Beck Nicholson starred in multiple sports while attending local Chestertown High School, excelling in baseball, football, and basketball. After graduating from Chestertown High at only sixteen years of age in 1931, Nicholson enrolled at nearby Washington College, where he continued to star in all three sports, excelling on the hardwood as a guard, the diamond as an outfielder, and the gridiron as a fullback and kicker. Hoping to pursue a career as a naval officer, Nicholson left for the Severn School in Annapolis in 1933 to prepare for entrance into the Naval Academy. However, after being rejected due to color-blindness, Nicholson returned to Washington to complete his education.

Following his graduation, Nicholson spent one year playing semi-pro ball, before signing with the Philadelphia Athletics as an amateur free agent in 1936. Although the twenty-one-year-old outfielder appeared briefly in an Athletics uniform that year, failing to hit safely in 12 official at-bats, he spent most of the next three seasons in the minor leagues, topping 20 homers and batting over .300 in both 1937 and 1938. Yet, in spite of the solid numbers Nicholson posted in each of those campaigns, the Athletics remained dissatisfied with his inability to make consistent contact at the plate, prompting them to trade him to the Washington Senators in August 1938. Subsequently assigned to Washington's minor league affiliate in Chattanooga, Nicholson developed into a top prospect under the watchful eye of manager Kiki Cuyler, who helped transform him into a feared power hitter by tinkering with his stance and teaching him to be more selective at the plate.

After Cuyler recommended Nicholson to Chicago's scouting staff, the Cubs purchased the young slugger from Washington for $35,000 on June 25, 1939. Nicholson then spent the remainder of the year playing right field for the Cubs, batting .295, hitting 5 homers, and driving in 38 runs, in 58 games and 220 official at-bats. Emerging as Chicago's top offensive threat the following season, Nicholson earned his first All-Star selection by batting .297, finishing second in the NL with 25 home runs and a .534 slugging percentage, and also ranking among the league leaders with 98 RBIs. Although Nicholson's batting average slipped to .254 in 1941, he once again placed near the top of the league rankings in homers (26) and RBIs (98). He followed that up with another productive year, hitting 21 homers, driving in 78 runs, and batting .294 in 1942. Meanwhile, Nicholson's 328 putouts and 18 assists led all NL right-fielders.

With Nicholson subsequently being excused from military duty due to his color-blindness, he remained behind while most of the game's best players entered the service during World War II. Asserting himself as the senior circuit's foremost slugger over the course of the next two seasons, Nicholson earned a third-place finish in the 1943 NL MVP voting by leading the league with 29 home runs and 128 RBIs, while also finishing among the leaders with 95 runs scored, 188 hits, 9 triples, a .309 batting average, and a .531 slugging percentage. Nicholson then nearly captured league MVP honors in 1944, finishing just one point behind St. Louis shortstop Marty Marion in the balloting after batting .287 and topping the circuit with 33 homers, 122 RBIs, 116 runs scored, and 317 total bases. By leading his league in home runs and RBIs in consecutive seasons, Nicholson joined legendary sluggers Babe Ruth and Jimmie Foxx as the only players to accomplish the feat, to that point.

Nicholson's power-hitting and outstanding offensive production made him extremely popular with Cubs fans, who typically chose to remain at Wrigley Field until their favorite player took his last turn at-bat, regardless of the score. Although Brooklyn fans tagged the six-foot, 205-pound Nicholson with the nickname "Swish" early in his career due to the ferocity of his swing, the fans at Wrigley referred to him affectionately as either "Big Bill" or "Nick." The tobacco-chewing Nicholson also grew to be quite popular with his teammates, with Cubs second baseman Don Johnson recalling, "Nick was one of the neatest guys you ever wanted to meet... built like a fullback, a quiet guy...he was a real good outfielder; covered more territory than you thought; I don't think I ever saw him throw to a wrong base."

Although Nicholson knocked in 88 runs and scored 82 times for the pennant-winning Cubs in 1945, he hit only 13 homers and batted just .243, as he began to suffer from the effects of the diabetes that caused his vision to gradually deteriorate over the course of the next several seasons. An injury-marred 1946 campaign followed in which Nicholson batted just .220, hit only 8 homers, and knocked in just 41 runs, in 105 games and 296 official at-bats. The veteran slugger then rebounded somewhat in each of the next two seasons, totaling 45 home runs and 142 RBIs from 1947 to 1948, even though he batted just .244 and .261, respectively.

With the thirty-three-year-old Nicholson clearly on the downside of his career, the Cubs elected to trade him to the Phillies for former batting champion Harry Walker following the conclusion of the 1948 campaign, Nicholson subsequently spent his final five big-league seasons in Philadelphia, never again serving as a full-time player. After losing 20 pounds during the first few months of the 1950 campaign, Nicholson was diagnosed with diabetes, forcing him to miss the rest of the season, including the World Series. Although he returned to play three more years, Nicholson spent most of that time pinch-hitting, before announcing his retirement after being released by the Phillies at the end of the 1953 season.

Yet, even though Nicholson failed to make a major impact on the playing field during his time in Philadelphia, he proved to be a steadying influence on the young *Whiz Kids* squad that captured the National League pennant in 1950, with Phillies utility infielder Putsy Caballero later

Bill Nicholson led the Cubs in home runs
eight times during the 1940s

commenting, "We all respected Bill Nicholson. He had been through what we hoped to go through. When he said something, we listened. He knew the pitchers in the league and would tell us what to expect in certain situations. He was a man's man."

Although Nicholson's reputation as a clubhouse leader seemed to make him a logical candidate for any managerial or coaching positions that became available following his playing days, he never received a single offer, prompting him to retire to his farm outside his home town of Chestertown, Maryland. He spent his remaining years there, before suffering a heart attack that took his life on March 8, 1996. Nicholson was eighty-one years old at the time of his passing.

Reflecting back on Nicholson's playing career, Allen Lewis, who covered the Phillies for *The Philadelphia Inquirer* during the 1950s and '60s, said, "He was a good ballplayer. As a slugger, he was above average....I think the fact he was a wartime ballplayer when he did his best work hurt his reputation. He would have been better known had it not been wartime."

Cub Numbers:

205 HR; 833 RBIs; 738 Runs Scored; 1,323 Hits; 245 Doubles; 53 Triples; 26 Stolen Bases; .272 AVG; .368 OBP; .471 SLG; .840 OPS

Career Numbers:

235 HR; 948 RBIs; 837 Runs Scored; 1,484 Hits; 272 Doubles; 60 Triples; 27 Stolen Bases; .268 AVG; .365 OBP; .465 SLG; .830 OPS

Cub Career Highlights:

Best Season: Nicholson most certainly had his two best seasons for the Cubs in 1943 and 1944, when he established himself as the senior circuit's top slugger. In addition to leading the league with 29 homers and 128 RBIs in the first of those campaigns, Nicholson finished third in runs scored (95), second in total bases (323), slugging percentage (.531), and OPS (.917), fourth in hits (188), sixth in batting average (.309), and seventh in on-base percentage (.386), posting career-high marks in four different offensive categories, en route to earning a third-place finish in the NL MVP voting. He followed that up by topping the circuit with 33 home runs, 122 RBIs, 116 runs scored, and 317 total bases in 1944, while also finishing second in the league in walks (93) and slugging percentage (.545), fifth in OPS (.935), seventh in doubles (35), compiling a batting average of .287, and leading all NL right-fielders with 306 putouts and 18 assists. It's an extremely close call, and either year would make an excellent choice. But, since Nicholson led the NL in four different offensive categories and came within one point of capturing league MVP honors in 1944, we'll go with that as his finest season.

Memorable Moments/Greatest Performances: Nicholson hit one of the longest home runs in the history of Wrigley Field in 1948, when he drove a ball just to right of the center field scoreboard that hit a building across Sheffield Avenue. Several years later, Roberto Clemente delivered a similarly majestic blow that traveled just to the left of the scoreboard.

Although the Cubs lost both ends of a doubleheader to the Pittsburgh Pirates on August 15, 1942, Nicholson had a tremendous day at the plate, collecting 6 hits, including 3 home runs and 2 doubles. After going 2-for-3, with a homer and double, during Chicago's 8-5 loss in Game One, Nicholson went 4-for-6, with 2 homers and a double, in the 8-7, 11-inning loss in the nightcap.

Exactly one week later, on August 22, 1942, Nicholson gave the Cubs a 5-4 win over Cincinnati by hitting a walk-off homer in the bottom of the 11th inning off right-hander Gene Thompson.

Nicholson again proved to be a thorn in the side of Cincinnati on July 18, 1943, when he homered and collected 4 hits and 4 RBIs during a 7-0 win over the Reds.

Nicholson had a similarly productive afternoon against St. Louis on September 19, 1943, going 4-for-5, with a homer, 4 RBIs, and 2 runs scored, during a 6-0 victory over the Cardinals.

Nicholson led the Cubs to a 12-6 win over Brooklyn on June 28, 1944 by collecting 3 hits, including a pair of homers, driving in 5 runs, and scoring 3 times.

Nicholson twice knocked in 6 runs in one game, doing so for the first time during an 11-3 win over the Phillies on July 28, 1946. Nicholson matched that career-high mark on April 20, 1947, when he homered twice—once with the bases loaded—during a 7-4 victory over the Cardinals.

In a case of déjà vu, Nicholson gave the Cubs a 2-1 win over Cincinnati on August 8, 1947 by hitting a walk-off homer in the bottom of the 11th inning, this time victimizing ace right-hander Ewell Blackwell.

Nicholson delivered another game-winning homer a little over one month later, on September 17, 1947, hitting a two-run blast in the bottom of the ninth inning against left-hander Dave Koslo, to give the Cubs a 12-10 victory over the Giants.

However, Nicholson had his greatest day at the plate on July 23, 1944, when, during a doubleheader split with the Giants, he went 5-for-6, with 4 home runs, 3 walks, 7 RBIs, and 6 runs scored. After Nicholson homered three times during Chicago's 7-4 win in the opener and reached the seats once again in the nightcap, New York manager Mel Ott paid him the ultimate tribute by having him intentionally walked with the bases loaded in the eighth inning of Game Two.

Notable Achievements:

- Hit more than 20 home runs six times, topping 30 homers once (33 in 1944).
- Knocked in more than 120 runs twice.
- Scored more than 100 runs once (116 in 1944).
- Batted over .300 once (.309 in 1943).
- Finished in double digits in triples once (11 in 1942).
- Surpassed 30 doubles twice.
- Posted slugging percentage in excess of .500 three times.
- Led NL in: home runs twice, RBIs twice, runs scored once, and total bases once.
- Finished second in NL in: home runs once, hits once, triples once, total bases once, bases on balls once, slugging percentage three times, and OPS once.
- Led NL outfielders in fielding percentage once.
- Led NL right-fielders in: putouts four times, assists twice, and fielding percentage twice.
- Ranks among Cubs career leaders in home runs (eighth) and bases on balls (10th).
- Hit three home runs in one game vs. New York Giants on July 23, 1944.
- Finished third in 1943 NL MVP voting.
- Finished second in 1944 NL MVP voting.
- 1943 *Sporting News* All-Star selection.
- Four-time NL All-Star (1940, 1941, 1943 & 1944).
- 1945 NL champion.

27

HANK SAUER

Acquired from Cincinnati in one of the best trades the Cubs ever made, Hank Sauer traveled a long and arduous road to the Major Leagues, first arriving in Chicago at thirty-two years of age in 1949. Yet, even though he joined the Cubs with nearly half his professional career already behind him, Sauer achieved stardom in the Windy City, with his prolific slugging earning him the nickname "The Mayor of Wrigley Field." En route to earning two All-Star selections and one league MVP trophy, Sauer hit more than 30 home runs four times, reaching the 40-homer plateau once. Serving as Chicago's primary power threat until Ernie Banks joined him in the Cubs' lineup in 1954, the towering 6'4", 200-pound outfielder also knocked in more than 100 runs three times. Even though the Cubs remained a non-contending team throughout his seven-year stay in Chicago, Sauer provided the hometown fans with many a thrill, establishing himself in the process as one of the most popular players in franchise history.

Born in Pittsburgh, Pennsylvania on March 17, 1917, Henry John Sauer grew up in the nearby suburb of Bellevue, where he attended high school, before taking a job at a federal Civilian Conservation Corps camp in 1935 to help support his family during the Great Depression. Although Sauer continued to work after he returned home in 1937, he also played baseball at the semi-pro level on weekends. Discovered by Yankee scout Gene McCann while participating in a local sandlot game, Sauer signed with New York, in whose farm system he spent the next two years playing first base. After being selected by Cincinnati in the 1939 minor league draft, Sauer remained in the minors for another five years, although he received brief trials with the Reds during the latter stages of both the 1941 and 1942 campaigns, going a combined 15-for-53 (.283), with 2 homers and 9 RBIs, while splitting his time between first base and the outfield.

Becoming increasingly frustrated with his inability to reach the Major Leagues, Sauer enlisted in the United States Coast Guard in 1944, where he spent most of the next two years serving his country during World War II. Discharged from the military in the spring of 1945, Sauer joined the Reds at midseason, hitting 5 homers, driving in 20 runs, and batting .293 over the next month, before tearing tendons in his ankle while sliding into third base. His season over and his running speed gone, Sauer subsequently found himself being optioned to Syracuse in the International League prior to the start of the ensuing campaign.

As it turned out, Sauer's demotion to Syracuse proved to be a blessing in disguise. In addition to learning the finer points of outfield play under Manager Jewel Ens, the 29-year-old Sauer received advice from Ens on how to improve his power production at the plate. Reflecting back on his time at Syracuse, Sauer recalled years later:

> *"Finally, I got that heavy 40-ounce bat. Jewel Ens, the manager at Syracuse, got me to use that big bat. Jewel said, 'Just give it 10 days.' I gave that 40-ounce bat 10 days, and that's when I had that tremendous minor league year. I've used it ever since. That heavier bat got me in the big leagues to stay. I was hitting a lot of home runs, but most of them were fouls. That's why Jewel wanted me to use the big bat. He said, 'Hank, you're a good contact hitter, but you're so fast with that bat that you're going to have to get something to slow you down.' So he ordered the 40-ounce Chick Hafey bat. From that day on, I still got around fast enough to pull the ball. I was already a pronounced pull hitter. That's [the bat] what made me, and I give Jewel Ens all the credit in the world for it."*

After hitting 21 homers, driving in 90 runs, and batting .282 in 1946, Sauer earned *Sporting News* Minor League Player of the Year honors the following season by hitting 50 homers, knocking in 141 runs, scoring 130 times, and batting .336. Sauer's exceptional performance earned him a return trip to Cincinnati, where, after laying claim to the Reds' starting left field job during the early stages of the 1948 campaign, he ended up hitting 35 homers, driving in 97 runs, and batting .260. Instructed by Reds manager Johnny Neun to hit the ball more to the opposite field in 1949, the right-handed hitting Sauer got off to a slow start, prompting Cincinnati to trade him to the Cubs for veteran outfielders Harry Walker and "Peanuts" Lowrey on June 15. Liberated from the restraints his former

Courtesy of RMYauctions.com

Hank Sauer (right) earned NL MVP honors in 1952 when he led
the league with 37 home runs and 121 RBIs

manager placed on him, Sauer responded by hitting 27 homers, knocking
in 83 runs, and batting .291 over the season's final 96 games, to finish the
year with 31 homers, 99 RBIs, and a .275 batting average. Recalling a
conversation he had with Cubs manager Frankie Frisch shortly after he
arrived in Chicago, Sauer revealed, "When they traded me to the Cubs,
manager Frankie Frisch said, 'Hank, I didn't get you to hit balls to right
field. I want you to hit home runs and drive in runs for me.' Well, that's
when I went crazy. I hit 31 home runs that year, and 27 of those came
with Chicago."

Sauer continued his outstanding play in 1950, earning All-Star honors
by finishing third in the league with 32 homers, while also knocking in 103
runs, scoring 85 times, batting .274, and leading all NL left-fielders with
12 assists. He followed that up with another solid year, concluding the
1951 campaign with 30 home runs, 89 RBIs, 77 runs scored, a .263 batting

average, and a career-high 18 outfield assists which placed him second in the league rankings.

Fast becoming a fan favorite at Wrigley, Sauer proved to be one of the few bright spots on a Cubs team that annually placed near the bottom of the NL standings. Indeed, *The Sporting News* referred to the man known affectionately to his teammates as "Honker" due to the prominence of his nose as "the most popular Cubs player since Bill Nicholson." After Sauer hit one of his signature home runs to left field, the fans seated in the bleachers typically displayed their fondness for him by showering the outfield with packages of his favorite chewing tobacco. Meanwhile, Sauer returned to Cubs fans the love they offered him, stating in author Carrie Muskat's book entitled, *Banks to Sandberg to Grace: Five Decades of Love and Frustration with the Chicago Cubs*, "You give the people of Chicago 100 percent of your ability and they will love you. You hit .220, but you give 100 percent and they love you....I think the people made me better than what I was....They were for me, and they made me feel like a millionaire."

Sauer's powerful wrists and muscular arms gave him tremendous bat speed, making him a dead pull-hitter, and prompting opposing teams to employ defensive shifts against him. In discussing Sauer in his book, *Stan Musial: The Man's Own Story*, Stan the Man claimed, "Against a packed shift toward third base, he seldom could hit to right field, but he could hit over the shift, if not through it."

Sauer often hit over the shift in 1952, when he earned NL MVP honors and his second All-Star nomination by leading the league with 37 home runs and 121 RBIs, while also scoring 89 times and batting .270. Sauer would have posted even better numbers had he not injured his neck early in September while sliding into third base, forcing him to spend most of the season's final month playing in pain. Yet, even though he hit only three homers the rest of the way, he still managed to tie Pittsburgh's Ralph Kiner for the NL lead in that department.

Sauer subsequently suffered through an injury-marred 1953 campaign in which he appeared in only 108 games due to a broken hand and a pair of broken fingers. Still, he finished with decent numbers, batting .263, hitting 19 homers, and driving in 60 runs, in just 395 official at-bats. Healthy again in 1954, Sauer returned to top form, establishing career-high marks in homers (41) and runs scored (98), while also knocking in 103 runs and batting .288. However, after the thirty-eight-year-old outfielder hit just 12 homers, knocked in only 28 runs, and batted just .211 in a part-time role the following year, the Cubs elected to trade him to the St. Louis Cardinals for journeyman outfielder Pete Whisenant prior to the start of the 1956 campaign. Upon learning of the deal, Sauer said, "I regret leaving Chicago because the fans were good to me."

Sauer ended up spending just one year in St. Louis, hitting 5 homers, driving in 24 runs, and batting .298 in a part-time role in 1956, before being released by the Cardinals at season's end. He subsequently signed with the Giants, with whom he spent his final three seasons, earning NL Comeback Player of the Year honors in 1957 by hitting 26 homers and knocking in 76 runs, in just 378 official at-bats. Reduced to occasional pinch-hitting duties by 1959, the forty-two-year-old Sauer announced his retirement following the conclusion of the campaign, ending his career with 288 home runs, 876 RBIs, and a .266 batting average. He then remained with the Giants for another thirty-five years, serving them first as a hitting coach, before moving into the front office, where he fulfilled a number of roles in player development, including scouting and serving as the director of the farm system. After finally retiring in 1993, Sauer lived another eight years, passing away at the age of eighty-four, on August 24, 2001. Following his passing, Sauer's son said that, in spite of his father's many years of service with the Giants, "In his heart, he was always a Cubbie. Chicago was a great town that was very good to him."

Cub Numbers:

198 HR; 587 RBIs; 498 Runs Scored; 852 Hits; 141 Doubles; 17 Triples; 6 Stolen Bases; .269 AVG; .348 OBP; .512 SLG; .860 OPS

Career Numbers:

288 HR; 876 RBIs; 709 Runs Scored; 1,278 Hits; 200 Doubles; 19 Triples; 11 Stolen Bases; .266 AVG; .347 OBP; .496 SLG; .843 OPS

Cub Career Highlights:

Best Season: Sauer had a big year for the Cubs in 1954, batting .288, driving in 103 runs, and establishing career-high marks in homers (41), runs scored (98), and OPS (.938). Nevertheless, the 1952 campaign would have to be considered his finest all-around season. In addition to leading the NL with 37 home runs and 121 RBIs, Sauer scored 89 times, batted

.270, compiled an OPS of .892, amassed 31 doubles and a career-high 301 total bases, and led all players at his position with 320 putouts, 17 assists, and 3 double plays. Sauer's outstanding performance, which earned him league MVP honors and his lone *Sporting News* All-Star selection, helped the Cubs finish the season with a .500 record, marking the only time in his seven years in Chicago they did not post a losing mark.

Memorable Moments/Greatest Performances: Sauer powered the Cubs to a 7-5 victory over Pittsburgh on May 27, 1950 by hitting a pair of homers and driving in 5 runs.

Sauer had another big day at the plate nearly one month later, on June 25, 1950, going 4-for-4, with 2 homers, 2 doubles, 4 RBIs, and 3 runs scored, during an 11-8 win over the Phillies.

Sauer defeated St. Louis almost single-handedly on August 14, 1951, when he collected 3 hits, a pair of homers, and 5 RBIs during a 5-4 victory over the Cardinals.

Sauer led the Cubs to an 8-6 win over the Giants on August 21, 1952 by driving in a career-high 6 runs with a pair of homers. Sauer's second homer of the contest, a three-run blast in the bottom of the seventh inning, provided the margin of victory.

Sauer twice homered three times in one game as a member of the Cubs, amazingly doing so both times against outstanding Phillies left-hander Curt Simmons. He accomplished the feat for the first time during a 7-5 win over the Phillies on August 28, 1950 in which he knocked in 4 of Chicago's 7 runs. Sauer again victimized Simmons on June 11, 1952, when he hit 3 solo homers, in leading the Cubs to a 3-2 victory over the Phillies.

Notable Achievements:

- Surpassed 30 home runs four times, topping 40 homers once (41 in 1954).
- Knocked in more than 100 runs three times, topping 120 RBIs once (121 in 1952).
- Topped 30 doubles twice.
- Posted slugging percentage in excess of .500 four times.
- Led NL with 37 home runs and 121 RBIs in 1952.

- Finished second in NL in total bases once and slugging percentage once.
- Led NL outfielders with 16 assists in 1949.
- Led NL left-fielders in: putouts twice, assists three times, and double plays once.
- Ranks among Cubs career leaders in home runs (ninth) and slugging percentage (fifth).
- Hit three home runs in one game twice (August 28, 1950 & June 11, 1952, both vs. Phillies).
- 1952 NL MVP.
- 1952 *Sporting News* NL Player of the Year.
- 1952 *Sporting News* All-Star selection.
- Two-time NL All-Star (1950 & 1952).

28

DERREK LEE

A powerful right-handed hitter who gave the Cubs outstanding run-production and a consistent bat in the middle of their lineup for the better part of seven seasons, Derrek Lee contributed significantly to two NL Central championship teams during his time in Chicago. En route to earning two All-Star selections and a pair of top-10 finishes in the NL MVP voting as a member of the Cubs, Lee hit more than 30 homers three times, knocked in more than 100 runs twice, and batted over .300 three times, putting together one of the most dominant seasons in recent memory in 2005, when he topped the senior circuit in six different offensive categories. An exceptional fielder as well, Lee annually ranked among the league's top players at his position in assists and fielding percentage, with the strapping first baseman twice earning Gold Glove honors. Meanwhile, Lee carried himself with class and dignity his entire time in the Windy City, making him a credit to the organization, both on and off the playing field.

Born in Sacramento, California on September 6, 1975, Derrek Leon Lee spent his early years living in Japan, where his father, Leon, and uncle, Leron, played professional baseball. After moving back to the States following the conclusion of their playing careers, Derrek attended Sacramento's El Camino High School, where he starred in both baseball and basketball. Recruited by several major colleges to compete in both sports following his graduation from El Camino, Lee initially committed to the University of North Carolina, whose head basketball coach, Dean Smith, hoped to make him the school's next point guard. However, the 6'5" Lee changed his plans when the San Diego Padres selected him with the fourteenth overall pick of the 1993 MLB Draft.

Lee subsequently spent most of the next four years advancing through the San Diego farm system, twice being named the organization's Minor

Courtesy of UCinternational

Derrek Lee led the National League
in six different offensive categories in 2005

League Player of the Year, before getting his first taste of the majors in 1997, when, garnering 54 official at-bats in 22 games, he batted .259 and hit his first big-league homer. But, with Wally Joyner ensconced at first base in San Diego, the Padres elected to include Lee in a package of players they sent to the Florida Marlins for ace right-hander Kevin Brown during the subsequent off-season.

Earning the starting first base job upon his arrival in Florida, Lee struggled somewhat as a rookie, hitting 17 homers and driving in 74 runs, but batting just .233 and striking out 120 times. After getting off to a slow start in 1999, Lee ended up spending most of the season with Triple A Calgary, where he performed well enough to earn a second chance with the Marlins the following year. Making the most of his opportunity, Lee posted solid numbers in 2000, concluding the campaign with 28 home runs, 70 RBIs, and a .281 batting average. He followed that up with another strong performance in 2001, hitting 21 homers, knocking in 75 runs, scoring 83 times, and batting .282. After another productive year in 2002, Lee helped the Marlins advance to the playoffs the following season by hitting 31 homers, knocking in 92 runs, scoring 91 times, and batting .271, while also earning Gold Glove honors for the first time in his career. However, after the Marlins won the World Series, they decided to make several cost-cutting moves, one of which involved trading Lee—an impending free agent—to the Cubs for Hee-Seop Choi on November 25, 2003.

After signing a three-year contract extension with the Cubs for $22.5 million, Lee had a big first year in Chicago, hitting 32 homers, driving in 98 runs, scoring 90 times, and batting .278. Improving upon those numbers significantly in 2005, Lee earned his first All-Star selection and a third-place finish in the NL MVP voting by knocking in 107 runs, placing second in the league with 46 homers and 120 runs scored, and topping the circuit with 199 hits, 50 doubles, 393 total bases, a .335 batting average, a .662 slugging percentage, and a 1.080 OPS.

Lee's increased willingness to drive pitches on the outer half of the plate to right field served him well in his banner year of 2005, making him a far more dangerous hitter. He also improved his pitch recognition and became more selective at the plate, drawing 85 bases on balls, which represented the third-highest total of his career. Yet, even though the prolific offensive numbers Lee posted garnered him a considerable amount of media attention, he contributed just as much to the Cubs with his outstanding defense at first base. Surprisingly nimble for someone who stood

6'5" tall and weighed 225 pounds, Lee proved to be particularly adept at stretching for errant throws and scooping them out of the dirt, instilling a great deal of confidence in his infield mates, particularly Aramis Ramirez, who saw his error total drop from 33 to 10 after Lee took over at first for the Cubs. Meanwhile, Lee handled his newfound fame with humility and grace, displaying the intelligence and level-headedness that remained such an integral part of his persona.

Unfortunately, Lee subsequently suffered through an injury-marred 2006 campaign in which he appeared in only 50 games due to a broken wrist he suffered in a collision with Rafael Furcal on a play at first base. With Lee out for most of the season, the Cubs tumbled to last place in the NL Central, finishing the season with a record of just 66-96. Although Lee returned at less than 100 percent the following year, finishing the season with just 22 homers and 82 RBIs, he still managed to compile a batting average of .317, score 91 runs, and place among the league leaders with 43 doubles, earning in the process his second All-Star selection. Lee posted solid numbers again in 2008, helping the Cubs capture their second straight NL Central title by hitting 20 homers, driving in 90 runs, scoring 93 times, and batting .291, before compiling a batting average of .545 during Chicago's three-game loss to Los Angeles in the NLDS.

Despite being limited to 141 games in 2009 by neck and back problems, Lee posted outstanding offensive numbers, finishing the season with 35 home runs, 111 RBIs, 91 runs scored, a .306 batting average, and an OPS of .972, en route to earning a top-10 finish in the league MVP balloting. However, after hitting just 16 homers, knocking in only 52 runs, and batting just .251 over the first four-and-a-half months of the ensuing campaign, Lee found himself headed for Atlanta when the Cubs traded him to the Braves for three minor leaguers on August 18, 2010. Upon learning of the deal, Lee told the Chicago media, "I understand what (Cubs GM) Jim Hendry is trying to do over here. I had a great time here. I grew as a player, grew as a person, but I didn't achieve the ultimate goal of winning the World Series, so that part is disappointing. The rest of my experience was nothing but positive."

In expressing his fondness for Lee, Hendry said, "He's had a tremendous career here, except for the year [2006] with his wrist injury. He's performed like an All-Star player, and an All-Star teammate, and an All-Star to deal with from the front-office side."

Meanwhile, star third baseman Chipper Jones revealed the excitement he felt over the prospect of Lee joining him in Atlanta, commenting, "It doesn't get any better; Outstanding character guy; Outstanding player. Defensively at first base, he's top-notch. And he gives us another right-handed presence in the middle of our lineup."

After spending the season's final six weeks in Atlanta, Lee signed with Baltimore as a free agent prior to the start of the ensuing campaign. He then split the 2011 season between the Orioles and Pittsburgh Pirates, posting a composite batting average of .267 and totaling 19 home runs and 59 RBIs in 113 games, before announcing his retirement when he became a free agent again at season's end. Lee left the game with career totals of 331 home runs, 1,078 RBIs, 1,081 runs scored, and 1,959 hits, along with a lifetime batting average of .281. After retiring as an active player, Lee accepted a position with the Cincinnati Reds, for whom he works as an advising batting coach to scouted players.

Cub Numbers:

179 HR; 574 RBIs; 578 Runs Scored; 1,046 Hits; 239 Doubles; 10 Triples; 51 Stolen Bases; .298 AVG; .378 OBP; .524 SLG PCT; .903 OPS

Career Numbers:

331 HR; 1,078 RBIs; 1,081 Runs Scored; 1,959 Hits; 432 Doubles; 30 Triples; 104 Stolen Bases; .281 AVG; .365 OBP; .495 SLG PCT; .859 OPS

Cub Career Highlights:

Best Season: Lee had a big year for the Cubs in 2009, earning a ninth-place finish in the NL MVP voting by batting .306, scoring 91 runs, and placing near the top of the league rankings with 35 homers, 111 RBIs, a .579 slugging percentage, and a .972 OPS. Nevertheless, there is little doubt that he had his finest season in 2005, when, in addition to driving in 107 runs, he established career-high marks in home runs (46), runs scored (120), on-base percentage (.418), hits (199), doubles (50), total bases (393), batting average (.335), slugging percentage (.662), and OPS (1.080), topping the senior circuit in each of the last six categories. Lee's extraordinary performance earned him his lone Silver Slugger and a third-place finish in the NL MVP balloting. Meanwhile, his outstanding defensive work at first base also earned him Gold Glove honors.

Memorable Moments/Greatest Performances: Lee had his first big game as a member of the Cubs on May 6, 2004, when he went 5-for-5, with a homer and 5 RBIs, during a lopsided 11-3 victory over the Arizona Diamondbacks.

Lee had another 5-for-5 afternoon a little over one month later, hitting safely in all five of his trips to the plate, homering once, and driving in 2 runs, in leading the Cubs to a 15-inning, 6-5 win over the Anaheim Angels on June 13, 2004.

Lee proved to be the difference in an 8-7 victory over the Cincinnati Reds on April 27, 2005, going a perfect 4-for-4, with 2 homers and 6 RBIs.

Lee defeated Pittsburgh almost single-handedly on May 17, 2005, going 4-for-4, with a double, 2 homers, and 4 RBIs, during a 4-3 win over the Pirates. Lee delivered the game's big blow in the top of the ninth inning, when his two-run homer off Pirates closer Jose Mesa provided the margin of victory.

Lee had a huge game against Los Angeles some two weeks later, leading the Cubs to a 9-5 win over the Dodgers on June 1, 2005 by going 5-for-5, with a homer and 4 RBIs.

Lee helped pace the Cubs to a 9-5 victory over the Milwaukee Brewers on July 2, 2009 by driving in a career-high 7 runs with a pair of homers, one of those being a fourth-inning grand slam off Milwaukee reliever Chris Smith.

Lee equaled his career-high mark in RBIs some six weeks later, going 3-for-3, with a pair of doubles and 7 runs batted in, during a 17-2 mauling of the Pirates on August 14, 2009.

Lee also delivered a pair of memorable late-inning home runs in 2009, with the first of those coming on June 19, when his solo blast off former Cubs teammate Kerry Wood (his second of the contest) in the bottom of the ninth tied the score with Cleveland at 7-7. The Cubs pushed across the winning run in the ensuing frame on an RBI single by Ryan Theriot. Lee provided similar heroics on August 1, when his leadoff homer in the top of the 10th inning off Florida closer Leo Nunez provided the winning margin in a 9-8 victory over the Marlins. Lee finished the game with 4 hits, 3 RBIs, and 2 runs scored.

Notable Achievements:

- Hit more than 20 home runs five times, topping 30 homers three times and 40 homers once (46 in 2005).
- Knocked in more than 100 runs twice.
- Scored more than 100 runs once.
- Batted over .300 three times, topping the .330-mark once (.335 in 2005).
- Surpassed 30 doubles five times, topping 40 two-baggers three times and 50 two-baggers once (50 in 2005).
- Compiled on-base percentage in excess of .400 twice.
- Posted slugging percentage in excess of .500 four times, topping the .600-mark once (.662 in 2005).
- Compiled OPS in excess of 1.000 once (1.080 in 2005).
- Led NL in: batting average once, hits once, doubles once, total bases once, slugging percentage once, and OPS once.
- Finished second in NL in home runs once and runs scored once.
- Led NL first basemen in assists once.
- Ranks among Cubs career leaders in slugging percentage (fourth) and OPS (fourth).
- Two-time NL Player of the Month.
- Two-time Gold Glove winner (2005 & 2007).
- 2005 Silver Slugger winner.
- Finished third in 2005 NL MVP voting.
- Two-time NL All-Star (2005 & 2007).

29

BILL BUCKNER

His reputation sullied by an error he committed on baseball's grandest stage, Bill Buckner rarely receives the credit he deserves for being one of the finest hitters of his generation. Over the course of a twenty-two-year major league career that spanned parts of four decades, Buckner compiled a lifetime batting average of .289, accumulated more than 2,700 hits, knocked in more than 1,200 runs, won a batting title, and played for two pennant-winning teams. Particularly effective during his eight-year stay in Chicago, "Billy Bucks," as he came to be known, batted over .300 four times, surpassed 30 doubles five times, and knocked in more than 100 runs and amassed more than 200 hits once each as a member of the Cubs. Yet, in spite of his many accomplishments, the mention of Buckner's name invariably elicits images in the minds of most people of the gimpy first baseman's futile attempt at fielding Mookie Wilson's slow ground ball down the first base line, which enabled the New York Mets to complete their miraculous comeback against the Boston Red Sox in Game Six of the 1986 World Series.

Born in Vallejo, California on December 14, 1949, William Joseph Buckner grew up just a few miles north, in the city of American Canyon. Excelling in both baseball and football while attending nearby Napa High School, Buckner earned All-State honors twice on the gridiron as a wide receiver, before abandoning any thoughts of pursuing a career in football when the Los Angeles Dodgers selected him in the second round of the 1968 MLB Draft.

After signing with Los Angeles, Buckner spent most of the next three seasons in the minors, although he also appeared briefly with the Dodgers in both 1969 and 1970, earning a late-season call-up in the second of those campaigns by compiling a .335 batting average at Triple A Spokane. Arriving in the big leagues to stay in 1971, the left-handed hitting Buckner spent most of the year platooning in right field, batting .277, hitting 5 homers, and driving in 41 runs, in just over 100 games and 350 official at-bats. Continuing to assume a part-time role the following year, Buckner batted .319, hit another 5 homers, and knocked in 37 runs, while splitting his time between first base and the outfield.

A regular member of the Los Angeles starting lineup by 1973, Buckner continued to see some action at first base, although he gradually transitioned to the outfield full-time following the emergence of Steve Garvey as an All-Star caliber player. Spending most of the next four seasons manning left field for the Dodgers, Buckner batted over .300 twice, making significant contributions to Los Angeles' pennant-winning ball club of 1974 by collecting 182 hits, finishing fourth in the league with a .314 batting average, knocking in 58 runs, scoring 83 times, and stealing a career-high 31 bases as the team's primary second-place hitter. Buckner had another solid year in 1976, driving in 60 runs, scoring 76 times, placing fourth in the league with 193 hits, swiping 28 bases, and batting .301.

Yet, in spite of Buckner's strong performance, the Dodgers decided to trade him and shortstop Ivan De Jesus to the Cubs for outfielder Rick Monday and pitcher Mike Garman on January 11, 1977. Still recovering from a staph infection to his ankle he contracted the previous year, Buckner became primarily a first baseman in Chicago. Meanwhile, despite spending virtually his entire time in the Windy City playing for non-contending teams with very little offensive firepower, Buckner developed into one of the National League's most consistent hitters. Although limited by ankle woes to fewer than 125 games and 500 total plate appearances in each of his first two seasons with the Cubs, Buckner posted batting averages of .284 and .323, respectively. Somewhat healthier in 1979, Buckner appeared in 149 games, batting .284, hitting 14 homers, knocking in 66 runs, and scoring 72 times. He followed that up with his finest season to-date, concluding the 1980 campaign with 10 home runs, 68 RBIs, 69 runs scored, 187 hits, 41 doubles, and a league-leading .324 batting average.

An excellent contact hitter, Buckner proved to be one of the most difficult men in all of baseball to strike out over the course of his career, fanning a total of only 453 times in just over 10,000 total plate appearances, and never striking out more than 39 times in any single season. On the flip side, Buckner rarely walked, drawing a total of only 450 bases on balls during his career. Primarily a line-drive hitter whose power gener-

Courtesy of Craig Johnson

Bill Buckner, during his time in Boston

ally manifested itself in doubles hit to the outfield gaps, Buckner never hit more than 18 home runs in a season. However, he compiled more than 30 doubles eight times, amassing as many as 46 two-baggers once, and topping the senior circuit in that particular category on two separate occasions.

As much as Buckner endeared himself to the fans at Wrigley with his excellent hitting, he became equally popular for his grittiness, determination, and old-school approach to the game. Although the ankle woes that Buckner began experiencing right around the time he joined the Cubs grew increasingly worse during his time in Chicago, robbing him of his once excellent speed, he remained an extremely aggressive base-runner, swiping as many as 15 bags in 1982. Possessing a burning desire to succeed, Buckner refused to accept losing graciously, taking particularly hard his own personal failures. Feeling an obligation to the hometown fans, Buckner stated during one difficult stretch of games, "You're a paid performer, and you're not performing too good, and the frustrations built up inside me. We're supposed to entertain, and we weren't. People have said that ballplayers make all this money, and so they don't care how they do. I think it's the opposite. You feel a responsibility to earn the money they're paying you. And losing makes you even more frustrated."

After hitting 10 homers, driving in 75 runs, and batting .311 during the strike-shortened 1981 campaign, Buckner got off to a slow start the following year, causing his frustrations to boil over in the Cubs dugout one day in the form of a fist-fight with Chicago manager Lee Elia. In addressing the events that transpired during the unfortunate incident, Buckner later explained, "Sometimes I can laugh off losing; it's the only way to keep your sanity. And, if you're doing well personally and can look yourself in the mirror, well, it helps. But, this time, things came to a head and I exploded." Buckner added, "I'm a fierce competitor, like Lee. And I went into his office, and we straightened it out."

Following his early struggles at the plate, Buckner ended up having his most productive offensive season as a member of the Cubs in 1982, earning a 10th-place finish in the NL MVP voting by hitting 15 homers, knocking in 105 runs, scoring 93 times, collecting 201 hits, and compiling a batting average of .306. He had another good year in 1983, concluding the campaign with 16 homers, 66 RBIs, 79 runs scored, a .280 batting average, and a league-leading 38 doubles. However, after Buckner got off to another slow start in 1984, the Cubs traded him to the Boston Red Sox for Dennis Eckersley and minor league infielder Mike Brumley on May 25, bringing to an end his lengthy stay in Chicago. Extremely unhappy to be leaving the Windy City, Buckner cried at the press conference held to announce the deal. He also left Chicago feeling a considerable amount of animosity towards Cubs special assistant and scout Charlie Fox, who he blamed for campaigning to have him traded throughout the winter, commenting, "I don't like Charlie, and he doesn't like me." In response, Fox railed, "Buckner's paranoid. Who does he think he is? Does he think his stuff doesn't stink? He's not that good."

Although Buckner's ankle problems grew increasingly worse during his time in Boston, he ended up posting excellent numbers his first three years with the Red Sox, performing particularly well in 1985, when, appearing in all 162 games, he hit 16 homers, knocked in 110 runs, scored 89 times, collected 201 hits, batted .299, and stole 18 bases. He followed that up by hitting a career-high 18 homers, driving in 102 runs, and batting .267 for Boston's 1986 AL championship ball club.

Yet, even though Buckner contributed greatly to the success the Red Sox experienced over the course of that 1986 campaign, he is remembered most for the miscue he committed in the bottom of the 10th inning of Game Six of the World Series that enabled the Mets to come away with a stunning 6-5 victory. With New York already having mounted a two-out, two-run rally that tied the score at 5-5, a hobbled Buckner allowed the game-winning run to cross the plate when he permitted Mookie Wilson's slow ground ball down the first base line to dribble between his legs. After the Mets won Game Seven as well, thereby depriving the Red Sox of their first world championship since 1918, Boston fans hung Buckner in effigy. With the beleaguered first baseman receiving death threats in the mail and constantly being heckled by the fans at Fenway Park the following season, Red Sox management decided to part ways with him on July 23, 1987. Buckner signed with California five days later, after which he spent the remainder of the year serving the Angels primarily as a designated hitter. Dealt to the Royals during the early stages of the ensuing campaign, Buckner spent the next two years in Kansas City, before ironically ending his career back in Boston in 1990, after signing with the Red Sox as a free agent. Although the fans at Fenway showed Buckner that they had forgiven him for his earlier miscue by according him a standing ovation during player introductions at the home opener on April 9, the love affair proved to be short-lived since Buckner announced his retirement some two months later after batting just .186 in 48 total plate appearances.

Following his playing days, Buckner moved his family to Boise, Idaho, where he invested in real estate and opened a car dealership. He also later returned to baseball, spending three years serving as a manager and hitting instructor at the minor league level, before leaving the game for good in 2014.

Cub Numbers:

81 HR; 516 RBIs; 448 Runs Scored; 1,136 Hits; 235 Doubles; 25 Triples; 56 Stolen Bases; .300 AVG; .332 OBP; .439 SLG; .771 OPS

Career Numbers:

174 HR; 1,208 RBIs; 1,077 Runs Scored; 2,715 Hits; 498 Doubles; 49 Triples; 183 Stolen Bases; .289 AVG; .321 OBP; .408 SLG; .729 OPS

Cub Career Highlights:

Best Season: Buckner arguably played his best ball for the Cubs in 1981, when he batted .311, led the league with 35 doubles, and posted career-high marks in slugging percentage (.480) and OPS (.829). However, with a player's strike shortening the season to just 113 games, he ended up hitting only 10 homers, driving in just 75 runs, and scoring only 45 times. Although Buckner won the batting title with a mark of .324 in 1980, his other numbers (10 homers, 68 RBIs, and 69 runs scored) were not particularly impressive. That being said, the feeling here is that Buckner had his finest all-around season for the Cubs in 1982, when, appearing in 161 games and accumulating 657 official at-bats, he hit 15 homers, knocked in 105 runs, batted .306, compiled an OPS of .783, and established career-high marks in runs scored (93) and hits (201). Buckner also led all NL first basemen with 159 assists and placed second among players at his position with a career-best 1,547 putouts.

Memorable Moments/Greatest Performances: Buckner led the Cubs to a victory over his former team on August 19, 1977, when he went 4-for-5, with a pair of homers and 5 RBIs, during a 6-2 win over the Dodgers.

Although the Cubs ended up losing a 23-22, 10-inning slugfest with the Phillies at Wrigley Field on May 17, 1979 that included 3 homers by

Dave Kingman and 2 by Mike Schmidt, Buckner had a huge day at the plate, going 4-for-7, with a grand slam homer and a career-high 7 RBIs.

Buckner helped pace the Cubs to a 9-4 victory over St. Louis on August 16, 1980 by going 4-for-5, with a homer, 3 RBIs, and 3 runs scored.

Buckner contributed to a 14-0 mauling of the Phillies on September 27, 1981 by going 3-for-5, with a pair of homers, a double, 4 RBIs, and 3 runs scored.

Buckner came up just a triple shy of hitting for the cycle on August 9, 1982, when he homered twice, doubled, singled, drove in 2 runs, and scored 3 times during a 9-2 win over Montreal.

Notable Achievements:

- Batted over .300 four times.
- Knocked in more than 100 runs once (105 in 1982).
- Surpassed 200 hits once (201 in 1982).
- Surpassed 30 doubles five times, topping 40 two-baggers once (41 in 1980).
- Led NL in: batting average once, doubles twice, at-bat-per-strikeout ratio twice, and at-bats once.
- Finished second in NL in hits twice and doubles once.
- Led NL first basemen in assists twice.
- August 1982 NL Player of the Month.
- Finished 10th in NL MVP voting twice (1981 & 1982).
- 1981 NL All-Star.

30

HEINIE ZIMMERMAN

Frequently criticized for his erratic play and characterized in baseball circles as a dim-witted eccentric, Heinie Zimmerman proved to be a study in unfulfilled potential. His legacy further tarnished by his banishment from the game due to unsubstantiated rumors of game-fixing, Zimmerman rarely receives credit for being one of the National League's top performers of the Dead Ball Era. Nevertheless, the fact remains that the versatile infielder wielded one of the period's most potent bats, annually placing among the NL leaders in numerous statistical categories. The first player of the "modern era" to win the National League Triple Crown, Zimmerman accomplished the feat while playing for the Cubs in 1912, topping the senior circuit with 14 home runs, 104 RBIs, and a .372 batting average. A powerful right-handed hitter, Zimmerman batted over .300 three times and finished in double digits in triples in five of his nine full seasons in Chicago. Yet, for some reason, the media preferred to focus on his shortcomings, with *Baseball Magazine's* F. C. Lane once writing, "Zimmerman might have been the greatest player, but he wasn't. Zimmerman has not, of late years, played his best game. Any time he wishes to exert himself he has the natural ability, but his temperament has been a big handicap."

Born to German immigrant parents in the Bronx, New York on February 9, 1887, Henry Zimmerman quit school at the age of fourteen and became a plumber's apprentice to help support his family. Continuing to play ball on weekends, Zimmerman honed his baseball skills on the local sandlots, gradually developing a reputation as one of the area's finest semipro players, before beginning his professional career as a second baseman with Wilkes-Barre of the New York State League in 1906. After being purchased by the Cubs during the latter stages of the 1907 campaign, Zimmerman spent the final three weeks of the season in Chicago serving as a backup infielder, appearing in 5 games and collecting 2 hits in 9 trips to the plate.

Continuing to function as a utility player in each of the next two seasons, Zimmerman struggled somewhat in the field, committing 28 errors in a total of 111 games, while splitting his time between second, short, and third. However, the 5'11", 176-pounder displayed from the very beginning an ability to hit major-league pitching, compiling a batting average of .292 in 1908, before posting a mark of .273 the following year. Zimmerman finally began to receive more significant playing time in 1910 after starting second baseman Johnny Evers suffered an ankle injury that forced him to miss more than a month of the season. Appearing in a total of 99 games, Zimmerman hit 3 homers, knocked in 38 runs, scored 35 times, and batted .284, while committing 33 errors in the field.

With Evers missing most of the ensuing campaign as well after suffering a nervous breakdown, the twenty-four-year-old Zimmerman became a full-time starter for the first time in his career. Spending most of his time at second, although he also saw some action at shortstop and third, Zimmerman emerged as one of the Cubs' top offensive threats, finishing the year with 9 home runs, 85 RBIs, 80 runs scored, 17 triples, a .307 batting average, and a .462 slugging percentage. Still, Zimmerman's shaky defense infuriated Manager Frank Chance, who pulled him from the field and briefly suspended him for "indifferent fielding" after he committed a pair of errors during the early stages of an August 7 contest against the Boston Braves.

Shifted to third base in 1912 following the return of Evers to full-time duty, Zimmerman had the finest offensive season of his career, leading the NL with 14 home runs, 104 RBIs, 207 hits, 41 doubles, 318 total bases, a .372 batting average, a .571 slugging percentage, and a .989 OPS, while also placing near the top of the league ranking with 95 runs scored, 14 triples, and a .418 on-base percentage. Zimmerman's fabulous performance prompted the local sportswriters to begin calling him "The Great Zim," a moniker that the Cubs third baseman embraced, often referring to himself in the third person under that same nickname.

Yet, there were those who considered Zimmerman to be merely the beneficiary of good fortune in 1912, with teammate Cy Williams later telling F. C. Lane in *Baseball Magazine*, "He was as good a hitter that year as I ever saw. And what was he doing? He was swinging at balls a foot over his head and driving them safe. You can get away with murder when the luck is with you."

Joe Tinker, though, disagreed with Williams' assessment, suggesting, "Why, do you know that fellow [Zimmerman] loses more hits through hard luck catches than I make. He has the strongest pair of hands and arms that I have ever seen on a human being."

Noted for swinging at balls well out of the strike zone, Zimmerman proved to be one of the Dead Ball Era's most aggressive hitters. He also became known as a mediocre fielder and a below-average runner, although he managed to steal more than 20 bases twice for the Cubs.

More than anything, though, Zimmerman developed a reputation as being someone who lacked intelligence, failed to take his profession seriously, and spent money freely, with one observer, who noted his fetish for lavish neckties, commenting, "Zim never knew how much money he had because he made the team's secretary his banker and 'touched' the secretary for five and ten-spots until his salary was gone, then economized until the roll was replenished."

Zimmerman followed up his exceptional 1912 campaign with two more strong seasons, batting .313 and placing among the league leaders with 9 home runs, 95 RBIs, a .490 slugging percentage, and an OPS of .868 in 1913, before knocking in 87 runs, scoring 75 times, and batting .296 in 1914. However, in addition to seeing his offensive numbers fall off to just 62 RBIs, 65 runs scored, and a .265 batting average in 1915, Zimmerman found his integrity being questioned by the members of the media for the first time. Described in *The Sporting News* as "one of the most interesting problems of baseball, a player whose energy is being misdirected and talents largely wasted," Zimmerman became known throughout the league as a "bad actor" who put forth a 100 percent effort only when he felt like doing so.

Although Zimmerman rebounded somewhat the following year to drive in 64 runs, score 54 times, and bat .291 through the first four and a half months of the campaign, the Cubs, having grown weary of his lackadaisical attitude and occasional mental lapses, elected to trade him to the New York Giants for standout second baseman Larry Doyle and two lesser players on August 28, 1916. After spending the remainder of the season in New York, Zimmerman went on to play for the Giants another three years, having his finest season for them in 1917, when he batted .297 and led the

Courtesy of Bain Collection at the Library of Congress

Heinie Zimmerman won the NL Triple Crown in 1912, when
he hit 14 homers, knocked in 104 runs, and batted .372

league with 102 RBIs. Impressed with the veteran third baseman's strong performance that year, *Baseball Magazine's* F. C. Lane wrote, "Zimmerman's disposition has not always been fortunate, and his all-round record hasn't been quite what it should have been. But there is no possible doubt that he is one of the greatest natural ballplayers who ever wore a uniform."

Unfortunately, Zimmerman's triumphant season ended in nightmare fashion when he batted just .120 and committed 3 errors during New York's loss to the Chicago White Sox in the 1917 World Series, with his involvement in a botched rundown in the sixth and final game of the fall classic resulting in him being unfairly ridiculed by the press. Subsequently branded as a buffoon in the newspapers, Zimmerman emerged from the World Series bitter and disillusioned, prompting him to experience a precipitous decline in offensive production in each of the next two seasons, while also displaying even less interest in the events that transpired on the field.

Everything finally came to a head for Zimmerman after the Giants acquired first baseman Hal Chase from the Cincinnati Reds prior to the start of the 1919 campaign. With Zimmerman striking up a quick friendship with the man who had been accused of fixing games several times during his career, Giants manager John McGraw curiously suspended both players indefinitely during the latter stages of the campaign. McGraw then sealed the fate of both men at the *Black Sox* trial in September of 1920, when he testified that he had sent Chase and Zimmerman home the previous year because he had strong evidence that they had been involved in fixing games. Subsequently banned from baseball by Commissioner Kenesaw Mountain Landis, neither Zimmerman nor Chase ever appeared in another Major League game.

Lacking the skills necessary to pursue any other form of labor, Zimmerman went back to work as a plumber in the Bronx, before supplementing his income by opening a speakeasy with the famous racketeer Dutch Schultz. He later worked as a steamfitter for a construction company as well. Zimmerman lived until March 14, 1969, when he passed away in his hometown of New York City at the age of eighty-two following a brief battle with cancer.

Cub Numbers:

48 HR; 566 RBIs; 513 Runs Scored; 1,112 Hits; 210 Doubles; 80 Triples; 131 Stolen Bases; .304 AVG; .343 OBP; .444 SLG; .787 OPS.

Career Numbers:

58 HR; 796 RBIs; 695 Runs Scored; 1,566 Hits; 275 Doubles; 105 Triples; 175 Stolen Bases; .295 AVG; .331 OBP; .419 SLG; .750 OPS.

Cub Career Highlights:

Best Season: Zimmerman unquestionably had the greatest season of his career in 1912, when he ranked among the NL leaders in 11 different offensive categories, leading the league in eight of those. Yet, even though the Cubs finished a very respectable third in the senior circuit, 11 ½ games behind the pennant-winning Giants, with Zimmerman winning the Triple Crown by leading the league with 14 home runs, 104 RBIs, and a .372 batting average, the Chicago third baseman surprisingly finished just sixth in the NL MVP voting.

Memorable Moments/Greatest Performances: Zimmerman helped the Cubs complete a doubleheader sweep of the Philadelphia Phillies on August 16, 1913 by leading them to an 8-3 victory in Game Two with 4 hits, a pair of homers, and 6 RBIs.

Zimmerman had another big day at the plate on May 31, 1914, going a perfect 3-for-3, with 2 doubles, 6 RBIs, and 1 run scored, during a lopsided 11-1 victory over the Cardinals.

Zimmerman had an extremely productive afternoon on July 23, 1914, when he led the Cubs to a 15-8 rout of the Phillies by going 4-for-5, with 3 RBIs and 4 runs scored.

However, Zimmerman had the biggest day of his career on June 11, 1911, when he paced the Cubs to a 20-2 win over the Boston Braves by driving in a franchise-record 9 runs with a pair of homers, a triple, and a single. Zimmerman also scored 4 times and stole a base during the game.

Notable Achievements:

- Finished in double digits in home runs once (14 in 1912).
- Knocked in more than 100 runs once (104 in 1912).

- Batted over .300 three times, topping the .370-mark once (.372 in 1912).
- Topped 200 hits once (207 in 1912).
- Finished in double digits in triples five times.
- Surpassed 30 doubles twice, topping 40 two-baggers once (41 in 1912).
- Stole more than 20 bases twice.
- Compiled on-base percentage in excess of .400 once (.418 in 1912).
- Posted slugging percentage in excess of .500 once (.571 in 1912).
- Led NL in: home runs once, RBIs twice, batting average once, hits once, doubles once, total bases once, slugging percentage once, and OPS once.
- Ranks among Cubs career leaders in triples (tied-10th).
- 1912 NL Triple Crown winner.
- Finished sixth in 1912 NL MVP voting.
- Three-time NL champion (1907, 1908 & 1910).
- Two-time world champion (1907 & 1908).

31

CHARLIE GRIMM

Nicknamed "Jolly Cholly" for his pleasant demeanor and upbeat personality, Charlie Grimm spent nearly fifty years serving the Cubs in one capacity or another. In addition to starting at first base for Chicago for 10 seasons, Grimm spent parts of 14 seasons managing the Cubs, leading them to three pennants and an overall record of 946-782 during that time. Grimm also served the Cubs as a broadcaster and front office executive, bringing joy to everyone with whom he came into contact in each position. Focusing here on his playing career, Grimm spent 12 of his 20 big-league seasons in Chicago, first joining the Cubs in 1925, after manning first base for the Pittsburgh Pirates the previous six years. An exceptional defender, Grimm led all NL first sackers in fielding percentage seven times, doing so on four separate occasions as a member of the Cubs. A solid hitter as well, Grimm batted over .300 four times and knocked in more than 80 runs three times during his time in Chicago. However, Grimm perhaps made his greatest contributions to the Cubs with his on-field leadership, spending his first several seasons in Chicago serving as team captain, before eventually transitioning into the role of player-manager, and, finally, manager.

Born in St. Louis, Missouri on August 28, 1898, Charles John Grimm developed a love of baseball at an early age. After dropping out of school at the age of twelve, Grimm began his lengthy association with Major League Baseball in an ancillary role, recalling years later, "On the weekends, I worked as a peanut vendor in old Robison Field, the Cardinals' park on Natural Bridge Road. That's where I really got started, shagging flies for the ballplayers before the games."

Grimm continued to develop his baseball skills while serving as Cardinals bat boy, eventually displaying so much potential that the Philadelphia Athletics signed him to a contract on July 28, 1916. Still only seventeen years old at the time, Grimm appeared in 12 games with the Athletics, before being sold to the Durham Bulls of the Class D North Carolina State League. After spending the next year-and-a-half in the minor leagues, Grimm joined the Cardinals in 1918, compiling a batting average of .220 in 50 games with his hometown team. He subsequently spent most of the ensuing campaign playing first base for the Little Rock Travelers of the Class A Southern Association, before being sold to the Pittsburgh Pirates, for whom he posted a .318 batting average in 14 games during the month of September.

Claiming Pittsburgh's starting first base job in 1920, Grimm struggled at the bat in his first full big-league season, driving in just 54 runs, scoring only 38 times, and batting just .227. However, he gradually developed into a solid offensive performer over the course of the next four seasons, having his biggest year at the plate for the Pirates in 1923, when he hit 7 homers, knocked in 99 runs, scored 78 times, and batted .345. The 5'11", 175-pound Grimm, who threw and batted left-handed, also emerged as arguably the National League's finest defensive first baseman during his time in Pittsburgh, leading all players at his position in fielding percentage three times, putouts once, and double plays once.

Yet, even though Grimm performed well for the Pirates on the field, team owner Barney Dreyfuss believed that his fun-loving ways proved to be too much of a distraction for his ball club. As a result, Dreyfus included Grimm in a six-player trade he completed with the Cubs on October 27, 1924 that sent the first baseman, future Hall of Fame infielder Rabbit Maranville, and pitcher Wilbur Cooper to Chicago, in exchange for pitcher Vic Aldridge, infielder George Grantham, and first base prospect Al Niehaus.

Although the Cubs finished last in the National League in 1925, Grimm found his new home very much to his liking, being named team captain his first year in Chicago. One of the few bright spots of an otherwise dismal campaign, Grimm hit a career-high 10 home runs, batted .306, and led the Cubs with 76 RBIs and a .354 on-base percentage. Grimm continued to post solid numbers in each of the next three seasons as the Cubs gradually emerged as pennant contenders, averaging 73 RBIs and 64 runs scored during that time, while compiling batting averages of .277, .311, and .294. Meanwhile, Grimm's exceptional glove work earned him a reputation as the senior circuit's finest defensive first baseman, with noted

Courtesy of Charlie Grimm

Charlie Grimm spent nearly half a century in Chicago
serving the Cubs in one capacity or another

baseball historian Bill James calling him "perhaps the best ever" defender at the position decades later.

Grimm's steady play and on-field leadership made him extremely popular with his teammates and the local fans. But it was his gregarious manner and affable nature that eventually helped him to become one of the most beloved players in franchise history. In addition to serenading fans before games with his singing and banjo playing, Grimm brought smiles to the faces of everyone with his comedic actions during contests. As renowned sportswriter and publisher J. G. Taylor Spink wrote in a 1945 edition of *The Sporting News*, "Charlie is a skilled mimic. Without any studied effort, he can imitate the walk, talk and actions of almost anyone in the National League. His impersonations of umpires keep the fans in stitches and give the players and fellow umpires many a chuckle (when he is not mimicking them)."

In discussing his on-field antics in his 1968 autobiography, Grimm wrote, "I had fun playing baseball. I tried to make it fun for my players after I became manager. I was 'Jolly Cholly,' and I always thought a pat on the back, an encouraging word, or a wisecrack paid off a lot more than a brilliantly executed work of strategy."

Although Grimm took a backseat to superstar teammates Rogers Hornsby and Hack Wilson during Chicago's pennant-winning campaign of 1929, he very quietly had one of his finest all-around seasons, finishing the year with 10 home runs, 91 RBIs, and a .298 batting average, despite missing 35 games in August and September with a broken hand. He followed that up with two more strong seasons, performing particularly well in 1931, when he knocked in 66 runs, batted .331, and compiled a career-high .393 on-base percentage. After team ownership expanded his role to that of player-manager in 1932, Grimm ended up leading the Cubs to the league championship, concluding the campaign with 7 homers, 80 RBIs, and a .307 batting average. Commenting on Grimm's managerial style years later, Cubs Vice President of Business Operations, E. R. Saltwell, noted, "The thing about Charlie is that he always saw something good in everything, no matter what the situation may be. He was never one to get down on himself or the players. He seemed to draw the best out in them."

Even though Grimm appeared in as many as 100 games in just one of the next four seasons, he continued to function in the dual role of player-manager until 1936, when he announced his retirement as an active player. During that time, Grimm led the Cubs to another NL pennant, doing so in 1935, when he started just two games at first base. Grimm remained manager in Chicago until July 20, 1938, when ownership replaced him at the helm with Gabby Hartnett.

Grimm subsequently spent the next four decades fulfilling various roles in the national pastime, primarily as a member of the Cubs organization. After spending three years in the broadcast booth, Grimm rejoined the Cubs as a coach in 1941. He then managed the American Association's Milwaukee Brewers for two years, before returning to Chicago to manage the Cubs in 1944. After guiding the Cubs to another pennant in 1945, Grimm continued to manage them until 1949, when he accepted a position as the team's vice president in charge of player operations. However, he left that post shortly thereafter, spending most of the next 13 seasons serving either as a manager or a coach at various levels. After a brief return to the broadcast booth, Grimm rejoined the Cubs' front office in 1964, remaining there until 1981, when he retired from the game. Grimm lived another two years, passing away at eighty-five years of age, on November 15, 1983, following a lengthy battle with cancer. After spending most of his adult life as a member of the Cubs organization, Grimm became part of Wrigley Field as well, with his wife subsequently adhering to his last wish by having his ashes scattered about the ballpark.

Cub Numbers:

61 HR; 696 RBIs; 596 Runs Scored; 1,454 Hits; 270 Doubles; 43 Triples; 26 Stolen Bases; .296 AVG; .349 OBP; .405 SLG; .755 OPS.

Career Numbers:

79 HR; 1,077 RBIs; 908 Runs Scored; 2,299 Hits; 394 Doubles; 108 Triples; 57 Stolen Bases; .290 AVG; .341 OBP; .397 SLG; .738 OPS.

Cub Career Highlights:

Best Season: Although Grimm compiled slightly better overall numbers in two or three other years, he made his greatest overall impact on the Cubs in 1932. In addition to hitting 7 homers, driving in 80 runs, scoring 66 times, batting .307, amassing 175 hits and 42 doubles, and recording a career-high 123 assists at first base, Grimm guided the Cubs to a record of 37-18 over the final two months of the campaign after replacing Rogers Hornsby as manager, enabling them to edge out the Pittsburgh Pirates for the National League pennant by four games.

Memorable Moments/Greatest Performances: Not known for his home-run hitting prowess, Grimm homered twice in one game just two times during his career, accomplishing the feat for the first time on June 13, 1925, when his two solo blasts gave the Cubs a 2-0 victory over the Boston Braves. Grimm again went deep twice in the same contest during a 9-4 win over Brooklyn on May 7, 1929.

Grimm had a big day at the plate on April 24, 1925, when he helped lead the Cubs to a 7-2 victory over the Pittsburgh Pirates by going 4-for-4, with a double, a pair of triples, 2 RBIs, and 2 runs scored.

Grimm had another 4-for-4 afternoon some six weeks later, on June 4, 1925, when, during an 11-9 win over Brooklyn, he homered, doubled, singled twice, drove in 4 runs, and scored 3 times.

Grimm posted nearly identical numbers on August 13, 1925, when he led the Cubs to an 8-5 victory over St. Louis by going 4-for-4, with a homer, double, 4 RBIs, and 2 runs scored.

Grimm had his biggest day of the 1926 campaign on April 23, when he went 4-for-4, with 4 RBIs and 1 run scored, during an 18-1 pasting of the Cincinnati Reds.

Grimm collected 5 hits in one game for one of two times in his career on June 18, 1928, when he led the Cubs to a lopsided 12-0 victory over the Boston Braves by going 5-for-6, with 3 RBIs and 2 runs scored.

However, Grimm topped that performance on June 21, 1931, when he had the only 5-for-5 day of his career, hitting safely in all 5 trips to the plate during a 7-6 loss to Brooklyn.

An outstanding postseason performer over the course of his career, Grimm posted a composite batting average of .364 in his two World Series with the Cubs. After batting .389, with a homer and 4 RBIs, against Philadelphia in the 1929 fall classic, Grimm batted .333 against the Yankees in the 1932 Series.

Notable Achievements:

- Batted over .300 four times, topping the .330-mark once (.331 in 1931).
- Finished in double digits in triples once (11 in 1931).
- Surpassed 30 doubles three times, topping 40 two-baggers once (42 in 1932).
- Led NL first basemen in double plays once and fielding percentage four times.
- Ranks among MLB career leaders in putouts (fifth) and double plays (seventh) by a first baseman.
- Finished eighth in 1931 NL MVP voting.
- Three-time NL champion (1929, 1932 & 1935).

32

BRUCE SUTTER

Referred to as "The Sandy Koufax of relievers" by St. Louis Cardinals manager Whitey Herzog, Bruce Sutter perfected and popularized the split-fingered fastball, establishing himself in the process as one of the greatest relief pitchers in baseball history. Over the course of his Hall of Fame career, Sutter became the only hurler to lead the National League in saves five times, retiring from the game in 1988 with 300 saves, which represented the third-highest total in history at the time. Spending his first five big league seasons in Chicago, Sutter earned four All-Star selections, two top-10 finishes in the NL MVP voting, and one Cy Young award as a member of the Cubs, before continuing his dominance in St .Louis, where he earned two more All-Star nominations, three more top-10 finishes in the league MVP balloting, and three top-five finishes in the Cy Young voting. The first pitcher to gain admittance to Cooperstown without starting a single game in the Major Leagues, Sutter compiled an ERA of less than 2.00 twice, recorded more strikeouts than innings pitched three times, and posted a WHIP under 1.000 twice, en route to earning NL Fireman of the Year honors on four separate occasions.

Born in Lancaster, Pennsylvania on January 8, 1953, Howard Bruce Sutter attended Donegal High School in nearby Mount Joy, where he played baseball, football, and basketball, serving as captain of the basketball squad and quarterback and captain of the football team. After choosing not to sign with the Washington Senators when they selected him in the twenty-first round of the 1970 amateur draft, Sutter briefly attended Old Dominion University. However, he ultimately elected to put his education on hold by signing with the Chicago Cubs as an undrafted free agent in 1971.

Sutter's professional career nearly ended before it began when he injured his arm while pitching in the minor leagues in 1973. Subsequently forced to undergo surgery to relieve a pinched nerve in his elbow, the young right-hander pitched ineffectively when he returned to the mound a year later, prompting the Cubs to seriously consider releasing him. However, minor league pitching instructor Fred Martin ended up saving Sutter's career by suggesting to him that he try throwing a forkball—a changeup in which the pitcher holds the ball with the index and third fingers split far apart. Sutter, though, had such huge hands that he turned the forkball into something else: a fastball with a devastating late sink. Fellow minor leaguer Mike Krukow, who also learned the pitch from Martin but never felt comfortable throwing it, later recalled, "He [Sutter] threw that thing all the time. As soon as I saw him throw it, I knew he was going to the big leagues."

After spending the next two years dominating minor league hitters, Sutter arrived in Chicago in May of 1976. Performing well for the Cubs over the season's final five months while continuing to fine-tune the pitch he relied on most heavily, the twenty-three-year-old rookie appeared in 52 games, compiling a record of 6-3, with 10 saves, a 2.70 ERA, and 73 strikeouts in 83⅓ innings of work. Sutter followed that up with a brilliant sophomore campaign in which he earned his first of five straight All-Star selections and a seventh-place finish in the NL MVP voting by going 7-3 with a 1.34 ERA, striking out 129 batters in 107⅓ innings of work, and finishing second in the senior circuit with 31 saves. Sutter performed so well for the Cubs over the course of that 1977 season that bumper stickers around Chicago read "Only The Lord Saves More Than Sutter." However, the Cubs used Sutter so frequently that they eventually had to shut him down with arm stiffness toward the end of the year, ruining any chance they had of winning the pennant.

Perhaps still a bit arm weary in 1978, Sutter saw his record fall to 8-10 and his ERA rise to 3.18. Nevertheless, he remained one of the game's top closers, ranking among the league leaders with 27 saves and striking out 106 batters in 99 innings pitched. Fully recovered by 1979, Sutter earned NL Cy Young honors and a seventh-place finish in the league MVP balloting by posting 6 victories, compiling an ERA of 2.22, topping the senior circuit with 37 saves, and striking out 110 batters in 101⅓ innings of work, while allowing the opposition just 67 hits and 32 bases on balls.

Courtesy of MEARS Online Auctions

Bruce Sutter earned NL Cy Young honors
while pitching for the Cubs in 1979

Sutter's dominance of National League hitters made a strong impression on teammates and opponents alike, with Cubs manager Herman Franks proclaiming, "He's the greatest relief pitcher that I've seen in my forty-five years of baseball."

In discussing Sutter's split-fingered fastball, Montreal Expos skipper Dick Williams suggested, "It's unhittable, unless he hangs it, and he never does. It's worse than trying to hit a knuckleball."

Cubs starting pitcher Ray Burris later commented, "He was lights out when he came in. As a starter, you knew if you got into the seventh or eighth inning that the game was pretty well sealed."

Meanwhile, Larry Bowa, who spent much of his career trying to hit against Sutter as a member of the Phillies and, later, the Cubs, stated, "I've never seen anybody, for a guy who didn't throw in the 90s…I've never seen anybody embarrass the big hitters like he (Sutter) did. He'd make them swing and miss at pitches that just disappeared out of the zone."

The thing that made Sutter's primary offering so devastating was that the ball came out of his hand with a spinning action that made it indistinguishable from a fastball. Yet, as the pitch appeared to be headed towards the strike zone as it approached home plate, it dropped clear out of the hitting zone some five feet away from the plate.

Although somewhat less dominant in 1980, Sutter had another excellent year, posting 5 victories, compiling an ERA of 2.64, leading the league with 28 saves, and recording 76 strikeouts in 102⅓ innings of work. Yet, in spite of his outstanding performance, the Cubs elected to send him to St. Louis at season's end when the bullpen-needy Cardinals came calling with a package of three players that included top prospect Leon Durham and slick-fielding third baseman Ken Reitz.

Sutter continued to excel in St. Louis, leading the National League in saves in three of the next four seasons, en route to earning two more All-Star selections, a pair of third-place finishes in the Cy Young voting, and three NL Reliever of the Year Awards. Particularly effective in 1984, Sutter compiled a brilliant 1.54 ERA and established career-high marks in innings pitched (122⅔) and saves (45), tying the single-season major league record in the last category in the process. He also helped the Cardinals capture the world championship in 1982 by recording a save and working 4⅓ perfect innings against Atlanta in the NLCS, before posting one win and two saves against Milwaukee in the World Series.

Sutter's magnificent pitching during his time in St. Louis prompted Cardinals manager Whitey Herzog to say, "He had the best makeup of any closer I've ever seen. He just cut the percentages down for me from 27 outs a game to 21."

Cardinals second baseman Tom Herr added, "I don't think people grasp how impressive it was for him to go two or three innings for a save. When you have to get six, seven, or eight outs, so many things can go wrong for a closer."

A free agent at the conclusion of the 1984 campaign, Sutter signed with the Atlanta Braves, with whom he spent the remainder of his career, never experiencing the same level of success. After saving only 23 games and compiling an inordinately high ERA of 4.48 in 1985, Sutter experienced arm problems that limited him to just 16 games the following year and forced him to miss the entire 1987 season. Ineffective again when he returned to action in 1988, Sutter elected to call it quits at the end of the year. In addition to totaling 300 saves, he ended his career with a record of 68-71 and an ERA of 2.83.

Looking back on his place in history and the manner in which the role of the closer has evolved through the years, Sutter, who became a minor league consultant for the Philadelphia Phillies in 2010, told *The USA Today* in 2005, "It's not good or bad, but closers have changed things. I don't think you are going to win a World Series without one. Where would the Yankees be without Mariano Rivera? Pitching two innings and coming back the next day—that's the stuff we did all season. Saves are not easy, but I think they are easier now. I warmed up in the seventh and maybe pitched. Then, in the eighth and maybe pitched. Lee Smith, Goose Gossage and I got a lot of seven-out saves."

Cub Numbers:

Record: 32-30; .516 Win Pct.; 2.39 ERA; 133 Saves; 493 IP; 494 SO; 1.055 WHIP

Career Numbers:

Record: 68-71; .489 Win Pct.; 2.83 ERA; 300 Saves; 1,042⅓ IP; 861 SO; 1.140 WHIP

Cub Career Highlights:

Best Season: Sutter performed brilliantly for the Cubs in his Cy Young campaign of 1979, going 6-6, with a 2.22 ERA, a league-leading 37 saves, and a WHIP of 0.977, while striking out 110 batters in 101⅓ innings of work. Nevertheless, he proved to be even a bit more dominant two years earlier, when, despite missing more than a month of the season with arm stiffness, he finished 7-3, with 31 saves and career-best marks in ERA (1.34) and WHIP (0.857). Sutter also struck out 129 batters and surrendered only 23 bases on balls, in 107⅓ innings of work, giving him a magnificent strikeout-to-walk ratio of better than 5-to-1. Particularly effective during the season's first half, Sutter compiled an ERA of 0.77 by the All-Star break, prompting former teammate Bill Buckner to later say, "In that first half of '77, Bruce was the most dominating pitcher I've ever seen. His ball broke straight down, and it felt like a six inning game for us."

Memorable Moments/Greatest Performances: Sutter earned a nine-out save on July 6, 1976, allowing no hits, 1 walk, and recording 5 strikeouts during a 4-0 win over San Diego.

Sutter performed heroically against St. Louis on June 1, 1977, surrendering 4 hits and 1 run over 5 innings, in a game the Cubs eventually won by a score of 4-3 in 13 innings. Sutter also recorded a career-high 9 strikeouts during the contest.

Sutter helped the Cubs defeat Cincinnati by a score of 16-15 in 13 innings on July 28, 1977 by tossing 3 hitless innings during which he yielded just 1 walk and recorded 6 strikeouts.

Yet, Sutter turned in his most memorable performance of the 1977 campaign on September 8, when he worked the final three frames of a 3-2, 10-inning win over Montreal, allowing just 1 hit and striking out 6 in earning the victory. Particularly dominant in his second inning of work, Sutter fanned sluggers Ellis Valentine, Gary Carter, and Larry Parrish on just 9 pitches in the ninth, making him the 12th NL pitcher in history to accomplish the 9-strike/3 strikeout half inning.

Sutter turned in another overpowering performance on May 12, 1978, when he worked 2⅓ perfect innings, striking out 5 of the 7 batters he faced, in picking up a save during a 9-7 win over the Dodgers.

Sutter proved to be equally dominant on June 26, 1978, when he fanned 5 of the 6 batters he faced, in earning a two-inning save during a 10-9 victory over the Mets.

Notable Achievements:

- Saved more than 25 games four times, topping 30 saves twice.
- Compiled ERA below 3.00 four times, posting mark under 2.00 once (1.34 in 1977).
- Compiled winning percentage of .700 in 1977.
- Threw more than 100 innings three times.
- Struck out more than 100 batters three times.
- Recorded more strikeouts than innings pitched three times.
- Posted WHIP under 1.000 twice.
- Led NL pitchers in saves twice.
- Finished second in NL with 31 saves in 1977.
- Ranks among Cubs career leaders in saves (second) and games finished (fourth).
- May 1977 NL Pitcher of the Month.
- 1979 NL Cy Young Award winner.
- 1979 *Sporting News* NL Fireman of the Year.
- 1979 Rolaids NL Relief Man of the Year.
- Finished in top 10 in NL MVP voting twice (1977 & 1979).
- Four-time NL All-Star (1977, 1978, 1979 & 1980).
- Elected to Baseball Hall of Fame by members of BBWAA in 2006.

33

LEE SMITH

Described by Pulitzer Prize-winning sportswriter Jim Murray in 1995 as "the best one-inning pitcher the game ever saw," Lee Smith spent his first eight big league seasons in Chicago, during which time he recorded more saves (180) than anyone else in franchise history. Working out of the Cubs' bullpen from 1980 to 1987, Smith surpassed 30 saves in each of his final four years in the Windy City, while also throwing more than 100 innings three times and recording more than 100 strikeouts once. Along the way, Smith established himself as arguably the most intimidating reliever of his time, with his imposing 6'6", 245-pound frame, cold stare, and 95 mph fastball weakening the knees of many an opposing batter. Remaining one of the top closers in the game after he left Chicago, Smith went on to save a total of 478 games for eight different teams over the course of his career, retiring in 1997 as the number one man on the all-time saves list.

Born in Shreveport, Louisiana on December 4, 1957, Lee Arthur Smith grew up some 50 miles southeast, in the small town of Jamestown, where he attended Castor High School. Looking back at the early stages of his athletic career, Smith recalled in Kevin Neary's book, *Closer: Major League Players Reveal the Inside Pitch on Saving the Game*:

> *"My first love was actually basketball, and I loved the Philadelphia 76ers with Bobby Jones, Dr. J, Moses Malone, and Maurice Cheeks....I was forced into playing baseball. I went to a very small high school growing up, and we didn't have enough guys to field the team, and that is why I had to play, so this way we had enough. With basketball you didn't need many things and, because my family didn't have much money, I grew up playing basketball. That is why I didn't get the chance to really know the game of baseball until I made it to the big leagues. I never played*

Little League, and I only played one year of baseball in high school."

Courtesy of Prisitne Auction

Lee Smith saved more games than
anyone else in franchise history

Scouted for the Cubs by legendary Negro League player and manager Buck O'Neil while in high school, Smith turned pro after Chicago selected him in the second round of the 1975 MLB draft with the twenty-eighth overall pick. He subsequently spent his first four minor league seasons working as a starter, before finally being converted into a reliever while pitching for the Double A Midland Cubs in 1979. After excelling at the Triple A level for the first five months of the ensuing campaign, Smith joined the Cubs in September, making a favorable impression on team management during the season's final month by winning his only two decisions, compiling an ERA of 2.91, and recording 17 strikeouts in 21⅔ innings of work.

A regular member of Chicago's bullpen in 1981, Smith served the Cubs primarily as a middle-inning reliever, going 3-6 with an ERA of 3.51, logging 50 strikeouts in 66⅔ innings pitched, and earning his first major league save. Smith really began to come into his own the following season after his boyhood idol, Ferguson Jenkins, returned to the Cubs after an eight-year absence. Later crediting Jenkins with simplifying his delivery, introducing him to the slider and forkball, and teaching him how to set up hitters, Smith assumed a more prominent role in 1982, when, sharing closing duties with Willie Hernandez and Bill Campbell, he posted 17 saves, compiled a record of 2-5 and an ERA of 2.69, and struck out 99 batters in 117 innings.

Emerging as one of baseball's top closers in 1983, Smith earned the first of his seven All-Star selections by compiling an ERA of 1.65, recording 91 strikeouts in 103⅓ innings of work, and leading the league with 29 saves and 56 games finished. Unfortunately, the Cubs performed dismally, finishing fifth in the NL East with an unseemly record of 71-91. As a result, Smith concluded the campaign with a personal mark of just 4-10. Nevertheless, his excellent pitching earned him a point in the NL Cy Young voting and eight points in the league MVP balloting.

Smith's rise to prominence coincided with his emergence as one of the most feared relief pitchers in the game, with one player telling writers Bruce Nash and Allan Zullo for their book, *Baseball Confidential*, that he considered one of the most daunting sights in the majors to be Smith throwing "pure gas from the shadows" of Wrigley Field, which did not have lights at the time. Meanwhile, fellow closer Kent Tekulve said, "Everything that Lee Smith did in his entire career was in slow motion, except what he did on the pitcher's mound. That is where he scared the shit out of the hitters. It was never fun to face Lee Smith!"

Although Smith's ERA rose to 3.65 in 1984, he helped the Cubs capture the NL East title by winning nine games, saving 33 others, and striking out 86 batters in 101 innings of work. However, he subsequently experienced the darkest moment of his career against San Diego in the NLCS, when, after earning a save in Game Two, he surrendered a two-run homer to Steve Garvey in the bottom of the ninth inning of Game Four that gave the Padres a series-tying 7-5 victory. San Diego went on to win Game Five as well, earning in the process a trip to the World Series.

With the Cubs posting a losing record in each of the next three seasons, Smith proved to be one of the team's few bright spots, amassing a total of 100 saves, while ranking among the league leaders in that category each year. Performing particularly well in 1985, Smith compiled a record of 7-4 and an ERA of 3.04, finished second in the league with 33 saves, and recorded a career-high 112 strikeouts in 97⅔ innings of work. He earned his second All-Star selection two years later by saving 36 games and striking out 96 batters over 83⅓ innings.

Although Smith's 36 saves in 1987 made him just the second pitcher, after Dan Quisenberry, to reach the 30-mark in four consecutive seasons, Chicago's growing concern over his increased weight and its effect on his knees, along with the veteran reliever's purported interest in playing for another team, prompted the Cubs to seek a viable trade partner for his services. GM Jim Frey finally pulled the trigger on a deal on December 8, 1987, when he traded Smith to the Boston Red Sox for pitchers Al Nipper and Calvin Schiraldi. In addition to saving a franchise record 180 games during his time in Chicago, Smith compiled an overall record of 40-51 and an ERA of 2.92 as a member of the Cubs.

While Nipper and Schiraldi subsequently accomplished very little during their relatively brief stays in the Windy City, Smith went on to save another 298 games for seven different teams over the course of the next 10 seasons, earning five more All-Star selections and three top-five finishes in the Cy Young voting along the way. Performing particularly well for the Cardinals in 1991 and 1992, Smith earned a runner-up finish in the Cy Young balloting in the first of those campaigns by going 6-3, with a 2.34 ERA and a league-leading and career-best 47 saves. He followed that up by topping the senior circuit with 43 saves in 1992, earning in the process a fourth-place finish in the Cy Young voting. After spending parts of the next five seasons with the Cardinals, Yankees, Orioles, Angels, Reds and Expos, Smith announced his retirement when Montreal released him during the latter stages of the 1997 campaign. He ended his career with 478 saves, which remained the major-league record until Trevor Hoffman surpassed it in 2006. Following his playing days, Smith accepted a position as a roving minor league pitching instructor for the San Francisco Giants—a post he continues to hold.

Cub Numbers:

Record: 40-51; .440 Win Pct.; 2.92 ERA; 180 Saves; 681⅓ IP; 644 SO; 1.255 WHIP

Career Numbers:

Record: 71-92; .436 Win Pct.; 3.03 ERA; 478 Saves; 1,289⅓ IP; 1,251 SO; 1.256 WHIP

Cub Career Highlights:

Best Season: Even though Smith concluded the 1983 campaign with a record of just 4-10, he pitched his best ball for the Cubs that year. In addition to leading the National League with 29 saves, Smith posted career-best marks in ERA (1.65) and WHIP 1.074, struck out 91 batters over 103⅓ innings, and yielded only 70 hits to the opposition, earning in the process one of his two All-Star selections as a member of the team and *Sporting News* NL Fireman of the Year honors for the only time.

Memorable Moments/Greatest Performances: Smith earned a nine-out save on April 24, 1985, surrendering just 2 hits and recording 5 strikeouts over the final three frames of a 5-2 victory over the Pittsburgh Pirates.

Smith turned in a dominant performance against Philadelphia on July 1, 1985, picking up a save during a 3-1 win over the Phillies by yielding 1 hit, 1 walk, and striking out 5 in his 2 innings of work.

Although the Cubs ended up losing their May 21, 1986 matchup with the Braves by a score of 9-8 in 13 innings, Smith performed heroically in relief, surrendering just 2 hits and 1 walk over 3⅔ scoreless frames.

Smith dominated Dodger batsmen on July 11, 1986, saving a 6-3 win for Scott Sanderson by allowing just 1 hit and striking out 5 over the final 2 innings.

Notable Achievements:

- Saved more than 30 games four times, saving 29 games one other time.
- Won 9 games twice.
- Compiled ERA below 3.00 three times, posting mark under 2.00 once (1.65 in 1983).
- Threw more than 100 innings three times.
- Struck out more than 100 batters once (112 in 1985).
- Recorded more strikeouts than innings pitched three times.
- Led NL pitchers in saves once and games finished twice.
- Finished second in NL in saves three times.
- Holds Cubs career records for most saves (180) and most games finished (342).

- Ranks among Cubs career leaders in pitching appearances (third) and strikeouts per nine innings pitched (seventh).
- Ranks third all-time in MLB history in career saves (478).
- Finished ninth in 1983 NL Cy Young voting.
- 1983 *Sporting News* NL Fireman of the Year.
- Two-time NL All-Star (1983 & 1987).

34

GLENN BECKERT

Extremely consistent, both in the field and at the bat, Glenn Beckert spent nine seasons in Chicago, during which time he served as a member of arguably the most famous infield in the rich history of the Cubs. A solid offensive player, Beckert topped 180 hits and 90 runs scored three times each, while also compiling a batting average in excess of .280 six straight times at one point, including posting a mark of .342 in 1971 that placed him third in the NL rankings. Teaming up with longtime double play partner Don Kessinger in the middle of the diamond, Beckert also established himself as one of the senior circuit's most reliable second basemen, annually placing among the top players at his position in putouts, assists, and double plays, en route to earning one Gold Glove and four consecutive All-Star selections.

Born in Pittsburgh, Pennsylvania on October 12, 1940, Glenn Alfred Beckert attended local Perry High School, before enrolling at Allegheny College, situated some ninety miles north of his hometown, in the city of Meadville. After spending the next four years starring at shortstop for the Gators, Beckert turned pro when the Boston Red Sox signed him as an amateur free agent in 1962. Subsequently plucked from Boston's farm system by the Cubs in the winter of 1962-63 in what was then called the "first-year draft," Beckert continued to play shortstop in the minor leagues for another two years, leading the Pacific Coast League in both putouts and assists in 1964, before being moved to second base by the Cubs in the spring of 1965 in an effort to solidify their infield following the death of former NL Rookie of the Year Ken Hubbs, who tragically lost his life in a plane crash one year earlier.

Although the right-handed hitting Beckert struggled at the plate in his first big-league season, batting just .239, with 3 homers, 30 RBIs, and 73 runs scored, he did an excellent job in the field, leading all NL second

Courtesy of MEARS Online Auctions

Glenn Beckert finished third in the NL
with a career-high .342 batting average in 1971

basemen with 494 assists, while also finishing fourth in putouts and second
in double plays turned. Far more comfortable at the bat in his sophomore
campaign of 1966, Beckert compiled a batting average of .287, knocked
in 59 runs, and collected 188 hits, which represented the fourth-highest
total in the senior circuit. Gradually assuming the number two spot in the
Cubs' batting order over the course of the season, Beckert struck out only
36 times in nearly 700 total plate appearances, beginning in the process a
four-year run during which he led the league in at-bat-to-strikeout ratio.

After another solid year in 1967, one in which he batted .280, scored 91 runs, and established career-high marks in homers (5) and doubles (32), Beckert earned a ninth-place finish in the NL MVP voting in 1968 by topping the circuit with 98 runs scored, while also finishing among the league leaders with 189 hits and a .294 batting average. Meanwhile, Beckert's outstanding defensive work at second base earned him Gold Glove honors for the only time in his career. Battling through injuries in each of the next two seasons, Beckert continued to display remarkable consistency, earning his first two All-Star selections by posting batting averages of .291 and .288, while scoring a career-high 99 runs in 1970.

Beckert's ability to put the ball in play made him an excellent second-place hitter, even though he rarely walked, drawing as many as 30 bases on balls just four times his entire career. Fanning only 243 times in nearly 5,600 total plate appearances over 11 big-league seasons, Beckert proved to be the most difficult player of his era to strike out. He also did an outstanding job of hitting behind the runner, often allowing sluggers Billy Williams and Ron Santo to step into the batter's box with men in scoring position. Meanwhile, Beckert worked extremely well in the field with shortstop Don Kessinger, giving the Cubs arguably the National League's top double play tandem of the period. In fact, Beckert and Kessinger joined first baseman Ernie Banks and third sacker Ron Santo in giving the Cubs baseball's most recognizable infield of the mid-to-late 1960s, with all four men starting virtually every game together from 1965 to 1969.

After batting somewhere between .280 and .294 in each of the previous five seasons, Beckert had his best year at the plate in 1971, concluding the campaign with a mark of .342 that placed him third in the National League, behind only Joe Torre (.363) and Ralph Garr (.343). Despite missing nearly a month of action due to injury, Beckert also scored 80 runs and collected 181 hits, earning in the process his third consecutive All-Star selection and an 11th-place finish in the league MVP voting. Although Beckert batted just .270 in 120 games the following year, he made the All-Star team for the fourth and final time, before being relegated to part-time duty in 1973 by injuries and advancing age, both of which compromised his performance.

With the Cubs subsequently electing to part ways with most of their older veterans following the conclusion of the 1973 campaign, they dealt Beckert to the San Diego Padres for outfielder Jerry Morales on November 7, 1973, ending the 33-year-old second baseman's 11-year association with the organization. Beckert left Chicago with career totals of 22 home runs, 353 RBIs, 672 runs scored, and 1,423 hits, a .283 lifetime batting average, a .318 on-base percentage, and a .348 slugging percentage.

Injuries continued to plague Beckert after he joined the Padres, limiting him to just 64 games and 172 official at bats in 1974. Released by San Diego after appearing in only 9 games over the first month of the ensuing campaign, Beckert chose to announce his retirement. Following his playing days, Beckert spent many years working as a trader at the Chicago Board of Trade, before eventually returning to his native Pittsburgh, where he currently resides.

Cub Numbers:

22 HR; 353 RBIs; 672 Runs Scored; 1,423 Hits; 194 Doubles; 31 Triples; 49 Stolen Bases; .283 AVG; .318 OBP; .348 SLG; .666 OPS

Career Numbers:

22 HR; 360 RBIs; 685 Runs Scored; 1,473 Hits; 196 Doubles; 31 Triples; 49 Stolen Bases; .283 AVG; .318 OBP; .345 SLG; .663 OPS

Career Highlights:

Best Season: Beckert had his best season as a hitter in 1971, when he established career-high marks in batting average (.342), on-base percentage (.367), and slugging percentage (.406). However, due, at least in part, to the 31 games he missed because of injury, Beckert's other numbers proved to be quite unspectacular. In addition to driving in 42 runs, scoring 80 times, and accumulating 181 hits, he hit just 2 homers, collected only 18 doubles, and finished just fifth among league second basemen in both putouts (275) and assists (382). Meanwhile, Beckert earned his lone top-10 finish in the NL MVP balloting in 1968 by leading the league with 98 runs scored, ranking among the leaders with 189 hits and a .294 batting average, and finishing second among players at his position with 356 putouts, 461 assists, and 107 double plays—figures that earned him Gold Glove honors. Factoring everything into the equation, Beckert had his finest all-around season in 1968.

Memorable Moments/Greatest Performances: Beckert compiled two of the longest hitting streaks in franchise history during his time in Chicago, with the first of those lasting from June 26 to July 22, 1968, a 27-game stretch during which he went 42-for-116 (.362), with 8 doubles and

21 runs scored. Beckert also hit safely in 26 consecutive games from April 15 to May 18, 1973, a period during which he went 38-for-107 (.355), with 9 doubles and 12 runs scored.

Beckert hit 2 home runs in one game for the only time in his career on July 1, 1965, when he led the Cubs to a 6-3 win over the Dodgers by knocking in 4 runs with a pair of homers.

Beckert helped lead the Cubs to a lopsided 12-3 victory over the Giants on September 10, 1966 by recording 3 hits and a career-high 5 RBIs.

Beckert had a big day at the plate against Cincinnati on July 30, 1967, collecting 4 hits and scoring 3 times during an 8-4 win over the Reds.

Beckert had a similarly productive afternoon against Los Angeles on July 21, 1968, going 4-for-5, with a triple, 2 RBIs, and 3 runs scored, during a 7-2 win over the Dodgers.

Beckert helped pace the Cubs to a 9-3 win over Houston on August 4, 1969 by going 5-for-6, with a pair of doubles, 2 RBIs, and 1 run scored.

Beckert had another big game against Houston on April 25, 1970, when he homered, singled 3 times, knocked in 2 runs, and scored 3 others during an 11-5 victory over the Astros.

Beckert had the only 5-for-5 day of his career on July 26, 1970, hitting safely in all 5 of his trips to the plate during a 7-6 win over the Braves.

Notable Achievements:

- Batted over .300 once (.342 in 1971).
- Topped 30 doubles once (32 in 1967).
- Led NL in runs scored once and at-bat-to-strikeout ratio five times.
- Finished third in NL with .342 batting average in 1971.
- Led NL second basemen in assists once.
- Finished second among NL second basemen in: assists four times, putouts twice, double plays three times, and fielding percentage once.
- 1968 Gold Glove winner.
- Finished ninth in 1968 NL MVP voting.
- Three-time *Sporting News* All-Star selection (1969, 1970 & 1971).
- Four-time NL All-Star (1969, 1970, 1971 & 1972).

35

CLAUDE PASSEAU

Although Claude Passeau did not join the Cubs until after he celebrated his thirtieth birthday, he earned a place in these rankings with his consistently outstanding pitching as a member of the team. Spending nine of his 13 big-league seasons in Chicago, Passeau pitched his best ball for the Cubs from 1939 to 1945, a seven-year stretch during which he compiled an overall record of 113-80, posted an ERA under 3.00 five times, threw more than 20 complete games three times, and tossed more than 200 innings each season. In addition to earning four All-Star selections and one top-10 finish in the NL MVP voting during that time, Passeau helped the Cubs advance to the 1945 World Series, where he turned in one of the greatest single-game pitching performances in the history of the fall classic.

Born in Waynesboro, Mississippi on April 9, 1909, Claude William Passeau grew up with very little, hoping to one day provide a better life for himself and his loved ones through sports. Establishing himself as an exceptional all-around athlete while attending Moss Point High School, Passeau garnered interest from multiple colleges as he neared graduation, with his primary suitors being Louisiana State University, in Baton Rouge, and Millsaps College, some 120 miles away, in Jackson, Mississippi. After initially deciding to attend LSU, Passeau ultimately elected to remain in his home state, accepting an athletic scholarship from Millsaps. He subsequently went on to earn 12 letters in four different sports over the next four years, starring in baseball, football, basketball, and track. Particularly proficient in the first two sports, Passeau excelled on the diamond as a pitcher, even though he never played high school ball. Meanwhile, he gained general recognition as the finest college quarterback in the state of Mississippi.

Preferring a career in baseball, Passeau played professional ball during his summers under an assumed name as a means of acquiring some much-needed experience. Performing for teams all over North America, Passeau usually remained with one ball club for two or three weeks, before moving on to another city. Impressed with the twenty-three-year-old right-hander's work on the mound, the Detroit Tigers signed him to a contract following his graduation from Millsaps, after which they assigned him to their minor league team in Des Moines, Iowa. Passeau spent most of the next three seasons in the minors, although he did make one brief appearance with the Pittsburgh Pirates in the final week of the 1935 campaign after they picked him up following his release by the Tigers a few weeks earlier.

Traded by the Pirates to the Phillies prior to the start of the 1936 season, Passeau spent the next three-plus years in Philadelphia, compiling an overall record of 38-55 during that time, while working as both a starter and a reliever. With his career apparently headed nowhere, the thirty-year-old Passeau received his big break on May 29, 1939, when the struggling Phillies dealt him to the Cubs for light-hitting outfielder Joe Marty, pitching prospect Ray Harrell, and Kirby Higbe, another young pitcher who went on star for the Dodgers during the early 1940s.

Inserted into the Cubs' starting rotation upon his arrival in Chicago, Passeau went on to post his first winning record as a major leaguer, going 13-9 over the season's final four months, to finish the year with an overall mark of 15-13. He followed that up with arguably his finest season, concluding the 1940 campaign with a record of 20-13, and ranking among the NL leaders with a 2.50 ERA, 124 strikeouts, 4 shutouts, 20 complete games, and 280⅔ innings pitched. After earning the first of three straight All-Star selections in 1941 by going 14-14 with a 3.35 ERA, Passeau earned a 10th-place finish in the NL MVP voting the following year by compiling a record of 19-14 and finishing among the league leaders with a 2.68 ERA, 278⅓ innings pitched, and a career-high 24 complete games.

Due to his somewhat advanced age, Passeau was excused from military duty during World War II, enabling him to retain his position as the ace of Chicago's pitching staff the next three seasons. Continuing to excel on the mound during that time, the lanky 6'3", 198-pound right-hander finished 15-12, with a 2.91 ERA, 18 complete games, and 257 innings pitched in 1943, before going 15-9, with a 2.89 ERA, 18 complete games, and 227 innings pitched the following year. Passeau then helped the Cubs

Courtesy of MEARS Online Auctions

Claude Passeau pitched one of the greatest games in World
Series history against the Detroit Tigers in the 1945 fall classic

capture the NL pennant in 1945 by compiling a record of 17-9, topping the circuit with 5 shutouts, and ranking among the league leaders with a 2.46 ERA and 19 complete games. Although the Cubs subsequently lost the World Series to the Detroit Tigers in seven games, Passeau performed magnificently in Game Three, allowing just one hit and one walk during a 3-0 Chicago win.

Hailed as one of the finest pitchers of the 1940s, Passeau drew praise from none other than Ted Williams, who wrote in his 1988 book entitled, *My Turn at Bat: The Story of My Life*, "Claude Passeau was always tough. He helped pitch the Cubs to the pennant in 1945. He had a fast tailing ball that he'd jam a left-handed hitter with, right into your fists, and, if you weren't quick, he'd get it past you."

Yet, in spite of the notoriety he received for his excellent work on the mound, Passeau felt unjustly persecuted by those who attempted to diminish his accomplishments by suggesting that he threw a spitball. While being interviewed by the Associated Press in 1997, Passeau displayed a card with the label "Spitballer" printed above his picture and stated, "They put it on my baseball card that I was a cheater. I couldn't throw a spitball if it was legal. I threw different speeds and sunk the ball, and slid it. I have been told it was one of the liveliest fastballs some of the scouts ever saw."

Despite going just 9-8 with a 3.13 ERA in 1946, Passeau made the All-Star team for the fourth and final time, before being demoted to the bullpen the following year, when he finished 2-6 with an uncharacteristically high 6.25 ERA. Released by the Cubs during the latter stages of the campaign, Passeau subsequently announced his retirement, ending his career with an overall record of 162-150, an ERA of 3.32, 188 complete games, and 1,104 strikeouts in 2,719 ⅔ innings pitched.

Following his playing days, Passeau retired to his home state of Mississippi, where he gained induction into the Mississippi Sports Hall of Fame in 1964. Passeau lived until August 30, 2003, when he died of natural causes at ninety-four years of age.

Cub Numbers:

Record: 124-94; .569 Win Pct.; 2.96 ERA; 143 CG, 22 Shutouts; 15 Saves; 1,914⅔ IP; 754 Strikeouts; 1.250 WHIP

Career Numbers:

Record: 162-150; .519 Win Pct.; 3.32 ERA; 188 CG; 26 Shutouts; 21 Saves; 2,719⅔ IP; 1,104 Strikeouts; 1.318 WHIP

Cub Career Highlights:

Best Season: Although Passeau also pitched extremely well for the Cubs in 1942 and 1945, his first full season in Chicago proved to be the finest of his career. In addition to placing second in the National League with 20 wins, a 2.50 ERA, and 124 strikeouts in 1940, Passeau finished fourth in the senior circuit in complete games (20) and innings pitched (280⅔), third in shutouts (4), and third in WHIP (1.133), establishing a career-best mark in the last category.

Memorable Moments/Greatest Performances: Passeau turned in his first dominant performance for the Cubs on May 17, 1940, when he yielded just 2 walks and a pair of singles to New York left-fielder Jo-Jo Moore during a 4-0 shutout of the Giants. Passeau also drove home 2 of Chicago's runs with a double.

Passeau came back to haunt his former team on August 20, 1940, when he tossed a three-hit shutout against the Phillies, defeating them by a score of 4-0.

Passeau experienced one of his most memorable moments on May 19, 1941, when, during a 14-1 victory over the Dodgers in which he surrendered just 4 hits, he hit the only grand slam home run of his career. Passeau finished the day with 5 RBIs.

Although he ended up losing the game by a score of 2-1, Passeau performed heroically against Cincinnati on April 19, 1942, allowing just 1 earned run and 7 hits over 14 innings.

During an 8-0 victory over Boston on August 11, 1945, Passeau tossed 7⅔ innings of no-hit ball, before surrendering a pair of singles to the Braves in the bottom of the eighth. He finished the game having allowed just those 2 hits, while recording 8 strikeouts.

However, Passeau's greatest individual performance came in Game Three of the 1945 World Series, when he yielded just 1 hit and 1 walk during a 3-0 victory over Detroit. The Tigers got their only safety of the game when slugger Rudy York singled to left field with 2 men out in the bottom of the second inning. Speaking to *The Sporting News* afterward, Passeau said, "I felt so good I began to tease the Detroit hitters. I am naturally fidgety—rub my fingers up and down my trousers, pick at my cap, pull at my belt, take my time in the box. I noticed it annoyed them, so I put it on more than ever."

Yet, Passeau is remembered equally for the dramatic two-out, three-run homer he surrendered to Ted Williams in the bottom of the ninth inning of the 1941 All Star Game that gave the American League a 7-5 victory over the National League.

Notable Achievements:

- Won 20 games in 1940.
- Surpassed 15 victories four other times, winning 19 games in 1942.
- Compiled ERA below 3.00 five times.
- Threw more than 200 innings seven times, topping 250 innings on three occasions.
- Tossed more than 20 complete games three times.
- Led NL pitchers in shutouts once and fielding percentage five times.
- Finished second in NL in: wins once, ERA twice, strikeouts once, and complete games once.
- Tied for eighth in Cubs history with 22 career shutouts.
- Finished 10th in 1942 NL MVP voting.
- Four-time NL All-Star (1941, 1942, 1943 & 1946).
- 1945 NL champion.

36

CARLOS ZAMBRANO

Combative, hot-tempered, and highly emotional, Carlos Zambrano often conducted himself in an unprofessional manner during his time in Chicago that reflected negatively on him and the entire Cubs organization. Whether quarreling with umpires, antagonizing opponents, or fighting with teammates, Zambrano frequently alienated himself from others around him with his immature behavior, making his 10 full seasons in the Windy City extremely turbulent ones. Nevertheless, the Venezuelan-born right-hander spent much of his time with the Cubs serving as the ace of their pitching staff, surpassing 16 victories three times, en route to compiling an overall record of 125-81 as a member of the team. A three-time All-Star, Zambrano also earned three top-five finishes in the NL Cy Young voting, helping the Cubs capture three NL Central titles in the process. Still, Zambrano's poor conduct tended to overshadow his strong pitching, leaving us with a somewhat skewed outlook towards his overall performance.

Born in Puerto Cabello, Carabobo, Venezuela on June 1, 1981, Carlos Alberto Zambrano signed with the Cubs as a sixteen-year-old amateur free agent in 1997 while still attending local U.E. Creacion Escuela High School. After spending most of the next four seasons in the minors, Zambrano made his big league debut in August of 2001, less than three months after celebrating his twentieth birthday. Appearing in six games over the final month of the campaign, mostly as a reliever, Zambrano failed to make much of an impression, going just 1-2 with a 15.26 ERA, and surrendering 11 hits and 8 bases on balls in only 7⅔ innings of work. Working as both a starter and a reliever the following year, Zambrano pitched somewhat more effectively, compiling an ERA of 3.66, while striking out 93 batters and yielding 94 hits over 108⅓ innings, although he also surrendered 63 bases on balls and won just four of his 12 decisions.

Inserted into the Cubs' starting rotation full-time in 2003, Zambrano began a string of six consecutive seasons in which he posted double-digit wins, concluding the campaign with a record of 13-11, an ERA of 3.11, and 168 strikeouts in 214 innings pitched, although he continued to struggle with his control, also walking 94 batters. Emerging as the ace of Chicago's pitching staff the following year, Zambrano earned his first All-Star selection and a fifth-place finish in the NL Cy Young voting by compiling a record of 16-8, striking out 188 batters in 209⅔ innings of work, and finishing fourth in the league with an ERA of 2.75. The 6'4", 275-pound right-hander posted similarly impressive numbers in 2005, going 14-6, with a 3.26 ERA and 202 strikeouts, while posting career-best marks in innings pitched (223⅓) and WHIP (1.146).

Zambrano's rise to prominence could be attributed largely to his varied pitching arsenal, which included his favorite offering—a heavy 88-92 mph sinker he used primarily to induce ground balls from the opposition. He also threw an 88-91 mph cut fastball, an 80-85 mph splitter, a 90-91 mph four-seam fastball, a 79-82 mph slider, and a curveball that generally reached somewhere between 68-72 mph on the radar gun. Meanwhile, Zambrano's outstanding hitting ability often enabled him to contribute to the Cubs' offense on those days he took the mound. Ending his career with a lifetime batting average of .238, 24 home runs and 71 RBIs, the switch-hitting Zambrano established a franchise record for pitchers by reaching the seats 23 times as a member of the Cubs. A three-time Silver Slugger winner, Zambrano also tied Ferguson Jenkins for the club's single-season home run record for pitchers by going deep six times in 2006.

Also performing well on the mound over the course of that 2006 campaign, Zambrano earned his second All-Star nomination and another fifth-place finish in the Cy Young balloting by tying for the NL lead with 16 victories, while also ranking among the league leaders with a .696 winning percentage, a 3.41 ERA, and a career-high 210 strikeouts. He followed that up with another strong performance in 2007, going 18-13, with a 3.95 ERA and 177 strikeouts.

Yet, even as Zambrano continued to further solidify his position of staff ace, team management grew increasingly concerned over his lack of professionalism and growing inability to control his temper. Behaving particularly poorly when he did not pitch well, Zambrano often blamed his failures on others, frequently expressing his dissatisfaction with his teammates in a highly confrontational manner. Attempting to downplay

Zambrano's boorish behavior, Cubs teammate Mark DeRosa told ESPN. com's Jerry Crasnick in September 2007:

> *"Carlos can't accept and move on quickly from people getting hits off him. That's good, in a way. But what's going to make him great in the coming years—and hopefully he'll learn this—is that he can still win those 6-4 ballgames. He doesn't have to shut out everyone every time. I think he feels a great sense of obligation to us as a team because we lean on him. Even though we have all the trust in the world in our two through five starters, he's the one guy, when he walks on the mound, we have to have that game."*

But, despite DeRosa's attempt to minimize the negative impact that Zambrano's conduct had on team morale, the pitcher far overstepped the boundaries of good judgment on June 1, 2007, when he became involved in a dugout altercation with teammate Michael Barrett after the Cubs catcher mishandled a pitch and committed a throwing error during the fifth inning of an 8-5 loss to Atlanta, leading to a mental meltdown of Zambrano, who subsequently allowed the Braves to score five runs. With Zambrano once again confronting Barrett in the clubhouse following the conclusion of the contest, the latter suffered a cut lip that resulted in a trip to Northwestern Memorial Hospital.

Following a rather uneventful 2008 campaign in which he compiled a record of 14-6 and an ERA of 3.91, Zambrano made headlines in each of the next three seasons with a series of emotional outbursts that garnered him a significant amount of negative media attention. Among his more notable temper tantrums are:

- After being ejected for arguing balls and strikes during a 2009 contest, Zambrano threw the game ball into the outfield and then proceeded to destroy the team's dugout Gatorade machine.
- After surrendering four runs to the Chicago White Sox in the bottom of the first inning of a June 25, 2010 game at U.S. Cellular Field, Zambrano mounted a furious tirade in the Cubs dugout, screaming in the face of first baseman Derrek Lee, who he apparently blamed for failing to field a sharply-hit ball off the bat of leadoff batter Juan Pierre. After the Cubs coaching staff separated the two players, manager Lou Piniella removed Zambrano from the game, later stating, "I'm embarrassed. Carlos should be embarrassed. We'll see exactly what comes out of this.

There's no question he has to control his emotions better than that. He's a grown guy and there's no need for it. I know darn well it's not going to be tolerated....We just couldn't tolerate that." Cubs GM Jim Hendry subsequently suspended Zambrano indefinitely and insisted that he undergo anger management.

- Following a 3-2, 10-inning loss to St. Louis on June 5, 2011, Zambrano criticized closer Carlos Marmol for his pitch selection, finding particular fault with the slider he threw to Ryan Theriot, which resulted in the game-tying double. Speaking to reporters in the clubhouse afterwards, an angry Zambrano fumed, "We should know better than this. We play like a Triple A team. This is embarrassing. Embarrassing for the team and the owners. Embarrassing for the fans. Embarrassed—that's the word for this team."

However, Zambrano finally went too far on August 12, 2011, when, after being ejected for throwing two pitches a bit too close to Chipper Jones in response to a series of Braves home runs, he cleaned out his locker from the visitors' clubhouse and told team personnel that he was retiring. Subsequently suspended by the Cubs for 30 days, Zambrano later apologized to the Cubs and their fans, saying that he wanted to "remain a Cub for life" and that he made his comments about retiring out of frustration. Having lost patience with Zambrano, team management placed him on the restricted list for the remainder of the year, bringing his season to a premature end after he posted a record of just 9-7 with an ERA of 4.82 in his 24 starts. Expressing the attitude of many of his teammates, veteran pitcher Ryan Dempster remarked, "He's [Zambrano's] made his bed. Let him sleep in it."

Seeking to rid themselves of the headache that Zambrano had become, the Cubs traded him to the Miami Marlins for undistinguished pitcher Chris Volstad following the conclusion of the campaign, bringing the former's lengthy stay in Chicago to an end. In addition to posting a record of 125-81 as a member of the Cubs, Zambrano compiled an ERA of 3.60 and struck out 1,542 batters, in 1,826⅔ total innings of work.

Zambrano ended up spending just one season in Miami, going 7-10 with a 4.49 ERA in 2012, before signing a one-year minor league contract with the Philadelphia Phillies when he became a free agent at season's end. Yet, even though Zambrano performed well at the Triple A level over

Courtesy of Jauerback

Carlos Zambrano spent 10 turbulent years in Chicago

the first few months of the 2013 campaign, the Phillies released him on July 25, essentially bringing his playing days to an end. After failing to catch on with another team, Zambrano officially announced his retirement from baseball on September 5, 2014, ending his career in rather ignominious fashion.

Cub Numbers:

Record: 125-81; .607 Win Pct.; 3.60 ERA; 9 CG; 4 Shutouts; 1,826⅔ IP; 1,542 Strikeouts; 1.319 WHIP

Career Numbers:

Record: 132-91; .592 Win Pct.; 3.66 ERA; 10 CG; 5 Shutouts; 1,959 IP; 1,637 Strikeouts; 1.331 WHIP

Cub Career Highlights:

Best Season: Although Zambrano posted a career-high 18 victories in 2007, he actually pitched better ball for the Cubs in both 2004 and 2006. In addition to leading all NL hurlers with 16 wins in the second of those campaigns, Zambrano ranked among the league leaders in ERA (3.41), winning percentage (.696), strikeouts (210), and fewest hits allowed per nine innings pitched (6.813), establishing career-best marks in each of the last two categories. Furthermore, Zambrano tied Ferguson Jenkins' franchise record for the most home runs in a season by a pitcher, reaching the seats six times in 2006. Nevertheless, the feeling here is that Zambrano had his best year on the mound for the Cubs in 2004, when, in addition to finishing fifth in the league with 16 wins, he ranked among the leaders with 188 strikeouts and a career-best 2.75 ERA. Zambrano also posted a WHIP of 1.216 that bettered the mark he compiled in either of the other two seasons (1.294 in 2006, and 1.331 in 2007).

Memorable Moments/Greatest Performances: One of the game's best-hitting pitchers, Zambrano often helped his own cause with his performance at the plate, with one such instance taking place on July 25, 2003, when his two-run homer in the top of the seventh inning helped the Cubs defeat Houston by a score of 5-3.

Zambrano again victimized Houston's pitching staff on June 11, 2007, when his solo homer in the bottom of the third inning provided the winning margin in a 2-1 victory over the Astros. Zambrano also recorded 8 strikeouts over 8 innings and yielded just 3 hits and 1 walk during the contest.

Zambrano had a big day at the plate against Pittsburgh on May 23, 2008, leading the Cubs to a 12-3 victory over the Pirates in which he allowed 6 hits and 2 runs in 7 innings of work by going 4-for-5 with 2 RBIs.

Zambrano knocked in what proved to be the winning run of a 3-2 victory over Cincinnati on August 21, 2008 with a solo homer in the bottom of the third inning. He also performed well on the mound, surrendering 6 hits and 1 run over the first seven innings, in earning the win.

Zambrano led a 15-hit assault against Arizona pitching that resulted in an 11-3 victory over the Diamondbacks on April 28, 2009 by going 3-for-4, with a homer, 2 RBIs, and 3 runs scored.

Zambrano drove home the decisive run of a 2-1 victory over Cincinnati on June 5, 2009 with a solo homer in the top of the fifth inning. He also performed extremely well on the mound, yielding 5 walks and just 2 hits over 6⅔ innings, before turning the game over to the Chicago bullpen.

Zambrano turned in his first dominant pitching performance for the Cubs on August 12, 2003, when he surrendered just 5 hits and recorded 10 strikeouts during a 3-0 shutout of Houston.

Zambrano proved to be equally dominant two starts later, when he took a no-hitter into the eighth inning before yielding 3 hits and 1 run to Arizona over the final two frames, en route to earning a complete-game 4-1 victory over the Diamondbacks on August 22, 2003.

Although the Cubs ended up losing their May 2, 2004 match-up with the Cardinals by a score of 1-0 in 10 innings, Zambrano performed brilliantly over the first seven frames, surrendering just 3 hits and striking out 12 batters, before being removed for a pinch-hitter in the top of the eighth.

Zambrano pitched even better in his next start, allowing just 2 hits and no walks during a complete-game 11-0 win over the Colorado Rockies on May 7, 2004.

Zambrano continued his exceptional run six days later, yielding just 2 hits and 1 run, while recording 11 strikeouts over the first 8 innings of a 7-3 victory over the Dodgers on May 13.

Zambrano turned in one of his finest all-around performances on June 5, 2006, when he allowed just 1 hit and 2 walks over the first 8 innings of an 8-0 shutout of the Houston Astros. Zambrano, who also homered and drove in 4 runs during the contest, had a perfect game until one out in the eighth inning, when he walked Mike Lamb and surrendered a single to Preston Wilson.

Zambrano dominated the White Sox on June 22, 2007, yielding just 3 hits and 1 run, while recording 12 strikeouts in 8 innings of work, in leading the Cubs to a 5-1 victory over their crosstown rivals.

Zambrano hurled a gem against San Francisco on September 25, 2009, allowing just a pair of harmless singles and recording 8 strikeouts, in shutting out the Giants by a score of 3-0.

However, Zambrano reached the high point of his career on September 14, 2008, when he tossed a no-hitter against Houston, defeating the

Astros by a score of 5-0. Zambrano, who recorded 10 strikeouts during the contest, walked just one batter and hit another.

Notable Achievements:

- Surpassed 16 victories three times.
- Posted winning percentage of .700 twice.
- Compiled ERA under 3.00 once (2.75 in 2004).
- Struck out more than 200 batters twice.
- Threw more than 200 innings five times.
- Led NL pitchers with 16 wins in 2006.
- Finished second in NL in wins once and winning percentage once.
- Ranks among Cubs career leaders in: strikeouts (second), strikeouts per nine innings pitched (10th), and games started (eighth).
- Threw no-hitter vs. Houston on September 14, 2008.
- Finished fifth in NL Cy Young voting three times.
- Three-time NL Pitcher of the Month.
- Three-time Silver Slugger winner (2006, 2008 & 2009).
- Three-time NL All-Star (2004, 2006 & 2008).

37

ANDY PAFKO

Known for his quick bat, powerful throwing arm, and acrobatic out-field play, Andy Pafko emerged as a fan favorite during his nine-year stay in Chicago, acquiring the nickname "Handy Andy" as a result of his defensive versatility. Earning All-Star honors as both a third baseman and an outfielder, Pafko made the NL squad four straight times between 1947 and 1950, hitting more than 20 homers twice, driving in more than 100 runs once, and batting over .300 three times during that four-year stretch. In all, Pafko topped 100 RBIs twice and compiled a batting average in excess of .300 on four separate occasions as a member of the Cubs, gaining him general recognition as one of the senior circuit's most dangerous batsmen.

Born in the small village of Boyceville, Wisconsin on February 25, 1921, Andrew Pafko grew up with his Slovak immigrant parents and siblings on a 120-acre farm, where he spent much of his youth milking cows—a chore he later credited with helping him develop the strong grip that eventually made him a major league hitter. After graduating from Boyceville High School, Pafko began his career in baseball as an amateur with Connorsville of the Dunn County League in 1939. He signed his first professional contract with the Class D Eau Claire Bears of the Northern League one year later, before joining Green Bay of the Wisconsin State League, for whom he batted .349 in 1941.

Impressed with Pafko's strong performance at Green Bay, Bill Veeck—owner of the Milwaukee Brewers (a minor league affiliate of the Cubs)—purchased the young outfielder's contract prior to the start of the 1942 season. After posting outstanding numbers the next two years while advancing through Chicago's farm system, Pafko joined the Cubs during the latter stages of the 1943 campaign, batting .379 and driving in 10 runs, in just 13 games and 58 official at-bats.

Granted a deferment from military service due to chronic high blood pressure, Pafko earned the Cubs' starting centerfield job in 1944, when, appearing in 128 games, he hit 6 homers, knocked in 62 runs, batted .269, and led all players at his position with 21 outfield assists. He followed that up with an exceptional 1945 campaign in which he earned a fourth-place finish in the NL MVP voting by hitting 12 homers, knocking in 110 runs, and batting .298 for the pennant-winning Cubs. Pafko subsequently suffered through an injury-marred 1946 season during which he sprained his ankle and fractured his arm, limiting him to just 65 games, 3 home runs, and 39 RBIs.

Pafko's health woes continued in 1947, when a kidney infection put him out of action for three weeks. Nevertheless, he ended up posting solid numbers, earning the first of his four consecutive All-Star selections by hitting 13 homers, driving in 66 runs, scoring 68 times, and batting .302. Shifted to third base the following year to replace Stan Hack, who announced his retirement at the end of the 1947 season, Pafko responded well to his change in positions. In addition to hitting 26 homers, knocking in 101 runs, scoring 82 times, and batting .312. Pafko led all NL third sackers with 314 assists and 29 double plays turned. Splitting his time between centerfield and the hot corner in 1949, Pafko had another good year, earning his third straight All-Star nomination by hitting 18 homers, driving in 69 runs, scoring 79 times, and batting .281.

Gradually establishing himself as an icon in Chicago with his strong play, Midwestern work ethic, and willingness to do whatever the Cubs asked of him, Pafko had good power, excellent speed, and one of the league's strongest throwing arms. Primarily a pull hitter, the right-handed swinging Pafko, who stood six-feet tall and weighed 190 pounds, employed an open batting stance that reminded some of New York Giants great Mel Ott. In discussing his hitting style years later, Pafko offered, "I hit some homers in my time, but I was thought of as a line drive hitter. Every now and then one of my liners would go high enough to clear the fence."

Quite a few of Pafko's drives cleared the outfield wall in 1950, as he ended up finishing second in the league with a career-high 36 homers. Pafko also drove in 92 runs, scored 95 times, and batted .304, earning in the process a 12th-place finish in the NL MVP voting. The Chicago outfielder's outstanding performance so impressed Cincinnati Reds' president Warren Giles that the future President of the National League stated that, if

Andy Pafko earned NL All-Star honors as both a third baseman and an outfielder during his time in Chicago

Courtesy of MEARS Online Auctions

he could choose any player in the senior circuit to help improve his struggling team, Pafko would be his choice.

In spite of Pafko's excellent play and popularity with the hometown fans, the Cubs elected to include him in an eight-player trade they completed with the Dodgers on June 15, 1951 that netted them, among others, outfielder Gene Hermanski and second baseman Eddie Miksis. The deal came after Pafko hit 12 homers, knocked in 35 runs, and batted .264 over the season's first 10 weeks. While Cubs fans lamented their hero's departure, Stan Musial later discussed in his book, *Stan Musial: The Man's Own Story,* the effect the trade had on Pafko, writing, "Andy was a strong hitter, a strong-armed fielder, and good defensively. He was steady, gave you a good day's work. I think he hated to leave the Cubs so much that he never was the same ballplayer."

Pafko actually performed well his first few seasons after he left Chicago, hitting 18 homers, driving in 58 runs, and batting .249 over the second half of the 1951 campaign, before helping the Dodgers capture the National League pennant the following year by hitting 19 homers, knocking in 85 runs, and batting .287. He also experienced the most surreal moment of his career during his time in Brooklyn, when, in the bottom of the ninth inning of Game Three of the 1951 playoffs, he found himself gazing hopelessly upwards into the left-field stands at the Polo Grounds as Bobby Thomson's *Shot Heard 'Round the World* sailed over his head, giving the Giants a stunning 5-4 come-from-behind victory over the Dodgers that earned them a trip to the World Series.

Dealt to the Braves following the conclusion of the 1952 campaign, Pafko spent his final seven seasons in Milwaukee, taking part in two more fall classics, and winning his lone world championship. He had his best year for the Braves in 1953, when he hit 17 homers, knocked in 72 runs, and batted .297. After assuming a part-time role from 1955 to 1959, Pafko announced his retirement shortly after Milwaukee released him on October 26, 1959, ending his career with 213 home runs, 976 RBIs, 844 runs scored, 1,796 hits, and a .285 batting average.

Following his playing days, Pafko remained with the Braves for another 14 years, serving them first as a coach (1960-1962), then as a minor-league manager (1963-1968), and, finally, as a scout (1969-1973). He also later scouted for the Montreal Expos. Unfortunately, Pafko developed

Alzheimer's in his later years, losing his battle with the dreaded disease on October 8, 2013, at ninety-two years of age.

Cub Numbers:

126 HR; 584 RBIs; 486 Runs Scored; 1,048 Hits; 162 Doubles; 40 Triples; 28 Stolen Bases; .294 AVG; .362 OBP; .468 SLG; .829 OPS

Career Numbers:

213 HR; 976 RBIs; 844 Runs Scored; 1,796 Hits; 264 Doubles; 62 Triples; 38 Stolen Bases; .285 AVG; .350 OBP; .449 SLG; .799 OPS

Cub Career Highlights:

Best Season: Although Pafko earned his lone *Sporting News* All-Star selection and only top-10 finish in the NL MVP balloting in 1945, he actually posted significantly better numbers in both 1948 and 1950, with the second of those campaigns being his finest all-around season. In addition to finishing runner-up in the senior circuit with 36 homers and a .591 slugging percentage in 1950, Pafko knocked in 92 runs, scored 95 times, and placed in the league's top 10 with a .304 batting average, a .397 on-base percentage, a .989 OPS, 8 triples, and 304 total bases, establishing career-high marks in five different offensive categories in the process. Perhaps most impressive, though, is the fact that Pafko struck out only 32 times, making him one of just a handful of players to ever finish a season with more home runs than strikeouts.

Memorable Moments/Greatest Performances: Pafko helped pace the Cubs to a 24-2 pasting of the Braves on July 3, 1945 by going 4-for-6, with 5 RBIs and 1 run scored.

Although the Cubs ended up losing their May 16, 1948 matchup with the Cincinnati Reds by a score of 13-11 in 10 innings, Pafko had a huge day at the plate, going 5-for-5, with a pair of homers, a double, 4 RBIs, and 4 runs scored.

Pafko again went 5-for-5 a little over one month later, doing so during a 5-2 victory over the Dodgers at Ebbets Field on June 19, 1948. He also knocked in 3 runs and scored once during the contest.

Pafko's 3-run homer in the top of the ninth inning proved to be the decisive blow in a 9-6 win over the Cincinnati Reds on April 18, 1950.

He finished the day 3-for-4, with a pair of homers, a double, 4 RBIs, and 2 runs scored.

Pafko had another big day against Cincinnati later in the year, collecting a homer, triple, and double, driving in 5 runs, and scoring 3 times during a 16-0 mauling of the Reds on July 2, 1950.

Pafko helped lead the Cubs to a 12-5 victory over the Dodgers on July 28, 1950 by going 3-for-4, with a pair of homers, a double, 3 RBIs, and 4 runs scored.

Even though the Cubs lost their August 2, 1950 contest with the Giants by a score of 8-6, Pafko turned in the finest performance of his career, driving in 5 of Chicago's 6 runs with 3 homers.

Notable Achievements:

- Hit more than 20 home runs twice, topping 30 homers once (36 in 1950).
- Knocked in more than 100 runs twice.
- Batted over .300 four times.
- Finished in double digits in triples once (12 in 1945).
- Surpassed 30 doubles once (30 in 1948).
- Compiled on-base percentage of .400 in 1943.
- Posted slugging percentage in excess of .500 three times.
- Finished second in NL in: home runs once; triples once; and slugging percentage once.
- Led NL outfielders in assists once and fielding percentage once.
- Led NL third basemen in assists once.
- Hit 3 home runs in one game vs. New York Giants on August 2, 1950.
- Finished fourth in 1945 NL MVP voting.
- 1945 *Sporting News* All-Star selection.
- Four-time NL All-Star (1947, 1948, 1949 & 1950).
- 1945 NL champion.

38

DON KESSINGER

The fourth and final member of Chicago's much-celebrated infield of the 1960s to make our list, Don Kessinger started at shortstop for the Cubs from 1965 to 1975, during which time he proved to be the National League's finest all-around player at the position. An exceptional defender with outstanding range and a strong throwing arm, Kessinger led all NL shortstops in assists four times, putouts three times, double plays four times, and fielding percentage once, en route to earning two Gold Gloves and six All-Star selections. Meanwhile, after spending his first few seasons struggling at the plate, the switch-hitting Kessinger eventually turned himself into a solid offensive performer, twice scoring more than 100 runs as the Cubs' leadoff hitter.

Born in Forrest City, Arkansas on July 17, 1942, Donald Eulon Kessinger created a name for himself while attending Forrest City High School by earning All-State and All-America honors in four different sports. Particularly proficient on the hardwood, Kessinger later noted, "I was better known for basketball in high school. I had the opportunity to go most any place I wanted in basketball." After fielding offers from several different colleges, Kessinger ultimately accepted an athletic scholarship from the University of Mississippi, where he earned All-SEC honors in both baseball and basketball from 1962 to 1964, as well as All-America honors in both sports in 1964. Presented with a chance to pursue a career in basketball following his graduation from Ole Miss, Kessinger recalled, "Several NBA clubs asked me, if they drafted me, would I play basketball. But I answered them honestly and said, 'No, I want to play baseball.' So that's what I did."

After being scouted and recruited by Leo Durocher, a former major league shortstop himself, Kessinger signed with the Cubs as an amateur free agent in 1964. He subsequently spent less than one full year in the minor leagues, before joining the Cubs two months into the 1965 campaign (although he also appeared in four games at the end of the 1964 season). Immediately anointed the Cubs' starting shortstop upon his arrival in the Windy City, Kessinger experienced difficulties both offensively and defensively as a rookie, batting just .201 in 106 games, while also committing 28 errors in the field.

Yet, in spite of Kessinger's frequent fielding miscues, his coaches and teammates remained convinced that he had all the skills necessary to develop into an elite defensive shortstop. Noting that Kessinger possessed superb range in the field and committed most of his errors on throws to first base, Chicago manager Lou Klein commented, "That doesn't worry me. This boy can play shortstop. That much I know....Put him down in your book. This boy will make it. And he'll make it big." Cubs third baseman Ron Santo echoed Klein's sentiments early in 1966, telling reporters, "When Kessinger first came up, he made a lot of mistakes. But, after all, he was young, green, and scared....He has as good an arm as any shortstop in the league, and he can make that play in the hole. There are still a few things that need polishing in his pivot work at second, but he and Beckert were clicking pretty well before the season was over." Jerome Holtzman of *The Sporting News* also praised Kessinger, writing, "There doesn't seem to be any question that he will be one of baseball's best shortstops in the near future."

Although Kessinger continued to perform somewhat erratically in the field for much of 1966, finishing second in the league with 35 errors, he began to emerge as one of the senior circuit's better defensive shortstops, leading all players at his position in assists for the first of four times. Meanwhile, in an effort to improve his offensive performance, the right-handed hitting Kessinger turned to switch-hitting. Working ceaselessly with coach Pete Reiser to learn how to bat left-handed, Kessinger overcame a poor first half to finish the 1966 season with a batting average of .274. Looking back at his experiment years later, Kessinger said, "I felt I had to do this to survive and remain in the big leagues. In retrospect, it was the right decision."

Even though Kessinger regressed somewhat at the plate in each of the next two seasons, compiling batting averages of just .231 and .240, he improved himself defensively to the point that he became absolutely indispensable to the Cubs because of his outstanding glove work. Performing

Seen here with his two sons, Don Kessinger earned two Gold
Gloves and six All-Star selections as a member of the Cubs

particularly well in the field in 1968, the lanky 6'1", 175-pound Kessinger
earned All-Star honors for the first of five straight times and the first of
his three consecutive *Sporting News* All-Star selections by leading all NL
shortstops with 97 double plays turned and a career-high 573 assists.

As Kessinger emerged as the senior circuit's finest defensive player at
his position, he became known for his patented "field, jump, and throw"
maneuver that has become a staple of major league shortstops in recent
years. Instead of fielding the ball, planting his feet, and firing overhand
to first base on grounders hit to the shortstop hole, the extremely athletic
Kessinger backhanded the ball, jumped in the air, rotated his body, and
released his throw to first base while still in mid-air. Although New York's
Derek Jeter later received much of the credit for perfecting this move,
Kessinger actually began using it some three decades earlier.

Kessinger continued his exceptional play in the field in 1969, earning Gold Glove honors for the first of two straight times by leading all

NL shortstops in every major defensive category. Meanwhile, he proved his worth as a leadoff hitter, driving in 53 runs, batting .273, and placing among the league leaders with 109 runs scored, 181 hits, and 38 doubles. Kessinger followed that up with another strong performance in 1970, earning his final *Sporting News* All-Star nomination by batting .266, scoring 100 runs, finishing second in the league with 14 triples, and leading all players at his position in assists for the third straight time.

Kessinger remained the Cubs' starting shortstop for another five years, earning three more All-Star selections, while finishing first among players at his position in putouts and double plays two more times each. He posted his best offensive numbers during that five-year stretch in 1972, when he batted .274, scored 77 runs, and compiled a career-high .351 on-base percentage. However, with Kessinger turning 33 years of age midway through the 1975 season, the Cubs elected to trade him to the St. Louis Cardinals for pitcher Mike Garman and infielder Bobby Hrapmann following the conclusion of the campaign. Upon learning of the trade, Kessinger said, "I have nothing but respect for the Cubs. I enjoyed my eleven years with them. I wish them nothing but the best for all concerned."

Kessinger ended up spending most of the next two seasons in St. Louis, starting at short for the Cardinals in 1976, and assuming a backup role the following year, before being dealt to the White Sox in August 1977. He spent the next two-plus years back in Chicago, serving as player-manager of the White Sox for the first few months of the 1979 campaign, before surrendering his post to Tony LaRussa in early August. Kessinger subsequently announced his retirement, ending his career with 14 home runs, 527 RBIs, 899 runs scored, 1,931 hits, a .252 batting average, a .314 on-base percentage, and a .312 slugging percentage.

After spending the first several years of his retirement away from the game, Kessinger accepted the position of head baseball coach at his alma mater, the University of Mississippi. He spent the next six seasons piloting the Rebels to an overall record of 185-153, before resigning his post to become Mississippi's Associate Athletics Director for Internal Affairs, while concurrently serving as Chair of the NCAA Baseball Rules Committee.

Cub Numbers:

11 HR; 431 RBIs; 769 Runs Scored; 1,619 Hits; 201 Doubles; 71 Triples; 92 Stolen Bases; .255 AVG; .315 OBP; .314 SLG; .629 OPS

Career Numbers:

14 HR; 527 RBIs; 899 Runs Scored; 1,931 Hits; 254 Doubles; 80 Triples; 100 Stolen Bases; .252 AVG; .314 OBP; .312 SLG; .626 OPS

Cub Career Highlights:

Best Season: Kessinger had his finest all-around season for the Cubs in 1969, when, in addition to batting .273 and establishing career-high marks in home runs (4), RBIs (53), and OPS (.698), he ranked among the league leaders with 109 runs scored, 181 hits, and 38 doubles, posting career-best marks in each of those categories as well. Kessinger also led all NL shortstops in putouts (266), assists (542), and fielding percentage (.976), earning in the process his first Gold Glove, his second selection to *The Sporting News* All-Star team, and a fifteenth-place finish in the league MVP voting (his best showing). Furthermore, he set a new single-season major league record for shortstops (since broken) by playing in 54 games without committing an error.

Memorable Moments/Greatest Performances: Kessinger had his first big offensive day for the Cubs on September 1, 1966, when he collected 4 hits, knocked in 1 run, and scored 3 times during an 11-3 rout of Cincinnati.

Kessinger helped lead the Cubs to a resounding 9-3 victory over the Braves on July 18, 1967 by going 4-for-5, with a pair of doubles, 2 runs scored, and a career-high 5 RBIs.

Kessinger had one of his best days at the plate on August 11, 1968, when he went 5-for-7, with 2 RBIs and 1 run scored, during a 15-inning, 8-5 win over the Cincinnati Reds.

Kessinger turned in one of his most productive offensive performances on April 22, 1970, when he homered, singled twice, drove in 3 runs, and scored 3 times during a 7-5 win over St. Louis.

Kessinger had another big game less than one month later, on May 18, 1970, when he went 4-for-6, with 2 RBIs and 4 runs scored, in leading the Cubs to a 12-5 victory over Cincinnati.

Kessinger came up big for the Cubs on August 31, 1971, when, during a 7-6 win over the Montreal Expos, he drove in the game's winning run with an RBI single to center field with the bases loaded in the bottom of the 10th inning. Kessinger finished the game 5-for-6, with 2 RBIs and 1 run scored.

However, Kessinger unquestionably had his greatest day at the plate on June 17, 1971, when he went 6-for-6, with 1 RBI and 3 runs scored, during a 10-inning, 7-6 win over the St. Louis Cardinals. Reflecting back on his exceptional performance, Kessinger told *Baseball Digest* in September 1975, "It was the kind of game you dream about, but never think will happen to you. I was 6-for-6, with 5 singles and a double, and I scored the winning run before a big crowd in our home ballpark. You can't hope to have a much more satisfying day than that."

Notable Achievements:

- Scored more than 100 runs twice.
- Finished in double digits in triples twice.
- Topped 30 doubles once (38 in 1969).
- Finished second in NL in doubles once and triples once.
- Led NL shortstops in: assists four times, putouts three times, double plays four times, and fielding percentage once.
- Two-time Gold Glove winner (1969 & 1970).
- Three-time *Sporting News* All-Star selection (1968, 1969 & 1970).
- Six-time NL All-Star (1968, 1969, 1970, 1971, 1972 & 1974).

39

FRANK SCHULTE

One of only four players in Major League history to surpass 20 home runs, 20 triples, 20 doubles, and 20 stolen bases in the same season, Frank "Wildfire" Schulte performed magnificently for the Cubs in 1911, when he became the first member of that exclusive club. However, while Schulte compiled easily the best numbers of his career that season en route to becoming the inaugural winner of the NL MVP Award (referred to at the time as the Chalmers Award), the hard-hitting outfielder proved to be much more than a one-year wonder during his time in Chicago. One of the National League's top sluggers of the Dead Ball Era, Schulte posted double-digit home run totals four times between 1904 and 1916, topping the senior circuit in that category twice. The left-handed hitting Schulte also topped the 100-RBI mark once, scored more than 100 runs once, collected more than 10 triples six times, and batted over .300 twice, all while doing a solid job of patrolling left field and right field at different times for the Cubs.

Born in Cochecton, New York on September 17, 1882, Frank M. Schulte displayed an affinity for baseball at an early age, spending his teenage years playing for various town and factory teams. The son of a German-born contractor who hoped to have his son follow in his footsteps, Schulte began his professional career with the Syracuse Stars of the New York State League in 1902, after turning down a $1,000 offer from his father to give up baseball. Heeding the advice of his more experienced teammates, some of whom previously played in the Major Leagues, Schulte fine-tuned his baseball skills and deepened his understanding of the game during his time at Syracuse, while compiling batting averages of .280, .294, and .307 over the course of the next three seasons. Discovered by Cubs scout George Huff while playing for the Stars, Schulte found himself headed for the Windy City when Chicago purchased his contract in August, 1904.

After making a favorable impression on Cubs management by hitting 2 homers, driving in 13 runs, scoring 16 times, and batting .286 in his 20 games with the club over the final three weeks of the 1904 campaign, Schulte claimed the starting left field job the following year. Appearing in 123 games and accumulating just under 500 official at-bats, the twenty-two-year-old Schulte had a solid rookie season, finishing the year with 1 home run, 47 RBIs, 67 runs scored, 14 triples, 16 stolen bases, a. 274 batting average, and 14 outfield assists. Schulte improved upon those numbers after being shifted to right field in 1906, helping the Cubs capture the first of their three straight National League pennants by hitting 7 homers, driving in 60 runs, scoring 77 others, topping the circuit with 13 triples, stealing 25 bases, and batting .281, while finishing fourth in the league with 18 outfield assists.

Although the Cubs repeated as NL champions in each of the next two seasons, they did so without much help from Schulte, who suffered through a pair of injury-marred campaigns. Returning to the team's everyday starting lineup in 1909, Schulte posted respectable numbers, finishing the season with 4 home runs, 60 RBIs, 57 runs scored, and a .264 batting average. However, the 5'11", 170-pound outfielder did not emerge as a truly elite player until the following year, when he topped the senior circuit with 10 homers, knocked in 68 runs, scored 93 times, accumulated 15 triples, batted .301, and finished third in the league with a .460 slugging percentage.

An extraordinarily eccentric individual, Schulte began to demonstrate his idiosyncratic nature more and more as he rose to prominence in the National League. After developing a fondness for actress Lillian Russell, who he watched perform in a play called *Wildfire* one year during spring training, Schulte named one of his racing trotters "Wildfire." When word got out that he had given that name to a horse, the local sportswriters hung the moniker on him. Schulte also caused those who knew him well to scratch their heads in response to his tendency to comb the streets looking for hairpins, since he believed that they predicted his future success in the batter's box. In addition to holding the belief that larger hairpins indicated greater success, he felt that a bent hairpin revealed the direction of his upcoming safety. Schulte's peculiar ways prompted teammate Joe Tinker to "doubt whether a quainter or more original character ever existed in the national pastime."

Frank 'Wildfire' Schulte is one of only four players
in MLB history to surpass 20 home runs, 20 triples,
20 doubles, and 20 stolen bases in the same season

After spending his first several years in Chicago playing the typical style of "small ball" prevalent throughout most of the Dead Ball Era, Schulte broke out in a big way in 1911. Perhaps aided by a somewhat livelier ball that the Major Leagues employed that season, Schulte topped the senior circuit with 21 home runs, 107 RBIs, a .534 slugging percentage, and 308 total bases, while also batting an even .300 and ranking among the league leaders with 105 runs scored and 21 triples. Schulte's exceptional performance earned him recognition as the first winner of the NL Chalmers Award, presented at that time to the Most Valuable Player in each league.

Although Schulte never again compiled such lofty numbers, he remained a productive player for the Cubs over the course of the next four seasons, annually placing among the league leaders in home runs. Performing particularly well in 1912 and 1913, Schulte hit 12 homers, knocked in 64 runs, scored 90 times, and batted .264 in the first of those campaigns, before hitting 9 homers, driving in 68 runs, scoring 85 times, and batting .278 the following year. However, with Schulte clearly on the downside of his career by 1916, the Cubs elected to include him in a four-player trade they completed with Pittsburgh on July 29, 1916, bringing to an end his thirteen-year stay in Chicago. Schulte left the Cubs as the last remaining link to the championship teams of 1906, 1907 and 1908.

After spending the remainder of the 1916 campaign in Pittsburgh, Schulte split his final two big-league seasons between the Pirates, Phillies, and Washington Senators, before spending another five years competing at the minor-league level. Following the conclusion of his playing career, Schulte settled down in Oakland, California, where he lived the rest of his life with his wife. Stricken with paralysis for a time in 1930, Schulte lived another nineteen years, passing away on October 2, 1949, just two weeks after celebrating his sixty-seventh birthday.

Cub Numbers:

91 HR; 713 RBIs; 827 Runs Scored; 1,590 Hits; 254 Doubles; 117 Triples; 214 Stolen Bases; .272 AVG; .330 OBP; .403 SLG; .733 OPS

Career Numbers:

92 HR; 793 RBIs; 906 Runs Scored; 1,766 Hits; 288 Doubles; 124 Triples; 233 Stolen Bases; .270 AVG; .332 OBP; .395 SLG; .726 OPS

Cub Career Highlights:

Best Season: Schulte had easily his greatest season in 1911, when he batted .300, stole 23 bases, and established career-high marks in home runs (21), RBIs (107), runs scored (105), hits (173), doubles (30), triples (21), total bases (308), walks (76), and slugging percentage (.534). By hitting 21 homers, Schulte became the first twentieth-century player to reach the 20-homer plateau. Meanwhile, his 21 homers, 21 triples, 30 doubles, and 23 stolen bases made him the first player in Major League history to top the 20-mark in all four categories in the same season, with only three other players accomplishing the feat since that time (Willie Mays, Curtis Granderson and Jimmy Rollins). Schulte also hit four grand slam home runs, which remained a single-season record until Ernie Banks established a new mark in 1955.

Memorable Moments/Greatest Performances: Schulte had a number of exceptional days at the plate during his outstanding 1911 campaign, with one of those coming on June 11, when he went 3-for-3, with a triple, double, 4 RBIs, and 4 runs scored, during a 20-2 pasting of the Boston Braves.

Schulte again tormented Boston's pitching staff on July 18 of that year, when he helped pace the Cubs to a 14-6 win over the Braves by going 3-for-4, with a homer, 4 RBIs, and 4 runs scored.

Schulte accomplished the rare Dead Ball Era feat of homering twice in one game on August 12, 1911, doing so during a 9-1 victory over St. Louis in which he also knocked in 5 runs.

Schulte continued his onslaught against National League pitching a few days later, when he homered and doubled in the same inning, drove in 5 runs, and scored twice during a 13-6 win over Boston on August 16.

Schulte had his last big day of the year on September 27, 1911, when he led the Cubs to an 8-0 victory over the Giants by going 4-for-4, with a homer, 2 doubles, 2 RBIs, and 3 runs scored.

Schulte helped the Cubs defeat Pittsburgh by a score of 12-2 on June 30, 1913 by going 3-for-4, with a homer, double, 6 RBIs, and 2 runs scored.

Schulte proved to be the difference in a 4-1 win over the Cardinals on September 7, 1913, hitting a pair of homers, knocking in 2 runs, and scoring 3 times.

Schulte turned in a tremendous all-around effort on June 12, 1916, going 4-for-5, with a homer, 2 runs scored, and a pair of stolen bases, during an 8-2 victory over the Giants.

An outstanding postseason performer during his time in Chicago, Schulte compiled a lifetime batting average of .321 in World Series play, driving in 9 runs and scoring 11 times in 21 total games. Hitting safely in 13 consecutive Series games at one point, Schulte collected at least one hit in all but two of the 21 games he started. Performing particularly well in his final two World Series appearances, Schulte batted .389 during the Cubs' five-game victory over Detroit in the 1908 fall classic, before posting a mark of .412 during their five-game defeat at the hands of the Philadelphia Athletics two years later.

Notable Achievements:

- Finished in double digits in home runs four times, topping 20 homers once (21 in 1911).
- Knocked in more than 100 runs once (107 in 1911).
- Scored more than 100 runs once (105 in 1911).
- Batted over .300 twice.
- Finished in double digits in triples six times, topping 20 three-baggers once (21 in 1911).
- Surpassed 30 doubles once (30 in 1911).
- Stole more than 20 bases five times.
- Posted slugging percentage in excess of .500 once (.534 in 1911).
- Led NL in: home runs twice, RBIs once, triples once, total bases once, and slugging percentage once.
- Led NL outfielders with 7 double plays in 1906.
- Led NL left-fielders with 24 assists in 1915.
- Ranks third in Cubs history with 117 career triples.
- Ranks third all-time in MLB history with 22 steals of home.
- First twentieth-century player to hit 20 home runs in one season.
- First twentieth-century player to surpass 20 homers, 20 triples, 20 doubles, and 20 steals in same season (1911).
- 1911 NL MVP winner.
- Four-time NL champion (1906, 1907, 1908 & 1910).
- Two-time world champion (1907 & 1908).

40

GUY BUSH

A key member of the Cubs' pitching staff during the pennant-winning campaigns of 1929 and 1932, Guy Bush spent parts of 12 seasons in Chicago, establishing himself during that time as one of the National League's most consistent winners. Despite spending much of his time in the Windy City being overlooked in favor of fellow Cub hurlers Charlie Root and Pat Malone, Bush won more games than either of his teammates from 1928 to 1934, a seven-year stretch during which the three men formed arguably the National League's top pitching trio. Compiling an overall record of 121-64 over the course of those seven seasons, Bush won at least 15 games each year, surpassing 18 victories on four separate occasions. The lanky right-hander also threw at least 15 complete games four times and tossed more than 250 innings twice, while also leading all NL hurlers in saves twice. Yet, like his longtime teammate Charlie Root, Bush is remembered most for surrendering a historic home run to Babe Ruth.

Born in the northeastern Mississippi town of Aberdeen on August 23, 1901, Guy Terrell Bush spent much of his youth working on his family's farm, leaving him little time for sports. However, after enrolling at nearby Tupelo Military Academy in 1916, the fifteen-year-old Bush quickly developed an affinity for baseball, making a strong impression on his high school coaches with his ability to deliver the ball to home plate with outstanding velocity. Choosing to pursue a career in baseball, rather than one as a soldier, Bush began playing semi-pro and independent ball in leagues throughout the northern part of the state following his graduation. He finally turned pro in 1923, when George Wheatley, president and scout of the Greenville (Mississippi) Swamp Angels, discovered him while pitching for a team situated in the small town of Shelby. Signed to a contract by Wheatley, Bush subsequently overpowered the competition in the Class D Cotton States League, prompting Chicago Cubs scout Jack Doyle to purchase his contract.

With the Cotton States League folding later in the year, Bush joined the Cubs in mid-September, throwing one scoreless inning of relief, before packing his bags for the winter. After compiling a record of 9-3 with the Wichita Falls Spudders of the Class A Texas League over the first two months of the ensuing campaign, "The Mississippi Mudcat," as he came to be known, returned to Chicago, where he spent the remainder of the year posting a mark of 2-5 and an ERA of 4.02 for the Cubs, while working as both a starter and a reliever. Bush continued to function in that dual role in 1925, when, appearing in 42 games and making 15 starts, he finished just 6-13 with a 4.30 ERA. However, the twenty-three-year-old right-hander spent countless hours working with veteran hurler Grover Cleveland Alexander, who he later credited with transforming him from a "thrower" into a "pitcher."

Although Bush again spent a considerable amount of time working out of the Chicago bullpen in 1926, he eventually earned a regular spot in the starting rotation, finishing the year with a record of 13-9 and an ERA of 2.86 that placed him fourth in the league rankings. Bush's outstanding performance prompted Irving Vaughan of the *Chicago Daily Tribune* to call him "one of the National League's outstanding finds" whose success resulted when he learned to "master a curveball and, also, his control." Despite missing an entire month of the 1927 season with a case of the mumps, Bush put together another solid year, going 10-10 with a 3.03 ERA. Fully healthy in 1928, Bush developed into one of the mainstays of Chicago's starting rotation, concluding the campaign with a record of 15-6 and an ERA of 3.83. Bush, though, did not emerge as a top-flight starter until 1929, when he helped the Cubs capture the NL pennant by going 18-7, with a 3.66 ERA, 18 complete games, and 270⅔ innings pitched.

The success that Bush experienced over the course of the 1929 season gained him a considerable amount of notoriety, with the local sportswriters portraying him as a good-natured country boy with a "deep Southern drawl" who learned about life, money, and baseball in the big city. Known for his extensive wardrobe, Bush also had a fondness for fast, luxurious cars. He also developed a reputation for his unusual delivery, which F.C. Lane described thusly in the November 1930 issue of *Baseball Magazine*:

Guy Bush compiled an overall record of 121-64
for the Cubs from 1928 to 1934

"On the hurling mound, Bush has developed a curious
"hop-toad" lunge that is unique. When he really bears down
on the ball, he actually springs forward and finishes up in a
squat position like a catcher reaching for a low pitch. This
freakish hop forward would be impossible to many pitch-
ers. Bush can do it by virtue of his lithe and wiry build, his
long thin legs."

In discussing his unorthodox delivery, Bush, who had a high windmill
windup, threw overhand to three-quarters overhand, and employed a high
leg kick and a long stride towards home plate, explained, "I found that I

can get more on the ball if I come forward with everything I got. I naturally throw myself off balance. In a tight, hard-pitched game, I'll generally skin my right knee."

Standing 6' tall and weighing only about 170 pounds, Bush appeared frail to most, with Cubs catcher Gabby Hartnett suggesting that his teammate's slight stature came from worrying too much. Yet, Chicago sportswriter Ed Burns commented that Bush is "stronger physically than he looks."

In spite of Bush's excellent work in 1929, *Baseball Magazine's* F.C. Lane wrote that he continued to be largely overlooked and underappreciated, claiming that he was "generally not rated as a great pitcher." Lane added that Bush approached the art of pitching cerebrally and "dissected every game with painstaking care."

Even though Bush compiled a record of 15-10 in 1930, his performance fell off dramatically, as he finished the year with an inordinately high 6.20 ERA. He followed that up by going 16-8 with a 4.49 ERA in 1931, before posting a mark of 19-11 and an ERA of 3.21 for Chicago's 1932 pennant-winning team. Bush then had arguably his finest season in 1933, going 20-12, with a 2.75 ERA, 20 complete games, and 4 shutouts.

Bush ended up spending just one more year in Chicago, finishing 18-10 with a 3.83 ERA in 1934, even though he missed nearly five weeks of the season due to a rib injury in June and an ear infection in July. With the veteran right-hander approaching his thirty-fourth birthday, the Cubs elected to include him in a five-player trade they completed with the Pittsburgh Pirates on November 22, 1934 that netted them pitcher Larry French and third baseman/outfielder Fred Lindstrom in return. Bush left Chicago having compiled an overall record of 152-101, along with a 3.81 ERA, 127 complete games, and 14 shutouts.

After leaving the Cubs, Bush spent the remainder of his career toiling in mediocrity, compiling a composite record of 24-35 over the course of the next four seasons, which he split between the Pirates, Boston Bees, and St. Louis Cardinals. While facing the Bees as a member of the Pirates in 1935, Bush surrendered the last two home runs of Babe Ruth's career, with homer number 714 traveling an estimated 600 feet over the right-field grandstand at Forbes Field. Although Bush announced his retirement after being released by the Cardinals on May 7, 1938, he mounted a brief comeback with the Cincinnati Reds at forty-three years of age in 1945, appearing in four games before retiring for good. Bush ended his career with an overall record of 176-136, a 3.86 ERA, 151 complete games, 16 shutouts, and 850 strikeouts in 2,722 innings of work.

Following his playing days, Bush spent a few years in Chicago running a tavern and working for the Pullman sleeping-car company. He also managed the Battle Creek Belles of the All-American Girls Professional Baseball League for parts of two seasons, before retiring permanently to Shannon, Mississippi, where he spent the remainder of his life raising vegetables and soybeans on his 50-acre farm. Bush passed away at the age of eighty-three, on July 2, 1985, after suffering a heart attack while tending to the garden at his home.

Cub Numbers:

Record: 152-101; .601 Win Pct.; 3.81 ERA; 127 CG; 14 Shutouts; 27 Saves; 2,201 ⅔ IP; 712 Strikeouts; 1.403 WHIP

Career Numbers:

Record: 176-136; .564 Win Pct.; 3.86 ERA; 151 CG; 16 Shutouts; 34 Saves; 2,722 IP; 850 Strikeouts; 1.399 WHIP

Cub Career Highlights:

Best Season: Bush performed well for Chicago's pennant-winning ball clubs of 1929 and 1932, earning a 10th-place finish in the NL MVP balloting in the first of those campaigns by going 18-7, with a 3.66 ERA, 18 complete games, a league-leading 8 saves, and a career-high 270 ⅔ innings pitched, before compiling a record of 19-11 and an ERA of 3.21 three years later. Nevertheless, the 1933 season would have to be considered the finest of his career. In addition to finishing second in the NL with 20 wins, Bush ranked among the league leaders with a .625 winning percentage, 259 innings pitched, a 2.75 ERA, 20 complete games, and 4 shutouts, establishing career-best marks in each of the last three categories.

Memorable Moments/Greatest Performances: Bush turned in his first dominant performance for the Cubs on August 17, 1926, when he tossed a two-hit shutout against the Giants, defeating them by a score of 7-0. With Bush not allowing any bases on balls during the contest, only singles by future Hall of Famers Fred Lindstrom and Mel Ott stood between him and perfection.

Bush turned in a memorable effort against Boston on May 14, 1927, when he worked all 18 innings of a 7-2 Cubs win over the Braves. Yielding 11 hits and 8 walks during the contest, Bush held on until his team finally pushed across 5 runs in the top of the 18th.

Bush again performed heroically on July 10, 1927, surrendering just 5 hits during a 1-0 victory over Brooklyn, in his first start back after missing the previous six weeks with a case of the mumps.

Bush dominated Cincinnati's lineup on September 9, 1928, allowing only a pair of harmless singles during a 2-0 win over the Reds.

Bush came within an eyelash of tossing a no-hitter on August 9, 1931, when official scorers ruled George Watkins' first-inning grounder, which Cubs' shortstop Woody English mishandled, a hit and not an error. Bush finished the 1-0 victory over the Cardinals having allowed just that 1 hit and 3 bases on balls.

Bush tossed another one-hitter a little over a month later, yielding only a single to first baseman Earl Sheely during an 8-1 win over the Boston Braves on September 13, 1931.

Bush threw back-to-back shutouts just three days apart in 1933, allowing Philadelphia only 3 hits during a 5-0 win over the Phillies on August 24, before yielding just 2 safeties during a 2-0 victory over the Dodgers on the 27th of the month.

Bush pitched one of the biggest games of his career on September 20, 1932, when he clinched the pennant for the Cubs with a 5-2 win over the Pittsburgh Pirates.

However, Bush turned in his finest clutch performance in Game Three of the 1929 World Series, when he outdueled Philadelphia's George Earnshaw by a score of 3-1, giving the Cubs their only win of the fall classic.

Notable Achievements:

- Won 20 games in 1933.
- Surpassed 15 victories six other times, topping 18 wins on three of those occasions.
- Posted winning percentage in excess of .700 twice.
- Compiled ERA below 3.00 twice.
- Threw more than 200 innings six times, topping 250 innings pitched twice.

- Tossed 20 complete games in 1933.
- Led NL pitchers in: saves twice, pitching appearances once, and putouts once.
- Finished second in NL in wins once and winning percentage twice.
- Ranks among Cubs career leaders in: wins (tied-sixth), innings pitched (ninth), and pitching appearances (fifth).
- Finished 10th in 1929 NL MVP voting.
- Two-time NL champion (1929 & 1932).

41

GREG MADDUX

Arguably the greatest pitcher of his time, Greg Maddux proved to be a study in consistency over the course of his twenty-three-year major league career, winning at least 15 games a record 17 consecutive times, en route to posting more victories (355) than any other hurler whose career began after 1950. In addition to reaching the 20-win plateau twice, Maddux surpassed 18 victories seven other times, topping the senior circuit in that category on three separate occasions. The Hall of Fame right-hander also led the league in ERA four times, WHIP four times, complete games three times, and shutouts and innings pitched five times each, earning in the process numerous individual accolades, including four NL Cy Young Awards, eight All-Star selections, and five *Sporting News* All-Star nominations. Although Maddux earned the vast majority of those honors while pitching for the Atlanta Braves, he first established himself as an elite hurler during his time in Chicago, posting at least 15 victories six times and winning the first of his record four straight Cy Young Awards as a member of the Cubs in 1992, before signing with Atlanta as a free agent during the subsequent off-season. And, after 11 brilliant seasons in Atlanta, Maddux returned to Chicago in 2004 to post another 38 victories for the Cubs over the course of the next three seasons.

Born in San Angelo, Texas on April 14, 1966, Gregory Alan Maddux spent much of his childhood in Madrid, Spain, where the United States Air Force stationed his father. After taking up baseball at an early age, Greg and his older brother, Mike, began training under the supervision of former major league scout Rusty Medar when the family returned to the States during the early 1980s. Despite starring on the mound for Valley High School in Las Vegas, Nevada, Maddux received few scholarship offers following his graduation in June of 1984 due to his skinny six-foot,

170-pound frame. As a result, the eighteen-year-old right-hander declared himself eligible for that year's Major League Baseball Draft, with Chicago Cubs scout Doug Mapson subsequently writing in his report to the ball club, "I really believe this boy would be the number one player in the country if only he looked a bit more physical."

After being selected by the Cubs in the second round of the draft at Mapson's behest, Maddux spent most of the next three seasons in the minors, before being summoned to the big leagues for the first time in September of 1986. Struggling on the mound during the season's final month, Maddux appeared in six games with the Cubs, compiling a record of 2-4 with an ERA of 5.52, and allowing 44 hits in only 31 innings of work. A regular member of Chicago's starting rotation the following year, Maddux fared no better, going just 6-14 with a 5.61 ERA, and yielding 181 hits over 155⅔ innings.

Having turned twenty two during the early stages of the 1988 campaign, Maddux began to display the form that eventually made him one of the game's most decorated pitchers by going 18-8 with a 3.18 ERA, and finishing among the league leaders with 249 innings pitched, 9 complete games, and 3 shutouts, en route to earning his first All-Star selection. Picking up right where he left off the following year, Maddux earned a third-place finish in the 1989 Cy Young voting by compiling an ERA of 2.95 and finishing second in the league with 19 victories (against 12 losses). Although somewhat less successful in each of the next two seasons, Maddux continued to perform well on the mound, totaling 30 victories for mediocre Cubs teams. Particularly effective in 1991, Maddux went 15-11 with a 3.35 ERA, led all NL hurlers with 263 innings pitched and 37 starts, finished second in the league with 198 strikeouts, and won the first of his record 18 Gold Gloves for his exceptional defensive work.

Although Maddux possessed neither an overpowering fastball nor a particularly sharp-breaking curveball, he rose to prominence primarily because of his pinpoint control, outstanding ball movement, and cerebral approach to his craft, which usually enabled him to anticipate the opposing hitter's thought process. Hall of Fame third baseman Wade Boggs marveled, "It seems like he's inside your mind with you. When he knows you're not going to swing, he throws a straight one. He sees into the future. It's like he has a crystal ball hidden inside his glove."

In discussing Maddux's ability to spot his pitches, Hall of Fame second sacker Joe Morgan suggested in Nino Frostino's *Right on the Numbers*, "Greg Maddux could put a baseball through a life saver if you asked him!"

Meanwhile, Hall of Fame outfielder Tony Gwynn discussed the strategy Maddux used to baffle opposing hitters, commenting, "He's like a meticulous surgeon out there. He puts the ball where he wants to. You see a pitch inside and wonder, 'Is it the fastball or the cutter?' That's where he's got you."

Having mastered his craft, particularly the art of starting his offering towards the batter's waist before having it break back over the inside part of the plate, Maddux earned NL Cy Young honors for the first time in 1992 by compiling a record of 20-11, an ERA of 2.18, and a league-leading 268 innings pitched.

Unfortunately, the 1992 campaign proved to be Maddux's last in Chicago for quite some time. A free agent at season's end, the twenty-six-year-old right-hander eventually signed with the Atlanta Braves after contract talks between Cubs general manager Larry Himes and Maddux's agent, Scott Boras, grew increasingly contentious, with both parties accusing the other of failing to negotiate in good faith. With the Cubs ultimately deciding to pursue other free agents, most notably José Guzmán, Dan Plesac, and Candy Maldonado, Maddux left the Windy City after seven seasons, choosing instead to ink a five-year, $28 million deal with the Braves.

Joining a pitching staff in Atlanta that already included standouts Tom Glavine and John Smoltz, Maddux quickly established himself as the ace of the Braves' starting rotation, winning his second straight Cy Young Award in his first year with his new team by going 20-10, with a league-leading 2.36 ERA, 1.049 WHIP, 267 innings pitched, and 8 complete games. Impressed with Maddux's cerebral approach to pitching, Smoltz commented, "Every pitch has a purpose. Sometimes he knows what he's going to throw two pitches ahead. I swear, he makes it look like guys are swinging foam bats against him."

Yet Maddux considered his plan of attack to be quite simple, noting, "I try to do two things: locate my fastball and change speeds. That's it. I try to keep it as simple as possible. I just throw my fastball to both sides of the plate and change speed every now and then. There is no special food or anything like that. I just try to make quality pitches and try to be prepared each time I go out there."

Maddux also constantly strove to attain an extremely high level of consistency, stating, "Consistency is something you can always improve on. You can be more consistent with your mental approach, the things you do physically on the mound. Instead of doing five good pitches an inning, try to make six. You can always do more of what you are doing well and try to be as consistent as you can be."

Maddux won his third straight Cy Young Award in 1994, going 16-6 with a league-leading 10 complete games and 1.56 ERA during the strike-shortened campaign, before becoming the first pitcher to capture four consecutive Cy Youngs the following year by leading all NL hurlers with a record of 19-2, a 1.63 ERA, 210 innings pitched, 10 complete games, and 3 shutouts. He then excelled for Atlanta during the postseason, compiling a combined record of 3-1, while posting an ERA of 1.13 against Cincinnati in the NLCS and a mark of 2.25 against Cleveland in the World Series, which the Braves won in seven games.

Maddux remained in Atlanta another eight years, contributing significantly to eight more division-winning ball clubs and two more pennant-winning teams during that time by compiling an overall record of 139-70. Performing particularly well in 1997 and 1998, Maddux finished 19-4 with a 2.20 ERA in the first of those campaigns, before going 18-9 with a league-leading 2.22 ERA the following year.

Maddux's continued excellence earned him the admiration and respect of everyone around the game, including the sport's other top hurlers. Randy Johnson suggested, "Greg Maddux is probably the best pitcher in all of baseball, along with Roger Clemens. He's much more intelligent than I am because he doesn't have a 95 or 98 mph fastball. I would tell any pitcher who wants to be successful to watch him, because he's the true definition of a pitcher."

Although Maddux remained an effective pitcher his entire time in Atlanta, his period of dominance ended in 2003, when he won 16 games but posted an inordinately high 3.96 ERA for the Braves. A free agent once more following the conclusion of the 2003 campaign, the thirty-seven-year-old Maddux elected to rejoin the Cubs, with whom he spent most of the next three seasons, compiling an overall record of 38-37 during that time. Yet, even though Maddux lacked the extraordinary pitching skills he possessed earlier in his career by the time he returned to Chicago, he continued to impress his teammates with his intellectual approach to his craft, with Cubs right-hander Ryan Dempster commenting, "Any pitcher on this team should have the pleasure of parking their butt next to him on the bench during games and learning whatever you can from him and then watching him when he is pitching."

Chicago outfielder Juan Pierre said of Maddux, "He's the definition of pitching. He's not overpowering, he doesn't have tremendous stuff, but he gets it done every day, day in and day out. It's good that I can tell my grandkids that I had the chance to play behind Greg Maddux, the Hall of Famer."

Maddux remained with the Cubs until the latter stages of the 2006 season, when they traded him to the Los Angeles Dodgers for infielder Cesar Izturis. He then split his final two-plus seasons between Los Angeles and San Diego, finally retiring at the end of the 2008 campaign with a career record of 355-227 that gives him the second most victories of any pitcher who began his career following the advent of the so-called "live ball" era in 1920, with only Warren Spahn's 363 wins surpassing his total.

Since retiring as an active player, Maddux has remained close to the game as a coach and a consultant, serving the Cubs as an assistant to General Manager Jim Hendry for two years, before joining the Texas Rangers organization in 2012. From Texas, he moved on to Los Angeles, where he spent only a few months serving as a special assistant to Dodgers President of Baseball Operations, Andrew Friedman, before accepting the position of pitching coach for the University of Nevada, where he continues to share his knowledge of pitching with the school's young hurlers, including his son, Chase.

The individual accolades continued to pour in for Maddux during his retirement, with the Baseball Hall of Fame opening its doors to him in 2014. Prior to that, though, the Braves inducted him into their own Hall of Fame during a ceremony held at Atlanta's Omni Hotel on July 17, 2009, with longtime Braves manager Bobby Cox commenting during the banquet festivities, "I get asked all the time was he the best pitcher I ever saw. Was he the smartest pitcher I ever saw? The most competitive I ever saw? The best teammate I ever saw? The answer is yes to all of those."

Cub Numbers:

Record: 133-112; .543 Win Pct.; 3.61 ERA; 47 CG; 14 Shutouts; 2,016 IP; 1,305 Strikeouts; 1.245 WHIP

Career Numbers:

Record: 355-227; .610 Win Pct.; 3.16 ERA; 109 CG; 35 Shutouts; 5,008⅓ IP; 3,371 Strikeouts; 1.143 WHIP

Cub Career Highlights:

Best Season: Maddux's first Cy Young campaign of 1992 proved to be easily his finest in Chicago. En route to earning *Sporting News* NL

Courtesy of ChrisB Photography

Greg Maddux won the first of his four NL Cy Young Awards
while pitching for the Cubs in 1992

Pitcher of the Year honors and an 11th-place finish in the NL MVP voting as well, Maddux topped the senior circuit with 20 wins, 35 starts, and a career-high 268 innings pitched, and also finished in the league's top three in ERA (2.18), WHIP (1.011), strikeouts (199), and shutouts (4).

Memorable Moments/Greatest Performances: Maddux turned in his first dominant pitching performance for the Cubs on May 11, 1988, when he yielded just 3 hits, no walks, and recorded 8 strikeouts during a 10-inning, 1-0 complete-game win over the San Diego Padres.

Almost exactly one year later, on May 13, 1989, Maddux lost a heart-breaking 1-0 decision to the Houston Astros, surrendering just 3 hits and 2 walks, in going the distance.

Maddux found himself involved in another pitcher's duel on June 21, 1989, this time allowing 6 hits and 4 walks over the first 10 innings of a game the Cubs ended up winning by a score of 1-0 in 11 innings. Maddux got credit for the victory, with the save going to Mitch Williams.

Out-dueling Philadelphia starter Jose De Jesus on October 2, 1991, Maddux earned a complete-game 1-0 victory over the Phillies by yielding just 3 singles, no walks, and recording 6 strikeouts.

Maddux saved one of his finest performances for the rival New York Mets on June 30, 1992, surrendering just 4 hits, 3 walks, and striking out 10, in earning a complete-game 3-1 win over the New Yorkers.

After returning to the Cubs prior to the start of the season, Maddux became a member of the 300-win club on August 7, 2004 by working the first 5 innings of an 8-4 victory over the Giants.

Notable Achievements:

- Won at least 15 games six times, topping 18 wins three times and 20 victories once (20 in 1992).
- Compiled ERA below 3.00 twice, posting mark under 2.50 once (2.18 in 1992).
- Threw more than 200 innings seven times, topping 250 innings pitched twice.
- Led NL pitchers in: wins once, innings pitched twice, games started four times, assists twice, putouts five times, and fielding percentage once.
- Finished second in NL in: wins once, strikeouts once, WHIP once, and innings pitched once.
- Ranks among Cubs career leaders in strikeouts (sixth) and games started (fifth).
- Ranks among MLB career leaders in: wins (eighth), strikeouts (10th), and games started (fourth).
- June 1988 NL Pitcher of the Month.
- 1992 *Sporting News* NL Pitcher of the Year.
- 1992 NL Cy Young Award winner.
- Finished third in 1989 NL Cy Young voting.
- Five-time Gold Glove winner (1990, 1991, 1992, 2004 & 2005).
- 1992 *Sporting News* All-Star selection.
- Two-time NL All-Star (1988 & 1992).
- Number 39 on *The Sporting News'* 1999 list of Baseball's 100 Greatest Players.
- Elected to Baseball Hall of Fame by members of BBWAA in 2014.

42

JAKE ARRIETA

Cast aside by the Baltimore Orioles after spending the early stages of his career struggling with his control and failing to display proper command of his pitches, Jake Arrieta has emerged as one of the National League's top hurlers since joining the Cubs midway through the 2013 campaign. En route to winning more than 70 percent of his decisions since arriving in Chicago, Arrieta has surpassed 18 victories and compiled an ERA under 3.00 two times each, earning NL Cy Young honors in 2015, when he put together one of the greatest seasons turned in by any pitcher in recent memory. Continuing his outstanding pitching this past season, Arrieta helped the Cubs claim their first world championship in more than a century by posting two victories against Cleveland in the 2016 World Series.

Born in Farmington, Missouri on March 6, 1986, Jacob Joseph Arrieta grew up in Plano, Texas, where he starred in baseball while attending Plano East Senior High School. Selected by the Cincinnati Reds in the 31st round of the 2004 MLB Draft following his graduation, Arrieta chose to put his professional career on hold, instead electing to enroll at Weatherford Junior College, for whom he posted a record of 6-2 and an ERA of 3.58 as a freshman, before transferring to Texas Christian University prior to the start of his sophomore year. Studying sports psychology while attending TCU, Arrieta also excelled on the mound for the Horned Frogs baseball team, performing particularly well as a sophomore, when he earned Mountain West Conference Pitcher of the Year and second-team All-America honors by compiling an ERA of 2.35 and leading all of college baseball with 14 wins.

Choosing to forego his final year of college eligibility after Baltimore selected him in the fifth round of the 2007 MLB Draft, Arrieta subsequently spent the next three years advancing through the Orioles' farm system, before finally making his big-league debut with them in June 2010. Failing to impress team management in his initial stint with the club, Arrieta compiled a record of 6-6 and an ERA of 4.66 during the season's final four months, while issuing 48 bases on balls in only 100 innings of work. Continuing to struggle on the mound the following year, Arrieta went 10-8 with a 5.05 ERA, prompting the Orioles to return him to the minor leagues for much of the ensuing campaign. After shuttling back and forth between Baltimore and the minors for most of the next two seasons, Arrieta finally received a reprieve when the Orioles included him in a four-player trade they completed with the Cubs on July 2, 2013 that also sent pitcher Pedro Strop to Chicago, in exchange for Scott Feldman and Steve Clevenger.

Arrieta, who became a target of scorn in Baltimore after a veteran player discovered a personal blog he kept as a rookie in which he derided the Orioles' spring training facilities, mocked the pitching mechanics of teammate Brad Bergesen, and questioned the physical condition of several of the team's more established players, gained a new lease on life after he arrived in Chicago, with Cardinals infielder Matt Carpenter, who played with Arrieta in college and served as a groomsman at his wedding, commenting, "The change of scenery was a good thing. When he got to Chicago, he felt like he could be himself. When he was in Baltimore, I felt like they kind of wanted him to be someone he wasn't."

Altering his pitching mechanics after he joined the Cubs, Arrieta wisely heeded the advice of pitching coach Chris Bosio, who suggested that the 6'4", 225-pound right-hander move to the third-base side of the pitching rubber and lower his arm slot. Doing so created more deception to his delivery and lent a "crossfire" effect to his pitches that helped keep opposing hitters off-balance and enabled him to pitch more effectively to both sides of the plate. In discussing Arrieta's new pitching motion, Colorado Rockies first baseman Mark Reynolds, an Orioles teammate in 2011 and 2012, noted, "It's really, really tough on a right-handed hitter. If you're standing in the box, he's on top of you, throwing right at you. You don't know whether to get out of the way, or swing, or take it."

After going 4-2 with a 3.66 ERA in his nine starts with the Cubs in 2013, Arrieta began to show the fruits of his labor the following year, when he compiled a record of 10-5, an ERA of 2.53, and a WHIP of 0.989, recorded 167 strikeouts, and yielded only 41 bases on balls in 156⅔ innings of work following his insertion into the starting rotation in early May.

Having perfected a cut fastball that became his signature pitch, Arrieta subsequently emerged as the senior circuit's best pitcher in 2015, earning NL Cy Young honors by going 22-6, with a 1.77 ERA, a WHIP of 0.865, 236 strikeouts, and a league-leading 4 complete games and 3 shutouts. Practically unhittable after the All-Star break, Arrieta won his last 11 decisions, limiting the opposition to one run or less in 13 of his final 16 starts.

Commenting on his former teammate's magnificent mound work, Mark Reynolds stated, "I always told him back in Baltimore he had the best stuff on the team. It was just a matter of time until he figured it out. You can't teach stuff."

Fellow Cubs hurler Dan Haren added, "He throws hard enough where the hitter has to commit. If he's getting ahead 0-1, 1-2, a hitter has to lock into a certain place. You don't have that much time with him because he throws so hard and it goes both ways. I do similar to what he does, where it's moving one way or the other. But it's like minus ten miles an hour. I actually had a pretty decent year doing that. I can't imagine having to face him."

In addition to his cutter, which resembles a slider and veers away from right-handed hitters at a speed of anywhere from 83 to 95 mph, Arrieta throws a four-seam fastball that approaches home plate at around 95 mph, a sinker he uses to induce ground balls from the opposition, a changeup with tailing motion that ranges somewhere between 86 and 89 mph, and a curveball that breaks straight down and typically registers about 80 mph on the radar gun.

In addressing the formidable nature of Arrieta's pitching repertoire, Giants catcher Buster Posey said, "The first thing that stands out is that he can throw the ball so hard and make it go both ways. You don't see a guy who can two-seam the ball at 95 and throw a cutter at 93, 94. Usually it's one or the other. And he's got a power curveball to go with them."

Expressing his admiration for the league's Cy Young Award winner, Dodgers first baseman Adrian Gonzalez suggested, "The only thing that can stop him now is injury. Hitters are in trouble facing this guy. He's just like Kersh [Clayton Kershaw]. Hitters are not going to adjust. C'mon. His stuff and confidence are that good."

Arrieta displayed his tremendous confidence shortly before the 2015 NL wild card game, when a Pirates fan tweeted at him, "Be ready for the sea of black" and included the hashtag "#CrowdIsGoingToEatYouAlive."

In response, Arrieta tweeted back, "Whatever helps keep your hope alive, just know, it doesn't matter." He then went out and tossed a 5-hit shutout against Pittsburgh, enabling the Cubs to advance to the NLDS.

Commenting on his teammate's brash behavior, Dan Haren said, "I could never do that. I feel like he just has that mentality. He's really comfortable with himself and confident in his stuff. He goes into every start just expecting to be dominant. I've had stretches in my career where I was really, really good. But still I would never go into a start thinking I was going to throw a no-hitter or, 'This is going to be a three-hit shutout.' Even my years where I was winning the ERA title or starting the All-Star Game, I went into every start worried about the other team."

Arrieta got off to another tremendous start in 2016, winning his first nine decisions, yielding one run or less to the opposition in six of his first nine starts, earning NL Pitcher of the Month honors in April, and making the All-Star team for the first time in his career. However, displaying less command of his cutter as the season wore on, Arrieta experienced a gradual decline in effectiveness, going just 6-6 after July 2. Nevertheless, he ended up posting excellent overall numbers, concluding the campaign with a record of 18-8, an ERA of 3.10, a WHIP of 1.084, and 190 strikeouts in 197⅓ innings pitched, while finishing first among NL hurlers in fewest hits allowed per nine innings pitched (6.294) for the second straight year. Arrieta then proved to be a key figure in the Cubs' successful run to their first world championship since 1908, defeating the Cleveland Indians twice in the World Series, while compiling an ERA of 2.38 against the American League champions. Still only thirty years old as of this writing, Arrieta will enter the 2017 season with an overall record of 54-21 as a member of the Cubs that gives him the fourth-best winning percentage (.720) in franchise history. He also has compiled an excellent 2.52 ERA and a franchise-record 0.985 WHIP during his time in Chicago.

Cub Numbers:

Record: 54-21; .720 Win Pct.; 2.52 ERA; 6 CG; 5 Shutouts; 634⅔ IP; 630 Strikeouts; 0.985 WHIP

Career Numbers:

Record: 74-46; .617 Win Pct.; 3.58 ERA; 6 CG; 5 Shutouts; 992⅔ IP; 907 Strikeouts; 1.161 WHIP

Cub Career Highlights:

Best Season: Arrieta had easily the finest season of his career in 2015, when he earned NL Cy Young honors and a sixth-place finish in the league MVP voting by topping the senior circuit with 22 wins, 3 shutouts, and 4 complete games, while also finishing second in ERA (1.77), WHIP (0.865), winning percentage (.786), and innings pitched (229), and placing third in strikeouts (236). Arrieta's 22-6 record and 1.77 ERA made him only the fifth pitcher to win at least 22 games with no more than 6 losses and a sub-2.00 ERA since the earned run became an official statistic in 1913. Particularly effective after the All-Star break, Arrieta surrendered just 9 earned runs in 15 starts and 107⅓ innings pitched, compiling in the process an ERA of 0.75 that represents the lowest second-half mark in MLB history. Arrieta's fabulous pitching, which earned him recognition as NL Pitcher of the Month in both August and September, prompted Cubs reliever Clayton Richard to comment, "No disrespect to major league hitters, but it was like you were at a high school game or a Little League game, and there's that one guy who just dominates. You just know the hitters don't have much of a chance. That's what it looked like - not just once, but every fifth day."

Memorable Moments/Greatest Performances: Arrieta had his breakout game for the Cubs on June 13, 2014, when he tossed 7 innings of two-hit shutout ball and struck out 9 batters, in earning a 2-1 victory over the Phillies at hitter-friendly Citizens Bank Park.

Arrieta proved to be even more dominant some two weeks later, when, during a 2-0 victory over the Red Sox on June 30, he worked 7⅔ no-hit innings before finally surrendering a single to Boston shortstop Stephen Drew. Turning the game over to the Chicago bullpen at that juncture, Arrieta left the contest having recorded 10 strikeouts and yielded just 1 walk and that lone hit.

Arrieta threw the first shutout of his career on September 16, 2014, when he allowed just 1 hit, 1 walk, and recorded a career-high 13 strikeouts during a 7-0 win over the Cincinnati Reds, who got their only safety of the game when Brandon Phillips doubled to left off Arrieta with one man out in the top of the eighth inning.

Arrieta turned in a tremendous all-around effort just eight days later, earning a 3-1 win over the Cardinals on September 24, 2014 by surrendering just 2 hits and 1 run over 7 innings, while knocking in a pair of runs with a fourth-inning triple. He also fanned 10 batters during the contest.

Arrieta led the Cubs to a 3-1 victory over the crosstown rival White Sox on July 12, 2015 by tossing a complete-game two-hitter, recording 9 strikeouts, and hitting his first career homer.

Arrieta turned in a number of brilliant performances during the second half of the 2015 campaign, with his finest effort coming on August 30, when he threw a no-hitter against Los Angeles, defeating the Dodgers by a score of 2-0. In addition to fanning 12 batters during the game, Arrieta allowed only two men to reach base—one on a third-inning error by Cubs second baseman Starlin Castro, and the other on a sixth-inning walk to Dodger shortstop Jimmy Rollins. Commenting on his ace right-hander's superb performance, Cubs manager Joe Maddon told *The New York Daily News*, "He [Arrieta] has that kind of stuff nightly. It's really crazy. The ball looks like a whiffle ball from the side. You can see the break on the slider and the curveball. Right now, he's pitching at a different level."

Arrieta again pitched magnificently on September 22, 2015, when he yielded just 3 hits and recorded 11 strikeouts during a 4-0 shutout of the Milwaukee Brewers.

Continuing his extraordinary run in his next start five days later, Arrieta surrendered just 1 hit and fanned 9 batters over the first 7 innings of a 4-0 victory over the Pittsburgh Pirates on September 27. Making things even sweeter, Arrieta launched the second home run of his career off Pittsburgh starter A.J. Burnett in the bottom of the second inning.

Arrieta again dominated Pittsburgh's lineup in the postseason, allowing just 5 hits and recording 11 strikeouts, in shutting out the Pirates by a score of 4-0 in the 2015 NL Wild Card Game.

Picking up right where he left off the previous year, Arrieta began the 2016 campaign by surrendering just 2 hits over the first seven innings of a 9-0 victory over the Anaheim Angels on Opening Day.

Arrieta tossed his second career no-hitter a little over two weeks later, fanning 6 batters and allowing 4 bases on balls during a lopsided 16-0 victory over the Reds in Cincinnati on April 21. Following the contest, Reds outfielder Jay Bruce stated, "Every time he [Arrieta] goes out there, he's got no-hit stuff. He's arguably the best pitcher in the game today." Meanwhile, in discussing his second no-hitter in his last 11 regular-season

Courtesy of Mateocubs

Jake Arrieta posted two victories for the Cubs
in the 2016 World Series

starts, Arrieta revealed, "I envisioned pitching like this, even when I had a 5.46 ERA in Baltimore. I expected to get to this point at some point, regardless of how long it took, or what I had to go through to get there."

Although Arrieta failed to get a decision in Game Three of the 2016 NLDS, surrendering 2 runs and 6 hits over the first 6 innings of a contest the Cubs eventually lost to the Giants by a score of 6-5 in 13 innings, he experienced one of his greatest thrills in the top of the second, when he gave Chicago an early 3-0 lead by hitting a three-run homer off Madison Bumgarner.

Arrieta came up big for the Cubs in Game Two of the 2016 World Series, helping them tie the Series at a game apiece by allowing just 1 run and 2 hits to Cleveland over the first 5⅔ innings of a contest they went on to win by a score of 5-1. He turned in another strong performance in Game Six, helping the Cubs even the Series for a second time by yielding 2 runs, 3 hits, and recording 9 strikeouts in another 5⅔ innings of work, in leading his team to a lopsided 9-3 victory. Arrieta concluded the fall classic with a record of 2-0, an ERA of 2.38, and 15 strikeouts in 11⅓ total innings of work, while surrendering only 5 hits to the American League champions.

Notable Achievements:

- Has won more than 20 games once, posing 18 victories another time.
- Has posted winning percentage in excess of .700 once (.786 in 2015).
- Has compiled ERA under 3.00 twice, posting mark below 2.00 once (1.77 in 2015).
- Has compiled WHIP under 1.000 twice.
- Has struck out more than 200 batters once (236 in 2015).
- Has thrown more than 200 innings once (229 in 2015).
- Has led NL pitchers in: wins once, shutouts once, complete games once, fewest hits allowed per nine innings pitched twice, putouts once, and assists twice.
- Has finished second among NL pitchers in: ERA once, winning percentage once, WHIP once, and innings pitched once.
- Holds Cubs career record for lowest WHIP (0.985).

- Ranks among Cubs career leaders in: winning pct. (fourth), strikeouts-to-walks ratio (sixth), fewest hits allowed per nine innings pitched (second), and most strikeouts per nine innings pitched (fourth).
- Has thrown two no-hitters (vs. Dodgers on August 30, 2015 & vs. Reds on April 21, 2016).
- Three-time NL Pitcher of the Month.
- Finished sixth in 2015 NL MVP voting.
- 2015 NL Cy Young Award winner.
- 2016 Silver Slugger winner.
- 2016 NL All-Star.
- 2016 NL champion.
- 2016 world champion.

43

BILL LEE

The staff ace of two pennant-winning Cubs teams, Bill Lee spent parts of 11 seasons in Chicago, proving to be one of the National League's best pitchers from 1935 to 1939. En route to compiling an overall record of 93-56 over the course of those five seasons, Lee surpassed 20 wins twice and 18 victories on two other occasions. The lanky 6'3", 195-pound right-hander also posted an ERA under 3.00 twice, leading all NL hurlers in that category once, while also finishing first in the senior circuit in winning percentage and shutouts two times each. A true workhorse, Lee also threw 20 complete games twice and tossed more than 250 innings five straight times, before his skills began to diminish due to a tired arm and failing eyesight that eventually led to blindness.

Born in Plaquemine, Louisiana on October 21, 1909, William Crutcher Lee spent two years pitching for Louisiana State University, before signing with the St. Louis Cardinals as an amateur free agent in 1929. Increasing his value by compiling a record of 71-31 over the course of the next four seasons while advancing through the Cardinals' vast farm system, Lee found himself headed to Chicago when St. Louis GM Branch Rickey sold him to the Cubs for $25,000 during the latter stages of the 1933 campaign.

Inserted into the Cubs' starting rotation early in 1934, Lee had a solid rookie season, going 13-14, with a 3.40 ERA, 16 complete games, 4 shutouts, and 214 innings pitched. He then joined Lon Warneke at the top of Chicago's rotation the following year, helping the Cubs win the NL pennant by posting a mark of 20-6 that gave him the league's best winning percentage (.769). The twenty-five-year-old right-hander also ranked among the league leaders with a 2.96 ERA, 3 shutouts, 18 complete games, and 252 innings pitched. Although Lee subsequently struggled somewhat

Bill Lee helped lead the Cubs to the pennant
in both 1935 and 1938

Courtesy of MEARS Online Auctions

in his lone start against Detroit in the World Series, surrendering 7 hits, 3 walks, and 4 runs over the first 7⅓ innings of Game Three, which the Cubs eventually lost by a score of 6-5 in 11 innings, he helped keep Chicago's hopes alive in Game Five by working the final three frames of a 3-1 Cubs win that extended the fall classic to a sixth game.

Lee had another excellent year in 1936, concluding the campaign with a record of 18-11, finishing among the league leaders with a 3.31 ERA, 20 complete games, and 258⅔ innings pitched, and topping the circuit with 4 shutouts. After a somewhat less successful 1937 season in which he finished just 14-15, even though he compiled a very respectable 3.54 ERA and threw 17 complete games and 272⅓ innings, Lee rebounded in a big way the following year. In addition to leading all NL hurlers with a record of 22-9, a 2.66 ERA, and 9 shutouts, Lee placed near the top of the league rankings with 19 complete games, 291 innings pitched, and 121 strikeouts. Lee's exceptional performance for the pennant-winning Cubs earned him All-Star honors for the first of two straight times and a runner-up finish to Cincinnati's Ernie Lombardi in the NL MVP voting.

Lee gradually developed into one of the National League's elite hurlers even though he did not throw particularly hard. Featuring a devastating curveball that buckled the knees of many a hitter, Lee depended largely on off-speed pitches to thwart the opposition. At the same time, though, he did an outstanding job of disguising his fastball with a signature high leg kick.

Lee continued to be a thorn in the side of opposing batters in 1939, going 19-15 with a 3.44 ERA, and finishing third in the league with 20 complete games and 282⅓ innings pitched. However, he never again came close to approaching those numbers. With his deteriorating eyesight making it difficult for him to see the catcher's signs or pitch with confidence, Lee slumped to a record of 9-17 and an ERA of 5.03 in 1940. He followed that up with two more lackluster seasons, going 8-14 with a 3.76 ERA in 1941, before compiling a record of 13-13 and an ERA of 3.85 in 1942. Although Lee began wearing glasses in the second of those campaigns in an effort to improve his vision, his eyes continued to degenerate. The veteran right-hander found his performance being further compromised by his ailing arm, which began to wear out after logging so many innings the previous few years.

Convinced that Lee had little left after he got off to a 3-7 start in 1943, the Cubs traded him to the Phillies for catcher Mickey Livingston on August 5. After going just 1-5 for Philadelphia the rest of the year, Lee compiled an overall mark of 13-17 for the Phillies over the course of the next season-and-a-half, before being dealt to the Boston Braves midway through the 1945 campaign. Lee remained in Boston until the end of 1946, when he signed as a free agent with the Cubs. Proving to be unsuccessful in his second tour of duty with the club, Lee announced his retirement after the Cubs released him during the season's final month. He ended his career with a record of 169-157, an ERA of 3.54, 182 complete games, 29 shutouts, and 998 strikeouts in 2,864 total innings of work.

Following his playing days, Lee returned to Plaquemine, Louisiana, where he had surgery to repair the detached retinas in both his eyes. Unfortunately, the operations did little good since irrevocable damage had already been done to his eyesight. Lee went blind shortly thereafter, spending the rest of his life in darkness, before passing away at the age of sixty-seven, on June 15, 1977.

Cub Numbers:

Record: 139-123; .531 Win Pct.; 3.51 ERA; 153 CG; 25 Shutouts; 9 Saves; 2,271⅓ IP; 874 Strikeouts; 1.330 WHIP

Career Numbers:

Record: 169-157; .518 Win Pct.; 3.54 ERA; 182 CG; 29 Shutouts; 13 Saves; 2,864 IP; 998 Strikeouts; 1.343 WHIP

Cub Career Highlights:

Best Season: Although Lee had a big year for the Cubs in 1935, going 20-6, with a 2.96 ERA, 18 complete games, and 252 innings pitched, he clearly had the finest season of his career in 1938. En route to earning a runner-up finish in the NL MVP balloting, Lee led the league with 22 victories, a .710 winning percentage, a 2.66 ERA, and 9 shutouts, establishing career-best marks in three of the four categories. He also placed near the top of the league rankings with 19 complete games, 291 innings pitched, and 121 strikeouts, posting career-high marks in each of the last two categories as well. Practically unhittable for extended periods of time during his signature season, Lee fashioned a pair of lengthy scoreless innings streaks, tossing 35⅓ consecutive scoreless frames, from May 23 to

June 7, before keeping the opposition off the scoreboard for 38⅓ straight innings, from September 5 to September 26.

Memorable Moments/Greatest Performances: Lee, who hit only 5 home runs his entire career, had his greatest day at the plate on May 7, 1941, when he homered twice during a complete-game, 11-2 victory over the Philadelphia Phillies. Lee also allowed just 5 hits and recorded 5 strikeouts during the contest.

Exactly seven years earlier, on May 7, 1934, Lee made his first major-league start a memorable one, yielding just 4 hits and 2 walks during a complete-game, 2-0 win over the Phillies.

Lee turned in another exceptional performance in his very next start, surrendering just a pair of singles during a 5-0 shutout of the Dodgers on May 12, 1934.

Lee hurled another gem later in the year, winning a 1-0 pitcher's duel with New York's Hal Schumacher on August 27, 1934. Lee allowed just 3 hits and 4 walks during the contest.

Lee got the better of Dizzy Dean on September 27, 1935, clinching the pennant for the Cubs with a 6-2 victory over Dean and the Cardinals.

Lee won a pair of 1-0 pitcher's duels in 1936, out-pitching Brooklyn's Van Mungo on April 29, and defeating New York's Carl Hubbell on July 13. Lee surrendered just 4 hits in each game.

Just a few days before Lee began the first of his lengthy scoreless innings streaks in 1938, he turned in one of his finest performances of the campaign, yielding just 5 hits over 10 innings, in earning a 1-0 complete-game victory over the New York Giants.

Lee highlighted the first of those streaks with a three-hit shutout of Boston on June 3 that the Cubs won by a score of 4-0.

Lee turned in his last dominant performance for the Cubs on May 28, 1942, when he surrendered just 6 hits and recorded 7 strikeouts during a 12-inning, 2-1 complete-game win over the Reds.

Notable Achievements:

- Won at least 20 games twice, surpassing 18 victories two other times.
- Posted winning percentage in excess of .700 twice.

- Compiled ERA below 3.00 twice.
- Tossed 9 shutouts in 1938.
- Threw more than 200 innings eight times, topping 250 innings pitched on five occasions.
- Tossed 20 complete games twice.
- Led NL pitchers in: wins once, winning percentage twice, ERA once, shutouts twice, assists once, and games started three times.
- Finished second in NL in innings pitched twice.
- Ranks among Cubs career leaders in: wins (ninth), shutouts (sixth), innings pitched (seventh), pitching appearances (10th), and games started (sixth).
- Finished second in 1938 NL MVP voting.
- Two-time NL All-Star (1938 & 1939).
- Two-time NL champion (1935 & 1938).

44

JOSE CARDENAL

A well-traveled outfielder who played for nine different ball clubs over the course of his eighteen-year major league career, Jose Cardenal proved to be one of the best players on some bad Cubs teams during the 1970s. Spending six seasons in Chicago, Cardenal compiled a batting average in excess of .290 five straight times and topped the .300-mark on two separate occasions as a member of the Cubs. The speedy Cardenal also scored more than 90 runs once and stole more than 20 bases four times during his time in the Windy City, while annually ranking among the leading players at his position in both putouts and assists. Yet, it is for his temperamental disposition and colorful persona that Cardenal is remembered most by Cubs fans.

Born in Matanzas, Cuba on October 7, 1943, José Rosario Domec Cardenal attended local Jose Marti Escuela High School, before signing with the San Francisco Giants as an amateur free agent in 1960. Although Cardenal performed well in the minor leagues over the course of the next five seasons, San Francisco's crowded outfield situation kept him off the big league roster for all but 29 games during that time, eventually prompting the Giants to trade him to the California Angels for catcher Jack Hiatt following the conclusion of the 1964 campaign. Cardenal spent the next three seasons playing centerfield for the Angels, having his best year for them in 1966, when he hit 16 homers, scored 67 runs, batted .276, and stole 24 bases.

Dealt to the Cleveland Indians for outfielder Chuck Hinton on November 29, 1967, Cardenal patrolled center for the Indians for the next two seasons, finishing second in the American League with 40 stolen bases in 1968, before finding himself on the move once again when Cleveland traded him to the St. Louis Cardinals for outfielder Vade Pinson prior to the start of the 1970 campaign. After driving in 74 runs, scoring 73 times, stealing 26 bases, and batting .293 for the Cardinals in 1970, Cardenal changed addresses once more midway through the 1971 season, joining the Milwaukee Brewers for the second half of the year, before being traded to the Cubs for outfielder Brock Davis and pitchers Jim Colborn and Earl Stephenson on December 3, 1971.

Shifted from center to right field upon his arrival in Chicago, Cardenal found his new home very much to his liking. Posting the best numbers of his career to that point, the twenty-eight-year-old outfielder hit 17 homers, knocked in 70 runs, scored 96 times, stole 25 bases, and batted .291 in his first year with the Cubs. He followed that up by hitting 11 homers, driving in 68 runs, scoring 80 times, and leading the team with a .303 batting average, 33 doubles, and 19 stolen bases in 1973, earning in the process recognition as the Cubs Player of the Year by the Chicago baseball writers. Cardenal continued his strong play for the Cubs in 1974, hitting 13 homers, knocking in 72 runs, scoring 75 times, stealing 23 bases, batting .293, and placing among the league leaders with a career-high 35 doubles.

Although Cardenal stood 5'10" tall and weighed only 155 pounds, he managed to post double-digit home run totals in each of his first three seasons with the Cubs because of his quick wrists, which gave him excellent bat speed. Nevertheless, he remained primarily a contact hitter whose bat typically produced many more line drives than long balls. Cardenal also displayed good range and a strong throwing arm in the outfield and outstanding speed on the base paths, recording more than 30 steals a total of four times over the course of his career.

In addition to his solid all-around play, Cardenal became known for his colorful persona, which made him a fan favorite at Wrigley Field. Sporting a gigantic afro, Cardenal also stood out for the manner in which he tucked his cap into his back pocket, and for his crouched batting stance and running style. Cardenal drew further attention to himself with a series of rather bizarre incidents that occurred during his time in Chicago, one of which took place in 1972, when he declared himself unfit to play because crickets in his hotel room had kept him awake all night. On another occasion, Cardenal refused to play because he claimed that a bad night's sleep had left him with an eyelid that would not close. Cardenal also once hit a policeman in the head with his own nightstick after arriving at O'Hare Airport to find the officer engaged in a heated argument with his wife over a parking violation.

Yet, in spite of his somewhat unconventional behavior, Cardenal continued to produce for the Cubs on the field in 1975, hitting 9 homers, driving in 68 runs, scoring 85 times, stealing 34 bases, and batting .317. He followed that up by batting .299 in 1976, although he experienced a steep decline in overall offensive production, concluding the campaign with only 8 homers, 47 RBIs, 64 runs scored, and an on-base percentage of .339. After Cardenal assumed a part-time role in 1977, the Cubs elected to trade him to Philadelphia for undistinguished pitcher Manny Seoane at season's end. Cardenal left Chicago having hit 61 homers, driven in 343 runs, scored 433 times, collected 864 hits, and compiled a batting average of .296 as a member of the Cubs.

Cardenal remained a part-time player in Philadelphia in 1978, before splitting his final two seasons between the Phillies, Mets, and Kansas City Royals, serving as a backup with all three teams. He retired at the end of the 1980 season, sporting career totals of 138 home runs, 775 RBIs, 936 runs scored, and 1,913 hits, a lifetime batting average of .275, an on-base percentage of .333, and a slugging percentage of .395.

Following his playing days, Cardenal entered into a lengthy career in coaching, serving on the coaching staffs of the Cincinnati Reds, St. Louis Cardinals, New York Yankees, and Tampa Bay Devil Rays, before spending five seasons as the senior advisor to the Washington Nationals general manager, during which time he tutored Alfonso Soriano on the finer points of playing the outfield. The Nationals relieved him of his duties following the conclusion of the 2009 season.

Cub Numbers:

61 HR; 343 RBIs; 433 Runs Scored; 864 Hits; 159 Doubles; 16 Triples; 129 Stolen Bases; .296 AVG; .363 OBP; .424 SLG PCT; .787 OPS

Career Numbers:

138 HR; 775 RBIs; 936 Runs Scored; 1,913 Hits; 333 Doubles; 46 Triples; 329 Stolen Bases; .275 AVG; .333 OBP; .395 SLG PCT; .728 OPS

Cub Career Highlights:

Best Season: Although the Chicago baseball writers named Cardenal Cubs Player of the Year in 1973 for hitting 11 homers, driving in 68 runs, scoring 80 times, stealing 19 bases, and batting .303, he actually compiled slightly better overall numbers in both 1972 and 1975. In addition to

Courtesy of Main Line Autographs

Jose Cardenal batted over .300 twice and stole more than 20
bases four times for the Cubs during the 1970s

hitting 9 homers, knocking in 68 runs, scoring 85 times, and swiping 34
bags in the second of those campaigns, Cardenal posted career-high marks
in hits (182), bases on balls (77), batting average (.317), and on-base percentage (.397). Meanwhile, Cardenal batted .291, drove in 70 runs, stole
25 bases, and established career-best marks in home runs (17), runs scored

(96), and slugging percentage (.454) in 1972. It's an extremely close call, but, since the Cubs posted a record of 85-70 in 1972, which represented their only winning mark of Cardenal's six-year tenure with the team, we'll go with that for his finest season.

Memorable Moments/Greatest Performances: Cardenal had his first big day at the plate for the Cubs on May 3, 1972, when he went 4-for-5, with a double, triple, 5 RBIs, and 2 runs scored, during a lopsided 12-1 victory over the Atlanta Braves.

Cardenal led the Cubs to a 5-1 win over the Mets on May 24, 1972 by driving in 4 runs with a pair of two-run homers.

Cardenal again proved to be a thorn in the side of the Mets later in the year, when he collected 3 hits, homered twice, and knocked in 5 runs, in leading the Cubs to an 18-5 win over their NL East rivals on September 16, 1972.

Cardenal provided all the offensive firepower the Cubs needed to defeat Los Angeles on May 31, 1975, homering twice during a 2-1 win over the Dodgers.

Cardenal had a huge game against Atlanta on August 31, 1975, going 4-for-5, with a double, 2 RBIs, and 1 run scored, in leading the Cubs to a 9-8 victory over the Braves in 10 innings. Cardenal delivered the game's winning run with a 2-out RBI single in the bottom of the 10th.

However, Cardenal turned in his finest performance as a member of the Cubs on May 2, 1976, when he went 6-for-7, with a homer, double, 4 RBIs, and 2 runs scored, during a 6-5 victory over the San Francisco Giants in which he drove home the winning run with an RBI single in the top of the 14th inning.

Notable Achievements:

- Batted over .300 twice.
- Scored 96 runs in 1972.
- Surpassed 30 doubles three times.
- Stole more than 20 bases four times, topping 30 thefts once (34 in 1975).
- Led NL left-fielders in: assists once, fielding percentage once, and double plays once.

45

KERRY WOOD

The author of one of the greatest single-game pitching performances in MLB history, Kerry Wood rose to prominence as a twenty-year-old rookie in 1998 when he recorded 20 strikeouts during a one-hit shutout of the Houston Astros. Although the hard-throwing right-hander subsequently suffered the misfortune of being plagued by injuries throughout much of his career, he established himself as one of the game's bright young stars his first few years in the league, fanning more than 200 batters in four of his first five seasons in Chicago, en route to earning one strikeout title and one All-Star selection. Unfortunately, Wood's consistently high pitch counts and aggressive style of pitching gradually took their toll on him, forcing him to spend significant portions of four seasons on the disabled list and miss the entire 1999 campaign after undergoing Tommy John surgery during the previous off-season. Nevertheless, after being moved to the bullpen by the Cubs in an effort to minimize the strain on his arm, Wood reinvented himself as a reliever, emerging as one of the National League's top closers in 2008, when he finished fourth in the senior circuit with 34 saves. He then spent the remainder of his career working out of the bullpen, before retiring from the game early in 2012, leaving behind him, through no fault of his own, a legacy of unfulfilled potential.

Born in Irving, Texas on June 16, 1977, Kerry Lee Wood grew up dreaming of one day playing in the Major Leagues, much like his childhood hero, Nolan Ryan. After spending his freshman year at local MacArthur High School playing shortstop for the school's baseball team, Wood transitioned to the mound as a sophomore, patterning his motion and demeanor on the hill after Ryan and fellow Texan Roger Clemens. Following his junior year at MacArthur High, Wood transferred to Grand Prairie High School, in Grand Prairie, Texas, where he established himself as a top pitching prospect by compiling a record of 14-0 and a brilliant 0.77 ERA as a senior, while also striking out 152 batters in only 81⅓ innings of work. The eighteen-year-old flamethrower's dominating performance so impressed Major League scouts that the Chicago Cubs selected him with the fourth overall pick of the 1995 MLB Draft. After watching Wood pitch both ends of a doubleheader for his high school team just a few days after drafting him, then-Cubs scouting director Al Goldis proclaimed, "I haven't seen a guy throw like this in ten years. If [Dwight] Gooden was in this draft, I would have taken Wood ahead of him."

Wood subsequently advanced rapidly through the Chicago farm system, performing so well at each stop that he earned serious consideration for a spot on the big league roster by the spring of 1998. However, with the Cubs feeling that the twenty-year-old phenom needed a bit more seasoning, they sent him to their Triple A affiliate in Iowa for the start of the campaign. Upon learning of Chicago's decision, then-Angels manager Terry Collins commented, "If the Cubs have five pitchers better than Kerry Wood, they'll definitely win the World Series."

Returning to the Cubs shortly thereafter, Wood joined Chicago's starting rotation in mid-April, after which he went on to earn NL Rookie of the Year honors by going 13-6 with a 3.40 ERA, and finishing third in the league with 233 strikeouts, in only 166⅔ innings pitched. Particularly impressive in his third start, Wood tossed a one-hit shutout against Houston in which he struck out 20 batters, joining in the process Roger Clemens as the only pitchers in MLB history, to that point, to record that many strikeouts in a nine-inning game. Dominating National League hitters throughout most of the campaign, Wood, whose pitching repertoire included a 96-98 mph fastball, an explosive slider, and a knee-buckling curveball that often froze opposing batters at the plate, would have compiled even better numbers had he not sprained his right elbow in late August, prompting the Cubs to shut him down for the rest of the year.

Wood suffered another injury the following spring, when he tore a ligament in his right arm in his first mound appearance, forcing him to undergo Tommy John surgery that kept him off the field for the entire year. Struggling somewhat upon his return to the Cubs in May of 2000, Wood appeared in only 23 games, posting a record of 8-7 and an ERA of 4.80. However, the 6'5", 210-pound right-hander displayed much of his old dominance the following year, when, despite being limited to 28 starts by various ailments, he finished 12-6, with a 3.36 ERA and 217 strikeouts, in 174⅓ innings of work.

Seeking to remain healthy for an entire year, and eager to shed the nicknames "Special K" and "Kid K", Wood adopted a new pitching philosophy in 2002, when, heeding the advice of veteran hurlers Kevin Tapani and Jon Lieber, he worked hard on improving his changeup and relied more heavily on his breaking pitches to retire opposing batters. Although Wood's new approach resulted in a record of only 12-11 and a rather pedestrian ERA of 3.66, he managed to establish career-high marks in starts (33) and innings pitched (213⅔), while also finishing third in the league with 217 strikeouts. Able to toe the rubber another 32 times in 2003, Wood earned the first of his two All-Star selections by going 14-11, with a 3.20 ERA and a league-leading 266 strikeouts.

Ironically, the 2003 campaign ended up being Wood's last as a full-time starter. Sidelined for nearly two months the following year with a strained triceps, Wood made only 22 starts, finishing the season with a record of just 8-9 and an ERA of 3.72. Experiencing further hardship in 2005, Wood made only 21 appearances, with just 10 of those being starts, before undergoing another surgery on his arm in late August. He then missed virtually all of the next two seasons with a variety of injuries that included a sore shoulder, a partially torn rotator cuff, and a knee ailment that required surgery to repair.

Nevertheless, displaying the fortitude and competitive spirit that once helped make him one of baseball's most highly-touted prospects, Wood returned to the Cubs in 2008, this time as a reliever. Excelling in his new role, the thirty-year-old right-hander earned All-Star honors by going 5-4 with a 3.26 ERA, finishing fourth in the league with 34 saves, and recording 84 strikeouts in 66⅓ innings pitched. A free agent at season's end, Wood signed with the Cleveland Indians, for whom he saved 20 games in 2009, before being dealt to the Yankees on July 31, 2010 after struggling on the mound over the season's first four months. Once again a free agent at the end of 2010, Wood returned to Chicago, where he compiled a record of 3-5 and an ERA of 3.35 for the Cubs in 2011 while working out of the bullpen, before announcing his retirement early the following year after pitching ineffectively in his first 10 appearances. Wood retired with a career record of 86-75, an ERA of 3.67, and 1,582 strikeouts in 1,380 innings pitched, giving him a lifetime strikeouts-per-nine-innings-pitched ratio of

10.317 that ranks second in MLB history to the mark of 10.610 posted by Randy Johnson. Wood compiled that impressive figure even though he made 14 trips to the disabled list over the course of his fourteen-year big league career.

Cub Numbers:

Record: 80-68; .541 Win Pct.; 3.67 ERA; 11 CG; 5 Shutouts; 35 Saves; 1,279 IP; 1,470 Strikeouts; 1.258 WHIP

Career Numbers:

Record: 86-75; .534 Win Pct.; 3.67 ERA; 11 CG; 5 Shutouts; 63 Saves; 1,380 IP; 1,582 Strikeouts; 1.267 WHIP

Cub Career Highlights:

Best Season: It could certainly be argued that Wood had his finest season in 2003, when he earned his first All-Star selection by establishing career-best marks in wins (14), ERA (3.20), complete games (4), shutouts (2), and strikeouts (266), leading all NL hurlers in the last category. Nevertheless, Wood proved to be slightly more dominant in 1998, when he captured NL Rookie of the Year honors by going 13-6 with a 3.40 ERA and recording 233 strikeouts, in only 166⅔ innings pitched. In addition to finishing third in the league in punchouts, Wood held opposing batters to a league-best .196 batting average and posted the best hits-per-nine-innings-pitched (6.318) and strikeouts-per-nine-innings-pitched (12.582) ratios in the senior circuit, setting a single-season franchise record in the last category.

Memorable Moments/Greatest Performances: A pretty fair hitting pitcher, Wood compiled a lifetime batting average of .171, with 7 homers and 32 RBIs, in only 346 official at-bats. Wood hit perhaps his most memorable home run on May 2, 2000, when, during an 11-1 victory over the Houston Astros in which he worked six strong innings in his first game back after undergoing Tommy John surgery the previous year, he delivered a two-run blast in his first trip to the plate.

Wood also helped his own cause on August 14, 2004, when, in addition to surrendering just 4 hits and recording 7 strikeouts over the first 8 innings of a 2-0 win over the Dodgers, he hit a solo home run off Kazuhisa Ishii in the bottom of the third inning.

Kerry Wood turned in the most dominant single-game
pitching performance in Cubs history in 1998,
when he struck out 20 Houston Astros

Far more comfortable on the mound, Wood turned in one of his most dominant pitching performances on August 26, 1998, when he struck out 16 batters and yielded just 3 hits and 2 runs over the first 8 innings of a lopsided 9-2 victory over the Cincinnati Reds.

Wood proved to be even more dominant on May 25, 2001, allowing just 1 hit, 2 walks, and recording 14 strikeouts, in earning a 1-0 complete-game victory over Milwaukee. The Brewers got their only hit of the game when second baseman Mark Loretta led off the top of the seventh inning with a single to left field.

Wood tossed another complete-game shutout on May 7, 2002, when he blanked the Cardinals on just 4 hits, striking out 9 St. Louis batsmen during an 8-0 Cubs win.

Wood hurled another gem on April 12, 2003, yielding just 3 hits and recording 13 strikeouts over the first 8 innings of a 4-0 win over the Pittsburgh Pirates.

Although Wood failed to earn a decision in a game the Cubs eventually won by a score of 4-2 in 17 innings, he turned in another dominant performance against the Brewers on May 15, 2003, surrendering 3 hits, 2 walks, and recording 13 strikeouts over 7 scoreless innings.

In a highly anticipated showdown between the only two men (at that time) ever to record 20 strikeouts in a nine-inning game, Wood got the better of Roger Clemens on June 7, 2003, defeating Clemens and the Yankees by a score of 5-2. Facing the Yankees in their first visit to Wrigley Field since the 1938 World Series, Wood yielded just 3 hits and 1 run over 7⅔ innings, while striking out 11 New York batters. Eric Karros delivered the game's big blow with a three-run homer off reliever Juan Acevedo in the bottom of the seventh inning.

Wood turned in a similarly dominant performance less than two weeks later, limiting the Reds to just 3 hits and 1 run, while striking out 9 batters, in earning a complete-game 4-1 victory over Cincinnati on June 18, 2003.

Wood continued his outstanding pitching the following month, recording 12 strikeouts and allowing just 3 hits and 1 run during a 5-1 complete-game win over the Florida Marlins on July 9, 2003.

Wood again dominated Florida's lineup just 10 days later, surrendering just 2 hits and recording 8 strikeouts, in going the distance to defeat the Marlins by a score of 1-0 on July 19.

Wood turned in another magnificent effort on September 17, 2003, allowing just 4 hits and fanning 11 batters during a 2-0 win over the New York Mets.

Wood performed brilliantly against Atlanta in the 2003 Division Series, earning wins in Games One and Five, to lead the Cubs to a berth in the NLCS. After recording 11 strikeouts and yielding just 2 runs and 2 hits over the first 7⅓ innings of a 4-2 victory in the Series opener, Wood surrendered just 1 run and 5 hits over 8 innings during Chicago's 5-1 win in the Game Five clincher.

Although the Cubs ended up losing Game Seven of the 2003 NLCS to the Marlins by a score of 9-6, with Wood failing to protect an early 5-3 lead, the Chicago starter experienced what he later called "My most memorable moment in baseball" in the second inning, when his two-out, two-run homer off Mark Redman tied the game at 3-3.

However, Wood unquestionably turned in the most noteworthy performance of his career in just his third start, surrendering only one hit and recording 20 strikeouts during a 2-0 victory over the Houston Astros on May 6, 1998. Wood, who hit one batter and allowed just a third-inning infield single to Houston shortstop Ricky Gutierrez during the contest, fanned the first five batters he faced, en route to becoming one of just four pitchers in MLB history to strike out 20 batters in a nine-inning game (Roger Clemens (twice), Randy Johnson and Max Scherzer are the others). In discussing Wood's performance, which many consider to be the most dominant pitching performance of all time, Astros Manager Larry Dierker told George Vass in the December 1998 edition of *Baseball Digest*, "That game reminded me a lot of the first time we saw [Nolan] Ryan in the sense that it seemed like, when the ball left his [Wood's] hand, it hit the catcher's mitt at the same time."

Notable Achievements:

- Struck out more than 200 batters four times.
- Threw more than 200 innings twice.
- Saved 34 games in 2008.
- Led NL pitchers in: strikeouts once, strikeouts per nine innings pitched twice, and fewest hits allowed per nine innings pitched twice.

- Holds Cubs record for most strikeouts in one game (20 vs. Houston on May 6, 1998).
- Holds Cubs single-season record for most strikeouts per nine innings pitched (12.582 in 1998).
- Ranks among Cubs career leaders in: strikeouts (third), strikeouts per nine innings pitched (third), and fewest hits allowed per nine innings pitched (fourth).
- 1998 NL Rookie of the Year.
- Two-time NL All-Star (2003 & 2008).

46

ALFONSO SORIANO

Taking a long and circuitous route to the city of Chicago, Alfonso Soriano began his career in professional baseball in Japan during the mid-1990s. From the Far East, Soriano traveled to the United States, where he played for the New York Yankees, Texas Rangers, and Washington Nationals, before finally arriving in the Windy City in 2007. Although Soriano spent most of his peak years playing for other teams, he still made significant contributions to the Cubs over parts of seven seasons, helping them capture two NL Central titles by surpassing 20 home runs six times and 100 RBIs once. And, after earning All-Star honors in each of his first two seasons in Chicago, Soriano later emerged as an elder statesman in the clubhouse, providing veteran leadership to several of his younger teammates.

Born in the baseball hotbed of San Pedro de Macoris, Dominican Republic on January 7, 1976, Alfonso Guilleard Soriano went to high school at Eugenio Maria de Osto, where he established himself as one of the area's most talented young ballplayers. First discovered by the Hiroshima Toyo Carp of Japan's Central League, whose Dominican Academy he entered at the age of eighteen, Soriano spent two years playing in the Japanese minor leagues, before making a brief appearance with the Carp in 1997. Unhappy with the treatment he received from team management, and weary of the rigorous Japanese training regimen, Soriano announced his retirement at the end of the 1997 campaign, thereby taking advantage of a loophole in the system that made him a free agent.

Subsequently signed by the Yankees, Soriano spent most of the next three years advancing through New York's farm system, although he also appeared in a total of 31 games at the major-league level during that time. Soriano arrived in the big leagues to stay in 2001, when, starting 156 games at second base for the Yankees, he hit 18 homers, knocked in 73 runs, scored 77 times, stole 43 bases, and batted .268. Developing into one of the league's most dynamic offensive players the following year, Soriano earned the first of his seven consecutive All-Star selections and a third-place finish in the AL MVP voting by hitting 39 homers, driving in 102 runs, amassing 51 doubles, batting .300, and topping the circuit with 128 runs scored, 209 hits, and 41 stolen bases. He again posted excellent numbers in 2003, concluding the campaign with 38 home runs, 91 RBIs, 114 runs scored, 198 hits, 35 steals, and a .290 batting average.

In spite of Soriano's outstanding offensive production, the Yankees elected to trade him to Texas for Alex Rodriguez when the Rangers made the controversial superstar available to them during the subsequent off-season. Soriano spent the next two years in Texas, totaling 64 home runs, 195 RBIs, and 179 runs scored during that time, en route to earning two more All-Star nominations and a pair of Silver Sluggers. But, with Soriano scheduled to become a free agent following the conclusion of the 2006 campaign, the Rangers dealt him to the Washington Nationals for a package of three players prior to the start of the season.

Soriano, who proved to be a below-average defender in his five full seasons at second base, initially balked at the idea of moving to left field when the Nationals suggested that he switch positions shortly after he arrived in Washington. However, he eventually accepted his inevitable fate, after which he went on to have a big year for the Nationals, becoming a member of the select 40-40 club in 2006 by hitting 46 homers and stealing 41 bases, while also knocking in 95 runs, scoring 110 times, and batting .277.

Soriano ended up spending just that one season in Washington, choosing to sign with the Cubs when they offered him a franchise-record eight-year contract worth nearly $136 million prior to the start of the 2007 campaign. Upon inking his deal with the Cubs, Soriano announced, "I love playing the outfield, and I love Chicago. I think the money isn't that important to me. I'm not looking for the money. I'm looking to be happy, and I think this is a good place for me to play and be happy."

After getting off to a slow start with the Cubs, batting .270, with no home runs and just one RBI during the month of April, Soriano eventually caught fire, earning his sixth straight All-Star selection by hitting 11 homers, driving in 18 runs, and batting .336 in June. Although he later missed three weeks in August after tearing his right quadriceps during an August 5 contest against the Mets, Soriano returned to the lineup to have a sensational month of September, leading the Cubs to the NL Central title by hitting 14 homers, knocking in 27 runs, and batting .320 over the season's final 29 games. Despite appearing in only 135 games, Soriano finished the year with 33 home runs, 70 RBIs, 97 runs scored, and a .299 batting average.

Experiencing further problems with his legs in 2008, Soriano found himself limited to just 109 games and 453 official at-bats, although he still managed to hit 29 homers, drive in 75 runs, score 76 times, steal 19 bases, and compile a batting average of .280, en route to earning All-Star honors for the final time. Able to appear in only 117 contests the following year due to an assortment of injuries, Soriano saw his offensive numbers slip to 20 homers, 55 RBIs, 64 runs scored, 9 steals, and a .241 batting average.

Never a particularly strong defender to begin with, Soriano became even more of a liability in the outfield as his range continued to diminish. In addition to leading all NL left-fielders in errors three straight times, Soriano occasionally misplayed fly balls, turning apparent outs into extra-base hits by the opposition. Soriano's defensive shortcomings caused something of a love/hate relationship to develop between himself and the fans at Wrigley, who cheered him whenever he drove a ball beyond the outfield wall or delivered a dramatic, game-winning hit, but also expressed their dissatisfaction with him whenever he committed a blunder in the field. It should be noted, though, that Soriano had a very strong throwing arm, enabling him to lead all NL outfielders in assists twice and double plays on four separate occasions.

Although Soriano totaled 50 home runs and 167 RBIs from 2010 to 2011, his descent into mediocrity continued, as he scored only 117 runs, swiped just 7 bases, and posted batting averages of just .258 and .244. Yet, as his career began to wind down, Soriano found other ways to contribute to the Cubs. In addition to improving his defense to the point that he led all NL left-fielders with a .996 fielding percentage in 2012, Soriano retained a positive outlook as the Cubs slid out of contention in the NL Central, accepting a lower slot in the batting order and becoming more of a team leader, including taking young players such as Starlin Castro under his wing. Having developed the best reputation in the clubhouse of anyone on the team, Soriano received praise from Cubs Manager Dale Sveum, who told MLB.com's Carrie Muskat in February 2012, "The guy [Soriano] works his butt off all the time. There's no doubt the fans lost a little faith in him sometimes with the things he does, but I think the fans have to understand he's probably the hardest-working guy in the clubhouse. That's always refreshing, and players love him to death. He's the most prolific guy in our lineup, and he's done it before."

After rebounding somewhat in 2012 by hitting 32 homers, driving in 108 runs, and batting .262, Soriano remained in Chicago until July 26, 2013, when the Cubs traded him back to the Yankees for minor leaguer Corey Black. Soriano subsequently performed extremely well for the Yankees over the season's final two months, hitting 17 homers, knocking in 50 runs, scoring 37 times, and batting .256, to finish the year with 34 home runs, 101 RBIs, 84 runs scored, and a .255 batting average. However, he slumped at the plate the following year, hitting just 6 homers, driving in only 23 runs, and batting just .221 over his first 67 games, prompting New York to release him on July 14. After sitting out the rest of the year, Soriano announced his retirement on November 4, 2014, telling the media, "I've lost the love and passion to play the game. Right now, my family is the most important thing. Although I consider myself in great shape, my mind is not focused on baseball." Soriano ended his career with 412 home runs, 1,159 RBIs, 1,152 runs scored, 2,095 hits, and a lifetime batting average of .270.

Cub Numbers:

Record: 181 HR; 526 RBIs; 469 Runs Scored; 898 Hits; 218 Doubles; 13 Triples; 70 Stolen Bases; .264 AVG; .317 OBP; 495 SLG PCT; .812 OPS

Career Numbers:

Record: 412 HR; 1,159 RBIs; 1,152 Runs Scored; 2,095 Hits; 481 Doubles; 31 Triples; 289 Stolen Bases; .270 AVG; .319 OBP; .500 SLG PCT; .819 OPS

Cub Career Highlights:

Best Season: Although Soriano hit 32 homers and knocked in 108 runs for the Cubs in 2012, he had his finest all-around season as a member of the team in 2007, when, in addition to hitting 33 homers and driving in 70 runs, he scored 97 times, accumulated 173 hits and 42 doubles, stole 19 bases, batted .299, and posted a career-high slugging percentage of .560,

Courtesy of Ben Grey

Alfonso Soriano hit more than 20 home runs
for the Cubs six times

en route to earning a 12th-place finish in the NL MVP voting. Soriano, who also led all league outfielders with 19 assists and four double plays, performed particularly well during the month of September, carrying the Cubs to the division title by batting .320, knocking in 27 runs, and hitting 14 homers, including seven of the leadoff variety.

Memorable Moments/Greatest Performances: Soriano had his first big game for the Cubs on June 4, 2007, when he went 5-for-5, with a homer, 3 RBIs, and 2 runs scored, during a 7-2 victory over the Milwaukee Brewers.

Later that month, Soriano endeared himself to Cubs fans by going a combined 6-for-13, with 3 home runs, during the team's three-game sweep of the crosstown rival Chicago White Sox at US Cellular Field from June 22 to June 24. Soriano, who homered in each game, led the Cubs to victories of 5-1, 2-1, and 3-0, single-handedly outscoring the entire White Sox offense in the process.

Soriano led the Cubs to an 8-1 win over the Reds at Cincinnati's Great American Ball Park on July 28, 2007 by collecting 3 hits, homering twice, knocking in 5 runs, and scoring 3 times.

Soriano had a similarly productive afternoon against Pittsburgh at Wrigley Field on September 22, 2007, driving in 5 runs with a double and a pair of homers during a 9-5 win over the Pirates.

After knocking in 4 runs with a pair of homers during a 7-4 victory over the Pirates one day earlier, Soriano continued his assault against Pittsburgh pitching on May 17, 2008, going 5-for-5, with a double, 2 homers, 3 RBIs, and 3 runs scored, during a 7-6 loss to the Bucs.

Soriano hit a number of big home runs for the Cubs over the course of the 2009 campaign, with one of those coming in just the second game of the season, when his solo shot off LaTroy Hawkins in the top of the eighth inning knotted the score with Houston at 2-2. Unfortunately, the Astros ended up winning the contest by a score of 3-2 in 10 innings.

Soriano again came up big for the Cubs just four days later, giving them a 6-5 win over the Milwaukee Brewers on April 11 by hitting a two-run blast off reliever Carlos Villanueva in the top of the ninth inning.

Soriano continued his heroics on April 17, when his two-run homer in the bottom of the eighth inning proved to be the decisive blow of an 8-7 victory over the St. Louis Cardinals.

Soriano delivered arguably his biggest hit of the year on July 27, 2009, when his grand slam homer in the bottom of the 13th inning gave the Cubs a 5-1 win over Houston.

Soriano paced the Cubs to an 8-1 victory over the Arizona Diamondbacks on July 13, 2012 by going 4-for-4, with 2 homers, 2 doubles, 5 RBIs, and 3 runs scored.

Soriano provided all the offensive firepower the Cubs needed to defeat Pittsburgh by a score of 4-1 on July 6, 2013, driving in all 4 of his team's runs with a pair of two-run homers.

Soriano hit 3 home runs in one game twice as a member of the Cubs, doing so for the first time on June 8, 2007, when he collected 4 hits and reached the seats 3 times during a lopsided 9-1 victory over the Braves. Soriano accomplished the feat again on September 6, 2008, when he went 4-for-5, with 3 homers, 5 RBIs, and 4 runs scored, during a 14-9 win over the Reds.

Notable Achievements:

- Hit more than 20 home runs six times, topping 30 homers twice.
- Knocked in more than 100 runs once (108 in 2012).
- Surpassed 30 doubles three times, topping 40 two-baggers twice.
- Posted slugging percentage in excess of .500 twice.
- Led NL outfielders in assists once and double plays three times.
- Led NL left-fielders in double plays four times and fielding percentage once.
- Ranks ninth in Cubs history with .495 career slugging percentage.
- Hit three home runs in one game twice (vs. Atlanta on June 8, 2007 & vs. Cincinnati on September 6, 2008).
- June 2007 NL Player of the Month.
- Two-time NL All-Star (2007 & 2008).

47

BILL MADLOCK

Although he spent just three of his 15 big league seasons in Chicago, Bill Madlock earned a place in these rankings with his exceptional hitting during his relatively brief stay in the Windy City. A four-time National League batting champion, Madlock won his first two titles while playing for the Cubs, en route to tying Riggs Stephenson for the highest career batting average (.336) in franchise history. Having most of his finest seasons for the Cubs and Pirates, Madlock batted well in excess of .300 in each of his three years in Chicago, leading the league with a career-high mark of .354 in 1975, before topping the circuit again the following year with an average of .339. Yet, even though Madlock won more batting titles over the course of his career than any other third baseman, with the exception of Wade Boggs, his reputation for being a mediocre fielder, a somewhat one-dimensional hitter, and a clubhouse distraction greatly diminished his legacy, preventing him from ever being seriously considered for the Baseball Hall of Fame.

Born in Memphis, Tennessee on January 2, 1951, Bill Madlock grew up in Decatur, Illinois, where he spent his formative years in organized baseball competing in the local youth leagues. After playing basketball, football, and baseball for four years at Decatur's Eisenhower High School, Madlock turned pro when the Washington Senators selected him in the fifth round of the secondary phase of the 1970 amateur draft. He spent the next four years in the minor leagues, before finally being summoned to the majors during the latter stages of the 1973 campaign after hitting 22 home runs, batting .338, and leading the Pacific Coast League in runs scored, while manning third base for Triple A Spokane. Starting 21 games at third for the Texas Rangers, who relocated from Washington two years earlier,

Madlock fared extremely well during the season's final month, compiling a batting average of .351 and hitting his first big league homer.

In desperate need of pitching, Texas traded Madlock and utility man Vic Harris to the Cubs for star hurler Ferguson Jenkins on October 25, 1973. Replacing longtime fan favorite Ron Santo at the hot corner in 1974, the twenty-three-year-old Madlock had a solid first year in Chicago, earning a third-place finish in the NL Rookie of the Year voting by hitting 9 homers, driving in 54 runs, scoring 65 times, and finishing fifth in the league with a .313 batting average, which represented the highest mark posted by a Cubs third baseman since Stan Hack batted .323 in 1945. Shattering the so-called "sophomore jinx" the following year, Madlock earned the first of his three All-Star selections and a 12th-place finish in the league MVP balloting by topping the circuit with a .354 batting average, while also hitting 7 homers, knocking in 64 runs, scoring 77 times, and ranking among the league leaders with 182 hits and a .402 on-base percentage. Madlock continued to perform at an extremely high level in 1976, when he led the league in batting with a mark of .339, joining in the process Roberto Clemente and Tommy Davis as the only right-handed hitters since 1960 to win multiple National League batting titles. Madlock also hit 15 homers, drove in 84 runs, stole 15 bases, and collected a career-high 36 doubles, en route to earning a sixth-place finish in the NL MVP voting.

Featuring a short, compact swing, the 5'11", 190-pound Madlock sprayed the ball to all fields, proving to be much more of a gap-to-gap line-drive hitter than a slugger over the course of his career. Yet, even though Madlock never hit more than 19 home runs in any single season, he had the ability to produce the long ball, reaching the seats at least 15 times in four different seasons, en route to amassing 163 career homers. Furthermore, Madlock rarely struck out, fanning a total of only 100 times in his three years with the Cubs, and never whiffing more than 53 times in any single campaign. In discussing his hitting style, Madlock revealed, "I didn't have this knack for going to all fields until I hit the major leagues. In my last year of Triple A ball, I considered myself a pull hitter...but, when I got up here and saw how these guys pitch, I shortened my stroke and started going to all fields."

Alan Trammell, who later played with Madlock in Detroit, marveled at his former teammate's swing, stating, "What a short stroke! I don't think I've ever seen a guy with a shorter stroke. This guy, when he played with us in '87, was basically on his way down and he was a little bit overweight, but he could still hit. He believed he could hit. He'd tell you he could hit. The good hitters do that."

Former catcher and major league manager Buck Martinez also praised Madlock's hitting ability, proclaiming, "He was Tony Gwynn before Tony Gwynn. He could hit whatever pitch you had and you couldn't fall into a pattern with him—and you couldn't establish one particular area of the plate because he had a swing for whatever you were featuring on any particular day."

Yet, in spite of his exceptional ability as a hitter, Madlock developed a reputation during his time in Chicago for being a somewhat moody player who occasionally chose to sit out against particularly tough pitchers. Madlock's fiery temperament and fierce competitive spirit, which earned him the nickname "Mad Dog," also caused him to be viewed by many as something of a "loose cannon." One of Madlock's more notable displays of temper during his Cub tenure occurred in August of 1975, when a profanity-laced tirade over a close call at first base earned him an ejection and a subsequent fine from the league office. Madlock received similar punishment for igniting a brawl between the Cubs and Giants on May 1, 1976 by charging the mound after being hit by a brushback pitch. He also made headlines later that year by criticizing Cubs pitchers for not "protecting him" from opposing hurlers' brushback pitches.

Troubled by Madlock's behavior, the Cubs finally decided to part ways with the two-time batting champion, trading him to the San Francisco Giants for All-Star outfielder Bobby Murcer prior to the start of the 1977 campaign. Madlock performed well for the Giants over the next 2 ½ seasons, batting .302 in 1977 and posting a mark of .309 the following year. However, he ultimately wore out his welcome in San Francisco as well, blackening the eye of teammate John Montefusco during a 1978 clubhouse altercation after the pitcher allegedly called the Giants "a team of losers."

Dealt to the Pirates on June 28, 1979, Madlock contributed significantly to Pittsburgh's successful run to the world championship, hitting 7 homers, driving in 44 runs, stealing 21 bases, and batting .328 over the season's final three months, before compiling a batting average of .375 and an on-base percentage of .483 against Baltimore in the World Series. Madlock spent most of the next five seasons in Pittsburgh, winning another two batting titles, earning two more All-Star selections, and having the most productive year of his career in 1982, when he batted .319, hit 19 homers, knocked in 95 runs, and scored 92 times. By leading the league in hitting in 1981 (.341) and 1983 (.323), Madlock became the first player in MLB history to win a pair of batting crowns with two different teams.

After leaving Pittsburgh during the latter stages of the 1985 season, Madlock split his final two-plus years between the Los Angeles Dodgers and Detroit Tigers, serving as a member of two more division championship ball clubs, before announcing his retirement when the Tigers released him following the conclusion of the 1987 campaign. He ended his career with 163 home runs, 860 runs batted in, 920 runs scored, 2,008 hits, a .305 batting average, a .365 on-base percentage, and a .442 slugging percentage.

Following his playing days, Madlock began a career in coaching, serving first as a coach for the Michigan Battle Cats in 1998, before becoming the hitting coach for the Detroit Tigers from 2000 to 2001. He later coached for the Triple A Buffalo Bisons and managed the Newark Bears. More recently, Madlock worked as an on-field operations supervisor for the Commissioner's office. He also has been regularly involved with international baseball and Alumni Association activities.

Despite often being portrayed by the media during his playing days as someone who frequently put his own interests before those of his team, Madlock revealed his true team spirit when he cited the 1979 World Series as easily the highlight of his career, stating, "Any time you win something as a team, and of course to get a chance to play with Willie Stargell was just great."

Meanwhile, seven-time AL batting champion Rod Carew spoke of Madlock's mental toughness and aggressive approach to the game, saying, "He was tough—tougher than the situation. You knew he was going to come through in every situation...People think Bill won batting titles and didn't do anything else. He was a hard-nosed player, he played the game hard; he knew how to play the game because he was brought up in an era where you had to know how to play the game."

Cub Numbers:

Record: 31 HR; 202 RBIs; 210 Runs Scored; 498 Hits; 86 Doubles; 13 Triples; 35 Stolen Bases; .336 AVG; .397 OBP; .475 SLG PCT; .872 OPS

Career Numbers:

Record: 163 HR; 860 RBIs; 920 Runs Scored; 2,008 Hits; 348 Doubles; 34 Triples; 174 Stolen Bases; .305 AVG; .365 OBP; .442 SLG PCT; .807 OPS

Cub Career Highlights:

Best Season: Although Madlock posted career-high marks in batting average (.354), hits (182), and triples (7) in 1975, he actually performed slightly better the following year. In addition to hitting 8 more homers (15), driving in 20 more runs (84), and stealing 6 more bases (15) in 1976, Madlock batted .339 and finished with career bests in doubles (36), slugging percentage (.500), and OPS (.912), en route to earning a sixth-place finish in the NL MVP voting, which proved to be his best showing.

Memorable Moments/Greatest Performances: Madlock had his breakout game for the Cubs on April 17, 1974, when he homered, doubled, walked twice, and scored a career-high 5 runs during an 18-9 blowout of the Pittsburgh Pirates.

Just three days later, on April 20, 1974, Madlock collected 4 hits and 2 RBIs during a 5-4 victory over the Philadelphia Phillies, driving in Billy Williams with the game's winning run with an RBI single to center field in the top of the 13th inning.

Madlock homered twice in one game for one of only two times as a member of the Cubs on September 24, 1974, when he reached the seats twice, collected 3 hits, and scored 3 runs during a 6-4 win over the Montreal Expos. He duplicated that feat on July 27, 1975, when he hit 2 home runs against New York left-hander Jerry Koosman, in leading the Cubs to a 4-2 victory over the Mets.

Although the Cubs lost to the Mets by a score of 9-8 in 10 innings one day earlier, Madlock had arguably the greatest game of his career, going a perfect 6-for-6, with a triple and 3 RBIs.

Madlock hit the lone grand slam of his Chicago tenure on June 18, 1976, when his seventh-inning blast with the bases loaded gave the Cubs a 6-4 win over the Atlanta Braves.

Madlock experienced one of the highlights of his career on the final day of the 1976 campaign, when he raised his average from .333 to .339 by going 4-for-4 during an 8-2 win over the Montreal Expos, edging out

Cincinnati Reds outfielder Ken Griffey (.336) for the NL batting title in the process.

Bill Madlock won two NL batting titles as a member of the Cubs

Notable Achievements:

- Batted over .300 three times, topping the .330-mark twice.
- Surpassed 30 doubles once (36 in 1976).
- Compiled on-base percentage in excess of .400 twice.
- Posted slugging percentage in excess of .500 once (.500 in 1976).
- Led NL in batting average twice.
- Finished second in NL in on-base percentage once and OPS once.

- Holds Cubs record (tied with Riggs Stephenson) for highest career batting average (.336).
- Ranks among Cubs career leaders in on-base percentage (fifth) and OPS (eighth).
- 1975 All-Star Game MVP.
- Finished sixth in 1976 NL MVP voting.
- 1975 *Sporting News* All-Star selection.
- 1975 NL All-Star.

48

WOODY ENGLISH

A member of the National League's inaugural All-Star team, Woody English spent 10 seasons in Chicago, starting at either shortstop or third base for the Cubs in seven of those. A solid hitter with a keen batting eye, English proved to be an excellent leadoff or number-two batter during his time in the Windy City, doing an outstanding job of setting the table for middle-of-the-lineup sluggers such as Hack Wilson, Riggs Stephenson, and Gabby Hartnett. One of the few players to surpass 200 hits and 100 walks in the same season, English accomplished the feat in 1930, when he scored 152 runs, helping to set up Hack Wilson's record-setting 191-RBI campaign. In addition to tallying a total of 400 runs between 1929 and 1931, English batted over .300 twice, compiled an on-base percentage in excess of .400 once, and accumulated more than 200 hits twice, all while serving as one of the Cubs' clubhouse leaders.

Born on a farm in Fredonia, Ohio on March 2, 1906, Elwood George English attended primary school in nearby Centerburg, before moving with his mother to Newark, Ohio in 1918 following the passing of his father at only thirty-four years of age. After playing second base for Newark High School, English remained active on the baseball diamond following his graduation, serving as a member of two different company teams while working part-time at local plants operated by the Pure Oil Company and the Firestone Tire and Rubber Company. Seeking to make baseball his livelihood, English began his semipro career as the starting shortstop for the Zanesville Grays in 1924. While at Zanesville, English caught the attention of former major league outfielder Al Schweitzer, who recommended the eighteen-year-old infielder to the Toledo Mud Hens of the Double A American Association.

After signing with Toledo, English suffered through a difficult 1925 campaign in which he batted just .220 in 131 games. Looking back at his time in Toledo, English later recalled, "I was probably pretty good with the glove, and I always had excellent speed, so I guess that is why they stayed with me while I was having trouble at the plate. Jimmy Burke was the manager that year. In 1926 Casey Stengel took over, and he was a real help to me in my hitting. Casey and I would go to the ballpark early and he would pitch to me and give me little tips here and there until my average began to pick up. I hit .301 that year and Casey was almost as happy about it as I was."

Purchased by the Cubs for $50,000 towards the tail end of the 1926 season, English arrived in Chicago the following spring, after which he went on to win the starting shortstop job as the season progressed. Appearing in 87 games as a rookie, English ended up batting .290, scoring 46 runs, and finishing second on the team with 23 sacrifice hits. Inserted into the leadoff spot in Chicago's batting order during the early stages of the ensuing campaign, English posted solid offensive numbers for the third-place Cubs, finishing the year with a .299 batting average and 68 runs scored, in only 116 games.

With the Cubs subsequently winning the National League pennant in 1929, English played a key role in their rise to prominence. In addition to batting .276, compiling a .352 on-base percentage, scoring 131 runs, and ranking among the top players at his position in double plays and fielding percentage, the twenty-three-year-old shortstop served as a buffer between newly-acquired superstar, Rogers Hornsby, and the rest of the team. Known for his surly disposition and prickly personality, Hornsby told team president Bill Veeck when he first joined the club that he "wanted a roommate who didn't talk in his sleep, didn't snore, didn't get up early and didn't come in late, didn't whistle while shaving, and didn't keep gin in his room." Meeting all of Hornsby's requirements, English ended up rooming with the temperamental second baseman, with who he often discussed opposing hitters and defensive strategy. Hornsby, who went on to claim NL MVP honors in his first season in Chicago, got along extremely well with the likeable, English, who rarely had a bad word to say about anyone.

Providing insight into English's overall impact on the team, a 1929 World Series preview noted, "Considered the clubhouse leader, even at the young age of twenty-three, Woody English is one of the few players on the squad who gets along with Hornsby, and his diplomacy has been vital in keeping the squad on an even keel." Meanwhile, English benefited from his relationship with Hornsby as well, revealing years later, "Hornsby liked me. He taught me quite a bit about hitting. I didn't weigh but 150 pounds. I choked the bat. He said, 'Woody, you stand closer to the plate. Stand about even with it, and, if anything, one foot a little bit in front of the other. Then you'll get that curve ball before it snaps off too fast.' He said, 'Push the ball past the pitcher. You can run good. Make the pitcher cover first base, and you'll beat him over there nine times out of ten."

English added, "You know, I liked the guy, because, see, he was so good to me, I couldn't help but like him, but a lot of players didn't like Rogers."

The smallish English, who stood 5'10" tall and barely weighed 155 pounds, compensated for his lack of size with his quickness and an extremely large pair of hands that aided him considerably in the field. Nevertheless, he never developed into anything more than an average defender, typically placing in the lower half of the league rankings in most fielding categories. Meanwhile, the right-handed hitting English's greatest strengths on offense lay in his abilities to consistently make contact with the ball, reach base via the walk, and use his speed to advance around the bases.

English followed up his strong 1929 campaign with an even better 1930 season, establishing career-high marks in nine different offensive categories, including home runs (14), RBIs (59), runs scored (152), hits (214), triples (17), and batting average (.335). Although the Cubs failed to repeat as National League champions, finishing a close second, two games behind the pennant-winning Cardinals, they established franchise records by leading the senior circuit with a .309 team batting average and 988 runs scored, with English's outstanding production at the top of the batting order contributing significantly to their record-setting performance.

English had another excellent year in 1931, earning a fourth-place finish in the NL MVP voting by batting .319, collecting a career-high 38 doubles, finishing third in the league with 117 runs scored and 202 hits, and leading all NL shortstops with 322 putouts. However, after missing all of April 1932 with a broken finger and losing his starting shortstop job to slick-fielding Billy Jurges, English never quite regained his earlier form. Spending most of his remaining time in Chicago at third base, English accumulated more than 500 official at-bats in a season just once more, doing so in 1932, when he batted .272 and scored 70 runs in 127 games. English subsequently posted batting averages of .261 and .278 in 1933 and 1934, respectively, while serving as a part-time player, before assuming a back-up role his last two years with the Cubs. Nevertheless, in spite of his diminished role, English spent his final five seasons in Chicago serving as team captain, even earning a spot on the National League roster in the first All-Star Game, played at Comiskey Park on July 6, 1933. Although English flied out in his only at-bat, he later identified his appearance in the Midsummer Classic as the biggest thrill of his career.

After English batted just .247 in 64 games in 1936, the Cubs elected to trade him to the Dodgers at season's end, bringing to a close his ten-year stay in Chicago. In discussing the details surrounding his departure years later, English revealed:

> *"I had no idea about it beforehand. Burleigh Grimes had been with the Cubs, and he went over to manage the Brooklyn Dodgers in 1937. At the end of the 1936 season, he told me that I would be playing for the Dodgers the next season. I said 'never.' But he was right. I was down at Hot Springs during the winter when I got a letter from Bob Lewis, the traveling secretary, which said, 'You are now the property of the Brooklyn baseball club.' I felt pretty bad about it because I had spent my whole career with the Cubs. You hate to leave a place where you had been for ten enjoyable years."*

English ended up spending his final two big league seasons in Brooklyn, retiring at only thirty-three years of age prior to the start of the 1939 campaign. Following his playing days, English spent several years working for a manufacturing plant in Chicago, before returning to the game from 1952 to 1954 as manager of the Grand Rapids Chicks of the All-American Girls Professional Baseball League. After the league disbanded, English returned to Newark, Ohio, where he spent the next seventeen years working for State Farm Insurance as a night supervisor, before retiring to private life in 1971. English lived another twenty-six years, passing away on September 26, 1997, at the age of ninety-one.

Cub Numbers:

Record: 31 HR; 373 RBIs; 747 Runs Scored; 1,248 Hits; 218 Doubles; 50 Triples; 51 Stolen Bases; .291 AVG; .368 OBP; .386 SLG; .754 OPS.

Courtesy of MEARS Online Auctions

Woody English accomplished the rare feat of surpassing 200 hits and 100 walks in the same season in 1930, when he scored a career-high 152 runs for the Cubs

Career Numbers:

Record: 32 HR; 422 RBIs; 801 Runs Scored; 1,356 Hits; 236 Doubles; 52 Triples; 57 Stolen Bases; .286 AVG; .366 OBP; .378 SLG; .743 OPS.

Cub Career Highlights:

Best Season: English had an outstanding all-around year in 1931, earning a fourth-place finish in the NL MVP voting by batting .319 and placing among the league leaders with 117 runs scored, 202 hits, 38 doubles, and 68 walks, while also leading all players at his position with 322 putouts. Nevertheless, English played his best ball for the Cubs the previous season, when, starting all 156 games and amassing a franchise-record 755 plate appearances, he established career-high marks in virtually every offensive category. In addition to hitting 14 home runs, batting .335, compiling a .430 on-base percentage, and posting a .511 slugging percentage, English placed near the top of the league rankings with 214 hits, 17 triples, 152 runs scored, and 100 bases on balls, while also setting a Cubs record by reaching base a league-leading 320 times.

Memorable Moments/Greatest Performances: English compiled one of the longest on-base streaks in franchise history from June 21 to July 26, 1929, reaching base safely at least once in 34 consecutive games during that time.

Although the Cubs lost their June 7, 1930 matchup with Brooklyn by a score of 12-9, English hit 2 home runs in one game for the only time in his career, finishing the day with 3 RBIs and 3 runs scored.

Even though English garnered just two official at-bats during a 17-3 mauling of the Phillies on August 18, 1930, he ended up scoring a career-high 5 runs, crossing the plate after singling once and drawing 4 bases on balls.

English nearly matched that total later in the year, going 4-for-6, with a double, 1 RBI, and 4 runs scored, during a 17-4 win over the Phillies on September 12, 1930.

English helped pace the Cubs to an 8-3 win over Pittsburgh on April 25, 1931 by going 4-for-5, with 2 RBIs and 3 runs scored.

English had a similarly productive afternoon against Philadelphia on May 16, 1931, leading the Cubs to a 17-6 rout of the Phillies by going 5-for-6, with a double, 2 RBIs and 3 runs scored.

Although Brooklyn defeated the Cubs by a score of 10-6 on July 19, 1931, English had the only 5-for-5 game of his career, collecting 5 singles and scoring a run during the defeat.

English had another big day against Brooklyn exactly two months later, going 4-for-4, with a double, triple, and 4 runs scored, during a 9-1 Cubs victory on September 19, 1931.

Notable Achievements:

- Batted over .300 twice, topping the .330-mark once (.335 in 1930).
- Scored more than 100 runs three times, topping 130 runs scored twice.
- Surpassed 200 hits twice.
- Finished in double digits in triples once (17 in 1930).
- Topped 30 doubles twice.
- Surpassed 100 bases on balls once (100 in 1930).
- Compiled on-base percentage in excess of .400 once (.430 in 1930).
- Posted slugging percentage in excess of .500 once (.511 in 1930).
- Led NL in games played twice and plate appearances twice.
- Finished third in NL in: runs scored twice, hits once, and triples once.
- Led NL shortstops in putouts once.
- Led NL third basemen in fielding percentage once.
- Holds Cubs single-season record for most plate appearances (755 in 1930).
- Finished fourth in 1931 NL MVP voting.
- 1933 NL All-Star.
- Three-time NL champion (1929, 1932 & 1935).

49

LEON DURHAM

A powerful left-handed hitter who earned two All-Star selections and one Silver Slugger as a member of the Cubs, Leon "Bull" Durham spent parts of eight seasons in Chicago, during which time he established himself as one of the team's most dangerous batsmen. In addition to hitting more than 20 home runs five times, Durham topped 90 RBIs twice and batted over .300 once, finishing third in the National League with a mark of .312 in 1982. An excellent base-runner as well early in his career, Durham twice stole more than 20 bases during his time in the Windy City, while also doing a solid defensive job at first base and in the outfield. Yet, in spite of the many contributions Durham made to the Cubs throughout much of the 1980s, he will always be remembered by fans of the team for committing one of the most costly errors in franchise history.

Born in Cincinnati, Ohio on July 31, 1957, Leon Durham attended Woodward High School, where he lettered for three years in baseball, basketball, and football. After earning high school All-American honors on the diamond in his senior year by hitting 16 home runs, batting .385, and compiling a record of 11-3 as a pitcher, Durham elected to postpone his college education when the St. Louis Cardinals selected him with the 15th overall pick of the 1976 MLB Draft.

Durham subsequently spent the next three years advancing through the St. Louis farm system, before earning American Association Rookie of the Year honors in 1979 by hitting 23 homers, driving in 88 runs, and batting .310 for Triple A Springfield. After spending the first two months of the ensuing campaign in the minors, Durham made his big league debut with the Cardinals on May 27, 1980. Appearing in 96 games and accumulating 303 official at-bats the rest of the year, the 6'2", 210-pound Durham

Courtesy of MEARS Online Auctions

Leon Durham hit more than 20 home runs
five times for the Cubs

earned a seventh-place finish in the NL Rookie of the Year voting by hitting 8 homers, knocking in 42 runs, and batting .271.

In much need of some offensive firepower, the Cubs elected to trade ace reliever Bruce Sutter to St. Louis for Durham, third baseman Ken Reitz, and utility man Ty Waller on December 9, 1980. Starting 83 games in right field for the Cubs during the strike-shortened 1981 campaign, Durham posted solid numbers in his first year in Chicago, hitting 10 homers, driving in 35 runs, scoring 42 times, stealing 25 bases, and batting .290. Splitting his time between center field and right the following year, Durham had arguably his finest offensive season, earning his first All-Star selection and lone Silver Slugger by hitting 22 homers, knocking in 90 runs, scoring 84 times, swiping 28 bases, and finishing third in the league with a .312 batting average. Although Durham earned All-Star honors again in 1983, he ended up missing a significant amount of playing time due to a series of injuries he sustained during the season's second half. Limited to only 100 games and 337 official at-bats, Durham concluded the campaign with just 12 home runs, 55 RBIs, 58 runs scored, and a .258 batting average.

With the Cubs making several moves during the subsequent offseason, including acquiring outfielders Bob Dernier and Gary Matthews from Philadelphia, Durham shifted to first base, where he replaced longtime fan favorite Bill Buckner. Excelling at his new post, Durham finished second among NL first basemen in assists and fielding percentage, while also ranking fourth in putouts. Meanwhile, he returned to top form on offense, helping the Cubs capture the NL East title and earning a 12th-place finish in the league MVP voting by hitting 23 homers, driving in 96 runs, scoring 86 times, and batting .279. Unfortunately, Durham's season ended disastrously, when, with the Cubs clinging to a 3-2 lead in the bottom of the seventh inning of the fifth and final game of the NLCS, he allowed Tim Flannery's sharp ground ball to go through his legs, leading to a pennant-clinching four-run rally by the San Diego Padres. Sadly, Durham's defensive miscue remains the defining moment of his career.

Still, even though Durham found it extremely difficult to live down his costly error his remaining time in Chicago, he had three more solid seasons for the Cubs before his skills began to diminish, averaging 23 home runs and 68 RBIs from 1985 to 1987, while posting batting averages of .282, .262, and .273. However, after getting off to a terrible start in 1988, Durham found himself headed to Cincinnati when the Cubs traded him to the Reds for undistinguished middle infielder Pat Perry and cash on May 19. With rumors of Durham's involvement with drugs abounding, the veteran first baseman appeared in only 21 games for Cincinnati, before entering a drug and alcohol rehabilitation center. Although Durham attempted a comeback with St. Louis the following year, he mustered just one hit in 18 official trips to the plate, forcing him into premature retirement at only thirty-two years of age. After several years of trying to get back to the majors, Durham accepted a coaching position within the Angels' organization in 1996. Since 2001, he has been serving as the hitting coach for the Toledo Mud Hens, the Triple A affiliate of the Detroit Tigers.

Cub Numbers:

Record: 138 HR; 485 RBIs; 474 Runs Scored; 898 Hits; 173 Doubles; 36 Triples; 98 Stolen Bases; .279 AVG; .362 OBP; .484 SLG PCT; .846 OPS

Career Numbers:

Record: 147 HR; 530 RBIs; 522 Runs Scored; 992 Hits; 192 Doubles; 40 Triples; 106 Stolen Bases; .277 AVG; .356 OBP; .475 SLG PCT; .831 OPS

Cub Career Highlights:

Best Season: Durham performed extremely well for the Cubs' 1984 NL East Division championship ball club, hitting 23 homers, batting .279, and establishing career-high marks in RBIs (96) and runs scored (86). However, he had his finest all-around season two years earlier, earning his first All-Star selection and lone Silver Slugger in 1982 by hitting 22 homers, knocking in 90 runs, scoring 84 times, and posting career-best marks in hits (168), doubles (33), stolen bases (28), batting average (.312), slugging percentage (.521), and OPS (.909), finishing third in the league in each of the last three categories.

Memorable Moments/Greatest Performances: Durham had his first big game for the Cubs on May 21, 1981, leading them to a 5-1 victory over the Cincinnati Reds by going 4-for-4, with a homer, double, 3 RBIs, and 2 runs scored.

Durham put together a pair of exceptional efforts in late June 1982, with the first of those coming on the 27th of the month, when he went 4-for-4, with a pair of doubles, 1 RBI, and 1 run scored, during a 4-2 win over the Cardinals. The very next day, Durham led the Cubs to a 6-4 victory over Pittsburgh by driving in 4 runs with a pair of homers and a triple. His second home run of the game—a two-run blast in the bottom of the seventh inning—provided the winning margin.

Durham paced the Cubs to a 10-7 victory over Atlanta on May 24, 1984 by collecting 3 hits and knocking in a career-high 6 runs with a pair of three-run homers.

Durham had another big day against Atlanta later in the year, leading the Cubs to a 5-0 win over the Braves on August 26, 1984 by driving in 4 runs with a pair of homers.

Durham came up big in the clutch on June 11, 1985, hitting a grand slam home run in the top of the eighth inning that turned a 3-1 deficit to the Montreal Expos into a 5-3 Cubs victory.

Durham gave the Cubs all the offense they needed to defeat Cincinnati on September 6, 1987, homering twice and knocking in all 3 Chicago runs during a 3-1 win over the Reds.

Nevertheless, there is little doubt that the seminal moment of Durham's career occurred in Game Five of the 1984 NLCS against the San Diego Padres. With the Cubs entering the bottom of the seventh inning holding a 3-2 lead and staff ace Rick Sutcliffe on the mound, they appeared to have an excellent chance of advancing to the World Series for the first time in nearly four decades. However, after Carmelo Martinez led off the home seventh with a walk and Gary Templeton sacrificed Martinez to second, everything quickly fell apart for the Cubs. San Diego pinch-hitter Tim Flannery subsequently hit a sharp ground ball towards first base that Durham allowed to go between his legs, permitting Martinez to score from second base. After an Alan Wiggins single, a Tony Gwynn double, and a Steve Garvey single plated 3 more runs, the Padres had a 6-3 lead they nursed the rest of the way, giving them the National League pennant. Durham's defensive miscue later became known as the "Gatorade Glove Play" because, before taking his position in the field that inning, he had Gatorade accidentally spilled on his glove by teammate Ryne Sandberg. Looking back at the incident, Durham, who earlier hit a two-run homer in the contest, stated in the 2004 book entitled, *Cubs: Where Have You Gone?*, "The media talks about the 'Billy Goat Curse' and errors and situations that caused the Cubs not to go further. If they would just try to forget about the past and think about what's going on now, maybe things could turn over for the Cubs. Let's live now and forget about the past."

Notable Achievements:

- Hit more than 20 home runs five times.
- Topped 90 RBIs twice.
- Batted over .300 once (.312 in 1982).
- Surpassed 30 doubles three times.
- Posted slugging percentage in excess of .500 three times.
- Stole more than 20 bases twice.
- Finished third in NL with .312 batting average in 1982.
- May 1984 NL Player of the Month.
- 1982 Silver Slugger winner.
- Two-time NL All-Star (1982 & 1983).

50

ANTHONY RIZZO

One of the key members of Chicago's world championship ball club of 2016, Anthony Rizzo has played a significant role in leading the resurgence the Cubs have experienced the past few seasons. Wielding a potent bat, the powerful first baseman has averaged 30 home runs and 92 RBIs over the course of his four full years in the Windy City, topping 30 homers three times and driving in more than 100 runs twice, while also scoring more than 90 runs on two separate occasions. More than just a slugger, Rizzo has batted at least .278 and compiled an on-base percentage close to the .400-mark in each of the last three seasons, en route to earning All-Star honors and a top-10 finish in the NL MVP voting each year. An excellent fielder as well, the 6'3", 240-pound Rizzo possesses surprising quickness and agility for a man his size, leading all players at his position in assists twice, while also annually ranking among the league leaders in putouts. Meanwhile, Rizzo's strong work ethic and unselfish nature have made him one of the Cubs' spiritual leaders, helping to create the positive clubhouse environment that proved critical during the team's successful run to the world championship this past season.

Born in Fort Lauderdale, Florida on August 8, 1989, Anthony Vincent Rizzo attended Stoneman-Douglas High School in nearby Parkland, before signing a letter of intent to enroll at Florida Atlantic University following his graduation. However, Rizzo's plans changed when the Boston Red Sox selected him in the sixth round of the 2007 MLB Draft. Signing with the Red Sox shortly thereafter, Rizzo spent the next three years advancing through Boston's farm system, during which time he had to undergo six months of chemotherapy after being diagnosed with Hodgkin's lymphoma in April 2008. Subsequently given a clean bill of health by his doctor, who told him he "could live a normal life," Rizzo resumed his baseball career the following spring, gradually developing a power stroke that he later credited to the easing of his swing and more effective use of his lower body.

Dealt to the San Diego Padres following the conclusion of the 2010 campaign, Rizzo received a ringing endorsement from Kevin Boles, his manager at Boston's minor-league affiliate at Salem. Boles, who previously managed star first baseman Adrian Gonzalez in the minor leagues, said of his latest protégé, "Rizzo reminds me a lot of Adrian Gonzalez... Rizzo is a bigger kid and has a little more power. Adrian is a little more of a contact hitter, but they had very similar styles of play...We thought very highly of Anthony Rizzo. He's going to be a heck of a player."

Rizzo ended up spending only one season in San Diego, batting just .141 in 49 games with the Padres in 2011, before being traded to the Cubs with right-handed pitcher Zach Cates for pitcher Andrew Cashner and minor-league outfielder Kyung-Min Na on January 6, 2012. Subsequently assigned to the Triple A Iowa Cubs at the start of the 2012 campaign, Rizzo hit 23 homers, knocked in 62 runs, and batted .342 over the first three months of the season, prompting the Cubs to summon him to the big leagues on June 26. Performing well in Chicago the rest of the year, Rizzo hit 15 homers, drove in 48 runs, scored 44 times, and batted .285 in his 87 games with the Cubs, establishing himself in the process as the team's first baseman of the future.

The twenty-four-year-old Rizzo slumped somewhat at the plate in 2013, finishing his first full season in the majors with a batting average of just .233 and 127 strikeouts. Nevertheless, he led a Cubs team that finished last in the NL Central with a record of 66-96 in several offensive categories, including home runs (23), RBIs (80), runs scored (71), and doubles (40). Although the Cubs once again finished last in the division the following year, concluding the 2014 campaign with a record of just 73-89, Rizzo had an extremely productive season, earning his first All-Star selection and a 10th-place finish in the NL MVP voting by knocking in 78 runs, scoring 89 times, batting .286, and ranking among the league leaders with 32 home runs, a .386 on-base percentage, and a .527 slugging percentage. Rizzo continued his outstanding play in 2015, helping the Cubs advance to the playoffs as a wild card by scoring 94 runs, batting .278, compiling a .387 on-base percentage, stealing a career-high 17 bases, and placing near the top of the league rankings with 31 home runs and 101 RBIs. The big first baseman's strong performance, which helped the Cubs improve their record to 97-65, earned him All-Star honors for the second straight time and a fourth-place finish in the NL MVP balloting.

As Rizzo emerged as arguably the Cubs' top offensive threat, he gradually assumed more of a role of leadership on the team, with veteran catcher David Ross commenting, "He (Rizzo) is probably the most important player we have on the team, just as far as his attitude and how he's able to get along with everybody and gets to know everybody."

Ross added, "Every time you're around him, whether you're on the field, or out to dinner, or any place, he wants everybody to have a good time. He's more worried about everybody else and puts himself second. Whether it's his at-bats, batting practice, or anything, he's quick to take a backseat to others. That's unusual for a superstar."

Beyond the positive example Rizzo sets in the clubhouse, he influences his teammates with the serious approach he takes to his craft. An extremely hard worker, Rizzo works out nearly every morning, almost never misses a game, and always hustles on the base paths. In discussing the manner in which Rizzo influences the other members of the team, Cubs pitcher Jon Lester suggests, "I think the whole leadership thing in baseball gets overrated. What I've seen over two years is that he's a leader because he goes out and plays hard every single day. He almost never takes a day off. Never takes at-bats off. Believe me, he's so important to us that everybody notices that. That's leadership."

Rizzo had another big year in 2016, earning his third consecutive All-Star selection and second straight fourth-place finish in the NL MVP voting by hitting 32 homers, scoring 94 runs, batting .292, and finishing second in the league with 109 RBIs and 43 doubles. He subsequently helped lead the Cubs to their first world championship in more than a century by hitting 2 homers, driving in 5 runs, and batting .320 against Los Angeles in the NLCS, before homering once, knocking in another 5 runs, scoring 7 times, batting .360, compiling an on-base percentage of .484, and posting a slugging percentage of .600 against Cleveland in the World Series. Rizzo will enter the 2017 campaign with career totals of 133 home runs, 416 RBIs, and 392 runs scored as a member of the Cubs—figures that are certain to increase dramatically over the course of the next several seasons. Still only twenty-seven years old as of this writing, Rizzo similarly appears destined to assume a much higher place in these rankings before his time in Chicago comes to an end.

Courtesy of Ben Grey

Anthony Rizzo knocked in 5 runs and batted .360
against Cleveland in the 2016 World Series

Cub Numbers:

Record: 133 HR; 416 RBIs; 392 Runs Scored; 720 Hits; 164 Doubles; 10 Triples; 34 Stolen Bases; .273 AVG; .366 OBP; .494 SLG PCT; .861 OPS

Career Numbers:

Record: 134 HR; 425 RBIs; 401 Runs Scored; 738 Hits; 172 Doubles; 11 Triples; 36 Stolen Bases; .267 AVG; .362 OBP; .483 SLG PCT; .845 OPS

Cub Career Highlights:

Best Season: Although Rizzo had a big year for the Cubs in 2015, earning a fourth-place finish in the NL MVP voting by batting .278, scoring 94 runs, and finishing among the league leaders with 31 homers, 101 RBIs, 38 doubles, and an OPS of .899, he performed slightly better this past season. En route to once again finishing fourth in the MVP balloting, Rizzo established career-high marks in 10 different offensive categories, including home runs (32), RBIs (109), hits (170), doubles (43), batting average (.292), slugging percentage (.544), and OPS (.928), placing second in the league in both RBIs and doubles. He also led all NL first basemen in assists.

Memorable Moments/Greatest Performances: After making his debut with the Cubs in late June of 2012, Rizzo quickly became a fan favorite at Wrigley by becoming the first player in franchise history to have three game-winning RBIs in his first five games with the team.

Shortly thereafter, Rizzo helped lead the Cubs to an 8-7 victory over the Mets on July 6 by going 4-for-5, with 3 RBIs. The hulking first baseman delivered the game's big blow in the top of the fifth inning, when he hit a three-run homer off New York starter Johan Santana.

Rizzo had the first two-homer game of his career later in the year, reaching the seats twice, driving in 6 runs, and scoring 3 times during a 13-9 win over the Pittsburgh Pirates on September 16, 2012. After homering in the previous frame, Rizzo delivered 4 runs with one swing of the bat in the bottom of the sixth inning, when he hit the first grand slam home run of his career.

Rizzo paced the Cubs to a 4-2 victory over the Miami Marlins on April 26, 2013 by collecting 3 hits and knocking in all 4 Chicago runs with a pair of two-run homers.

Rizzo gave the Cubs a 5-3 walk-off win over Miami on June 6, 2014, when his two-run homer off Marlins reliever Kevin Slowey in the bottom of the 13th inning plated the game's final 2 runs. He finished the day with 2 hits and 4 RBIs.

Rizzo provided similar heroics on May 23, 2015, when his three-run homer off Arizona reliever Enrique Burgos in the top of the ninth gave the Cubs a 9-6 victory over the Diamondbacks. Rizzo's game-winning blast gave him 6 RBIs on the day, tying his single-game high.

Rizzo again proved to be a thorn in the side of Arizona pitchers on April 7, 2016, when he led the Cubs to a 14-6 win over the Diamondbacks by going 3-for-4, with a homer, triple, single, 6 RBIs, and 3 runs scored.

Notable Achievements:

- Has hit more than 30 home runs three times, topping 20 homers on another occasion.

- Has knocked in more than 100 runs twice.
- Has surpassed 30 doubles three times, topping 40 two-baggers twice.
- Has posted slugging percentage in excess of .500 three times.
- Has finished second in NL in: home runs once; RBIs once; and doubles once.
- Has led NL first basemen in assists twice.
- Ranks among Cubs career leaders in slugging percentage (10th) and OPS (10th).
- 2014 Branch Rickey Award winner.
- 2016 Silver Slugger winner.
- 2016 Gold Glove winner.
- 2016 Wilson Defensive First Baseman of the Year.
- Has finished in top 10 in NL MVP voting three times, placing in top five of balloting twice.
- Three-time NL All-Star (2014, 2015 & 2016).
- 2016 NL champion.
- 2016 world champion.

SUMMARY AND HONORABLE MENTIONS

(The Next 25)

Having identified the 50 greatest players in Chicago Cubs history, the time has come to select the best of the best. Based on the rankings contained in this book, the members of the Cubs all-time team are listed below. Our squad includes the top player at each position, along with a pitching staff that features a five-man starting rotation, a set-up man, and a closer. I have listed a second team as well, whose catcher I took from the list of honorable mentions that will soon follow.

Cubs First-Team Starting Lineup:

Player:	Position:
Kiki Cuyler	RF
Ryne Sandberg	2B
Billy Williams	LF
Ernie Banks	SS
Hack Wilson	CF
Ron Santo	3B
Mark Grace	1B
Gabby Hartnett	C

Cubs First-Team Pitching Staff:

Mordecai Brown	SP
Ferguson Jenkins	SP
Ed Reulbach	SP
Hippo Vaughn	SP
Grover Cleveland Alexander	SP
Charlie Root	SU
Bruce Sutter	CL

Cubs Second-Team Starting Lineup:

Player:	Position:
Stan Hack	3B
Billy Herman	2B
Riggs Stephenson	LF
Andre Dawson	CF
Sammy Sosa	RF
Frank Chance	1B
Joe Tinker	SS
Johnny Kling	C

Cubs Second-Team Pitching Staff:

Lon Warneke	SP
Claude Passeau	SP
Carlos Zambrano	SP
Guy Bush	SP
Greg Maddux	SP
Kerry Wood	SU
Lee Smith	CL

Although I limited my earlier rankings to the top 50 players in Cubs history, many other fine players have performed for the fans at Wrigley over the years, some of whom narrowly missed making the final cut. Following is a list of those players deserving of an honorable mention. These are the men I deemed worthy of being slotted into positions 51 to 75 in the overall rankings. The statistics they compiled during their time with the Cubs, and their most notable achievements as a member of the team are also included.

51 – Pat Malone (P, 1928-34)

Cub Numbers: 115-79; .593 Win Pct; 3.57 ERA; 106 CG; 15 Shutouts; 9 Saves; 1,632 IP; 878 Strikeouts; 1.351 WHIP

Notable Achievements:

- Surpassed 20 wins twice, topping 15 victories three other times.
- Compiled ERA under 3.00 once (2.84 in 1928).
- Threw more than 200 innings five times, tossing more than 250 innings on three occasions.
- Threw 22 complete games in 1930.

- Led NL pitchers in: wins twice, strikeouts once, shutouts once, and complete games once.
- Two-time N.L champion (1929 & 1932).

52 – Rick Sutcliffe (P, 1984-91)

Cub Numbers: 82-65; .558 Win Pct; 3.74 ERA; 40 CG; 11 Shutouts; 1,267⅓ IP; 909 Strikeouts; 1.315 WHIP

Notable Achievements:

- Surpassed 16 victories three times, winning 18 games once.
- Posted winning percentage in excess of .900 once (.941 in 1984).
- Compiled ERA under 3.00 once (2.69 in 1984).
- Threw more than 200 innings three times.
- Led NL pitchers in wins once and winning pct. once.
- Holds Cubs single-season record for highest winning percentage (.941 in 1984).
- August 1984 NL Pitcher of the Month.
- Finished fourth in 1984 NL MVP voting.
- 1984 NL Cy Young Award winner.
- Finished second in 1987 NL Cy Young voting.
- 1987 Lou Gehrig Memorial Award winner.
- 1987 Roberto Clemente Award winner.
- 1987 *Sporting News* NL Comeback Player of the Year.
- Two-time *Sporting News* NL Pitcher of the Year (1984 & 1987).
- Two-time *Sporting News* NL All-Star selection (1984 & 1987).
- Two-time NL All-Star (1987 & 1989).

53 – Augie Galan (OF, 1934-41)

Cub Numbers: 59 HR; 435 RBIs; 549 Runs Scored; 912 Hits; 166 Doubles; 46 Triples; 90 Stolen Bases; .277 AVG; .363 OBP; .409 SLG PCT; .771 OPS

Notable Achievements:

- Batted over .300 twice.
- Scored more than 100 runs three times.
- Topped 200 hits once (203 in 1935).
- Finished in double digits in triples twice.
- Surpassed 30 doubles twice, reaching 40-mark once (41 in 1935).
- Stole more than 20 bases twice.

- Led NL in runs scored once and stolen bases twice.
- Led NL left-fielders in fielding pct. once and double plays once.
- Finished ninth in 1935 NL MVP voting.
- 1936 NL All-Star.
- Two-time NL champion (1935 & 1938).

54 – Orval Overall (P, 1906-10, 1913)

Cub Numbers: 86-43; .667 Win Pct; 1.91 ERA; 95CG; 28 Shutouts; 1,135 IP; 729 Strikeouts; 1.078 WHIP

Notable Achievements:

- Surpassed 20 victories twice.
- Posted winning percentage in excess of .700 twice.
- Compiled ERA under 2.00 four times.
- Posted WHIP under 1.000 once (0.996 in 1909).
- Struck out more than 200 batters once (205 in 1909).
- Tossed 9 shutouts in 1909.
- Threw more than 200 innings three times, topping 250-mark twice.
- Threw more than 20 complete games twice.
- Led NL pitchers in shutouts twice and strikeouts once.
- Ranks among Cubs career leaders in: ERA (fourth), winning percentage (ninth), WHIP (seventh), shutouts (fifth), and fewest hits allowed per nine innings pitched (third).
- Four-time NL champion (1906, 1907, 1908 & 1910).
- Two-time world champion (1907 & 1908).

55 – Rick Reuschel (P, 1972-81, 1983-84)

Cub Numbers: 135-127; .515 Win Pct; 3.50 ERA; 65 CG; 17 Shut-outs; 3 Saves; 2,290 IP; 1,367 Strikeouts; 1.312 WHIP

Notable Achievements:

- Surpassed 20 victories once, winning 18 games another time.
- Compiled ERA under 3.00 twice.
- Threw more than 200 innings eight times, tossing more than 250 innings on three separate occasions.
- Led NL pitchers in: starts once, putouts twice, and assists once.
- Ranks among Cubs career leaders in: strikeouts (fifth), innings pitched (sixth), and starts (second).

- Four-time NL Pitcher of the Month.
- Finished third in 1977 NL Cy Young voting.
- 1977 *Sporting News* NL All-Star selection.
- 1977 NL All-Star.

56 – Frank Demaree (OF, 1932-33, 1935-38)

Cub Numbers: 49 HR, 396 RBIs, 392 Runs Scored, 820 Hits, 131 Doubles, 26 Triples, 21 SB, .309 AVG, .360 OBP, .434 SLG PCT, .794 OPS

Notable Achievements:

- Knocked in more than 100 runs once (115 in 1937).
- Scored more than 100 runs once (104 in 1937).
- Batted over .300 three times, reaching .350-mark once (.350 in 1936).
- Surpassed 200 hits once (212 in 1936).
- Topped 30 doubles twice.
- Compiled on-base percentage of .400 in 1936.
- Led NL right-fielders in double plays once and fielding percentage once.
- Had six hits in one game vs. St. Louis on July 5, 1937.
- Finished seventh in 1936 NL MVP voting.
- Two-time NL All-Star (1936 & 1937).
- Three-time NL champion (1932, 1935 & 1938).

57 – Johnny Kling (C, 1900-1908, 1910-1911)

Cub Numbers: 16 HR; 438 RBIs; 397 Runs Scored; 963 Hits; 156 Doubles; 51 Triples; 119 Stolen Bases; .272 AVG; .317 OBP; .358 SLG PCT; .675 OPS

Notable Achievements:

- Batted over .300 once (.312 in 1906).
- Finished in double digits in triples once (13 in 1903).
- Stole more than 20 bases twice.
- Led NL catchers in: putouts six times, assists twice, fielding percentage twice, double plays once, and caught-stealing percentage once.
- Four-time NL champion (1906, 1907, 1908 & 1910).
- Two-time world champion (1907 & 1908).

58 – Keith Moreland (OF, 3B, C, 1B, 1982-87)

Cub Numbers: 100 HR; 491 RBIs; 394 Runs Scored; 912 Hits; 153 Doubles; 12 Triples; 19 Stolen Bases; .281 AVG; .341 OBP; .429 SLG PCT; .770 OPS

Notable Achievements:

- Hit more than 20 home runs once (27 in 1987).
- Knocked in more than 100 runs once (106 in 1985).
- Batted over .300 twice.
- Surpassed 30 doubles three times.

59 – Rogers Hornsby (2B, 3B, 1929-32)

Cub Numbers: 58 HR; 264 RBIs; 245 Runs Scored; 392 Hits; 91 Doubles; 10 Triples; 3 Stolen Bases; .350 AVG; .435 OBP; .604 SLG PCT; 1.309 OPS

Notable Achievements:

- Hit more than 30 home runs once (39 in 1929).
- Knocked in more than 100 runs once (149 in 1929).
- Scored more than 100 runs once (156 in 1929).
- Batted over .300 three times, hitting .380 in 1929.
- Surpassed 200 hits once (229 in 1929).
- Surpassed 30 doubles twice, reaching 40-mark once (47 in 1929).
- Compiled on-base percentage in excess of .400 twice.
- Posted slugging percentage in excess of .500 twice, topping the .600-mark once (.679 in 1929).
- Led NL in: runs scored once, total bases once, slugging percentage once, and OPS once.
- Finished second in NL in doubles once and on-base percentage once.
- Finished third in NL in: home runs once, RBIs once, batting average once, and hits once.
- Led NL second basemen in assists once and double plays once.
- Holds Cubs single-season records for most runs scored (156) and most hits (229), both in 1929.
- Hit three home runs in one game vs. Pittsburgh on April 24, 1931.
- 1929 NL MVP.

- 1929 *Sporting News* All-Star selection.
- Two-time NL champion.

60 – Kris Bryant (3B, 2015-Present)

Cub Numbers: 65 HR; 201 RBIs; 208 Runs Scored; 330 Hits; 66 Doubles; 8 Triples; 21 Stolen Bases; .284 AVG; .377 OBP; .522 SLG PCT; .900 OPS

Notable Achievements:

- Has hit more than 20 home runs twice, topping 30 homers once (39 in 2016).
- Has knocked in more than 100 runs once (102 in 2016).
- Has scored more than 100 runs once (121 in 2016).
- Has surpassed 30 doubles twice.
- Has posted slugging pct. in excess of .500 once (.554 in 2016).
- Led NL with 121 runs scored in 2016.
- Has finished third in NL in home runs once and total bases once.
- Hit three home runs in one game vs. Cincinnati on June 27, 2016.
- 2015 NL Rookie of the Year.
- August 2016 NL Player of the Month.
- 2016 NL MVP.
- Two-time NL All-Star (2015 & 2016).
- 2016 NL champion.
- 2016 world champion.

61 – Jimmy Sheckard (OF, 1906-1912)

Cub Numbers: 17 HR; 291 RBIs; 589 Runs Scored; 907 Hits; 172 Doubles; 46 Triples; 163 Stolen Bases; .257 AVG; .374 OBP; .346 SLG PCT; .720 OPS

Notable Achievements:

- Scored more than 100 runs once (121 in 1911).
- Finished in double digits in triples three times.
- Stole more than 30 bases three times.
- Drew more than 100 bases on balls twice.
- Compiled on-base pct. in excess of .400 once (.434 in 1911).
- Led NL in: runs scored once, bases on balls twice, on-base percentage once, and sacrifice hits twice.
- Led NL outfielders in assists twice and double plays once.

- Holds Cubs single-season record for most walks (147 in 1911).
- Four-time NL champion (1906, 1907, 1908 & 1910).
- Two-time world champion (1907 & 1908).

62 – Rick Monday (OF, 1972-76)

Cub Numbers: 106 HR; 293 RBIs; 441 Runs Scored; 690 Hits; 114 Doubles; 26 Triples; 37 Stolen Bases; .270 AVG; .366 OBP; .460 SLG PCT; .826 OPS

Notable Achievements:

- Hit more than 20 home runs three times, surpassing 30 homers once (32 in 1976).
- Scored more than 100 runs once (107 in 1976).
- Posted slugging percentage in excess of .500 once (.507 in 1976).
- Finished third in NL with 32 home runs in 1976.
- Led NL outfielders in double plays once and fielding percentage once.
- Hit three home runs in one game vs. Philadelphia on May 16, 1972.

63 – Jack Pfiester (P, 1906-1911)

Cub Numbers: 70-40; .636 Win Pct; 1.85 ERA; 72 CG; 17 Shutouts; 1,028⅓ IP; 482 Strikeouts; 1.059 WHIP

Notable Achievements:

- Won 20 games in 1906.
- Posted winning percentage in excess of .700 twice.
- Compiled ERA under 2.50 five times, posting mark below 2.00 on three occasions.
- Posted WHIP under 1.000 twice.
- Threw more than 250 innings twice.
- Tossed 20 complete games in 1906.
- Led NL pitchers with 1.15 ERA in 1907.
- Finished second in NL in ERA once and WHIP once.
- Four-time NL champion (1906, 1907, 1908 & 1910).
- Two-time world champion (1907 & 1908).

64 – Jody Davis (C, 1981-88)

Cub Numbers: 122 HR; 467 RBIs; 350 Runs Scored; 834 Hits; 159 Doubles; 11 Triples; 7 Stolen Bases; .251 AVG; .313 OBP; .416 SLG PCT; .729 OPS

Notable Achievements:

- Hit more than 20 home runs twice.
- Surpassed 30 doubles twice.
- Led NL catchers in: putouts once, assists once, double plays twice, and caught stealing percentage once.
- Finished 10th in 1984 NL MVP voting.
- 1986 Gold Glove winner.
- Two-time NL All-Star (1984 & 1986).

65 – Larry French (P, 1935-41)

Cub Numbers: 95-84; .531 Win Pct; 3.54 ERA; 87 CG; 21 Shutouts; 8 Saves; 1,486 IP; 642 Strikeouts; 1.324 WHIP

Notable Achievements:

- Surpassed 15 victories four times.
- Compiled ERA below 3.00 once (2.96 in 1935).
- Threw more than 200 innings five times.
- Led NL pitchers in shutouts twice and putouts once.
- Tied for 10th all-time on Cubs with 21 shutouts.
- 1940 NL All-Star.

66 - Shawon Dunston (SS, 1985-1995, 1997)

Cub Numbers: 107 HR; 489 RBIs; 563 Runs Scored; 1,219 Hits; 226 Doubles; 48 Triples; 175 Stolen Bases; .267 AVG; .295 OBP; .407 SLG PCT; .702 OPS

Notable Achievements:

- Surpassed 30 doubles twice.
- Stole more than 20 bases four times, topping 30 steals once (30 in 1988).
- Led NL shortstops in: putouts three times, assists once, and double plays once.
- 1989 *Sporting News* NL All-Star selection.
- Two-time NL All-Star (1988 & 1990).

67 – Carl Lundgren (P, 1902-1909)

Cub Numbers: 91-55; .623 Win Pct; 2.42 ERA; 125 CG; 19 Shutouts; 6 Saves; 1,322 IP; 535 Strikeouts; 1.214 WHIP

Notable Achievements:

- Surpassed 17 victories three times.
- Posted winning percentage in excess of .700 three times.
- Compiled ERA under 2.50 four times, posting mark below 2.00 twice.
- Threw more than 200 innings three times.
- Tossed more than 20 complete games three times.
- Finished second in NL with 1.17 ERA in 1907.
- Three-time NL champion (1906, 1907 & 1908).
- Two-time world champion (1907 & 1908).

68 – Bob O'Farrell (C, 1915-1925,1934)

Cub Numbers: 27 HR; 255 RBIs; 253 Runs Scored; 529 Hits; 88 Doubles; 31 Triples; 23 Stolen Bases; .279 AVG; .364 OBP; .401 SLG PCT; .765 OPS

Notable Achievements:

- Batted over .300 twice.
- Compiled on-base percentage in excess of .400 twice.
- Finished second in NL with 79 bases on balls in 1922.
- Finished third in NL with .439 on-base percentage in 1922.
- Led NL catchers in: putouts once, assists twice, double plays, and caught stealing percentage once.
- 1918 NL champion.

69 – Starlin Castro (SS, 2B, 2010-2015)

Cub Numbers: 62 HR; 363 RBIs; 391 Runs Scored; 991 Hits; 186 Doubles; 31 Triples; 75 Stolen Bases; .281 AVG; .321 OBP; .404 SLG PCT; .725 OPS

Notable Achievements:

- Batted over .300 twice.
- Surpassed 200 hits once (207 in 2011).
- Finished in double digits in triples once (12 in 2012).

- Surpassed 30 doubles four times.
- Stole more than 20 bases twice.
- Led NL in: hits once, games played once, and at-bats three times.
- Finished second in NL with 12 triples in 2012.
- Led NL shortstops in putouts twice and assists twice.
- Three-time NL All-Star (2011, 2012 & 2014).

70 – Vic Saier (1B, 1911-17)

Cub Numbers: 53 HR; 379 RBIs; 436 Runs Scored; 738 Hits; 140 Doubles; 58 Triples; 116 Stolen Bases; .265 AVG; .354 OBP; .414 SLG PCT; .768 OPS

Notable Achievements:

- Finished in double digits in triples three times, amassing more than 20 three-baggers once (21 in 1913).
- Surpassed 30 doubles once (35 in 1915)
- Stole more than 20 bases three times.
- Led NL with 21 triples in 1913.
- Finished second in NL in home runs once and bases on balls twice.
- Holds Cubs single-season record for most triples (21 in 1913).
- Finished sixth in 1913 NL MVP voting.

71 – Charlie Hollocher (SS, 1918-1924)

Cub Numbers: 14 HR; 241 RBIs; 411 Runs Scored; 894 Hits; 145 Doubles; 35 Triples; 99 Stolen Bases; .304 AVG; .370 OBP; .392 SLG PCT; .762 OPS

Notable Achievements:

- Batted over .300 four times, topping the .340-mark twice.
- Surpassed 200 hits once (201 in 1922).
- Surpassed 30 doubles once (37 in 1922).
- Stole more than 20 bases twice.
- Compiled on-base percentage in excess of .400 three times.
- Led NL in hits once and total bases once.
- Finished second in NL with .379 on-base percentage in 1918.
- Led NL shortstops in fielding percentage twice.
- 1918 NL champion.

72 – Harry Steinfeldt (3B, 1906-1910)

Cub Numbers: 9 HR; 332 RBIs; 339 Runs Scored; 696 Hits; 120 Doubles; 28 Triples; 92 Stolen Bases; .268 AVG; .334 OBP; .346 SLG PCT; .680 OPS

Notable Achievements:

- Batted over .300 once (.327 in 1906).
- Finished in double digits in triples once (10 in 1906).
- Stole more than 20 bases twice.
- Led NL in RBIs once and hits once.
- Finished second in NL with .327 batting average in 1906.
- Led NL third basemen in fielding percentage three times.
- Four-time NL champion (1906, 1907, 1908 & 1910).
- Two-time world champion (1907 & 1908).

73 – Manny Trillo (2B, 3B, 1B, SS, 1975-78, 1986-88)

Cub Numbers: 32 HR; 300 RBIs; 265 Runs Scored; 708 Hits; 94 Doubles; 15 Triples; 23 Stolen Bases; .261 AVG; .321 OBP; .342 SLG PCT; .663 OPS

Notable Achievements:

- Led NL second basemen in assists four times and double plays once.
  Finished third in 1975 NL Rookie of the Year voting.
- 1977 NL All-Star.

74 – Ivan De Jesus (SS, 1977-1981)

Cub Numbers: 14 HR; 173 RBIs; 414 Runs Scored; 756 Hits; 115 Doubles; 31 Triples; 154 Stolen Bases; .261 AVG; .330 OBP; .336 SLG PCT; .667 OPS

Notable Achievements:

- Scored more than 100 runs once (104 in 1978).
- Finished in double digits in triples once (10 in 1979).
- Surpassed 30 doubles once (31 in 1977).
- Stole more than 20 bases five times, topping 40 thefts twice.
- Led NL with 104 runs scored in 1978.
  Led NL shortstops in: assists twice; putouts once; and double plays once.
- Hit for cycle vs. St. Louis on April 22, 1980.

75 – Ron Cey (3B, 1983-86)

Cub Numbers: 84 HR; 286 RBIs; 250 Runs Scored; 467 Hits; 99 Doubles; 3 Triples; 4 Stolen Bases; .254 AVG; .337 OBP; .447 SLG PCT; .784 OPS

Notable Achievements:

- Hit more than 20 home runs three times.
- Surpassed 30 doubles once (33 in 1983).
- Posted slugging percentage in excess of .500 once (.508 in 1986).
- Led NL third basemen in fielding percentage once.

GLOSSARY

Abbreviations and Statistical Terms

AVG. Batting average. The number of hits divided by the number of at-bats.

CG. Complete games pitched.

CL. Closer.

ERA. Earned run average. The number of earned runs a pitcher gives up, per nine innings. This does not include runs that scored as a result of errors made in the field and is calculated by dividing the number of runs given up, by the number of innings pitched, and multiplying the result by 9.

HITS. Base hits. Awarded when a runner safely reaches at least first base upon a batted ball, if no error is recorded.

HR. Home runs. Fair ball hit over the fence, or one hit to a spot that allows the batter to circle the bases before the ball is returned to home plate.

IP. Innings pitched.

MVP. Most Valuable Player

NL. National League

NLCS. National League Championship Series

NLDS. National League Division Series

OBP. On-base percentage. Hits plus walks plus hit-by-pitches, divided by plate appearance.

OPS. tOn-base plus slugging.

RBI. Runs batted in. Awarded to the batter when a runner scores upon a safely batted ball, a sacrifice or a walk.

RUNS. Runs scored by a player.

SB. Stolen bases.

SLG. Slugging percentage. The number of total bases earned by all singles, doubles, triples and home runs, divided by the total number of at-bats.

SO. Strikeouts.

SP. Starting pitcher.

SU. Set-up reliever.

WHIP. Walks plus hits per inning pitched

WIN PCT. Winning percentage. A pitcher's number of wins divided by his number of total decisions (i.e. wins plus losses).

BIBLIOGRAPHY

Books:

DeMarco, Tony, et al., *The Sporting News Selects 50 Greatest Sluggers*.
    St. Louis: The Sporting News, a division of Times Mirror Magazines,
    Inc., 2000.

Shalin, Mike, and Neil Shalin, *Out by a Step: The 100 Best Players*
    Not in the Baseball Hall of Fame. Lanham, MD: Diamond
    Communications, Inc., 2002.

Thorn, John, and Palmer, Pete, eds., with Michael Gershman, *Total*
    Baseball. New York: HarperCollins Pub., Inc., 1993.

Williams, Ted, with Jim Prime, *Ted Williams' Hit List*. Indianapolis, IN:
    Masters Press, 1996.

Videos:

Ritter, Lawrence and Bud Greenspan. *The Glory of their Times.* Cappy
    Productions, Inc., 1985.

The Sporting News' 100 Greatest Baseball Players. National
    Broadcasting Co., 1999.

Internet Websites:

BaseballLibrary.com. *The Ballplayers*. http://www.baseballlibrary.com/
    baseballlibrary/ballplayers.

Society for American Baseball Research. "SABR Baseball Biography
    Project." Last modified November 12, 2016. http://sabr.org/
    bioproject.

MLB Advanced Media. "Historical Stats." Last modified January 20,
    2016. http://www.mlb.com/stats.historical/individual.

Baseball Almanac, Inc. "The Ballplayers: A Baseball Player
    Encyclopedia." http://www.baseball-almanac.com/players/
    ballplayers.shtml.

Sports Reference LLC. "Players." Last modified December 20,
    2016. http://www.baseball-reference.com/players.